Milton on Film

Medieval & Renaissance Literary Studies

General Editor:

Rebecca Totaro

Editorial Board:

Originally titled the *Duquesne Studies: Philological Series* (and later renamed the *Language & Literature Series*), the ***Medieval & Renaissance Literary Studies Series*** has been published by Duquesne University Press since 1960. This publishing endeavor seeks to promote the study of late medieval, Renaissance and seventeenth century English literature by presenting scholarly and critical monographs, collections of essays, editions and compilations. The series encourages a broad range of interpretation, including the relationship of literature and its cultural contexts, close textual analysis, and the use of contemporary critical methodologies.

MILTON
ON FILM

ERIC C. BROWN

DUQUESNE UNIVERSITY PRESS
Pittsburgh, Pennsylvania

Copyright © 2015 Duquesne University Press
All rights reserved

Published in the United States of America by
Duquesne University Press
600 Forbes Avenue
Pittsburgh, Pennsylvania 15282

Library of Congress Cataloging-in-Publication Data

Brown, Eric C.
    Milton on film / Eric C. Brown.
        pages cm
    Includes bibliographical references and index.
    Includes filmography.
    ISBN 978-0-8207-0476-0 (cloth : alk. paper)
    1. Milton, John, 1608–1674—Film adaptations. 2. Milton, John, 1608–1674
Paradise lost. 3. Film adaptations—History and criticism. 4. English literature—
History and criticism. I. Title.

    PR3588.B75 2015
    821'.4—dc23

                                                                    2014034973

∞ Printed on acid-free paper.

For my parents, Richard and Elizabeth

Contents

Illustrations

Acknowledgments

I wish to thank first my colleagues at the University of Maine at Farmington, and especially Clint Bruce, Kristen Case, Daniel P. Gunn, Michael K. Johnson, and Sabine Klein for their suggestions and feedback on earlier drafts of this material. Much appreciated institutional support came from the Office of the Provost, as well as Jonathan Cohen and the Division of Humanities and Associate Provost Rob Lively. I also want to thank Shari Witham in Humanities for her tireless contributions, Tim Hupp for his help with media reproduction, and Sarah Otley and the staff at Mantor for securing so many interlibrary loans. My thanks also to the University of Maine System for a Trustee Professorship in 2011–12 that provided release time and research support. I have benefited immeasurably from students in several seminars on Milton and film at both UMF and Harvard University; for those lively and wide-ranging discussions, I am deeply indebted.

The seeds for this study were planted years ago at Harvard University, during a Milton seminar with Barbara Lewalski, and I am forever grateful not only for her wisdom and guidance but also for her reading in its entirety my own attempt at a rather long screenplay adaptation of *Paradise Lost*. Laura Knoppers and Greg Semenza have been guiding lights, and for their groundbreaking work in Milton and popular culture and their previous readings and discussion of material in this book and elsewhere, my continued gratitude. I am fortunate for an opportunity recently to talk about Milton and film with Christopher Ricks, and I am grateful for his input, as I am for other mentors in earlier times who shaped my thinking on Milton, including Burton Hatlen, Gale Carrithers,

Josephine Roberts, and Lawrence Sasek. Anonymous readers for Duquesne University Press made important and formative comments on the present manuscript, and I extend my appreciation for their careful and considerate work. And not only for championing a film of *Paradise Lost*, but also for sharing with my students his insights and his fascination with the poem, my thanks to Vincent Newman.

Happily, this book has also depended frequently on the kindness of strangers. For their generous assistance and encouragement, my thanks to Christian Algar at the British Library; Amy Cosgrove at the University of Otago; Mimi Colligan, Bridget Gayle, and Chelsea Weathers and the staff of the Harry Ransom Center, which also granted me a Warren Skaaren Film Research Endowment Fellowship to review the John Collier collection; Roberta Basano and Elena Boux at the Museo Nazionale del Cinema in Torino; Robbie Butcher at the Charlotte White Center; Josie Walters-Johnston at the Library of Congress; Kristine Krueger and Lea Whittington at the Academy of Motion Picture Arts and Sciences; Anthony Slide; the staff at the Houghton Library; Katie Trainor at the Museum of Modern Art; and Ryan Breen and John Funk at Vincent Newman Entertainment. For their inexhaustible knowledge of magic lantern slides, my thanks also to Terry and Deborah Borton, Richard Crangle, Jack Judson, Lester Smith, and Kentwood Wells.

Finally, this book could not have happened without the support and encouragement of my family and friends, and I thank especially David Bordes, Lauren Bordes, Maggi Brown, Michael Carolin, Janine Collins, Kilene Conrad, Anne Gaiennie, Laura Jackson, Rick Martinec, Jason Moore, Michael Palmer, Elizabeth Simon, and Rod Willey. What little I can say here is not enough to thank my mother and father, my brother, Shawn, and my sisters, Liza, Amanda, and Molly. For my wife, Lisette, and three sons, Griffin, Ivan, and Oliver, this last sentence has been a long time coming. Your thousand daily decencies have meant everything.

Introduction

"*Paradise Lost...*was an interstellar science fiction epic before the genre existed, and its sense of spectacle was cinematic long before the invention of cinema."
—Christopher R. Miller, *New York Times*

"Okay. Don't write this down, but I find Milton probably as boring as you find Milton. Mrs. Milton found him boring, too. He, uh, he's a little bit long-winded, he doesn't translate very well into our generation, and his jokes are terrible."
—Dave Jennings, professor of English, *Animal House*

On a summer night in 1713, the renowned English essayist Joseph Addison attended a show of royal fireworks upon the Thames with "two or three fanciful friends." Addison found the display dazzling: an "agreeable confusion" of "innumerable blazing stars and meteors," "pillars of flame" and "clouds of smoke." "Every rocket," he wrote admiringly, "ended in a constellation," filling the air with "a shower of silver spangles." One of his less fanciful friends, however, thought the exhibition terribly disappointing and inappropriate, depicting such incongruous allegories as "Chastity with a body of fire." This unnamed companion offered an alternative design for a fireworks display, one "which he thought would be very amusing, if executed by so able an artist as he who was at that time entertaining us." According to Addison, "The plan he mentioned was a scene in Milton":

> He would have a large piece of machinery represent the Pan-daemonium, where — "from the arched roof / Pendant by subtle magic, many a row / Of starry lamps, and blazing cressets, fed / With Naphtha and Asphaltus, yielded light / As from a sky — " This might be finely represented by several illuminations disposed in a great frame of wood, with ten thousand beautiful exhalations of fire, which men versed in this art know very well how to raise. The evil spirits at the same time might very properly appear in vehicles of flame, and employ all the tricks of Art to terrify and surprise the spectator. We were well enough pleased with this start of thought, but fancied there was something in it too serious, and perhaps too horrid, to be put in execution.[1]

The imagined pyrotechnics here are inspired by the "subtle magic" of Pandaemonium but also by further iterations of its false fires and chemical glamour. There is something of a sham about the whole project, a figurative hollowness within the "great frame of wood," as it summons up the abyssal horrors of *Paradise Lost* not just as a source for public entertainment but also as the elements of pure spectacle. The didactic allegory of Chastity has given way to an entirely literal-minded presentation of pomp: a commodious wooden edifice for Satan's palace, "ten thousand beautiful exhala-tions of fire" for the starry lamps and blazing cressets. In the cli-max, evil spirits would replace the boring, edifying virtues, turning the lesson into an evening of tricks, terror, and surprise without any apparent moral lessons. Addison's conflicted response — initially enthused by the proposed image, then unsure of the depths to which it might sink — captures well several tensions in play: the lurid draw of John Milton's horrifying visions and their aptness for spectacle, the unforeseeable effects of their successful imitation, and the irony (or inappropriateness) of drawing superficial pleasure from such sublime imaginings.

Addison's reaction also models two competing and seemingly incompatible narratives that have described Milton's relationship to the cinema since its beginnings. In the first, Milton's sprawling and sublime imagination anticipates, epitomizes, and defines the very limits of cinematic representation. The extraordinary ineffabil-ity of a work like *Paradise Lost* can only be fully realized in a filmic medium, which could render to the eye what Roland Mushat Frye calls the central visual problem of the poem: its dedication to the "indescribable and the inaccessible."[2] In the second model, there is something too *serious* about the poet to translate into any popular medium, and film registers as an especially resistant form. Not only for its mass-market, commercial exigencies but also for its compressions and concisions of whatever might be called "Miltonic," the language of the cinema has seemed hostile to the accommodation of Milton's weighty verse and grand style.

This book takes up the dual history of Milton and the cinema, in which even the horrid, as for Addison, has served as both incitement and deterrent for adapting his work. From the earliest protocinematic inventions, Milton has figured as the quintessential subject of increasingly spectacular visual entertainment: mechanical pantomimes and spectacles in the eighteenth century, panoramas, dioramas, musical extravaganzas, and magic lantern shows in the nineteenth. The tradition reached its latest highpoint in the Opening Ceremony of the 2012 London Olympics, in which the vision of Addison's friend was partly realized during a sequence director Danny Boyle titled "Pandemonium."[3] For centuries, *Paradise Lost* has been regarded as the perfect choice for artists wishing to showcase the newest technologies and special effects. With each generational shift arrives the promise of fulfilling as never before Milton's sublime visual aesthetics, a process of legitimization that underscores both the power of new technical forms and their limitations. For what seems most constant in the advance of Miltonic spectacle, and its eventual passage into film, is the distance between the advance and its imagined end, what Michel Foucault called the permanent gap between "an inaccessible norm and the asymptotic movement that strives to meet in infinity."[4] A snapshot of this asymptotic movement can be glimpsed in the proclamation of Robert Burford, a purveyor of the panorama shows popular in the early 1800s, who said of his choice to present a scene from Milton, "It having been long and generally admitted that no style of painting could portray these subjects with so much interest and appearance of reality, it occurred to him that [the panorama] might be adapted to the higher branches of the art with increased effect, and embody, with unrivalled boldness and grandeur, the most sublime and stupendous imagery."[5]

With the advent of film, the medium changed while the rhetoric of exclusivity remained—the cinema would surpass the panorama and every other visual art form, just as Burford had once supposed the panorama would supplant the lower branches of painting. At the turn of the twentieth century, the contest to best represent Milton's poetic imagination was renewed partly as an effort to authenticate this new medium. The cinema began to fashion itself as the final innovation, a universal pictorial language, exclusively capable of accommodating the infinite vastness and "indescribability" of all things sublime, and Milton again served as touchstone. Indeed, D. W. Griffith suggested 100 years ago that works like *Paradise Lost* could never be successfully adapted by anything but the new cinema: "Say that you had just written 'Paradise Lost' and wished to have it produced on the stage. To whom would you go?...The motion picture has taken all of these works, has deemed none of them too 'highbrowed,' and has 'got them across.' Perhaps the production was not always perfect, or wonderfully artistic, but the big idea was still there, still intact, and it reached the hearts of the spectators."[6] The condensation of high and low in Griffith's vision speaks to cinema's own anxieties over its position as a legitimate art form in the early 1900s, but it has also proven prescient: because of its massive popular appeal, film remains a contested medium as a form of high art, and adaptations of literary classics are still evaluated not merely on whether they capture the "big idea" or reach the hearts of millions, but on whether the production was also as wonderfully artistic as the original—an unattainable (and often undesired) perfection.[7]

In its first throes, cinema was especially subject to the hue and cry of those defending the superiority of traditional artistic forms and resisting the cinema's attempts to appropriate and displace the antique pen of a majestic poet. As one reviewer of an early silent film adaptation of Milton complained, "To prostitute Milton's noble work in such a way is an artistic crime."[8] Similar objections persist in the present day: the announcement in October 2005 of a feature-film Hollywood adaptation of *Paradise Lost* met with a mixture of excitement and distress. Diane K. McColley posted a representative grievance: "the idea of a film version of *Paradise*

Lost horrifies me. Images stick in people's heads and become icons that disable the imagination, which words leave free to re-see over and over."[9] A movie house, in this reading, is still the last place true lovers of Milton want to see him, a place far removed from the liberties of his vast poetic vision.

Not long after the Hollywood adaptation began gaining momentum, Gregory Semenza offered a compelling point on this preservation of Milton as sanctified art: "there's the sense that Milton is the last figure that can be protected from the tentacles of pop culture, so there is some resistance to this movie."[10] This intriguing statement raises a number of questions. Putting aside the issue of whether Milton is truly the last (literary?) figure to submit to the kraken of popular culture (or whether he *should* be protected), one wonders: within what groups does this sense of overprotection pervade? Milton scholars? Not if such titles as *Milton in Popular Culture, Is Milton Better than Shakespeare?*, or *Why Milton Matters* are a reliable index.[11] Making Milton more accessible, or at least opening up a debate as to the merits of such accessibility, seems desirable in the classroom as well.[12] At any rate, would a small cadre of Milton obscurantists win out if the culture monster were truly *interested* in Milton? Perhaps the real question, then, is what exactly has shielded Milton from its attentions for so long? The poet himself seems to possess formidable natural immunities, but the issues with transferring Milton from page to screen have as much to do with the idiosyncrasies of the film industry as with the place of Milton (and his verse) in the popular imagination. While other canonical classics are made and remade for the screen—*Hamlet, Pride and Prejudice, Great Expectations*, and so forth—no feature-length production of *Paradise Lost* has ever been successfully mounted. It remains the greatest literary work never filmed.

In *Film Adaptation and Its Discontents*, Thomas Leitch suggests that cinematic versions of certain literary texts—*Gone with the Wind* or *The Lord of the Rings*—must shoulder the burden of "exceptional fidelity." That is, certain texts are seen in "quasi-scriptural terms" by both popular and academic audiences, "a particular kind of sacred writing whose adaptation demands unusual fidelity under unusually severe penalties."[13] This seems to have been the case with *Paradise Lost* from almost the very beginning. In Andrew Marvell's dedicatory verse for the 1674 edition, he worries

> that some less skilful hand
> (Such as disquiet always what is well,
> And by ill imitating would excel)
> Might hence presume the whole Creation's day
> To change in Scenes, and show it in a Play.

One "ill" imitation Marvell had in mind, John Dryden's operatic *The State of Innocence and the Fall of Man,* had already foundered. Dryden reportedly sought permission from Milton first to "tag his verses" by adapting the poem into his own rhymed couplets, and ended up concocting a massively unstageable drama that was never successfully performed. Marvell concluded that he need not be concerned over the poem's contamination by lesser imitators:

> I am now convinc'd, and none will dare
> Within thy Labours to pretend a share.
> Thou hast not miss'd one thought that could be fit,
> And all that was improper dost omit:
> So that no room is here for Writers left,
> But to detect their Ignorance or Theft.[14]

And this judgment has proven, to a degree, prophetic. This is not to say there has been a shortage of attempts, including those who would follow Dryden's path to adapt for the stage: from operas by Joseph Haydn (1798) and Krzysztof Penderecki (1978) to twenty-first century musical theater.[15] But *Paradise Lost* has largely remained, like God's own Mount, unassailable, the attempts of lesser beings to storm it and reshape it into some new kingdom—perhaps after a day or two of skirmishing—easily thwarted.

In their book *Milton in Popular Culture,* Laura Knoppers and Gregory Semenza make a number of perceptive observations about why Milton has been developed so differently from other canonical writers:

> One factor might be genre and original audience. Unlike Shakespeare—whose plays were performed in the public theaters of Southwark and constituted the equivalent of Renaissance popular entertainment—Milton's complex prose and poetry were geared

toward a fit audience, though few. Milton's high epic style and content seem to require an imposingly broad knowledge of the Bible and classical texts. Further, whereas Shakespeare was lauded within ten years of his death as a poet for all time, Milton's extensive prose writings, which explicitly spell out his positions on religious, political, and gender issues, locate him precisely in mid-seventeenth-century conflicts. As a result, Milton becomes seemingly more difficult to dislodge and appropriate for contemporary and popular concerns.[16]

Of all these impediments—the complexity, the allusiveness, the selective audience—the greatest may be the explicitness of Milton's moral and theological convictions and justifications. Even if there is serious debate as to their nuances, or how much from the prose tracts carries over into the sensibilities and decisions of Milton the poet, compared to the great unknown of Shakespeare's personal ideology the difference is immeasurable.[17] This tends to be the informing rationale for those appropriations of Milton that identify him as ideologically stodgy or intractable. Milton also has a complex relationship with his scriptural source material, material that is, at least on a basic narrative level, more present to a mass, moviegoing audience than, say, Holinshed, Plutarch, Ovid, or Cinthio are to an audience attending a performance of Shakespeare. While the latter's literary debts are typically restored or acknowledged only through editorial intervention—one discovers Arthur Brooke's *The Tragicall History of Romeus and Juliet* by reading Shakespeare and not the other way around—audiences will immediately correlate Milton's narrative with its biblical prefiguration. A general audience may be surprised that much of their conception of Adam, Eve, and the serpent is, in fact, due to Milton's influence, for his sway in the popular imagination differs most from Shakespeare's in one crucial way: attribution.

Milton's heterodoxies and often transgressive appropriation of scriptural matter—a model more for radicalism than stodgy intractability—have often successfully overwritten the biblical narrative. An Eden without Satan seems almost heretical, though he is never mentioned by name in Genesis. But so successful has been Milton's overwrite that it has developed into the master narrative, even as it has become ironically detached from him. Similarly, Milton is behind many cinematic treatments of free will and predestination, omniscience and omnipotence and human agency, the nature of evil, rebellion, romantic revolutionary spirit, though the attribution to "Milton" is routinely subsumed. One of the directions of the present study is to recuperate some of this material from its detachment, connecting moments of Miltonic appropriation to these broader signals while also emending the notion itself that Milton's place in the popular imagination has become distended. Particularly in certain filmic genres and subgenres, even the name Milton has become sufficiently charged to bear a number of conventional associations.

In this respect, there is a distinction between attempts to adapt a work like *Paradise Lost* in full and more localized appropriations of or allusions to Miltonic material. There is natural resistance and manifold difficulty in adapting poetry, even narrative poetry, into feature films, and this extends to writers beyond Milton, though the cinematic *citation* of poetry is relatively widespread. But *Paradise Lost* complicates this even further in its rich polyphony and modulations of disparate styles (Barbara Lewalski observes a full spectrum, "colloquial, dialogic, lyric, hymnic, elegiac, mock-heroic, denunciatory, ironic, oratorical, ornate, plain").[18] Though the Homeric epics have been routinely adapted into films — *Troy* (dir. Wolfgang Petersen, 2004) is but one recent example — these are typically mined for their tales and not the manner of their telling. Milton's complex prosody is so strongly characteristic that to lose its effect must seem to alter essentially what "Milton" means. In this way, *Paradise Lost* has more in common with a work like Dante's *Inferno* or Joyce's *Ulysses* than with the *Odyssey*.

Dante, in fact, presents an interesting foil to Milton in the popular imagination. Amilcare A. Iannucci's argument in the introduction to *Dante, Cinema, and Television* that even a film like *The Devil's Advocate*, which makes a number of explicit articulations of Milton, is nonetheless far more dependent on Dante (even pointing out that the official website uses Dante rather than Milton as its guide) may be taken as representative.[19] Dante — often presented as a lusty (but still pious) Italian — seems cooler, more easily fetishized than Milton's puritanical Englishman.[20] And yet, cinematically speaking, even this advantage has not resulted in a spate of *Divine Comedy* projects. Perhaps this is because in another important way it shares with *Paradise Lost* a distinct disadvantage for mass production: prolific nudity. It is hard to overestimate the problems for a blockbuster film raised by the nakedness of Adam and Eve—not to mention the expressive sex life presented by Milton. When one considers the possible audiences a feature production would most hope to entice (those who paid for Mel Gibson's 2004 *The Passion of the Christ*, say), it is easy to see why this has proven a steady complication.

Does Milton still have a place in the array of quasi-scriptural texts? Will critics rail upon seeing an actor like Bradley Cooper playing Satan in a mainstream Hollywood film the same way Charles Lamb did upon seeing Boydell's Shakespeare Gallery, "To be tied down to an authentic face . . .! To confine the illimitable!"[21] Certainly reactions such as McColley's maintain this feeling that the limitlessness of Milton should never be contained. But does *Paradise Lost* qualify for such burdens of "exceptional fidelity" in the same way that *The Lord of the Rings, Harry Potter,* or even the Shakespeare Gallery might? Not only does *Paradise Lost* lack the legion of popular fans, it seems also now to occupy a more contested position in the curriculum than literary lions like Shakespeare or Jane Austen. In an interesting turn, Alvin Snider is content to concede that, in the kind of popularity contest provoked by books like Nigel Smith's *Is Milton Better than Shakespeare?*, Milton will never come out on top until he is authenticated at the box office: "To the rhetorical question posed by the title, the common reader might respond that the playwright has a distinct advantage, that only when directors can cast Jude Law or Ethan Hawke in *Comus* or *Samson Agonistes* will the later writer stand much of a chance."[22] The countercurrents here—to preserve Milton's elite position, and keep his imagination unbounded, he must be kept from popular film, but in order to surpass Shakespeare he must be subjected to a Hollywood treatment—underscore the central paradox of Milton as a literary figure.

Snider's rebuke to Smith's project is playful, I think. His casting examples have an absurdist bent—would anyone believe more in Milton's greatness after seeing the pillars muscled down onto the Philistines by Ethan Hawke?—and the schoolyard bravura of Smith's title lends itself to a lighter touch. But what sits behind

Snider's example is the tacit idea that such performances would never actually happen. The very mooning over the lack of suitable Milton leading men discloses serious anxiety not only over Milton's position in the gigantomachia with Shakespeare—an anxiety among Miltonists that Stanley Fish terms "popular culture-envy"—but in the idea of placing Milton on film at all.[23] It has been said that in contemporary culture a major film version has become the final ful- fillment of all great literary works, themselves only prefigurements of this quasi-divine treatment. If so, the repeated distancing effects and deferrals of placing *Paradise Lost* on film have left a lingering sense of incompleteness in its cultural arc.[24]

The various resistances to Milton on film further contribute to his particular relationship with popular cultural forms, and vice versa. When Milton is circulated in mainstream cultural produc- tions, he tends to signify even more than Shakespeare a literary elitism and almost insurmountable obscurity. The standard line, as suggested above, has become that, whereas Shakespeare was "for all time," a universal mind who could speak to the groundlings and the intelligentsia with equal skill, Milton contented himself with his fit audience and injected so much of himself into his work that he became time bound. It is an argument reiterated by Hiroko Sano in tracing the (non)influence of Milton in Japan: "I contend that a primary reason that has dampened his introduction and reception in Japanese scholarship and culture—one that only exacerbates the linguistic and social ones—is Milton's strong authorial per- sona. While 'gentle' Shakespeare is myriad-minded and protean, 'Puritan' Milton refers to and reveals himself in all his works."[25] Sano urges various ways to popularize Milton despite these obsta- cles: "Perhaps we need to foster entertainment as in Shakespeare's plays. *Samson Agonistes* could be performed as a Japanese Noh play"; and also, "the scale of Milton's cosmos from hell to heaven, along with the war of angels, is extraordinary. Spectacular film- making based on Milton's epics might be possible. . . . In translat- ing Milton's epics into film, Japan might well make a significant contribution with its state-of-the-art animation and computer graphics."[26] In Sano's narrative, it is Shakespeare who has been acting as Milton's Satan, dynamic and shape-shifting, while Milton has assumed the burden of the God of *Paradise Lost,* so revelatory as to become uninteresting. But, in fact, the kind of "spectacular filmmaking based on Milton's epics" Sano imagines has also been imagined and even enacted by many others, and often in preference to Shakespeare. For despite all manner of encumbrance, Milton surfaces again and again in the history of the cinema.

Well before Griffith offered his take on *Paradise Lost* as the perfect example of a text that would be realized fully only on film, directors were using Milton to express the new possibilities of the medium. The first successful attempt at adapting *Paradise Lost* in a motion picture was Luigi Maggi's silent era work *Satan, or the Drama of Humanity* (1912), which included the war in heaven, temptation of Adam and Eve, and construction of Babel by the Sons of Cain, all derived from Milton's poem. A few years later, Vachel Lindsay cites George Bernard Shaw making a point similar to Griffith's: "Failures of the spoken drama may become the stars of the picture palace. And there are the authors with imagination, visualization and first-rate verbal gifts who can write novels and epics, but cannot for the life of them write plays. Well, the film lends itself admirably to the succession of events proper to narrative and epic, but physically impracticable on the stage. *Paradise Lost* would make a far better film than Ibsen's *John Gabriel Borkman,* though *Borkman* is a dramatic masterpiece, and Milton could not write an effective play."[27] Lindsay interprets Shaw's remarks to mean "the pouring hosts of demons and angels," which he terms "one kind of a Crowd picture"—that is, a film whose scope may present the "sea of humanity" and contain all its multitudes.[28] It is a vision of Milton on film, his idea of the war in heaven as a consummately cinematic sequence, that maintains throughout the modern era. The most famous commentary is that of Soviet filmmaker Sergei Eisenstein, who proclaimed in his book *Film Sense* that "there is much in [*Paradise Lost*] that is very instructive for the film-maker," and that "Milton is particularly fine in battle scenes."[29] Some critics have seen his 1938 masterpiece *Alexander Nevsky* as a direct adaptation of those battle scenes—the "pouring hosts" of seemingly infinite figures rendered as a battle on the ice between Russian and Teutonic troops.[30]

The roots of Milton on film are even deeper and go back to the pre-cinematic entertainments of the preceding centuries. The very scene imagined by Addison's fireworks companion—the raising of Pandaemonium—was in fact constructed in the late 1700s by the French painter and stage designer Philippe Jacques de Loutherbourg using a protocinematic device he dubbed the "Eidophusikon." Loutherbourg had been displaying moving pictures as early as 1781, all to rave reviews. The following year he added the most celebrated part of his performance, a vision of Satan rallying his troops and creating his infernal palace, based on *Paradise Lost*. One early study of Milton's influence cites Loutherbourg's Pandaemonium show as the " 'movies' of the day" for the "contemporary of Johnson or Cowper."[31] Derivative exhibitions of the Eidophusikon emerged later in America by Charles Willson Peale, and Milton also proved popular during the vogue of panoramas and magic lantern shows throughout the 1800s.

Such popularity was further driven by the illustrations of Milton's poetry by William Blake, Gustave Doré, Henry Fuseli, John Martin, J. M. W. Turner, and others.[32] However, even here a familiar resistance to Milton can be sensed. John Knowles reports this exchange after Fuseli had opened the Milton Gallery in 1799: "On one occasion, a coarse-looking man left his party, and coming up to him, said, 'Pray, Sir, what is that picture?' Fuseli answered, 'It is the bridging of Chaos: the subject from Milton.'—'No wonder,' said he, 'I did not know it, for I never read Milton, but I will.'—'I advise you not,' said Fuseli, 'for you will find it a d__d tough job.'"[33] Of all *Paradise Lost* artists, those most influential upon the cinema have been Martin and Doré. Both illustrators were widely circulated as part of pre-cinematic performances, and the colorization and mechanization of those illustrations in magic lantern entertainments mark not only an aesthetic alteration of their work but also a desire to see Miltonic material performed.

This continues into the twentieth century, where the film materials for Maggi's watershed adaptation used Doré freely. D. W. Griffith based his designs for *The Sorrows of Satan* (1926) on Doré's etchings as well, and Merian C. Cooper did the same for *King Kong* (1933): "Cooper wanted the jungle to be realistically unreal: it had to have a dawn-of-creation feeling, and for this he insisted that [Willis] O'Brien and his men should copy Gustave Doré's steel engravings for Milton's *Paradise Lost.*"[34] Cooper describes "the lighting, jungle, the foliage" as "direct from Doré." The aerial shots, in particular, were cribbed from the Eden of *Paradise Lost:* "the jungle sets were built on three large tables. On those tables were a series of plate-glass panes on which [Mario] Larrinaga and [Byron] Crabbe painted sections of the jungle and skies, all copied directly from Doré."[35] Most recently, Vincent Newman, the producer of the Hollywood adaptation of *Paradise Lost* first announced in 2005, recounts how he brought along Doré's illustrations while first pitching the film to give an indication of the awesome spectacles the project would involve if only they could add some "electricity" to them.[36]

Other twentieth century treatments of Milton cast more broadly his cinematic sensibilities and effectualness. Richard Wilbur, for instance, describes how his own "mind's eye must have been conditioned by motion pictures": "Whenever, for example, I read *Paradise Lost,* I, 44–58 (the long shot of Satan's fall from Heaven to Hell, the panorama of the rebels rolling in the lake of fire, the sudden close-up of Satan's afflicted eyes), I feel that I am experiencing a passage which, though its effects may have been suggested by the spatial surprises of Baroque architecture, is facilitated for me, and not misleadingly, by my familiarity with screen techniques."[37] Here is the sense of panoramic expansiveness, but also the facility of screen techniques to move rapidly between multiple perspectives, to train, as it were, the mind's eye into similar movements, rather than vice versa. It is the power of Milton's imagination not to have needed such training but, rather, to have anticipated and cultivated the very techniques that the availability of motion pictures shapes for Wilbur. Thomas Merton likewise observes that "there are times when [*Paradise Lost*] is structured like a movie or even like a comic strip. Milton sometimes has a very modern imagination."[38]

In the late 1960s, several *Paradise Lost* feature-film projects looked like they might take flight. Of these, a script by John Collier, shopped around to most of the important directors of the day—Ingmar Bergman, Federico Fellini, Sydney Pollack—was at once the most successful and most disastrous. The producer Martin Poll envisioned an avant-garde, surrealist bit of late 1960s psychedelia, while Collier was laboring to represent Adam, Eve, and the angels as a combination of Henrik Ibsen's *A Doll's House* and Stanley Kubrick's *2001: A Space Odyssey*. After beginning with much ardor, the project eventually disintegrated, leaving Collier to publish the final script as a book he called *Milton's Paradise Lost: Screenplay for Cinema of the Mind*. In Collier's treatment, he writes Eve as the true hero, is wildly sympathetic to the revolutionary spirit of Satan, and willfully excludes all action (he would call it inaction) in heaven—no God, no war, no theodicy. Collier's bold but strange screenplay for the mind failed to generate much interest in this form, either; a piercing attack by John Updike in the *New Yorker* was the death-knell for *Cinema of the Mind* and likely hindered other efforts at reviving Collier's script for the screen.

By the end of the twentieth century, claims for the cinematic qualities of Milton's poetry reached new levels of exuberance. Reviewing the film *City of Angels* for the *New York Times* in the late 1990s, Christopher R. Miller notes the spate of pop-culture angels (including "a tour of the New Age section of any Barnes & Noble...to say nothing of *Angels in America*, *Highway to Heaven* and *Touched by an Angel*,") but argues that "Milton gave us some of the most memorable depictions of angels ever written, far more sublime than our contemporary images of kindly enablers or wistful lost souls." As a result, Miller avers that *Paradise Lost* "was an interstellar science fiction epic before the genre existed, and its sense of spectacle was cinematic long before the invention of cinema. The battle between good and bad angels, for instance, demands the computer-morphing technology of a James Cameron. When Satan is struck by Michael's sword, he bleeds an ethereal substance before the wound closes up as if nothing has happened—just like the liquid-metal Terminator 2."[39]

In the same spirit, James Hynes writes in the *New York Times*, " 'Paradise Lost' is full of spectacular effects that would do a summer blockbuster proud. The battle in heaven in Book VI cries out for Peter Jackson and thousands of digital extras like those in his 'Lord of the Rings' movies; you've got to love a battle scene that ends with whole mountains being flung through the air. And the moment in Book X when Satan and his demons are turned into a sea of writhing snakes begs to be seen in all its computer-animated glory."[40] Edward M. Cifelli, introducing the Signet Classic edition, asserts that "Readers have always thrilled to Milton's heroic superheroes and indestructible arch-villains, characters who may remind younger readers of similarly immune-to-harm figures in twenty-first-century comic books, movies, television shows, and computer games."[41] With slightly more restraint, John Shawcross advises us that films such as *The Devil's Advocate* and *The Matrix* continue to evidence Milton's contemporary relevance: "The great advances of science and space travel which a movie such as the first *Matrix* exploits have reminded viewers of Satan's voyage in *Paradise Lost* through Chaos. . . . The Blind Neo has thus been seen as a counterpart to Milton."[42] In his study of the different challenges of adapting various genres in *The Cambridge Companion to Literature on Screen,* Brian McFarlane writes, "Personally, I'm waiting for someone to realize that Milton's *Paradise Lost* contains a wonderful story told in a language of surpassing grandeur; if ever there was a challenge to filmmakers, this is it."[43] And in 2008, the four hundredth anniversary of Milton's birth, the *New Yorker* featured a piece on his "enduring relevance," calling him "far more our contemporary than Shakespeare."[44] Finally, Vincent Newman's Hollywood adaptation of *Paradise Lost* remains in development in 2014 and has the potential to alter the entire landscape of Milton on film, including somewhat irrevocably his place in the popular imagination.

But even with all this exuberance, the failure of a film like Collier's calls further attention to the 100 years that have now passed since Griffith first imagined *Paradise Lost* as a major motion picture, a vision yet to be realized. Indeed, mounting a production of *Paradise Lost* has stood as a symbol for all that is wrong with Hollywood adaptations at least as far back as 1961, when Patrick Dennis skewered the idea in his celebrity spoof, *Little Me: The Intimate Memoirs of that Great Star of Stage, Screen, and Television, Belle Poitrine.* The plucky heroine of Dennis's faux autobiography receives a letter from an old and obsequious colleague, Dudley du Pont, promising her the lead in a brand new film: "Ducky, *don't* spread this around to those old bitches in H'wood, but I *think* I've found *the* film divine for you and *Prettykins* to do next. This old side-kick of mine, Milton, has written the most heavenly thing called *Paradise Lost* and it's a natch for pix!" Lest Belle worry that she won't have full creative control over the material, Dudley continues, "Milton is absolutely buried in St. Giles's and wouldn't make a bit of trouble about your changing bits about. He's a perfect pet, although there is unpleasant talk about his being blind now and again. However, if you rush $10,000 to me I can promise you that Milton will be as still as the grave and not lift a pinkie to interfere with anything you want to do to *Paradise Lost*." This particular Hollywood branding promises to cover all the most important parts of the poem — "Ivor and I rather see you and Lover Boy in simply celestial things by Lanvin and then a flashback to the Garden of Eden with the two of you in absolutely *miniscule* rhinestone fig leaves and things too divine." Belle reports on the artistic success of the film, which "created a furor," and explains how she "did part of the story in the present where Eve is a rich Junior Leaguer who wants to lead Adam, a young, idealistic architect, astray (with flashbacks to the Garden of Eden) until the modern Eve happens to stumble into the Four-Square Gospel and get saved. In the end she and Adam marry and settle down happily on a big ranch, with a lovely apple orchard."[45] As Dudley seems to imply, the production might make Milton roll over in his grave, but as a direct result he won't raise a finger to disturb the set. Dennis's line about *Paradise Lost* being "a natch for pix" suggests pretty plainly that it is just the opposite, or at least that the superficial attentions to burlesque costume, domestic melodrama, and happy endings exploited by Hollywood will turn it into a most unnatural commodification of the poem (fig. 0.1).[46] Thus, *Paradise Lost*, notwithstanding its energetic promotion by Griffith, Eisenstein, Collier, and others, stands as a work particularly, and peculiarly, *resistant* to both cinematic adaptation and popular approval. As we shall see, this condition has not prevented a number of ambitious attempts to overcome that resistance, though the battle has been routinely uphill.

Fig. 0.1. Belle Poitrine as Eve, camping it up on the set of *Paradise Lost*.
Courtesy of Ralph Crocker.

Milton's Visual Imagination

Concurrent with issues of popular appeal and literary travesty-ing is a strong tradition of regarding *Paradise Lost* as intrinsically "unfilmable."[47] The satirical treatment by *Belle Poitrine* is, after all, only a slight incarnation of the broader problem of the sublime collapsing into the ridiculous, and in this complication the role of Milton's visual imagination is central. When the latest Holly-wood *Paradise Lost* was first listed on the Internet Movie Database (IMDb), a running thread appeared almost immediately: "*Paradise Lost* is not filmable," with postings that debated the difficulties of representation—how to present God, for instance, in a way that "isn't laughable"—as well as the merits of Milton's visuals. Most lamented what might be lost in translation. According to one post, "*Paradise Lost* is a world of total light, total darkness, infinity, and the sublime, and can simply not work as film."[48] Such rhetoric draws on the long history of *Paradise Lost* and the sublime, mostly refracted through the lens of Samuel Johnson, who pronounced of Milton, "The characteristic quality of his poem is sublimity. He sometimes descends to the elegant, but his element is the great. He can occasionally invest himself with grace; but his natural port is gigantic loftiness. He can please when pleasure is required; but it is his peculiar power to astonish."[49] This statement has for centuries provided a powerful vector for understanding Milton's visual imagination and has been offered as evidence both for and against Milton's suitability for the cinema. While the translation of Milton's visuals into mainstream film has long been among the most compelling reasons to adapt *Paradise Lost,* such trans-mediation is also at the crux of the difficulties.

The cinematic qualities of Milton's verse, or the Miltonic qual-ities of the cinema, are promoted in the earliest descriptions of film in a shared discourse of the sublime: transport, limitlessness, a perspective above and beyond the mundane reality. Moreover, it was immediately apparent to the first filmmakers that the cinema was not only a new medium but also a medium that could bind all others to it. Even before the era of talkies, film was seen as an epic force, one that could universalize experience and appropri-ate or subsume other art forms. Painting, sculpture, music, dance, tragedy, comedy, and story in all its forms—the novel, the short story, the narrative poem—could be absorbed into the cinema. In this way, film seemed to share that encompassing plenitude of the poetic epic, its movement through and mastery of a number of modes and registers—the lyric, pastoral, heroic, elegiac, hymnal, historical.

As Joseph A. Wittreich remarks on Milton's poetic and prophetic designs, "Expanding consciousness, extending it into the infinite—these objectives require a transcendental form, one capable of subsuming all perspectives; they necessitate one central form capable of embracing all others."[50] For the early twentieth century, this central form was the cinema. That the sublime magnitudes of Milton's imagination were doing the work of the filmmaker can be seen in the press for Maggi's 1912 adaptation: "it requires an undeniable boldness to set oneself to such a task, to (attempt to measure up to) Milton, but cinematography has made such enormous progress in recent times as to allow even this audacity, and we leave this trial convinced of our victory, convinced of allowing the spectator to witness the titanic battles between heaven and earth, which the minds of poets have seen and transferred to impassioned words and immortal verse."[51] As grander, more panoramic manifestations of the cinema have arisen, up to the surround-sound IMAX 3D cinemagical hyperrealism of the modern movie theater, Milton has seemed an even more compatible figure. Film director Alex Proyas, for several years attached to direct the Hollywood production, imagines that *Paradise Lost* has finally caught up with moviegoers' taste for epic fantasy: "I've sometimes thought that only an insane person would want to make this movie, because it's visually audacious and has to live up to a classic poem that is so beloved. I don't think the visuals could have been done justice until now, which is the great fun of being a film director in this modern age of visual effects."[52]

Proyas proposes that the poem can finally be "done justice" because the cinema has fulfilled its promise of presenting, as Griffith put it, the "big idea," but now without having to apologize that the production itself might not be "wonderfully artistic." The synthesis Proyas sees in the "modern age of visual effects" announces, effectively, a cinematic sublime for which *Paradise Lost* seems to have been attached all along. But the idea of ineffability in *Paradise Lost* opens up other questions—what is the nature of

Milton's visual imagination, and how much travestying of those visuals must be suffered to approximate them on film? Are the "visual effects," by virtue of being both *visual* and *effects,* still representing anything at all consistent with the poem itself? Milton's reputation for presenting things unpresentable is not straightforward, though Johnson pinpoints the basic problem: "Another inconvenience of Milton's design is, that it requires the description of what cannot be described."[53] Such indescribability has been challenged by cinema's claims for a universal language, and for visual effects that transcend the limits of form. But the point is less whether cinema can represent the ineffable than whether, in adapting Milton, it needs to. For Milton's solutions to the problem of ineffability make the poem and its visualizations more representable than some critics have allowed. Much of this is accomplished through the various accommodations in the poem, the interventions of the poetic narrator or of Raphael or Michael, but much depends on a dialectic of the sublime and the particular in Milton's visuals that produces a highly cinematic visual experience.

Harold Bloom sees an irremediable disjunct between what the cinema can sustain and what Milton does in the poem. Recalling Eisenstein's eager underwriting of Milton as "prophetic of cinema," Bloom worries whether *Paradise Lost* "will survive our visual age of information, where only Shakespeare, Dickens, and Jane Austen seem able to survive television and cinematic treatment. Milton requires mediation: he is learned, allusive, and profound. Like James Joyce and Borges in our century, blindness helped to stimulate both a baroque verbal richness and a visual clarity, neither of which are easily transferable to the screen. The blurred montages of our cinema would not accommodate *Paradise Lost.*"[54] Bloom settles on a number of questionable positions here. His observations on the estrangement of Milton from Shakespeare, Dickens, and Austen on the grounds of the need for additional mediation are reasonable enough, and some of these issues have been discussed above. Still, in what ways does film fail to mediate learnedness, allusion, or profundity? Bloom further resorts to a conventional hierarchy of film and higher art, in which the cinema stands in for popular culture and a consequent dilution or reduction of those higher forms into something parochial, circumspect, and shallow. But even if one agrees with this position, surely some of these same issues trouble productions of other canonical authors. What really propels Bloom's reading is Milton's "verbal richness" and "visual clarity" that seem antithetical to the language of the screen and its "blurred montages." There is certainly validity to Bloom's underscoring of the competing signifying systems at work, though it holds to old ideas of fidelity in supposing film incapable of presenting "verbal richness," or overlooking the kinds of "inevitable supplement" that cinematization produces.[55] By "visual clarity," Bloom seems to suggest that Milton is rigidly pictorial, authoring vivid but ultimately discrete presentations of isolated tableaux. Contra Eisenstein, who saw Milton's poetry as an almost ideal representation of the art of dialectical montage, Bloom sees nothing of what Gilles Deleuze refers to as the "movement-image" of the cinema. Instead, the frames of Milton's scenes are set in place, unfolding without that sense of duration that marks cinematic time. This argument seems to misrepresent the tradition of Milton as a poet of the ineffable, of scenes that break containment, unless by clarity Bloom means a radical focus or exposure to some transcendent truth that depends on but belies the visual, something akin to Kant's dynamic sublime.

A more nuanced critique of Milton's visual imagination, almost the opposite of Bloom's, is that of T. S. Eliot. Eliot supposed that Milton's blindness contributed to a fault in his "visual imagination," such that he produced in his poetry not the particular but the archetypal.[56] Thus, of *Paradise Lost* Eliot writes, "I do not think we should attempt to *see* very clearly any scene that Milton depicts: it should be accepted as a shifting phantasmagory."[57] This becomes a fortunate fault in Eliot's opinion since he affirms that "no setting, other than that which he chose in *Paradise Lost,* could have given him such scope for the kind of imagery in which he excelled, or made less demand upon those powers of visual imagination which were in him defective.... [A] more vivid picture of the earthly Paradise would have been less paradisiacal. For a greater definiteness, a more detailed account of flora and fauna, could only have assimilated Eden to the landscapes of earth with which we are familiar."[58] This criticism has sometimes been repeated as a general defect in the visual imagination of the poem, though at least in Eliot's second essay on Milton it is rather more refined. There, Eliot allows Milton to "excel" in a particular kind of visual imagery: "Milton is at his best in imagery suggestive of vast size, limitless space, abysmal depth, and light and darkness."[59] This is a minor reworking of Johnson's observation regarding *Paradise Lost,* and an effect similar to what Christopher Ricks locates in the "traditions of grandeur": "the heroic example of Homer and Virgil, the sublimity of the Bible, the European dignity of a style that deliberately does not limit itself to the vernacular."[60]

Eliot's swat left a lasting mark, though it is apparent that he does not so much abase Milton's "visual imagination" in totality as to ascribe a different *kind* of seeing to Milton, one in fact well suited to the cinematographic (and as ill suited to the theatrical). If it is a lofty vagueness, it is also encompassing, involuted (its narrative structure, particularly its use of the epic simile, continually offers up new bursts of scene that can carry us from the depths of hell to "*Norway* foam"), and lavishly intricate. And there are significant ways in which Eliot's charge falls short: when he wrote earlier in his essay on Blake that "Milton's celestial and infernal regions are large but insufficiently furnished apartments filled by heavy conversation," he was musing on the "historical thinness" of "Puritan mythology."[61] But this quip is insufficient to account for the extensive infernal and celestial trappings independent of (and incongruous with) that mythology: the "*Gorgons* and *Hydras,* and *Chimeras* dire" (*PL* 2.628), for instance, that model the monstrosities in Milton's hell. Or the array of empyreal troops Abdiel espies in heaven: "all the Plain / Cover'd with thick embattl'd Squadrons bright, / Chariots and flaming Arms, and fiery Steeds, / Reflecting blaze on blaze" (6.15–18). Milton's apartments are not entirely bare.

Eliot might argue that even Milton's monsters are a bit vague — there is no monstrous blazon, and the syntax at once suggests that hell is full of fabulous creatures and that his hell overleaps them so that they are "Abominable, inutterable, and worse / Than Fables have yet feign'd, or fear conceiv'd" (*PL* 2.626–27).[62] But this seems less an aversion to the presence of detail than a way of formulating it by absence: his hell gestures at a blanket of "darkness visible," but Milton does not require his reader to sustain this paradox. Nor is his heaven a starched sheet of endless, blank light. But the multiplicity of detail they conceal can only be glimpsed in concentrated moments. Consequently, Eliot may as well criticize the impossibility of reading two books simultaneously. For often when Milton seems like he could drift into something purely ineffable or hyperbolic — the "gigantic loftiness" of "*Leviathan,* which God of all his works / Created hugest that swim th' Ocean stream" (*PL* 1.201–02) — he focuses that vision into concentrated moments of particular detail — the sea-beast's "scaly rind" (1.206) — that create a dialectic between the sublime and the irreducible image.

In *Milton and the Ineffable,* Noam Reisner makes a similar reading of this combinatory work: the "poetic vision is one of sinewy, often luxuriantly tactile, concreteness, which is nevertheless strangely unreal and ephemeral, where images evoking raw materials such as gold, silver, pearl, and other precious minerals are shaped into the 'sparkling orient gems' (3.506) and 'liquid pearl' (3.518) of heaven's ineffable fabric, as well as into the enameled opulence of Paradise's equally ineffable and quite un-natural 'nature's boon' (4.242), where rivers run on 'orient pearly and sands of gold' (4.239)."[63] Marshall Grossman's sense of the poem's overall arc agrees with this "concreteness" that is "nevertheless strangely unreal"; he argues that Milton "conflates two visions — one temporal, empirical, mimetic; the other eternal, revelatory. These visions are double, but each is projected into the single linear discourse of a poetic narrative."[64] Closest to my reading of the dialectic between Milton's endless scope and concentrated detail are two recent essays on visual perspective in Milton's epic similes that both borrow from the language of cinema to unpack the poet's technique. Miklos Peti argues that the similes enforce a "shift from the narrator's wide-angle perspective to the focus on...the concrete aspect of the moment...and zooming in on precise detail," a "rapid oscillation of perspectives" that negotiates "the panoramic with the closely focused."[65]

Along the same lines, Julia Staykova discusses "the preoccupation of the Miltonic simile with topoi of observation," "evident from the sheer number of similes that depict a figure watching a view, often a mutable view, the outlines of which dissolve while they are being watched."[66] In cinematic terms, the Miltonic simile "fastens upon a significant image and zooms in, inviting the reader to linger in purposeful contemplation," while its "slow, protracted syntactic rhythm captures the flow of visual stimuli in a consciously specular space" in ways analogous to "slow motion camera shots."[67] It is evidenced, too, in Northrop Frye's account of the movement between books of *Paradise Lost:* "Throughout the first two books we move through shadowy and indefinite gloom, and then, at the opening of the third, are plunged quite as suddenly into blinding light, where only after our pupils have contracted again can we observe such details as the pavement of heaven which 'Impurpled with celestial roses smiled.' "[68] This sense of telescoping movement enacts Milton's visuals in a way outside of either acute clarity or impaired focus. Indeed, it is a quality of the sublime to activate a similar dialectic between subject and boundless object, immanence and transcendence; it is not only a shift in subjectivity but also an interchange of state.

I am in basic agreement, then, with Wittreich's contention that *Paradise Lost* is "pictorially energized," and further that Milton was "intent upon transcending the limitations of his medium by devising for literature a new optical system." As Wittreich puts it, "Not simply descriptive (indeed to be distinguished from simple description), this pictorialism involves the imitation of visual processes; it creates visual impressions, or images, in order to render visual experiences; and such experiences are a continual assault on the reader's mind, on his interpretive faculties."[69] While Wittreich places this effect in the tradition of *ut pictura poesis,* it is helpful in understanding not only Milton's theory of visuality but also how (and why) film has appropriated and incorporated what is essentially a filmic approach to language.

This is exemplified in the film *Angels and Insects,* Philip Haas's 1995 adaptation of A. S. Byatt's novella *Morpho Eugenia,* which maintains some of Byatt's allusions to *Paradise Lost* while visually foregrounding the Edenic imagery of the epic. Moreover, the relatively lengthy quotation it carries over from the novella acts as a kind of embedded montage, an irruptive movement-image in the film's visual tableau. Early on, the Victorian naturalist William Adamson (Mark Rylance) is freshly returned to England from work in the rainforests of South America and is now sojourning on a rich country estate. Living up to his namesake, this Son of Adam strolls the grounds with his Eve-like love interest, the seemingly immaculate Eugenia Alabaster (Patsy Kensit). As William reflects on the paradisiacal qualities of the New World, including nakedness of its inhabitants, a stream choked with lilies and weeds recalls for him the connections he would make along the Amazon to Milton's Eden. The screenplay cleaves closely to the novella: "These floating clumps of twigs and grasses even remind me of the great floating islands of upturned trees, creepers and bushes that make their way down the great river. I used to compare those to the passage in *Paradise Lost* where Paradise is cast loose after the Deluge." Overhearing this exchange, the eagerly attentive governess, Matty Crompton (Kristin Scott Thomas), completes the thought by quoting Milton in full:

> Then shall this Mount
> Of Paradise by might of Waves be mov'd
> Out of his place, push'd by the horned flood,
> With all his verdure spoil'd, and Trees adrift
> Down the great River to the op'ning Gulf,
> And there take root an Island salt and bare,
> The haunt of Seals and Orcs, and Sea-mews' clang.[70]
>
> (*PL* 11.829–35)

At this gushing forth of verse, Eugenia can only mutter, "Clever Matty."

The evocation of Milton's Eden works on a few levels here: on the surface it bedecks the pastoral English landscape with the ornaments of innocence. William frames this triptych of Milton-Amazon-Alabaster estate at least partly to compliment his hosts and suggest to Eugenia, and to himself, that the Edenic new world is an imitation not only of the English imagination but also of her own primal innocence. Later, when William discovers (with Matty's coaxing) Eugenia's dark past, including an incestuous relationship with her brother, the reference to a postlapsarian, dislocated Eden can be seen as foreshadowing this disillusionment.

In effect, the secret of the Alabaster estate is that its whitewashed innocence belies its postdiluvian condition, a once fertile garden become a barren island of beasts and scattered wreckage. Calling on these particular lines of Milton—a fallen and displaced garden, a grotesque new world—permits the twin narratives of innocence and experience to coexist briefly before unraveling in the film's later acts. But it also evinces again Milton's dialectical vision, his "pictorial energies" that move in the film from old world to new, and in the poem from past to present to future, from old, floating clumps of weed and the bare, featureless island to the piercing precision of a seagull's cry. Milton's entire visual sequence, as Eisenstein pointed out, is really a montage, a series of shots that the film at once adopts and electrifies, even as it slows down its own movement to register the Miltonic quotation.

Adapting Milton

The following chapters trace the development of Milton on film from its origins, including those that depend on a visual experience of the poem. Many of these instances of Milton are, however, not concerted adaptations of his work. In the critical vocabulary of adaptation studies, they might be called "appropriations," a term that suggests both a willful, self-conscious intertextuality and, as other critics note, a typically contestatory one as well, or citations, borrowings, imitations, incorporations.[71] As noted earlier, not all films are eager to announce their debt to Milton overtly, and a conscious attention to Milton is not typically sustained across the broader narrative. Of course, in some cases the allusion *is* the announcement. It may be as blunt as the conspicuous display of some copy of *Paradise Lost*, as happens in a number of films, including perhaps most famously a desolate library scene in *Star Trek II: The Wrath of Khan* (dir. Nicholas Meyer, 1982). Some of these adaptive acts possess the qualities Julie Sanders ascribes to citation as opposed to quotation, namely, that "quotation can be deferential or critical, supportive or questioning.... Citation, however, presumes a more deferential relationship; it is frequently self-authenticating, even reverential, in its reference to the canon of 'authoritative,' culturally validated, texts."[72] But as Knoppers and Semenza point out, "While some evocations of Milton may be largely to signal, in Pierre Bourdieu's term, 'good taste' and hence to enforce class distinctions, not infrequently, Milton is challenged, subverted, or appropriated in radical contexts to support values or reshape or seem to invert those of the historical poet."[73] This hardly ever reaches the level of subversion seen in Shakespearean appropriations. While Douglas Lanier observes the "strong parodic strain in Shakespop," even when "the object of parody is typically not Shakespeare at all but the stultifying decorum that surrounds him," quotations of Milton rarely blend into parody, usually because the parodying text cannot depend on the kind of double access, or recognition across classes, credited to Shakespeare.[74] (There are significant exceptions to this, however, particularly in film genres that have historically appropriated Milton most heavily.)

A lack of familiarity further compromises the interrelated pleasures of similarity and difference in experiencing the adapted work, what Linda Hutcheon calls "repetition without replication, bringing together the comfort of ritual and recognition with the delight of surprise and novelty."[75] Hutcheon is no doubt right to assert that "adaptation is unavoidably a kind of intertextuality *if the receiver is acquainted with the adapted text,*" a problem with additional repercussions for Milton and the lack of acquaintance projected back onto his works by those adapting him.[76] As Sanders argues, "the spectator or reader must be able to participate in the play of similarity and difference perceived between the original, source, or inspiration to appreciate fully the reshaping or rewriting undertaken by the adaptive text."[77] For Milton, this interplay depends on a number of complicating factors, not least the relative unfamiliarity of the actual text, in this case, following Gérard Genette's scheme, the hypotext, when compared to its cultural transformations and projections.[78] How different, for instance, is Milton's description of Pandaemonium from the sense that word has accrued in the past centuries—from Satan's desperate but precise attempt to organize and plan to a modern cliché for utter chaos. This study is less concerned, then, with the hierarchies of adaptation, the belatedness or derivativeness of a work, than with the processes of appropriation and the production of meaning across and between works. I follow Hutcheon in eschewing post-Romantic idealizations of pure imagination and the sanctity of originality for models of intertextuality that describe the permeability and deep openness of texts, those "mosaics of citations that are visible and invisible, heard and silent."[79]

Reading these acts of appropriation forestalls the notion of a passing allusion or a throwaway line. I thus extend here to filmic citation some of the same functions that critics have applied to adaptation more broadly, especially as creative rereadings or reinterpretations.[80] Particularly in light of Milton's tendentious history on film, theories of adaptation that stress its repetition of form or its advertised affinity with its source text are less helpful in tracing what, exactly, "Milton" is performing cinematically. Some of these film examples thus require a reconsideration of Hutcheon's conclusion that adaptation must necessarily be "an announced and extensive transposition of a particular work or works." Such a definition disqualifies "allusions to and brief echoes of other works," because they are not "extended engagements," as well as unacknowledged "appropriations" that might better be called "plagiarism."[81] But because it is surely difficult to quantify the transpositional effect of one text upon another only by measuring the duration of an echo, or the prominence of an acknowledgment, I will prefer the idea that even a drop of Milton goes a long way. This seems especially the case in the specific spatiality of the cinema and the translation from verbal to visual signifying systems, when bold banners heralding *Paradise Lost* or a *Pandemonium Shadow Show* carry a different, and often recurring, weight than a corresponding syntactical moment in a novel.

Even brief appropriations can bring with them the same transpositional force as adaptations, unmooring the narrative in time and place. And so meaning in these moments shifts on fault lines less apparent and less extensive than some critics have allowed. It is perhaps less difficult to argue that a film such as *The Wrath of Khan* adapts in some sense *Paradise Lost,* given its prominent display in one scene of the book itself. And Gregory Machacek thoughtfully describes how such allusions, even when brief, serve as "phraseological adaptations" that engage a number of dynamic reading responses and whose "impact...on the meaning of a literary work can be significant and far-reaching."[82] But even without that explicit signal, the narrative, characterization, thematics, and other qualities of the film are clearly coordinated via Milton. Simply put, a work does not need to be called *Paradise Lost* (and even less "Milton's *Paradise Lost*") to be enmeshed in the complications of intertextuality—though magnification may occur in works that do (say, Clifford Odet's *Paradise Lost* or Toni Morrison's *Paradise*); nor should a work that alludes to *Paradise Lost* only in passing be overlooked as an ultralocal textual punctuation isolated from the interplay of the work as a whole.

Adaptation theorists have discussed widely the effects as a text passes from one medium or genre to another, and it is worth pointing out that most of that discussion has concerned the adaptation of novels into film. Thus, Leitch poses as a question for adaptation studies: "Is it possible for a film to recreate what might be assumed to be specifically literary aspects of its source that challenge medium-specific models of adaptation by indicating unexpected resources the cinema brings to matters once thought the exclusive province of literature (almost always, in this case, the novel)?"[83] Hutcheon notes the "adaptogenic" qualities of the "linear realist novels"—those by Dickens, Ian Fleming, Agatha Christie—"are more often adapted than those of Samuel Beckett, James Joyce, or Robert Coover." And as she points out, according to Mark Axelrod even when such "radical" works are adapted they are "reduced to a kind of cinematic homogenization."[84] While the latest Hollywood adaptation of *Paradise Lost* invites a number of new considerations and examinations of what transposing from a poetic to a filmic medium entails, it is also significant that many other appropriations of Milton on film are themselves adaptations of novels in which Milton has been put to use. As a result of this connection to a prior, mediating text, Miltonic film adaptations often present as prominently writerly or frankly bookish.

This excessive literariness develops on film as either an investment, at some point, in the authority of the written word or a display of books themselves, including those films favoring the "book insert" technique of coyly depositing a tome or two of Milton (sometimes among other luminaries) into the shot. In other adaptations, this visual cue is replaced as a voice-over, in which the film begins with the corresponding opening lines of the adapted work—often recited lovingly by an author figure or central protagonist, before the narrative plunges into radical departures. This parallels what John M. Desmond and Peter Hawkes call the "concentration strategy" in adapting short stories to feature films, where a film might parallel its source closely at the start before expanding into new narrative directions.[85] Milton films, *mutatis mutandis,* tend to dramatize the tension between the literary and the appropriative in similar fashions, betraying both an anxiety over their own relationship as films to a literary forerunner and a willingness to recombine, reinterpret, and recontextualize the original. That these films should be so preoccupied with other texts underscores the difficulty in transposing Milton into something cinematic—many channels often need to be crossed before such a transition can be sanctioned and successful.

Chapters 1 and 2 here trace the origins of Milton's cinematic presence through the earliest spectacular dramatizations of his work, including Dryden's opera, Parisian pantomimes, Loutherbourg's Eidophusikon, museum sideshows, and Broadway extravaganzas. I explore specifically protocinematic entertainments such as panoramas, moving dioramas, magic lantern shows, phantasmagoria, and amusement park attractions, all of which have grappled with and exploited Milton to varying degrees of success. The protocinematic effects of these entertainments are bound up with Milton's own conditioning of spectacle in *Paradise Lost* while serving also to anticipate the first realizations of the cinematic sublime at the turn of the twentieth century.

Chapter 3 focuses on the transition to early cinema, including such silent era films as Luigi Maggi's *Satana, or the Drama of Humanity* (1912), Bertram Bracken's *Conscience* (1917), and D. W. Griffith's *The Sorrows of Satan* (1926), alongside the development of a new cinematic sublime. In *Satana,* a film that has received scant attention in Milton studies, Satan battles the hosts of heaven, tempts Adam and Eve, helps commit the first murder, constructs the first weapons, and foments the destruction of the tower of Babel. In *Conscience,* an impassioned Milton reciting *Paradise Lost* to his daughters serves as prologue to the ensuing morality tale, much of which draws on (and substitutes for) the epic. Griffith's *The Sorrows of Satan,* adapted from Marie Corelli's best-selling novel, dramatizes the war in heaven (via Doré's images of Milton's angels) and creates a satanic figure at once seductive and repulsive.

In the fourth chapter, on the ambivalence of the Miltonic film, I explore the myriad ways Milton and his poetry have been adapted, appropriated, and rejected by filmmakers throughout the twentieth and twenty-first centuries. The disparate critical assessments of Milton's aesthetics form the groundwork for his equivocal place in the cinema, where he has been both embraced and eliminated. This chapter culminates in the story of the greatest motion picture never made, the John Collier/Martin Poll *Paradise Lost* collaboration in the late 1960s. I examine in particular Collier's substantial correspondence with his agent, producer, artistic director, and other figures involved in the adaptation, tracing the often extreme runs of excitement and objection.

In chapters 5 and 6, I discuss the influence of Milton on the two genres that borrow from him most: supernatural, angelic warrior films, a sort of apocalyptic subgenre of the superhero film, and horror films, instancing many of the richest examples of Miltonic appropriations. Milton's visions of angelic combat and the war in heaven have impacted a host of angelic warrior films, while various representations of Satan assume the sympathetic qualities attributable to Milton's fallen angel and popular subgenres such as the vampire film maintain a close alliance with Milton's characterization of the diabolical. At least as often, horror adaptations have turned to Milton's Pandaemonium as an instantiation of contemporary anxieties over loss of selfhood, the threat of endless and unknowable space, hive mentality, and the rise of overpowering, faceless industry.

Finally, in the conclusion I consider the latest effort to bring *Paradise Lost* to the screen, the production by Vincent Newman and Legendary Pictures. Newman's film at one time promised a star-studded cast, a budget in excess of 100 million dollars, and extreme special effects. The spectacle of innumerable legions of angels in 3-D combat was one of the compelling selling points, but a red flag to some purists. The film remains in development and could still become a watershed moment in the study of Milton, informing visuals for the poem for a generation of potential readers and forging an entirely new level of popular identifications. The film's initial promise and ultimate discontinuation remains a major story in this narrative, perpetuating the ideas that first sprang under fireworks on the banks of the Thames three centuries ago: Milton's poetry continues to inspire unimaginable sublimity, the greatest spectacles ever presented, while at the same time seeming a bit too serious for an evening out.

Milton and the Staging of Spectacle

Before anything by Milton was projected onto a film screen, his work served as a source for spectacular entertainments. Many of these appropriations and adaptations turned to Milton at least in part because they hoped to reproduce in three dimensions the stunning visual effects of *Paradise Lost*. Prior to turning more fully to films with sustained engagements with Milton—and to attempts to adapt *Paradise Lost* for the screen—it will be helpful to look deeper into the rise of spectacle in the preceding centuries, when appropriations of Milton anticipate similar moves in the modern cinema. From John Dryden's ambitious opera *The State of Innocence, and Fall of Man* (1677) to Giovanni Niccolo Servandoni's Parisian pantomime *The Fall of the Rebel Angels* (1758) to Philippe Jacques de Loutherbourg's protocinematic hybridization of the stage, the Eidophusikon (1781), Milton's epic was the core text for those wishing to push the representational limits of their art. Indeed, the ineffability of Milton's design was regarded as a model and a challenge to the very idea of the spectacular. If spectacle could be more than just extravagance and promiscuous display, if it could somehow sublimate those energies into intellectual expansiveness, a new art of formless control, Milton was the poet to shepherd it.[1] The nature of spectacle in *Paradise Lost* has, however, been the subject of some debate. In the wake of T. S. Eliot's critique of Milton's visual imagination, and Harold Bloom's identification of "verbal richness" and "visual clarity," it is worth reviewing exactly what sort of spectacle Milton propounded, and to what degree he avoids spectacle as part of a reformed doctrine.[2]

While there was a general exaltation of the word over the image in most Puritan practice, Milton was not limited by the kinds of extreme objections to spectacle litanized by William Prynne in *Histrio-mastix* (1633):

> the mercies of God the Father; the merits and soule-saving passion of God the Sonne; the consolations, joyes and graces of God & the holy Ghost; the wisedome, power, goodnesse, eternity, omnipotency, mercy, truth and alsufficiency of the sacred Trinity, *which are onely able for to fill the soule:* the word, the promises of the God of truth; the eternall joyes of Heaven; the fellowship of the blessed Saints and Angels, to ravish, solace, and rejoyce his soule upon all occasions: on these he may cast the eyes, yea fix the very intentions and desires of his heart: in these his affections may even satiate themselves, and take their full contentment, without any subsequent repentance, sinne, or sorrow of heart: Those then who cannot satisfie their soules with these celestiall Spectacles, and soule-ravishing delights, in which all Christians place their complacency and supreme felicity, it is a sure character, that they have yet no share in Christ, no acquaintance with the least degrees of grace, no interest in Gods favour, no true desire of grace, of Heaven, and everlasting life.[3]

As Protestant accommodation discourse made clear, the representation of divine things, beyond the human capacity of understanding, was nonetheless permitted "by offering a mode of description that was neither literal nor figurative": "transcendent scriptural truths could be conveyed to finite human comprehension, without distortion or misrepresentation, by the condescension of the ineffable and the upward reach of human intelligence, sometimes assisted by the Holy Spirit."[4] Joad Raymond makes a convincing case that Milton depends on accommodation "to justify what would otherwise be an unsustainable, even outrageous, incursion in the unknown."[5] Thus, Raphael's "likening spiritual to corporal forms" is motivated equally by Adam's active interpretation of the word and by a metonymic rather than metaphorical relationship between his narrative and some higher truth. Milton is not spinning an allegory but a series of likenesses and approximations, informed by his own prophetic inspiration in a way that clearly parallels the recitation of Raphael. In this way, the "celestial spectacles" favored by Prynne are representable across a full array of poetic indicators.

Even when Milton marks a clear division between what the eyes and mind may see, as in the successive modes Michael uses to relate to Adam the course of biblical history, an orthodox Protestant preference of the word for the image, Milton presses the dialectic of sedulous detail and the limits of "mortal sight." Because "Objects divine / Must needs impair and weary human sense,"[6] Michael shifts from a panoramic enactment of biblical history to verbal language alone. And yet his first move under this new method of narration is to describe the confusion and erasure of languages after the fall of Babel; the "jangling noise of words unknown" (*PL* 12.55) becomes a reminder to Adam that in the transmission of eternal visions neither image nor word can be taken without some recourse to acts of accommodation. These acts make sense of the failed image—the collapsed tower that reaches to heaven but never quite achieves it—but this image also succeeds as a reformed spectacle, transformed from a grand monument of brick and "black bituminous gurge" spewed from "the mouth of Hell" to a "hubbub strange" that all of heaven looks down upon, meeting with "great laughter" the greatest of comic pratfalls (12.41, 42, 60, 59).

The politics of spectacle in the mid-seventeenth century were additionally complicated by the ostentatious, saturnalian displays of the Restoration, and critics have found in *Paradise Lost* signs that Milton had become predominantly a poet celebrating the "paradise within" over classical heroic triumphs and displays of power.[7] As Laura Knoppers argues, Milton "opposes the tumult of Bacchic celebration" and the "tedious pomp that waits / On Princes."[8]

She sees Milton as reorienting and repurposing the Roman excess of Charles's return to England for a privatized joy in *Paradise Lost*. This movement inward, which Knoppers convincingly argues is in response to the "misguided" and "perverse" displays of public, politicized joy celebrating the triumphs of Charles, may be compared with the broader critical tradition of seeing Milton as moving steadily away from public life and, by the time of *Paradise Lost*, toward the "paradise within."[9]

But Milton seems at odds with himself in the proem to book 9 in which he decries how earlier heroic texts would "dissect / With long and tedious havoc fabl'd Knights / In Battles feign'd" (*PL* 9.29–31) and where he openly prefers "the better fortitude / Of Patience and Heroic Martyrdom" that poets have left "unsung" (9.31–33). This is a hard sell after the "shiver'd armor" (6.389) and overturned chariots of the war in heaven over which Milton lingers, or the dissected melees between Gabriel and Moloch, Uriel and Adramalech, Raphael and Asmadai, Abdiel and Ariel/Arioch/Ramiel (though it is true that Raphael shows some restraint, since he "might relate of thousands" [6.373]). Or when Milton describes the very "Races and Games" or "Knights / At Joust and Tournament" (9.33, 36–37) that he rejects here during the "swift Race" of "Olympian Games" interlude in book 2, when the fallen angels are likened to "Aery Knights" burning the heavens "with feats of Arms" (2.529–38). It is especially difficult to believe the narrator when he describes himself as "Nor skill'd nor studious" in such "Artifice or Office mean" (9.41–42, 39). But Milton's point in the proem is not exclusively the avoidance of this sort of romantic spectacle, but that such dissections are not the "chief maistry" (9.29) or highest argument of heroism. He is most concerned with the climax of his work here, the psychomachia of the Fall, rather than the proper presentation of war and war games.

Knoppers further argues that in depicting hell, "the poem mediates divine power by showing not a hell of grisly eternal punishment (contrast Dante's *Inferno*, for instance), but...an inner state of misery."[10] But a wholesale substitution in Milton's hell of inner misery for the kinds of grotesque, Dantean punishments promoted in the Restoration spectacles Knoppers outlines—the executions of the regicides, the exhumations and decapitations of Cromwell,

Ireton, and Bradshaw—draws an incomplete picture. There are various kinds of grotesque and material punishments in Milton, best exemplified in the complicated explorations undertaken by the fallen angels in *Paradise Lost* 2.570–628. The sequence has confused some critics who miss the prolepsis of the passage, which anticipates in present tense the visitations of "all the damn'd" (2.597), who will be dragged by "harpy-footed Furies" (2.596) to feel the

> bitter change
> Of fierce extremes...
> From Beds of raging Fire to starve in Ice
> Thir soft Ethereal warmth, and there to pine
> Immovable, infixt, and frozen round.   (2.598–602)

This is obviously quite Dantean, though Milton even exacerbates the punishments by having the sinners ferried over the "Lethean sound" from one kind of torture to another. Moreover, guarding the "sweet forgetfulness" of the Lethe is (in a bit of a shock) none other than Medusa, who terrifies and threatens the sinners with her power to petrify.[11] The contrapasso punishments of the fallen angels in book 10 are also influenced by Dante—they are turned into snakes, biting into fruit of "bitter Ashes," "writh[ing] thir jaws / With soot and cinders fill'd" (10.566, 569–70), undergoing contorted metamorphoses that mimic in their "contagious" spread the very network of sedition plotted on the night of Satan's rebellion in heaven. There, Milton is further crafting a visual tableau—a "multitude" of the forbidden tree upon which the primal scene is enacted. It may be that Milton's spectacularization of hell is less about the transference of public to private energies than an articulation of the broader dialectic at work in the poem between conceptual extremes—here the endless, almost kaleidoscopic forest of trees and snakes, still sampled at close range in the jaws full of soot and cinders. Each part reflecting the whole, Milton's respiring visual structure imitates those angels who in battle fight as if "in strength each armed hand / A Legion" (6.231–32).

One of the poem's most spectacular moments occurs when Sin grants Satan passage through the nine-fold gates of hell, and the "infernal doors" spring open onto the cosmos with "jarring sound" and "harsh thunder" (*PL* 2.880–82):

> Before thir eyes in sudden view appear
> The secrets of the hoary deep, a dark
> Illimitable Ocean, without bound,
> Without dimension, where length, breadth, and highth,
> And time and place are lost.   (2.890–94)

It is, Milton insists twice, "a wild abyss" as well as "the Womb of nature, and perhaps her Grave" (2.910–11). Satan "Stood on the brink of hell and look'd a while, / Pondering his voyage" (2.918–19), and as he assesses this panorama of primordial chaos, the poem sets before the reader a mixture of warring atoms, unprincipled matter, star fields of nebulous elemental clusters where "*Chance* governs all" (2.909). These are the "dark materials" Philip Pullman made famous, the launching point for *Paradise Lost* as space odyssey, and it is a scene that defies the imagination. It assaults and overwhelms the senses not only with its infinite vistas but also "with noises loud and ruinous" (2.921), the very clamor of Armageddon, of worlds torn apart and sundered from the heavens. Satan's first leap into this "vast vacuity" (2.932) almost sends him plunging into oblivion. He, like the reader, must gradually find his footing, stabilize, to fix the images one step at a time—as the winding enjambments of the passage take rest in the metrically stolid lockstep of his journey: "O'er bog or steep, through strait, rough, dense, or rare, / With head, hands, wings, or feet pursues his way, / And swims or sinks, or wades, or creeps, or flies" (2.948–50). It makes for an easy cinematic opening—the curtains part, we plunge into the extradimensionality of the images, the vistas and horizons driving past and around the viewer.[12] The viewer is virtually absorbed into the extra space, but again Milton tends to match this vertiginous effect with framed shots of exquisite detail, as with the "scaly rind" of his monstrous Leviathan.

Neither spectacle nor luxury is the sole province of the satanic. Barbara Lewalski, noting of "Milton's representations of Hell, Heaven, and Eden" that "All are in process," finds in heaven "courtly magnificence," where "martial parades, warfare, pageantry, masque dancing, feasting, lovemaking, political debate, the protection of Eden" all provide "an ideal of wholeness."[13] That is, in the dynamic movements that keep Milton's worlds spinning, celestial spectacle works toward a totalizing grandeur, every straw spun into gold, every molecule of space elevated to instance an eternal beauty. This can be seen in book 2, which begins and ends with two visual counterpoints that echo and revise one another—the splendored seat of Satan and the lavish and bejeweled gates of heaven. At the opening, "Satan exalted sat" upon his

> Throne of Royal State, which far
> Outshone the wealth of *Ormus* and of *Ind*,
> Or where the gorgeous East with richest hand
> Show'rs on her Kings *Barbaric* Pearl and Gold. (*PL* 2.1–4)

At the close, Satan wheels away to seek the "Opal Towr's and Battlements adorn'd / Of living Sapphire, once his native seat" (2.1049–50). The bookended scenes are linked by the explicit exchange Satan has made of one "seat" for another, trading empyreal gems for a reasonable facsimile of earthly excess. And yet Satan's ersatz throne, also a perversion of the deity's, serves not as a contradiction but as a foil for the adornments of heaven, bringing out their gleam until heaven becomes a spectacle to end all others.

Similarly, when Milton wishes to glorify Michael's earthly appearance, his blazon includes a treasury of spectacular items: "lucid arms," a "military Vest of purple," a "starry helm," and "glistering Zodiac" (*PL* 11.24–47). They are there to make an impression upon Adam not of ineffability but of divinely regal display, and perhaps to stir emulation. Miltonic spectacle tends to mobilize subject and object in this way, to provide at once a fixation and loss of scale and perspective, a glaring vision that becomes the surest way of seeing. There is resemblance in all this to a Deleuzian "respiration," that filmic "alternation between epic and intimate scenes, intensity and respite, tracking-shot and close-up, realistic and unrealistic sequences."[14] It is an effect of spectacle that subsequent artists have been tempted to adapt and remotivate, this dialogical movement between the image and its indefinite sublimation. But the formless control Milton sustained, the autonomic naturalness of Deleuze's "respiration," could not often be recaptured.

Dryden's *State of Innocence*

By all accounts, the first attempt to stage the spectacle of Milton's *Paradise Lost* was Dryden's rhymed rendering, *The State of Innocence, and Fall of Man: An Opera Written in Heroique Verse, and Dedicated to her Royal Highness, the Dutchess*.[15] There are a few famous shreds of anecdotal evidence that Dryden sought out Milton in person for the express purpose of receiving his permission for the project: "Mr. Dryden... went with Mr. Waller in Company to make a Visit to Mr. Milton, and desire his Leave for putting his Paradise Lost into Rhime for the Stage. Well, Mr. Dryden, says Milton, it seems you have a mind to Tagg my Points, and you have my Leave to Tagg 'em, but some of 'em are so Awkward and Old Fashion'd that I think you had as good leave 'em as you found 'em."[16] This sounds like a mixed blessing: Milton acquiescing, perhaps reminded of his own plans for a dramatic telling of *Adam Unparadis'd*, but in language that makes Dryden simply modish. (Lewalski imagines Milton might have agreed to this adaptation in the hopes that "those who saw the stage version might be led back to the original, much as we might be led by a film to read the better book.")[17] In contrast to Milton's own "old-fashioned" verse, Dryden's rhymes are like aglets sported by the faddish and "tagged" to the end of ribbons, an ostentatious (and jangling) display of fashionable superfluity. His last remonstrance — that Dryden might be better off leaving his lines entirely alone — sounds equally equivocal: Dryden might coax Milton's blank verse into something dainty and newfangled, but Milton says because his lines are awkward to begin with, he expects a grotesque result, a silk purse out of a sow's ear. It is easy enough to gather the underlying message, however: Dryden's rhymes, those "inventions of a barbarous age," are the true grotesques, and Milton's warning not to alter his lines both a political riposte to Dryden's royalist poetics and a fair admonition that trying to adjust Milton's matter to the "modern bondage" of couplets will prove disastrous. As it turns out, Milton was right: Dryden's play was a failure as an opera, never performed, and serves mostly as a bellwether for centuries of similar frustrated attempts to tease out Milton's sublime effects from the verse that created it.[18]

Dryden himself was not an ardent defender of the work. When *The State of Innocence* was published in 1677, he claimed that the libretto had been completed "at a Months warning" and "not since Revis'd."[19] This marks the piece as one of either great haste or exceeding economy, but may also have been Dryden's way of compensating for the play's deficiencies. In his preface to *Amboyna* he also used the excuse of the play being "written in a Moneth" to explain its many "defects" ("the Subject barren, the Persons low, and the Writing not heightened with many labored Scenes").[20] Dryden asserts that his primary reason for issuing *The State of Innocence,* "an OPERA which was never acted," was to reassert his authorial control over a text that had been supposedly circulating widely in manuscript throughout England and on the continent. He claimed, perhaps spuriously, that "many hundred Copies of it" had been "dispers'd abroad without my knowledge or consent: so that every one gathering new faults, it became at length a Libel against me."[21] However, of the surviving manuscripts, none demonstrates any such accumulation of error, and the substantive textual variants that do exist are fairly minor. Dryden's act of recuperation may still have been genuine, but what pervades in the preface is a sense of artistic degradation. The prefatory matter included a commendatory verse from Nat Lee that seemed even to Dryden embarrassingly commendatory, as well as a dedicatory epistle to the Duchess of York, an epigraph from Ovid, and Dryden's essay defending (or excusing) his method of adaptation, "The Authors Apology for Heroique Poetry; and Poetique Licence."[22] In that essay, Dryden reveals a great deal of self-consciousness about the relationship between Milton's original and his own adaptation. He declares from the start, "I should be sorry, for my own sake, that any one should take the pains to compare them together: The Original being undoubtedly, one of the greatest, most noble, and most sublime POEMS, which either this Age or Nation has produc'd."[23] Some of this may be conventional posturing, but the combination of Dryden's defensiveness and modesty produces a feeling that the adaptation was, at the least, inchoate. Milton begins to sound like "the great Inhibitor, the Sphinx who strangles even strong imaginations in their cradles," Dryden the epigone who reputedly remarked of him, "This Man...Cuts us All Out, and the Ancients too."[24]

The fact that *The State of Innocence* was never performed furthers this sense of inferiority, though the failure to mount the opera may have been driven less by its art than by politics—Lewalski is convinced that Dryden likely intended the opera as part of the celebrations around the wedding of James and Mary of Modena and that the "unpopularity of that match made grand festivities unwise."[25] Conversely, Joad Raymond suggests that the play was never performed "because it was unfinished," and that it "carries several marks of a text awaiting further revision: the songs and music are unevenly distributed, and one scene (2.2) is in blank verse."[26] Raymond does not, however, offer any reason why Dryden would have left it unfinished in the first place. James Anderson Winn offers the fullest explanation on the possible reasons for the failure, arguing that the play's budget simply priced it out of production at Drury Lane: "staging it effectively would have cost thousands of pounds, too big a gamble for a company down on its luck." Other factors may have figured: Winn suggests both that "appropriate music may have been impossible to procure" and that "the possibility that someone would accuse Dryden of heretical language or take offense at the very idea of a religious opera may have been among the reasons why the King's players preferred the safely pagan *Ariane*."[27]

There have also been those who argued the play was never meant to be performed at all, primarily based on the problem of representing Adam and Eve's nudity. Johnson called it "a tragedy in heroic rhyme, but of which the personages are such as cannot be decently exhibited on the stage."[28] Following the same thread, Walter Scott also singled out the nakedness in Eden: "the costume of our first parents, had there been no other objection, must have excluded the 'State of Innocence' from the stage, and accordingly it was never intended for representation."[29] This position has been dismissed by those who point to the long history in England of staging Adam and Eve as part of the mystery cycles, and to Dryden's own stage direction that the woman in Eve's dream be "habited" like her.[30] Undoubtedly the manner of habiting Adam and Eve has traditionally been one of the significant directorial decisions in bringing them to the stage. William Tydeman notes that in one of the earliest records, that of the Anglo-Norman *Adam,* "Adam and Eve wear garments of glory in Paradise. Adam and Eve shall take their places before [God], Adam wearing a red tunicle, but Eve in the white garments proper to a woman, with a white silk headdress"; after the Fall, these "solemn vestments" are exchanged for "poor garments sewn with figleaves."[31] But costuming of this sort gives way in most other records to what Tydeman calls "the medieval equivalent of the modern body-stocking or leotard and tights."[32] Thus, Adam and Eve (usually played by a man) wore a variety of outfits to give, paradoxically, the illusion that they were shamelessly naked and not merely signifying innocence.

There were various innovations in the "body-suit": "in 1538 Adam and Eve are simply listed as 'neckend' but in a later list we are informed that they are 'in lybkleider, alls nacket [in body-clothing, as if naked],' and a 1583 entry confirms that they wore 'Lybkleidern uber den blossen lyb [body-clothing over the bare skin].'" Meanwhile, "the 1565 inventory of the Norwich Grocers' Guild who presented the Creation includes '2 costes [coats] and a payre hosen for Eve, stayned [dyed]' and 'A cote and hosen for Adam, steyned.'" Finally, in the Cornish staging of the *Creation of the World,* "Adam and Eve are to be 'aprlet in whytt lether,' but they act as if naked, for there are to be 'fig leaves redy to cover ther members,' and . . . there are 'garmentis of skynnes to be geven to Adam and Eva by the angell.'"[33] Such precedents only begin to address the problem of adapting Milton's Adam and Eve, who are not only unashamed in walking about unclothed but also make love before the Fall and engage in lascivious sex after it.[34] Dryden's couple never goes that far on stage, though Eve in particular relates graphically the experience of her intercourse with Adam, provoking Lucifer's envy and perhaps pushing the boundaries of comfort for opera-goers.

I would argue that Dryden's attempts at reconciling the sublime in Milton with the limited possibilities of the stage are at the heart of its representational problems in *The State of Innocence.* Not coincidentally, astronomical budgets, religious sensitivity, and the problem of "habiting" Adam and Eve are frequent explanations for why cinematic adaptations of *Paradise Lost* have been generally unsuccessful. But it is in furnishing Milton's sublime images for the stage that Dryden creates an unstageable production. His adaptation anticipates a number of other pressures that emerge in later attempts to adapt *Paradise Lost* for the cinema: how to manage the allusive and weighty poetry for a popular audience, how and where to compress the epic action (Dryden, like Collier in the 1960s, seems to have seen the story as a domestic melodrama between Adam, Eve, and Lucifer, cutting almost all of the war, as well as God and the Son), and how to make manifest the unimaginable, to transform sublimity into spectacle.[35] Some of its solutions recur in the adaptations of succeeding centuries— easing the verse into something more vernacular, incorporating dumb shows, dance, and musical numbers to minimize the dependence on Milton's language, and most importantly relying on cutting-edge technologies to push the limits of representation into a suitably Miltonic—and so ineffable—realm.[36]

Dryden's opening scene is also his most striking. In fact, he packs so much into the first vision that there is hardly enough energy left to sustain the remaining acts:

> The first Scene represents a Chaos, or a confus'd Mass of Matter; the Stage is almost wholly dark: A symphony of Warlike Music is heard for some time; then from the Heavens, (which are opened) fall the rebellious Angels wheeling in the Air, and seeming transfix'd with Thunderbolts: The bottom of the Stage being opened, receives the Angels, who fall out of sight. Tunes of Victory are play'd, and an Hymn sung; Angels discover'd above, brandishing their Swords: The Music ceasing, and the Heavens being clos'd, the Scene shifts, and on a sudden represents Hell: Part of the Scene is a Lake of Brimstone or rowling Fire; the Earth of a burnt colour: The fall'n Angels appear on the Lake, lying prostrate; a Tune of Horrour and Lamentation is heard.[37]

Here in the span of two scenic shifts is both a parallel to Milton's own opening in book 1 and an overture for the drama in its entirety. Dryden begins with the summation of the war, the rebel angels "Hurl'd headlong flaming from th' Ethereal Skie / With hideous ruine and combustion down / To bottomless perdition," and matches in the indefinite pace of "Warlike Music...heard for some time" the contained Miltonic interval of "Nine times the Space that measures Day and Night" (*PL* 1.45–47, 50). Dryden transmutes Milton's flames and combustion into fixed bolts of lightning, piercing the angels "wheeling in the air." It is a type of visual catachresis, a baffling combination of the kinetic and the static: flashes of light frozen in space, riveted angels spinning in gyres. Such is Dryden's Chaos and "confused Mass of Matter." When these paradoxical representations give way to the "Lake of Brimstone," for which Dryden also adopts Milton's impeccable phrasing of "rowling," there is a sudden and palpable condensation of action. The immediate contrast of angels above, "brandishing swords" to the "tunes of victory," and the leaden thud of angels "lying prostrate" to a "tune of horror," narrates the fall of all that has been and all that is to come. Visually, the scene must have been quite confusing: angels on wires crisscrossing the stage, a symphony of music fading in and out, the floor being opened, more angels waggling swords high above, and all in Dryden's version of "darkness visible": a blacked-out stage where action for the actors would have been as dizzying as for the spectators.

Scott may have been the first to decry the implausibility of such spectacles: "stage directions...supply the place of the terrific and beautiful descriptions of Milton. What idea, except burlesque, can we form of the expulsion of the fallen angels from heaven, literally represented by their tumbling down upon the stage? Or what feelings of terror can be excited by the idea of an opera hell, composed of pasteboard and flaming rosin?"[38] But as Lawrence suggests, such effects were already current in French and Italian opera, though "Had it reached the stage just when it was written, *The State of Innocence* would have been the most elaborate spectacle seen up to that time in an English theatre."[39] Vinton A. Dearing catalogues a number of stage directions in Drury Lane opera at the time that suggest "effects like the opening display of *The State of Innocence* were possible," though almost all his examples come after the theater's opening in 1674 (when it was referred to as a "Plain Built House" with no "Scenes" or "Machines").[40] In Nathaniel Lee's own *Sophonisba* (April 1675), for instance, there is the direction "The Scene drawn, discovers a Heaven of blood, two Suns, Spirits in Battle, Arrows shot to and fro in the Air: Cryes of yielding Persons, &," while in works such as John Crowne's *The Destruction of Jerusalem* (January 1677) and Lee's *Mithridates* (February 1678), there is evidence for increased use of machinery: "An Angel descends over the Altar" and afterward "ascends"; "An Image of Victory descends with two Crowns in her hands."[41] But Dearing's comparisons never fully embody the careful orchestration and technical wizardry of Dryden's opening. All of the directions he cites, for instance, use the word "ascend" or "descend" or "arises," a simple verticality purposefully disrupted in *The State of Innocence*. And the "Heaven of blood" in *Sophonisba* seems far more pictorial, its archers shooting "to and fro" much more systematic and axial than the chaos and confusion of Dryden's wheeling, "rowling" spirits.[42]

Dryden's own articulation of his adaptative approach shows that he was striving to reproduce the sublimity of Milton, to translate a writerly poetic imagination into a new and somewhat experimental medium: "Imagining is, in it self, the very heighth and life of Poetry. 'Tis, as Longinus describes it, a Discourse, which, by a kind of Enthusiasm, or extraordinary emotion of the Soul, makes it seem to us, that we behold those things which the Poet paints, so as to be pleas'd with them, and to admire them."[43] The preface thus makes a bold retreat to more meager classicisms—that the imagination produces images for pleasure and admiration—and Dryden never makes the case for a more ambitious transposition of his own "painted poem." In his commendatory verse, Nat Lee captures (and rejoices at) this very conversion of Milton's illimitable for Dryden's sensible: "So when your Sense his mystic reason clear'd, / The melancholy Scene all gay appear'd; / New light leapt up, and a new glory smil'd."[44] As Bernard Harris glosses the line, Lee celebrates Dryden's effort at "presenting the product to the sophisticated gaze and literary taste of the court," and "to have penetrated arguments conveyed in obscure metaphors and translated them into sensible, tangible, concrete, and above all reasonable language."[45] Dryden, for his part, seems to recognize an unintended reduction, that in shining a clear light on Milton's complicated mysticism he has, in fact, fallen short of those sublime effects described by Longinus: "I wish I could produce any one example of excellent imaging in all this Poem: perhaps I cannot: but that which comes nearest it, is in these four lines, which have been sufficiently canvas'd by my well-natur'd Censors. 'Seraph and Cherub, careless of their charge, / And wanton, in full ease now live at large: / Unguarded leave the passes of the Sky; / And all dissolv'd in Hallelujahs lye.'"[46] What Dryden seems to approve of most here is the oblique inexpressibility conveyed in the line "all dissolv'd in Hallelujahs." What others had complained of as an absurdity (Dryden quotes one critic, "I have heard...of Anchove's dissolv'd in Sauce; but never of an Angel in Hallelujahs"), Dryden presents as the closest his work comes to achieving Milton's sublimity—to dissolving even into song the poetic force of Milton's angels.

Elsewhere in the preface, Dryden is more conservative, describing the problem of representing the unrepresentable by resorting to the same language of accommodation Milton employs in *Paradise Lost*:

> how are Poetical Fictions, how are Hippocentaures and Chymaeras, or how are Angels and immaterial Substances to be Imag'd; which some of them are things quite out of Nature: others, such whereof we can have no notion?...The answer is easie to the first part of it. The fiction of some Beings which are not in Nature...has been founded on the conjunction of two Natures, which have a real separate Being. So Hippocentaures were imag'd, by joining the Natures of a Man and Horse together....For Immaterial Substances we are authoriz'd by Scripture in their description: and herein the Text accommodates it self to vulgar apprehension, in giving Angels the likeness of beautiful young men. Thus, after the Pagan Divinity, has *Homer* drawn his Gods with humane Faces: and thus we have notions of things above us, by describing them like other beings more within our knowledge.[47]

The problem for Dryden is that Milton's accommodating acts are bound up with a poetics of inexpressibility, while the accommodations of the stage are freighted with concretized restrictions, the mechanics of performer and performance. When Dryden attempts to reproduce Milton's ineffabilities, as in the opening stage direction or the dissolving angels, defying convention and the pleasing clarity celebrated by Lee, the work seems unpresentable. When he falls back solely on "vulgar apprehension," on approximations and refinements, merely "tagging" verse as if, as Lee puts it, he "cou'd well dispose" what Milton had only "rudely cast," the potency of the sublime effects becomes hopelessly enervated.[48]

That this latter path seems to have been the dominant one is suggested by Andrew Marvell's barbed prefatory poem in the second edition of *Paradise Lost,* released a few months after Dryden's play was registered. Whether Marvell had read Dryden's manuscript or had only heard at secondhand of his visit to Milton, his condemnation of the effort is crushing:

> Jealous was I that some less skilful hand
> (Such as disquiet always what is well,
> And by ill imitating would excel)
> Might hence presume the whole Creation's day
> To change in Scenes, and show it in a Play.
> Pardon me, Mighty Poet, nor despise
> My causeless, yet not impious, surmise.
> But I am now convinc'd, and none will dare
> Within thy Labours to pretend a share.
> ⋯⋯⋯
> Well mightst thou scorn thy Readers to allure
> With tinkling Rime, of thy own sense secure;
> While the *Town-Bayes* writes all the while and spells,
> And like a Pack-horse tires without his Bells:
> Their Fancies like our Bushy-points appear,
> The Poets tag them, we for fashion wear.[49]

Lewalski observes that in singling out Dryden's adaptation, Marvell wants to "exemplify the folly of trying to contain genius and inspiration within conventional norms."[50] He does so not only by referencing Dryden's "tagged" rhymes, the bells and whistles of an inferior and beastly poet, but by earlier in the poem expressing succinctly the dialogics of Milton's epic: its "delight and horror," its "gravity and ease." (One of Marvell's most biting lines is also easy to miss: his fears of a "less skilful hand" transforming *Paradise Lost* into a play are "causeless"—this seems intended to be a painful reminder of Dryden's failure to mount the opera and implies, at least in this immediate context, that it was because of the play's

aesthetic defects rather than political or financial circumstances.)
Contra Lee's ebullient celebration of *The State of Innocence* as
"gay," "light," "mild," and "gawdy," Dryden seems conscious in
his own preface of the terrible sublimities alluded to by Marvell.
The fact that his play was never performed can be read as the greatest indicator that, at least to some degree, he succeeded too well
in achieving them.

The remainder of Dryden's drama never quite matches the
intensity of the opening, though he reverts again and again to
extravagant special effects and narrative involutions that contribute to the unstageability. Devils "rise up and fly" from off their
fiery lake, the palace of Pandaemonium surges up from the stage,
and in an intriguing entr'acte, Dryden dramatizes the "the Sports
of the Devils; as Flights and Dancing in Grotesque Figures: and a
Song expressing the change of their condition; what they enjoy'd
before; and how they fell bravely in Battel, having deserv'd Victory
by their Valour; and what they would have done if they had
Conquer'd."[51] This parallels Milton's interlude in book 2, when
the fallen host engage in their Olympiad and "sing / With notes
Angelical to many a Harp / Thir own Heroic deeds and hapless
fall / By doom of battle" (*PL* 2.547–50). But what in Milton reads
as an infinitely looping *mise en abyme,* in which the fallen angels
take up the poem they themselves inhabit and sing aimlessly around
and around the tale of their tale, becomes in Dryden not an ironic
moment of narcissistic self-referentiality, but an expression of the
gap between source and adaptation. Dryden's sports and songs
here re-narrate not the play but the poem, driven into the interstitial spaces between acts 1 and 2, a sort of nowhere land outside
but dependent on the text where the enabling narrative — the war
in heaven as recited in *Paradise Lost* — becomes endungeoned. Yet
Dryden goes even further, not only appropriating and condemning, but also suggesting a new song, a new theme: not only what
they lost, but also what they hoped to gain — "what they would
have done if they had Conquer'd." It is a remarkable and ambitious addition, but one from which Dryden ultimately shies. The
seed to surpass Milton's vision is there, to reimagine the source as
the devils themselves are reimagining the doom of battle, but there
the text stops short. Dryden's new song is left to fall through the

cracks, even as it leaves a last, empty imprint of the full design of Dryden's adaptive plan.

The angels, meanwhile, in their many instances of deus ex machina, do not merely descend to earth by cloud: they career. In Lucifer's case, this is done against a backdrop of celestial motion and sophisticated lighting: "The Scene changes; and represents above, a Sun, gloriously rising, and moving orbicularly: at a distance, below, is the Moon; the part next the Sun enlightened, the other dark. A black cloud comes whirling from the adverse part of the Heavens, bearing Lucifer in it; at his nearer approach, the body of the Sun is dark'ned."[52] Not to be outdone, Uriel next comes slanting down from the heavens on a swift chariot drawn by white horses, and his arrival rekindles the light of the sun that Lucifer has momentarily eclipsed. Later, Gabriel and Ithuriel likewise descend on clouds only after "flying cross each other," and in the device's greatest *coup de théâtre,* "The Cloud descends with six Angels in it; and when it's near the ground, breaks; and on each side, discovers six more: they descend out of the Cloud. *Raphael* and *Gabriel* discourse with Adam, the rest stand at distance."[53] It is hard to regard such spectacles as anything but the sensational corollary of Dryden's tagged verse—if Milton's Uriel descends on an indefinite sunbeam, Dryden's must drive the latest souped-up chariot; if Milton's Raphael comes down like a phoenix, gradually and majestically unfurling his six seraphic wings, Dryden's must sail a self-generating embryonic cloud, unwinding not just wings but entire angels (and those in nice, symmetrical array) that explode onto the scene in a blinding "floud of light."[54] Dryden's visual effects at once acknowledge and attempt to supersede the sublimity of *Paradise Lost.*

The Dream of Eve is the centerpiece of Dryden's drama. Here Milton's version of Eve's vision becomes reconfigured as a kind of dumb show in which Lucifer stages, much like his counterpart in *Paradise Regained,* a sensuous masque: "*Lucifer* sits down by *Eve,* and seems to whisper in her ear. A Vision, where a Tree rises loaden with Fruit; four Spirits rise with it, and draw a canopie out of the tree, other Spirits dance about the Tree in deform'd shapes, after the Dance an Angel enters, with a Woman, habited like *Eve.*"[55]

The Angel then offers a song—the only finished set piece in the drama—tempting the Woman into a rehearsal of the Fall to come. The entirety of the dream sequence is less technically demanding than Dryden's other directions, though it still involves much intricate machinery, as when "Two Angels descend" and "take the Woman each by the hand, and fly up with her out of sight."[56] What stands out most, perhaps, is the way Dryden absorbs the dream of Milton's Eve as a presentiment of his own opera. Milton's Eve, who wants nothing more than not to be "Earth confin'd" (*PL* 5.78), but "in the Air" to "Ascend to Heav'n" (5.78, 79, 80), recalls to Adam how "Forthwith up to the Clouds" she "flew, and underneath beheld / The Earth outstretcht immense, a prospect wide / And various" (5.86–89). These desires are played out literally in the dumb show of Dryden's Eve. But in *Paradise Lost*, Eve also "wond[ers]" at her "flight and change / To this high exaltation" (5.89–90), and as she wonders she sinks back into her own sleeping form, a vertiginous prefigurement of the Fall. In *The State of Innocence*, Eve's dream double never comes back to earth but vanishes "out of sight." What Dryden could not reproduce from Milton—the cosmoramic perspective of Milton's Eve—he adapts into an infinite vanishing point. By thus also erasing the conceit of rising and sinking as emblematic of Eve's fall, the opera can also revel in its primary artistry—the visual spectacle of three-dimensional flight—as not only a flouting of metaphor (Dryden's dream preenacts and discloses rather than alluding or signifying) but also as a kind of fulfillment of what Milton/Eve could only imagine.

In the opera's final act, when Adam and Eve receive their visions of human history (put forth by Raphael rather than Michael, whom Dryden cuts), the couple view both "A battle at land, and a Naval fight."[57] These generalized images of war are meant to instance the "many shapes of death" in *Paradise Lost*, book 11. Contending that "the great vision of the future history of man has been sacrificed for a pageant of contemporary war so present to the mind of the time that it is instantly and simply oppressive to the spirit," Bernard Harris reads the simple descriptor "Naval" as an indicator for the Third Anglo-Dutch War.[58] There certainly may be shades of that conflict, but the deliberate indefiniteness of the images suggests once again Dryden's attempts to harness the power of Milton's indescribability. And in this masterstroke of compression, which is also a dilation—a stage direction without end, a globalizing if not universalizing of space (land and sea), and a kind of sublimation of Milton's war in heaven, cut from Dryden but alluded to here again in absence (land and sea and not air)—Dryden comes closest to denying and duplicating Milton's original. Winn points out that "*The State of Innocence* reversed what Dryden hoped would be the direction of his career: he was planning to retire from the stage to write an epic poem, yet this opera was an exercise in turning epic into drama."[59] It was an exercise that others would soon take up, with much the same uneven success.

Dryden himself would go on to stage spectacles at Dorset Garden that rivaled the technical demands of *The State of Innocence*, though he apparently never attempted to rework or remount the Milton adaptation. The lavish *Albion and Albanius* (1684–85), with its "stunning profusion of complex scenes and machines" and "Poetical Hell" in act 2 (scenes Judith Milhous assures us were, this time at least, "not just the playwright's pipedream") perhaps comes closest to the vision Dryden laid out in his earlier opera.[60] However, the opera did experience at least one curious revival: as a play in the puppet theater. The *Spectator* advertised the performance, which was competing against a revival of Dryden's *Tempest* at Drury Lane: "At Punch's Theatre, in the Little Piazza, Covent-Garden, to Day and to Morrow, the 15th and 16th of this instant February, will be presented an Opera call'd, The State of Innocence, or the Fall of Man. With Variety of Surprising Scenes and Machines, particularly the Scene of Paradise in its primitive Station, with Birds, Beasts, and all its ancient Inhabitants: The Subtilty of the Serpent in betraying Adam and Eve; a diverting Dialogue between Signior Punchanella [*sic*] and Madamoiselle Sousabella Pignatella, and other Diversions too long to insert here."[61] There is little of Dryden's narrative here, but a sustained emphasis on spectacle—the "surprising" portrayal of paradise, the menagerie of the garden (and whatever else is subsumed in "ancient Inhabitants"). And the interlude between Punch and his wife, if anything like their "dancing merrily in the ark" during a performance of the Deluge, promises additional exuberance (or a burlesque of Adam and Eve's domestic discord).[62] But in this reduced theater, the "scenes and machines" that never materialized for Dryden were at last set in motion.

PANTOMIME SPECTACLE

Some 80 years after the publication of Dryden's libretto, Giovanni Niccolo Servandoni's spectacular pantomime *The Fall of the Rebel Angels* premiered in Paris on March 12, 1758. Servandoni was well established by this point as the premier designer of spectacle in Paris and beyond. Diderot memorialized him as "a great stage designer, great architect, good painter, and sublime decorator," while he is perhaps most famous today as the designer of the façade of the church of Saint-Sulpice.[63] Born in 1695 in Florence, he moved to Paris in 1724 and quickly rose in prestige, first with the Royal Academy of Music, the Opera, where he was the chief painter and decorator for a number of lavish sets, and then as a designer for grand outdoor spectaculars. In 1729–30, he crafted a number of larger-than-life celebrations for the birth of the dauphin, including a gargantuan scene on the Seine:

> The structure was in the form of two mountains united at their base, representing the Pyrenees and symbolizing the alliance between France and Spain. Some waterfalls, trees, plants, Tritons, Nereides, and other sea creatures populated the composition. The two mountains floated on two boats richly decorated with gold and shells. The boats also supported orthogonal structures representing the temples of Pleasure and Joy, occupied by the musicians. On either side, two floating terraces covered with colored sand and patterns of grass supported two rocks on which two bronze statues again represented [Spain and France]. Elaborate fireworks were also staged and divided into two acts. For about an hour, fireworks were launched from various sea monsters, and the two mountains transformed into volcanoes. Then, from the centre of the two mountains, a powerful light simulated the rising of the sun. At the same time, a giant rainbow linked the two mountains, and on top, the goddess Iris floated on a cloud.[64]

The representational possibilities of such spectacles whetted Servandoni's appetite for a more profound space than even the generous dimensions of the Paris Opera could provide. He may also have desired more control over operational procedures: an eyewitness report in *The Political State of Great Britain* reports that the simulation of the sun could not be accomplished in the allotted time, and the climax of the performance—Iris rising on her Rainbow, with its promise of a new covenant between France and Spain—was too "unwieldy and unmanageable" to be controlled, and so did not appear.[65] And so in 1738, Servandoni received permission to use the Salle des Machines of the Tuileries, whose vast reaches had made it unfit acoustically to house operatic works. The stage in the Salle des Machines was recorded as an amazing 132 feet deep (while only 30 feet wide at the proscenium opening), and its machinery—estimated to cover some 2,400 square feet—could handle even "three hundred divinities" descending on clouds.[66]

Each spring from 1738 to 1742, Servandoni presented there a new spectacle. His first effort was a towering diorama of Saint Peter's in Rome that included dramatic shifts in light alongside other trompe l'oeil effects to present to spectators an immersive realism. Servandoni's express purpose, he claimed, was to make manifest the famous basilica for those unable themselves to travel to Italy (a rationale that anticipated the great panoramas of the nineteenth century). The claim is an interesting motivation here because Servandoni's design was itself a re-creation of a painting by his mentor Giovanni Paolo Pannini. And it is this very act of re-creating other art forms—Servandoni, in fact, saw them as comfortably miscible, as attested to in his detailed descriptions of the stagings, in which painting, acting, architecture, music, and mechanics all merged into one encompassing spectacle—that seemed most to trouble critics, some of whom, for instance, saw the presentation of marvels as the sole domain of epic poetry. This bold remapping of the boundaries between disciplines inevitably dovetailed with Servandoni's efforts at erasing the edges of the stage itself. The illusory effects of the Saint Peter's diorama depended upon a technique in which Servandoni had been trained in Italy, the *scena per angolo* or oblique perspective design, which decentered the viewing subject and established manifold vanishing points. Such techniques "create the illusion of an endless extension to the stage...precisely because the boundaries of the virtual space could not be grasped," and Servandoni accented the effect with towers, trees, and other vertical structures that appeared to soar beyond the frame of the stage.[67] The natural depths of the Salle des Machines stage obviously made such effects as towering backdrops even more believable and helped to draw the spectators further into the scene, creating a vertiginous sensation in multiple dimensions. Marc Olivier reads the event as a seamless transmedial adaptation: "Servandoni's spectacle brings the painting to life with meticulous attention to authenticity and detail, including a vault seventy feet high."[68] The precise identification of Servandoni's creation here is difficult to articulate: is it a painting come to life? (Indeed, does it remain still, primarily, a painting?) Is it a sculpture? An architectural model? It is surely not another basilica, though the vaulted heights render it quite differently from the two-dimensional panoramas that hoped to achieve the same verisimilitudes.

Despite the lifelike quality of the work, the initial diorama of St. Peter's was in other ways quite poised—there was no live acting or singing, simply the dynamism of the decor. While the power of this effect alone was affirmed by those who attended (Quatremère de Quincy called it a "drama without words that keeps the mind interested in the scenic action through the eyes only"),[69] Servandoni would address the limitations of static images in his subsequent spectacles. After *Pandora* in 1739, the impresario allowed for the addition of pantomime actors who could bring "some kind of life to this spectacle."[70] Thus, *The Descent of Aeneas into Hell*, *The Adventures of Ulysses*, and *Hero and Leander* all featured muted dramatic action that supplemented the real focus—the play of light and machine (and what Olivier sees more broadly in Servandoni's work as "the confrontation of nature and technology").[71] The dramatic action, however, rarely went much beyond that of a glorified *tableau vivant*.

So exorbitant were the productions that, after *Hero and Leander*, Servandoni could no longer afford to put them on, and he returned to his more lucrative work with the Opera, not reprising his spectacles in the Salle des Machines until 1754. With the

important addition of orchestral accompaniment, he then produced in succeeding years *The Enchanted Forest* (based on Tasso's
Gerusalemme liberata), *The Coronation of Constantine, The
Conquest of the Mongols, The Triumph of Wedded Love,* and, finally,
The Fall of the Rebel Angels (*La chute des anges rebelles*), taken from
Milton's *Paradise Lost.* As a group, Servandoni's entertainments
were wildly popular and played to packed houses. Consequently,
they were also regarded increasingly by contemporary theater critics as vulgar abominations. Of *The Enchanted Forest,* Grimm wrote,
"Geminiani's music is…detestable, and the acting of the mimes
shamefully mediocre. The marvelous is the sole domain of the epic
poet; the desire to realize one's fantasies leads to puerility."[72] It
remained for Servandoni to prove that the marvelous could be produced not just by epic poetry but the sublimity of the theater as
well, but his choice of Milton seems ultimately to have proven a
fatal mistake.

Like his other spectacles, *The Fall of the Rebel Angels* was a
mechanical pantomime, a mute spectacle, featuring extraordinary
fulminations and pyrotechnics but little dramatization of character or attention to dramatic plot. That is not to say there was
not action: in its first two acts, the entertainment covered most
of Milton's books 1 and 2, with a third act dramatizing the war
in heaven. It promised a dazzling display of light and shadow that
"should produce on the mind all the effect one expects from a
silent spectacle."[73] And like Raphael, Servandoni claims he "gives
bodily form to spiritual things and presents within these sensible
figures that which would surpass the limits of the human mind."[74]
The subject matter will show to advantage all the artistry of painting and perspective and "ingenious movement of machinery," all
to the accompaniment of some 160 musicians. Servandoni hews
closely to Milton's original throughout those sequences it attempts
to represent, though making a Procrustean cut of much of the
larger narrative. The opening scene begins with a river of fire, dark
subterranean caverns of Divine Justice, and Satan discovered in
all his fallen misery and pride floating on the lake of fire. He ral-
lies his troops amid earthquakes and trembling rocks, while in the
third scene the stage becomes dominated by a volcanic mountain
spewing great gouts of (painted) flame. Deep veins of silver, gold,

and sparkling jewels crease the rocks. Satan assumes his place on a dragon chariot to direct the building of Pandaemonium from these raw materials.

The second act takes up after the building: Pandaemonium is revealed, the demons discovered in its midst. Satan presides on his high throne amid a palace oozing pagan iconography: a baldaquin covered in Egyptian hieroglyphs, mysterious candelabras, and other markers of demonic worship. The council in hell follows, with Satan surrounded not only by his principals but such lesser Miltonic figures as Chemos, Baalim, Astaroth, Tammuz, Rimmon, and Dagon, the Egyptian deities Osiris, Isis, and Horus, and assortments of demons in varied forms. The final act assumes the action of Milton's sixth book, the war in heaven, though the production makes it seem as if this assault follows upon the war council: Satan leaves hell through thick dark clouds and flashes of lightning. A "troupe innumerable" of demons follows, and at the sound of trumpets battle is joined in heaven. Michael, Raphael, Gabriel, Uriel, Abdiel, and even Azael and Zophiel join in defense of heaven, but they are temporarily defeated by the demonic horde. Servandoni makes efficient use of the profusion of boulders in the opening sets, as the demons bring these with them to heaven (the entire terrain was lifted magically into the air by the theater's colossal machinery). He then adapts the mountain-throwing from the second day of the war in Milton, and these pieces of hell-rock briefly overwhelm the loyal angels (fusing, too, the idea of Satan's "materials dark and crude" from "deep underground" as part of his cannonade in *Paradise Lost* 6.478). In the grand finale, the clouds part all at once to reveal the Son in his blazing chariot, advancing on the rebel host with terrible thunder and lightning until the last of the rebels has fallen.

Servandoni had been pitching similar *Sturm und Drang* effects since his first offering, *Pandora*, in 1739:

> The show will open with a depiction of chaos, and once the viewers have gazed at this for a while, then this formless mass in all its parts will move and expand to the sound of thunder and flashes of lightning. Each element will take the place that Nature intended for it: fire, represented by transparencies, will soar into the highest regions....Earthquakes, volcanoes, firestorms, overturned

boulders, thunder, lightning, and everything that may help depict universal disorder will be used for this extravaganza, which will last more than an hour in continual motion. To enrich and enliven this performance, we have employed everything that architecture, painting, and mechanics could provide.[75]

The resemblances here to *The Fall of the Rebel Angels* suggest at least some recycling of properties and mechanisms: boulders, fiery transparencies, tempestuous noise, Pandora and Pandaemonium. But even the language has remained continuous: he describes the same fusion of the arts, the same animation of space, all against a cosmography of chaos and disharmony. Between Servandoni's first and last spectacles is also a commitment to the soundlessness of the actors: while Servandoni's adaptation of Milton is one of the most literal, scene-by-scene depictions of Milton's poem, there is along the way not a single utterance of Milton's poetry. It is a primary example of the difficulties in adapting *Paradise Lost* and the inadequacies of technical effect: when "Milton" is stripped of his verse, his visions become delimited, derivative, trite, and manqué. But when his verse is maintained, it seems to complicate and impede those same visions. It is a tension that emerges, sometimes explosively, in every attempt to adapt Milton's poem. And it seems to have been the case most pronouncedly with Servandoni.

Jeanne Bouché reports that Servandoni's repeated debts contributed to the eventual bankruptcy of the Tuileries spectacles. He spared no expense in his productions and finally had nothing but expense. Bouché adds further that the demise of Servandoni's spectacles owed something to the reasonable fears that the theater would eventually catch fire, brought about by the scores of daring (and open) flames Servandoni favored. More damning still, however, was the intensification of critical attacks.[76] Since the first spectacle, Servandoni had to withstand the criticisms of elitist theatergoers who saw the glorification of English pantomime as both base and needlessly conspicuous. By the time of *The Fall of the Rebel Angels,* the enchantment of the spectacle had been almost completely dissipated, driven by the treatment of the Miltonic subject matter. The *Journal Encyclopédique* described the attempt as too conservative and too tainted by "l'amour-propre,"[77] a self-consciousness that spoiled the effect of the original. Another reviewer in *L'année littéraire* found the show's execution quite unspectacular and sounded the death-knell for Servandoni's extravagant shows.[78] Diderot writes that *The Fall of the Rebel Angels* was so poorly done "that it fell beyond recovery at the very first performance."[79]

According to *L'année littéraire*, Satan's appearance on the flaming lake was not sufficiently "magical." The scene of the infernal council was painted in too light a color to seem terrifying and the actors themselves were too static. Satan in particular did not meditate on his lot vehemently enough. Causing further disappointment was the absence of any of Milton's monsters—his "*Gorgons* and *Hydras,* and *Chimeras* dire" (*PL* 2.628). Notwithstanding others' anxieties over fire, the reviewer complained that the flames of the volcanic mount were only painted and not really gushing lava. Even the design of Pandaemonium showed itself to be the work of a "student" and not a "grand master" (it was credited to M. de Wailly, not Servandoni himself): the Doric columns supporting Satan's throne were too small, "the candelabras had the air of a magic lantern by the form and not by the effect," and the hieroglyphs were poorly arranged.[80] In this critique, there is perhaps some lingering effect of Voltaire's pronouncement that Milton's Pandaemonium was a "ridiculous" "contrivance," full of mismatched styles and ludicrous effects that might as well fit a mock-heroic piece as an epic of high seriousness.[81] As for Servandoni's war in heaven, the demons were far too orderly, the rocks too small to impress, the clouds too uniform and rectangular, the "Glory" (the machine intended to support the divine forces) too poorly lit. In short, the spectacle failed at its primary goal of immersing its audience in the verisimilitude of the scene. It is evident that even with all the technical artistry available to him, Servandoni's failure seemed driven mostly by the limits of his stagecraft. One of the overriding criticisms was that there was far too little *motion* involved, and what motion there was came across as plainly artificial, mechanical.

The reviewer's final comment is perhaps the most revealing: "I am all the more angered and surprised, as I truly enjoy these sorts of spectacles, and I still remember having previously seen, with much pleasure, *The Descent of Aeneas into Hell, The Enchanted Forest,* and many other works worthy of the grandeur of the place they were staged, and of the connoisseurs they drew to attend."[82] A preference for Aeneas over Satan, or the demonic battles of *The Enchanted Forest* over the war in heaven, may be idiosyncratic. But Servandoni was sensitive to the differences as well, hoping in his *Description* that, "since the Chevalier Servandoni is making an effort to reconcile the ideas of his author, he hopes that he will not be blamed for exposing on the stage things which in any other spectacle would appear risky, even out of place."[83] While the performance visibly recycled efforts from previous seasons, Servandoni's adaptation of *Paradise Lost* failed not because of its resemblances but despite them. The Salle des Machines shut down after the season, and after being transformed and converted into an operatic theater (with improved acoustics) was never in use again in its capacity as a space for spectacle. Servandoni's efforts at achieving a "scenic action" that could captivate the mind through the eyes alone, however, would be taken up and remodeled by others seeking innovative entertainments as the eighteenth century continued.

In 1763, a decade after Servandoni but clearly influenced by his work, another pantomime attempted to accommodate even more of the poem, including the temptation and fall of Eve: Louis Josse's production *L'origine du monde et la chute du premier home, pièce en cinq actes tirée du Paradis perdu de Milton.*[84] Josse's work seems to have been the template for a nineteenth century adaptation that Martin Meisel calls "the climax of spectacular scriptural illustration in the French theater": Adolphe Philippe D'Ennery and Ferdinand Dugué's adaptation of Milton, *Le paradis perdu: Drame en cinq actes et douze tableaux.*[85] A free mixture of *Paradise Lost* and Byron's *Cain, Le paradis perdu* premiered in March 1856 at Le Théatre de L'Ambigu-Comique and is notable not only for its éclat effects but also for following Milton's verse quite closely and for appropriating a number of his secondary characters. The opening tableau presents the fallen angels roiling and howling in the bituminous lake against a backdrop of thunder, lightning, and

waves of flame; a few scattered legionnaires still cling to the edges
of the abyss, while Satan is chained to a rock front and center.
After an initial speech that ranges from anguish to defiance, Satan
then begins a dialogue not with Beelzebub but with an Angel
of Mercy ("L'Ange du Pardon") in a scene clearly indebted to
Shelley's *Prometheus Unbound.* In the exchange, Satan is chas-
tised and offered a chance at redemption. D'Ennery and Dugué
then unload as retorts almost all of Satan's best lines from the first
book of *Paradise Lost:* "tout n'est pas perdu! il me reste la volonté
inflexible, la soif insatiable de la vengeance et une haine immor-
telle comme la sienne!" and, of course, "Salut, tenebreuse hor-
reur!...salut, monde infernal! Mieux vaut régner dans l'enfer que
server dans le ciel!" (that is, "All is not lost; the unconquerable
Will, / And study of revenge, immortal hate" and "Hail horrors,
hail / Infernal world"; "Better to reign in hell than serve in heaven"
[*PL* 1.106–07, 250–01, 263]).[86]

The usual suspects join Satan in the gulf—Beelzebub, Belial,
Moloch (Mammon is missing)—but speaking parts are also
afforded Chemos (Chamos) and Adramalech, while Ramiel,
Mulciber, Azazel (Azaziel), and Ashtaroth (Astaroth) are among
the named attendant *démons.* The second tableau, incorporating
most of these figures, features the raising of Pandaemonium: "A
vast edifice shining with bizarre splendors; it is supported by columns of molten metal and is bounded by an immense area; under
the arched roof hang long lines of sparkling lamps. In the middle
of the palace, a magnificent throne."[87] The palace is conveyed in
mostly Miltonic terms—the metallic columns, the "ample spaces,"
and the "arched roof" from which "Pendant by subtle Magic many
a row / Of Starry Lamps and blazing Cressets...yielded light."
Especially compelling is the gloss on the bizarre magnificence
of its design—astounding and eclectic but also garish, orgu-
lous. It is an impression one can receive from Milton's description, with its hodgepodge of architectural styles, influences, and
allusions, but this phrasing also captures the sense that the image
of Pandaemonium, so tempting to produce on stage, is always
ultimately incomprehensible. The dramatic climax of the subsequent scene occurs when Azaziel and Astaroth unfurl the infernal

standards, trailing like meteors, and the ensuing hurl of defiance as swords burst from scabbards and the fallen angels cry out to heaven en masse. It is perhaps the central trope of the production's first act: an irrepressible volcanism, erupting from the lake of fire, the mouth of Satan, the exhalation of Pandaemonium, and the clamor of angels ready to break loose upon the earthly paradise.

D'Ennery and Dugué include a brief scene with Satan meeting Sin and Death at the gates of hell, though they have purged the meeting of much of its dramatic and affective tension. Sin and Death are now both daughters of Satan, and they mostly serve to enunciate the scope of Satan's upcoming voyage through the "empire of chaos." Death has no lines herself, though she joins in chorus with Sin to curse humankind as the final words of act 1. The second act begins with a tableau of Adam and Eve in Eden and covers the action of the Fall. It is necessarily compressed—Satan first appears complaining about what a "spectacle" Adam and Eve are making of themselves, and he is then confronted by Gabriel, who attempts to banish him back to hell with a touch of his sword. This has the opposite effect of Ithuriel's spear, as Satan disappears but leaves behind a suspicious-looking serpent in his place. In the next scene, which encompasses the entire temptation and fall of Eve, Satan wastes only a few lines before regaining his own shape, and it is in this form that he conducts the remainder of his encounter. Adam falls quickly thereafter, and without much objection. One significant alteration in the staging of the Fall and of Milton's poem here is the final scene of the second act, in which Gabriel arrives to deliver God's justice. Satan also bears witness, along with Sin, Death, and the entire complement of fallen angels. They are countered by the host of heavenly angels, who have also descended with Gabriel. Their collective appearance changes the punishment of Adam and Eve into a rather public shaming, even as it serves as a kind of redux of the war in heaven. As Gabriel prepares to lead Adam and Eve from Eden, Satan and his fellows prepare to leap upon them and begin their colonization of earth: "the damned creatures are ours, let us pursue them!" But Gabriel blocks him, declaring God's will that Adam and Eve are to be spared death so that they may atone in life for their sin. At the archangel's beckoning, the angels of the Lord ("les anges du

Seigneur") then draw their flaming swords and prepare to battle once more the fallen host. Satan cries out again in defiance, "man has sinned!...the earth is ours!"[88] But it is there the act ends, a perpetual suspension of this second war that becomes transposed into the final three acts of the play, as Satan continues his depredations on humankind.

The play generally leaves Milton behind at this point, dramatizing the murder of Abel and the riotous acts of the children of Cain, including the ruin of a temple (after which Satan, Moloch, Chamos, Belial, and Adramalech return for a dance number). The final act, an arresting production of the Deluge, was singled out by Charles Dickens in his recounting of the play. Dickens, who apparently attended the opening night along with Wilkie Collins, was compelled partly by the "wildest rumours...as to the un-dressing of our first parents."[89] Of the performance itself, which clocked in at some four-and-a-half hours ("the waits between the acts being very much longer than the acts themselves"), Dickens observed,

> The play is a compound of *Paradise Lost* and Byron's *Cain;* and some of the controversies between the archangel and the devil, when the celestial power argues with the infernal in conversational French, as "Eh bien! Satan, crois-tu donc que notre Seigneur t'aurait exposé aux tourments que t'endures à présent, sans avoir prévu," &c. &c., are very ridiculous. All the supernatural personages are alarmingly natural (as theatre nature goes), and walk about in the stupidest way.... The people are very well dressed, and Eve very modestly. All Paris and the provinces had been ransacked for a woman who had brown hair that would fall to the calves of her legs—and she was found at last at the Odéon. There was nothing attractive until the 4th act, when there was a pretty good scene of the children of Cain dancing in, and desecrating, a temple, while Abel and his family were hammering hard at the Ark, outside, in all the pauses of the revel. The Deluge in the fifth act was up to about the mark of a drowning scene at the Adelphi; but it had one new feature. When the rain ceased, and the ark drove in on the great expanse of water, then lying waveless as the mists cleared and the sun broke out, numbers of bodies drifted up and down. These were all real men and boys, each separate, on a new kind of horizontal sloat. They looked horrible and real. Altogether, a merely dull business; but I dare say it will go for a long while.[90]

Dickens's review contains many of the standard complaints about *Paradise Lost* adaptations: the loss of grandeur, the epic style of Satan turned to colloquialism, the divine and godlike turned into pedestrian figures who "walk about in the stupidest way," and the general conversion of Miltonic spectacle into dull, mechanical set pieces. The distinction Dickens makes between the "alarmingly natural" supernatural elements and the "real" bodies that drift up and down after the flood shows that his desires for the show were, nevertheless, mixed. The more real Eve seemed, the more ridiculous and less like Milton's Eve she became (even if Dickens imitates Milton in singling out just one physical trait of Eve as essential—long hair). Contrarily, the more real the horrors of the flood, the greater Dickens's approval, and the closer to Miltonic spectacle it became: quiet, concentrated images that work not primarily as visual effects but imaginative prompts, the indescribable devastation of the Deluge as specific corpses. That the Deluge seemed best to translate Milton's sublime effects contributed to its place as a mainstay in future adaptations and strongly influenced a subsequent American production of *Paradise Lost* that aimed even higher in its degree of spectacle than its French forerunner.

MILTON ON BROADWAY

One of the more ambitious spectacularizations of Milton in the nineteenth century was a musical extravaganza called *The Deluge, or Paradise Lost,* which debuted on Broadway at Niblo's Theater in New York City on September 7, 1874. The Brothers Kiralfy, Imre and Bolossy, had come to America five years prior after careers as stage performers, choreographers, and directors, first in their native Hungary and eventually in theaters from Vienna and Verona to Paris and London. They specialized in the stage spectacle, a genre that Barbara Barker places between "the realistic theater that began early in the nineteenth century and the birth of cinema at the onset of the twentieth."[91] Barker argues that "Bolossy's work is, in fact, the ultimate aesthetic expression of a cycle of realistic-pictorial theater production that led directly to film. Throughout his career he constantly endeavored to create artificially what constituted the very essence of the cinema, pictures in motion. In his attempt to achieve ever-greater reality, he and his contemporaries evolved techniques that were used by early filmmakers; crossfades from scene to scene and dissolves as one set melted into the next are but two examples."[92] The Kiralfys "pushed the technology of the stage to its limits," creating the Victorian equivalent of a modern Super Bowl halftime show, and by 1874 they had already enjoyed tremendous success in New York City with the theatrical bonanza *The Black Crook*, a revival of a spectacle that had been popular the year before the Kiralfys' arrival in America. (They were still a year away from their adaptation of Jules Verne's *Around the World in Eighty Days*, which featured an onstage elephant borrowed from P. T. Barnum.)[93] They brought core elements of *The Deluge* over from D'Ennery and Dugué's *Le paradis perdu* that had appeared nearly two decades prior. The Kiralfys kept the basic plot and some of the dialogue but introduced new dance numbers, including the "Grand Ballet and Bachanale" and the "Grand Ballet Fantasie: The Daughters of Eve," incorporating some 250 dancers. They also engaged an English actress, Julia Seaman, to take on the role of Satan—the *New York Times* reviewer approved her "deep and powerful voice," her "earnestness and declamatory skill, and perfect self-possession."[94] The show was meant to put the extravagant in extravaganza—as Bolossy Kiralfy remembers it, "We spared no expense to reproduce the biblical stories as artistically and realistically as possible."[95] It ran for five acts, beginning with Satan in the garden of Eden, comprising the first murder and the wayward rites of the sons of Cain (who performed a wanton ballet that, even with its "taint of sin," seemed to please audiences), and finishing with the cataclysmic Flood.[96] It was this final act that proved the show's undoing from the very start. According to Bolossy Kiralfy, *The Deluge* "was the first American production to introduce a stage rainfall, which came from an immense water tank installed above a special metal floor."[97] The emptying of this "immense water tank" was supposed to incite a "war of elements" amid "appalling darkness" and "rush of waters," all to signify the awesome wrath of God. Unfortunately, as Kiralfy recalls, on opening night "the mechanism malfunctioned and nearly drowned our cast." That night the show went on but did not end until around one in the morning.

While Kiralfy suggests that the "fiasco did not deter good audiences during the two-month run," the flood malfunction clearly irked the reviewer for the *Times,* whose account the next day ranged from the snarky to the scathing, likely contributing to the show's relatively short run:

> "The Deluge" has little to commend it to notice save the scenery and pageantry with which its scenario is illustrated....These incidents are set forth by a prodigious quantity of action on the part of a concourse of persons who are equally unanimous and energetic in Pandemonium and on earth; by much dialogue, and by dances, marches, and tableaux....*Eve* is portrayed by Miss Lillie Macdonald, whose appearance speaks volumes for the nutritious quality of the food supplied by the garden of our first parents. Mr. J. Stretton, a gentleman with excellent intentions and slender gifts, represents *Cain,* and the remainder of the roles are in competent hands. The performance passed off with considerable smoothness until the last act, and several bright and effective scenes, a fine display of silks and armor worn by comely damsels, and an animated ballet were heartily applauded. Act the fifth, for which the assemblage waited forty-five minutes, proved, however, a complete disappointment, and the terrific war of the elements, the appalling darkness, and the rush of waters—all of which were advertised and therefore expected—resolved themselves into a vision of stage carpenters wrestling with squares of unruly scenery; and drowned humanity, rising from the vasty deep and wading into the wings in full sight of the spectator.[98]

That the show's *coup de théâtre* turned into something out of "The Miller's Tale" can hardly have encouraged audiences, even with the lavish costumes, splendiferous pageantry, and lively ballets. In turn, Kiralfy simply concluded that "the idea of a deluge, biblical or not, did not excite most Americans."[99] The show was tweaked midway through its run, introducing new (and curious) acts, including the famed dancer Betty Remmelsberg and a troupe of Alpine yodelers. Notwithstanding these new trumperies, the Niblo production closed for good on November 14, 1874.

The "prodigious quantity of action" for which the Kiralfys' grand spectacle was striving can be felt in the almost kaleidoscopic poster advertising the performance (see fig. 1.1). It is a Milton

Fig. 1.1. Advertisement for the Kiralfy Brothers' "Grand Spectacle of *Paradise Lost*." *Courtesy the Library of Congress.*

gallimaufry: the popular images from John Martin, Gustave Doré, and others swirl about, as if caught in a permanent eddy, while the cast (and Kiralfys) clutter the rest of the frame. These were clearly the kinds of visuals the extravaganza was attempting to reproduce, as the panoramas had before, only to give them a supremely kinetic energy.[100] It is the kind of temptation Milton's imaginative scenes played out over and over in these nineteenth century entertainments: the drive to fill the unfillable, to circumscribe the illimitable, to hold within one frame—a stage, a poster, a 10,000 square foot revolving canvas—the vast imagination of *Paradise Lost*.[101] In 1877, after Bolossy Kiralfy had fallen on hard financial times, he licensed *The Deluge* to tour California and later exported it internationally to moderate acclaim. When it reached the South Pacific, it was still advertised as "A mammoth show," a "Grand spectacular drama," that "illustrates Milton's 'Paradise Lost' in a dramatic form, supported by a full company of actors and actresses, numbering about forty."[102] In this scaled-down, moveable version, Seaman remained as Satan, amid a host of other Miltonians: "Abel, Cain, Adam, Eve, Tophet, Ithuriel, Mammon, Raphael, &c.," and in addition to the scenery of Pandaemonium and Eden, the advertisement notes also a "panorama of the aerial voyage of his Satanic Majesty."[103] If the lofty heights of Milton's poem seemed repeatedly unattainable, this did not, at least, deter the will of Victorian showpeople from continuing to aspire to conquer them.

SUBTLE MAGIC: LOUTHERBOURG'S EIDOPHUSIKON

The rampant energies and sweeping scope of Miltonic epic were managed in ways no less sublime by another of the inheritors of Servandoni's spectacular techniques: Philippe Jacques de Loutherbourg. Born in Strasbourg in 1740, Loutherbourg arrived in England at the age of 31, already having been elected to the French Academy for his talents as a landscape painter. David Garrick took him on at Drury Lane as a painter and scene designer, where the inventive Loutherbourg flourished—and fashioned himself as the successor to the spectacular work of Servandoni.[104] He was the "first artist in Western Europe to devise an act drop or scenic curtain," among other innovations.[105] In England, he was heralded as "the first artist who showed our theatric directors that by a just disposition of light and shade, and a critical preservation of perspective, the eye of the spectator might be so effectually deceived in a playhouse, as to be induced to mistake the produce of art for real nature."[106] Enlarging on these sentiments, Martin Meisel calls him the "essential...link between the two manifestations of sublimity, pictorial and theatrical."[107] His most ingenious contribution to the specific history of Miltonic spectacle rests on a fantastical device he termed the "Eidophusikon, or Representation of Nature" (sometimes also glossed in contemporary notices as "Various Imitations of Natural Phenomena, represented by Moving Pictures").

The Eidophusikon debuted in Leicester Square, in Loutherbourg's private residence, on February 26, 1781. A meticulous assemblage of painted pasteboard scenes, wooden miniatures, functional three-dimensional models, and mechanical movement all combined with dramatic sound and advanced lighting effects to produce a series of natural landscapes that attained a kind of virtual realism. The audience sat in a darkened space, itself an unusual phenomenon for the time, while the scenes played out before them in what almost every critic writing on the subject has recognized as a key forerunner of the cinema.[108] The advertisements for the performance gloss the range of scenarios on display:

> various Imitations of NATURAL PHENOMENA, represented by moving pictures, Invented and Painted by Mr. DE LOUTHERBOURG in a Manner entirely New. The performance divided into five Scenes; 1st Aurora, or the Effects of the Dawn, with a View of London from Greenwich Park. 2d. Noon, the Port of Tangier in Africa, with the distant view of the Rock Gibralter and Europa Point. 3d. Sun-set, a view near Naples. 4th, Moonlight, a View in the Mediterranean, the Rising of the Moon contrasted with the Effect of Fire. Four TRANSPARENT PICTURES will be exhibited, An Incantation, A Sea Port; a conversation of sailors of different nations. Winter, a view in the Alps, a Woodcutter attacked by wolves: and a summer evening, with cattle and figures. A sonata on the harpsichord. The conclusive scene A STORM and SHIPWRECK. Between the Acts of the Performance, SINGING by Mrs. Arne. The Performance accompanied and the music by Mr. Michael Arne.[109]

These scenes share a central concern with the fluctuations of time: modulations of light over the course of a day, from a misty dawn along the busy Thames to the stark noonday sun of an African coast, to the mild Italian sunset and finally a calm moonlit evening. (The latter scene further featured the silvery moonlight contrasted with the bright and fiery illumination of a lighthouse, as if natural light were in contest with artificial.) Two of the four transparencies, forming part of the scenic interludes, also address the theme of seasonal fluctuation: winter wolves and summer kine. The conclusive storm and shipwreck pitch together all of the mild action in the preceding scenes to create a disturbance of sound, a staccato of lightning, and what for one attendee, William Henry Pyne, was Loutherbourg's greatest achievement, a synesthetic art Pyne termed the "picturesque of sound."[110] In fact, as later accounts reveal, the Eidophusikon was consciously aimed at a complete sensory immersion so that the threshold scenes of rising and setting were imitative of a greater transformation in the audience, blending the subject and object of the performance until all sense of separation between spectator and scene was lost. As one contemporary review put it, "He resolved to add motion to resemblance. He knew that the most exquisite painting represented only one moment of time of action, and though we might justly admire the representation of the foaming surge, the rolling ship, the gliding water, or the running steed; yet however well the action was depicted, the heightened look soon perceived the object to be at rest, and the deception lasted no longer than the first glance. He therefore planned a series of moving pictures, which should unite the painter and the mechanic; by giving natural motion to accurate resemblance."[111]

Loutherbourg's choice of scenes also provides the allure of the exotic. Only one is definitely domestic, and even that is freighted with traffic and trade, a metonymy of imperial agency: the river Thames as the conduit for English expansion. As Chandler and Gilmartin point out, "natural and urban layers seem to alternate and interconnect in this taking in of the great metropolis," even as it "offered representation of the wider world with which the great metropolis communicated, its ports and other points of contact."[112] The Italian, African, and Alpine scenes are conventionally romantic, to be sure, but they are also transporting and vaguely touristic, a series of virtual postcards from the Rock of Gibraltar, the city of Naples, the Swiss Alps. Even the "conversation of sailors of different nations" suggests the global reach of the performance. But the advertisement also hints at something decidedly unnatural, if not outright hostile, about Loutherbourg's scenes from nature, particularly in the transparencies. Amid all the tranquility of a Greenwich morning and Mediterranean night, grazing cattle and lumbering sailors, Loutherbourg sets the scene of the woodcutter attacked by wolves. It is the only instance, prior to the shipwreck finale, that even gestures at conflict or, for that matter, bears any narrative thrust. In this scenario, he provides a central character and some lupine antagonists, and though the attack must have been perpetually arrested, as on a Grecian urn, the tension of the woodcutter's position stands out against the almost exclusively docile scenes around it.[113] It is a preliminary instance of Loutherbourg's interest not only in imbuing scenes drawn from life with "natural motion" but also in exploring the anxieties produced by nature, fiction, and fancy.

The promise of an "incantation" as part of the first transparency further suggests that Loutherbourg wanted his audience to enter a sacred space, one set apart from rather than imitative of natural time. After all, his audience was to witness a condensation of time, from sunrise to moonrise, and a compression of space, a world in a grain of sand, an immersion not only in a virtual reality but unreality. To disrupt the mundane in this way, Loutherbourg inevitably risked but also increasingly invited a degree of incoherence: the conversation of sailors from different nations, types for Babel and confusion, the serenity of moonlight contrasted with fire. Even the view from Tangiers, drawing the eye past the Pillars of Hercules, the classical *ne plus ultra*, threatens to lead one, like Dante's Ulysses (or Europa herself), into the ocean's oblivion. Such transgressive pressures, like the initial incantation, serve as reminders of Loutherbourg's later embrace of the occult, a preoccupation perhaps only incipient at the time of the Eidophusikon but fully fledged later in his life when he befriended the infamous alchemist Cagliostro and similar figures.[114]

The relatively high cost of admission, five shillings, reflected the elaborate and sumptuous setting: well over 100 spectators could luxuriate on crimson seats after passing through a gallery of Loutherbourg's own romantic paintings. The theater space was compact but ornate, with "panels painted in the richest style with festoons of flowers, musical instruments, etc., heightened in gold...and at the upper end is a seat of state between two pillars of the Ionic order, fit for a princely visitor."[115] The gathering concentrated upon the small stage, stripped of its apron and framed to serve as a kind of grand and dilated shadow box. Though no precise records of its construction survive, contemporary accounts suggest its effects were nothing less than magical. (One account of the show's opening night bemoans how "the audience will not keep their seats; the eagerness of curiosity is so great").[116] Pyne offers the most detailed contemporary account of Loutherbourg's full program, adding, moreover, that "the scenes which he described were so completely illusive, that the space appeared to recede for many miles."[117] In certain cases, a dioramic effect was achieved by blending and foregrounding natural materials *in parvo:* the Greenwich heath, for example, was effected by "minute mosses and lichens."[118] Stephen Herbert suggests the basic arrangement: "The pictures themselves were probably painted on very fine material in translucent colours, and light was then projected on to them from behind at variable distances through adjustable coloured glass, added luster being obtained by means of reflecting mirrors. The scenes were shown through an aperture measuring 8 by 6 ft."[119] This vibrant collage, framed to narrow and focus the viewers' attention, simultaneously overloaded the visual field and inveigled the spectator into desiring its overwhelming illusions.

On the last day of January 1782, Loutherbourg exhibited for the first time a new final scene, *the* "Grand Scene from Milton," as it was advertised: "SATAN arraying his TROOPS on the Banks of the FIERY LAKE with the RAISING of the PALACE of PANDEMONIUM, from Milton."[120] This "miniature Gothic movie scene," as Iain McCalman calls it, was the climactic but far from only alteration in the program.[121] An array of new settings and motions included Niagara Falls, a rainy view of the "Castle, Town, and Cliffs of Dover," and, off the coast of Japan, a waterspout lit three different ways.[122] Elements of explicit or implicit danger still present themselves—one reviewer described the waterspout as expressing "all the brightness of phosphoric vapour," shooting into the sky until the vortex "seems to threaten destruction to every approaching object."[123] The show was bigger, louder, and more complex. McCalman rightly contends that this program was also "much more recognizably a popular commercial show," appealing to touristic and nationalist tastes alike.[124] The turn to Milton shares some of these nationalistic tendencies, though the legitimizing authority of the Milton of the Enlightenment was on the verge of giving way to the Romantic and all its Blakean subversiveness.

A vivid account of the scene is given by Pyne, probably from a showing in 1786, when the Eidophusikon was briefly revived at Exeter Change after a four-year hiatus:

> But the most impressive scene which formed the finale of the exhibition, was that representing the region of the fallen angels.... Here, in the foreground of a vista, stretching an immeasurable length between mountains, ignited from their bases to their lofty summits, with many coloured flame, a chaotic mass rose in dark majesty, which gradually assumed form until it stood, the interior of a vast temple of gorgeous architecture, bright as molten brass, seemingly composed of unconsuming and unquenchable fire. In this tremendous scene, the effect of coloured glasses before the lamps was fully displayed: which, being hidden from the audience, threw their whole influence upon the scene, as it rapidly changed, now to a sulphurous blue, then to a lurid red, and then again to a pale vivid light, and ultimately to a mysterious combination of the glasses, such as a bright furnace exhibits, in fusing various metals. The sounds which accompanied the wondrous picture, struck the astonished ear of the spectator as no less preternatural; for, to add a more awful character to peals of thunder, and the accompaniments of all the hollow machinery that hurled balls and stones with indescribable rumbling and noise, an expert assistant swept his thumb over the surface of the tambourine, which produced a variety of groans, that struck the imagination as issuing from infernal spirits.[125]

What stands out first in Pyne's description is less the precise details than the indefiniteness of the presentation: the "immeasurable" distances, the "chaotic mass," "unconsuming and unquenchable fire," and especially that "mysterious combination" of light, a kind of darkness visible. Apparent, too, is the full sensory assault—the "awful...peals of thunder," the "indescribable rumbling and noise," the infernal groans—an utter immersion in a deranged and dimensionless, preternatural space. Curiously, Pyne does not mention the horde of fallen angels here, who appear as part of a second movement in the scene, but another contemporary review fills in the missing details:

> The fifth scene closes the grand climax. It borrows not its light from the rising or setting sun, nor derives its splendor from the moon. It is a flight, which only the genius of Loutherbourg could reach. It is a view of the Miltonic Hell, cloathed in all its terrors. The artist hath given shape and body to the imaginations of the immortal bard, and presents to the wrapt and astonished sense, the fiery lake bounded by burning hills. He follows closely the descriptions of the poet. Belzebub and Moloch, rise from the horrid lake, and Pandemonium appears gradually to rise, illuminated with all the grandeur bestowed by Milton, and even with additional properties, for serpents twine around the doric pillars, and the intense red changes to a transparent white, expressing thereby the effect of fire upon metal. Thousands of Demons are then seen to rise, and the whole brightens into a scene of magnificent horror. The lightning exhibits all the varied and vivid flashes of the natural phenomenon, and the thunder includes every vibration of air, and shock of element which so often in its prototype, strikes terror and admiration on the mind.[126]

Where Pyne foregrounded the unnaturalness of the transporting effects, here the emphasis is on the naturalizing of Milton's imagination—giving it "shape and body," making it comprehensible. The detailing of the serpents on the pillars, and the naturalized lighting ("the effect of fire upon metal") and sound ("all the varied and vivid flashes of the natural phenomenon"), combine to give the sense that this is a so-called realistic representation of Milton's hell. The import of the scene is not ineffability but recognition.

Foremost among the reasons Loutherbourg turned to Milton must be the cultural capital gained for his enterprise by invoking high art—McCalman makes a convincing case that Loutherbourg's indulgence in popular entertainment had serious repercussions for his reputation as an elite artiste. But the addition of the Pandaemonium scene marks a fairly radical departure from the previous scenes—it now stretches credulity to say that the Eidophusikon is displaying scenes from "nature." In generating scenes of literary fancy, it can be regarded as one more in a succession of spectacles of the sublime, each chosen not only for the variety of light and tone but with idea of transporting the viewer. Indeed, Loutherbourg's Pandaemonium scene seems a type of the "gothic sublime," in the words of David Morris, "a vertiginous and plunging—not a soaring—sublime, which takes us deep within rather than far beyond the human sphere. The eighteenth century sublime always implied (but managed to restrain) the threat of lost control. Gothic sublimity—by releasing into fiction images and desires long suppressed, deeply hidden, forced into silence—greatly intensifies the dangers of an uncontrollable release from restraint."[127] Interestingly, neither of the contemporary accounts mentions Satan, which is either a sign of the very repressions Morris sees in the Gothic sublime or an underwhelmed omission. In fact, the omission of Satan from the accounts supports the idea that Satan—or something signified by him, the majesty of the individual, say—was not the central effect. It is, rather, the multiplicity of the demonic, the unrestrained abundance rather than the stately ruin of the archfiend, that most connected with the audience. The audience is repeatedly forced to identify with the masses in turmoil.

Apart from hoping to lend legitimacy to his project, there are a number of other reasons Loutherbourg may have turned to this scene. First, as Pyne's account reveals, the "chaotic mass" rising up achieves some of the same condensation of effect and tumult as the storm at sea. Infernal thunder and lightning were taking the place of the sea tempest, and the monstrous sounds of Pandaemonium were every bit as important as the visuals. In fact, it is the "groaning" of the demons—that chalkboard scraping of the tambourine—that generates the most "preternatural" effect. The demonic energy rampant in the scene must have been terrifying, if the smoke and fire of the belching mountain were not enough.[128] This seems to resonate too with the earlier transparency of the woodcutter attacked by wolves—the threat of the many against the one, of things unmanageable and wild irrupting into the fabric of quotidian placidity. If the lake of burning fire offered Loutherbourg the chance to combine some of his favorite tropes—oceanic maelstroms, garish strokes of light (Denis Diderot once remarked of one of his paintings, "the sun is so fervid, so hot on the horizon, that it is more like a conflagration than a sunset, and one is tempted to cry to its sitting shepherdess, 'Run, if you don't want to be burned'")—it also marked the only attempt to draw them from a literary source.[129] But it was a source so full of the same energies he was cutting from the natural world that it permitted him to draw implicit analogies between the real and unreal: the troops of Satan become another twining, writhing mass—the visual equivalent of tempestuous waves and foaming water. The palace formed from the very soils of hell and its backdrop of "burning hills" replicates the theatrical engineering with which Loutherbourg was himself engaged.

The greatest influence of all, then, may have been Milton himself, whose description of the hellish palace must have inspired Loutherbourg with its theatrical artificiality: the "subtle magic" that suspends the "starry lamps and blazing cressets" (*PL* 1.727–28), the incantatory "dulcet symphonies and voices sweet" (1.712) that bring the building into being as if breathing it forth, raising it "like an exhalation" (1.711). Even in that motion it resembles one of Loutherbourg's stage curtains being raised to the proscenium. In short, the creation of Pandaemonium imitated poetically the very effects he was attempting to achieve in his darkened theater.[130] No one as interested in stage lighting as Loutherbourg could avoid being drawn to Milton's use of "Naphtha and Asphaltus" that "yielded light / As from a sky" (1.729–30). But Pandaemonium is a complex structure, not least because it constitutes extremes of both the natural and artificial.[131] It is birthed from the "bowels of their mother Earth" who is "rifled" for her "treasures," creating a "spacious wound" in a foreshadowing of the later raping of Sin by Death and the mutilation of her womb (1.687–89). These natural but ill-gotten materials are then worked "with wondrous art" (1.703) into the labored sculptures and frescoes of the palace, crafting what many critics read as a garish distortion of classical beauty—a pagan shrine of "wealth and luxury" (1.722), striving

like "Babel" (1.694) (and recalling those confused sailors) ostenta-
tiously to rival the art of heaven. The short ekphrastic sequence is
full of such superfluities: the "golden architrave," the "bossy sculptures graven," the ceiling of "fretted gold" (1.715–17). Satan's
capitol becomes a blend and a blurring of elements, a grotesque
triumph of art over nature joined with a grand illusion.

A watercolor by Edward Francis Burney (ca. 1782) offers the
only contemporary image of the Eidophusikon, and his work captures the protocinematic feel of the space: a group of figures gathered to stare into a three-dimensional alternate reality that appears
much like a modern silver screen (see fig. 1.2). But what is most
immediately striking is the contrast between Burney's rather placid
watercolor and the reports of Pyne and the papers—what Pointon
calls the performance's "sense of horror," "a terror originating in
human horror of the unnatural."[132] Burney's scene, at first blush,
looks positively unhorrific—in fact, it is hard to imagine a more
staid and tempered setting; in several figures the controlled pos-
tures border on indifference.[133] The two children look attentive
but hardly more so than if they were watching a garden grow. The
figure on the far right might as well be a chaperone or pedagogue,
scrutinizing the scene with his magnifying scope, detachedly
appreciating the intricacies and mechanisms.[134] On the left side,
the bowing man suggests a social tryst, a genteel offer to be seated.
When such vignettes are framed by the terrifying Pandaemonium
we have come to believe Loutherbourg was staging (and even in
Burney's sketch, the central image of Satan and his troops seems
incensed and minatory), they open a number of questions. For
instance, where, one wonders, are the horrible groans? Or rather,
why do they seem to have such little effect? Where is the potency in
this "Grand Scene" of harried demigods and distracted observers?
Burney's work evokes a number of these ironies, but perhaps self-
consciously so, suggesting there is something prurient, subversive,
in the intimate gazing upon this demonic scene.

First, the picture calls attention to its own act of framing in
relation to that of the Eidophusikon itself. Within the latter's
frame, Burney shows Satan on a raised dais, a stage-within-the-
stage, aligning the arraying of Satan's troops with the arrangement of the Georgian figures on and around the bench who also

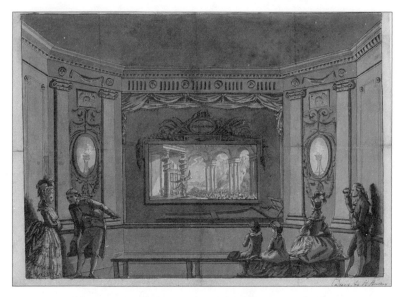

Fig. 1.2. Edward Francis Burney, watercolor of Pandaemonium scene (ca. 1782). © *Trustees of the British Museum.*

serve as spectators. With almost perfect symmetry, the frame of the painting sits squarely around the design of the room itself, while the foregrounded figures provide a countervalence for the fallen angels in the distance. The left of the picture is dominated by the bowing man, whose gaze is squarely on the lady, apparently newly arrived, and who is gesturing for her to take a seat. But if it is a genial or romantic moment, it is heavily ironized by the scene behind—the troops before Pandaemonium joining Satan just as the lady accepts the courtesies of the diffident man. With a dramatization of *Paradise Lost* as a backdrop, it is difficult for any seeming courtesy or enticement between man and woman to appear entirely innocent, and there is something of the spider welcoming the fly into the parlor here. The man's outward gaze, ignoring completely the dramatic action of Pandaemonium itself, is counterpoised by the intent, even magnified gaze of the party on the right. The woman and children are spellbound, their seeming innocence yet another contrast with the fallen angels before them, while the man directs his monocular toward the stage. There is a touch of ambiguity in the latter figure: he seems to be gazing at least partly not at Satan but at the tryst across the room, the kind of voyeurism Milton builds into *Paradise Lost* when Adam and Eve are spied on in Eden, "Imparadis't in one another's arms" (*PL* 4.506). The weight of the Eidophusikon scene is similarly skewed: Satan alone on the left (that sinister side), the bulk of his troops to the right and below him. Herbert reports that this particular scene "was supported by more than music: the delighted audience was almost deafened by the dreadful sounds appropriate to this horrific scene. As legions of hideous shrieking demons arose at the summons of their chief, a volcano began to erupt liquid fire to the accompaniment of lightning and claps of thunder. 'The lightning,' wrote a reviewer, 'exhibits all the vivid and varied flashes of that natural phenomenon and the thunder includes every vibration of air and shock of element which so often in its prototype strike terror and admirations on the mind.'"[135] This cacophony bravely contrasts the seeming placidity of the spectators in Burney's watercolor. One must conclude either that the rave reviews were hyperbolic, or that Burney was crafting a more complicated picture than has been acknowledged.

On May 31, 1782, the Eidophusikon closed again, this time with falling attendance and prices—the five-shilling admission a year earlier had been cut in half. Midway through this run, the original climax of the show—the shipwreck, which the Pandaemonium scene had replaced—was reintegrated to serve as the conclusion to the first of two acts, with Milton still serving as the grand finale. Combined with the loss of interest over the spring, this revision of the program problematizes the popular appeal of the Pandaemonium scene. Historians have followed Altick in asserting, "Except for one or two hints that it was on tour, nothing more is heard of the Eidophusikon from its closing in Lisle Street in May 1782 to its opening at Exeter Change on 30 January 1786."[136] This is, however, a significant inaccuracy. The *Morning Post and Daily Advertiser* actually reports the run of shows at Exeter Change as early as March 17, 1784, this time with "humorous recitals by Mr. Cresswick," and again in December

1784 with new scenes to join the shipwreck and Pandaemonium standards.[137] (There was even a special Christmas Eve showing, still featuring Satan, along with selections from the *Messiah* on harp and pianoforte.)[138] It continued to play in various incarnations throughout the first half of 1785, though by May it had been largely pared down and incorporated into other exhibits, with only the Milton scene still being presented. The Exeter Change venue allowed for a greater seating capacity—around 200. Still, the novelty had worn off by 1784 and the profile of the performances had diminished. It was revived with slightly greater fanfare on January 30, 1786, so as to represent a contemporary shipwreck, that of the *Halsewell,* and present an "exact, awful, and tremendous Representation of that lamentable Event."[139] (By this time, the apparatus had been sold off by Loutherbourg and was in the hands of another showman named Chapman.) The resurrection of Loutherbourg's device for the demonstration of the *Halsewell* wreck is an interesting bit of showmanship since the "exact" representation was really a redesign of Loutherbourg's earlier scene and a case of art imitating art. Though submerged in the broader marketing discourse of rebranding and renovation, the mimetic appeal of the disaster also shares with the imaginative pull of the "unnatural horrors" of Pandaemonium that vicarious pleasure in fear and catastrophe. This exhibition closed on May 12 and was struggling to seem current: it began to include other sensational acts, bringing in, "immediately previous to the Grand Scene from Milton," a performance by "the astonishing Phenomenon Sieur Borowlaski, the celebrated Polish Dwarf," who would "perform select Pieces on the English guitar."[140]

In May 1785, the American painter Charles Willson Peale opened in Philadelphia his own version of the Eidophusikon (now the rather prolix "Perspective Views with Changeable Effects; or Nature Delineated, and in Motion"), eventually including seven scenes that also (shamelessly) culminated in Milton's Pandaemonium. The title was soon abbreviated to "Moving Pictures," and Peale's biographer credits this as the first use of the phrase in America.[141] The show lasted from seven to nine o'clock, and was even air-conditioned, though Peale's facsimile lacked the luxuriant atmosphere of Loutherbourg's gilded halls. The text of Milton's description of Pandaemonium was included in the printed program, but Peale did not stop there. In what his biographer describes as "two poets, Peale and Milton, together out beyond the flaming ramparts of the world," Peale composed his own verse ("to be chanted softly to an appropriate air") to accompany the unrolling of Pandaemonium.[142]

In Peale's version of the scene, a series of incendiaries leads finally to a ritualized moment where Peale's poetry forms a kind of incantation: "The flames were naturally represented in motion assending with clouds of smoke and repeated flashes of lightning, with Imps of various fanciful forms flying through the fire, and Satan appears with a staff passing through the flames, and musick is heard with the words":

> Rise Pandamoniam Rise
> amidst sulphurous fume
> Whose rolling smoke assend the skies
> will burn and not consume.
> [the verse repeats]
> ever burning n'er consuming
> with hotest fire ever fuming
> ever burning n'er consuming
> with hotest—with hotest fire
> ever burning, with hotest—
> with hotest fire, ever burning
> with hotest, with hotest fire
> ever fuming.[143]

Earlier versions of Peale's accompaniment are equally as effusive if not quite such panting doggerel. The tenor of Peale's verse seems to be the paradoxical appearance of the fire, "fuming" but not "consuming," and in that he underscores the dualities of his artifice, sustaining the kinds of tensions Loutherbourg was so interested in exploring. Peale apparently staged Satan and the "imps" quite differently, however—creating airborne figures and arming Satan with a mage's staff rather than the spear of Loutherbourg (and Milton). Perhaps by having Satan "pass through the flames," he locates the power of the scene more centrally in that figure, whereas Loutherbourg highlighted the hideous masses. Certainly, in that sense, Peale's verse becomes a kind of paean to Satan's power of resistance (his chants refer to Satan's power over the flames rather than to their torturous effect—undying flames that continue to burn, and punish, eternally). At any rate, it does not appear the poetry swayed the audience to sympathize more fully with Milton, as Peale had first hoped (as in his earliest attempt at the chant, "To raise by art the stately pile / we will essay our skill / To make it grand and in a stile / befiting Milton's will").[144]

As Sellers makes clear, Peale hastened to include topical scenes after the visions of Milton grew stale (no mention is made of the effect upon the audience of Peale's soft chanting). In addition to musical interludes, Peale "for a while hired someone to do readings from Milton and Shakespeare." The reader, one Mr. George, however, "offended Peale by slipping in double-entendres, and the musicians proved very expensive and failed to show up." Consequentially, Peale installed "a mechanical barrel organ capable of reproducing thirty tunes, which played between scenes, sometimes with vocal accompaniment."[145] The show, which suffered from mechanical difficulties and lengthy intermissions, received a tepid response and, with dwindling receipts, closed after two years. It was exhibited for audiences during the Constitutional Convention in 1787 and then sold three years later to a traveling showman. Peale, for his part, soon turned his attentions elsewhere (namely, to the building of his museum of natural history).

The final movements of the Eidophusikon are rather more ignominious than its celebrated origins might have promised. Back in London, Chapman once more tried the Eidophusikon in February 1793, this time at the Great Room, Spring Gardens, but its age was showing. Its purveyor attempted to liven it up with sideshow marvels—the music of the Mozart disciple Master Hummel, and "George Saville Cary's 'Comic Songs, Readings and Imitations,' the latter being of 'many characters of the past and present age' including contemporary actors and actresses." A veteran of the Paris and London entertainment scene, the magician Sieur Comus also played a limited engagement in May. The double bill with an illusionist also drawing on Milton's poetry appears coincidental—though Altick relates that this Comus, not entirely unlike Milton's, specialized in "Cards, Caskets, Rings, Watches, Medals, Sympathetick Clocks, and many Magical Deceptions."[146] In 1799, a new Eidophusikon went on display at Panton Street, Haymarket, this time with only occasional mention of Milton—though there was the return of Comus, this time with "astonishing and pleasing Operations, *viz.* Rhapdology, Mathematics, Steganography, Palingenesis, Phylacteria, Capiromance, and many wonderful Performances on the Dodecahedron."[147] By January 1800, the Eidophusikon even featured a mind-reading dog ("le chien savant"). A few months later, on March 21, 1800, the Eidophusikon was consumed in a fire that reportedly began in a neighboring brothel.[148] The Haymarket Eidophusikon, however, had just begun a new series of scenes only days before: an eruption of Mount Etna with "volumes of smoke" and "streams of lava."[149]

In 1973, a scaled-down reconstruction of the Eidophusikon was exhibited at the Iveagh Bequest, Kenwood House, London. One of the curators, Lindsay Stainton, described the technical creativity involved: "it was made on eighteenth-century principles, with hand-wound winches (i.e. no electric motor to raise the scene). The cyclorama effect was created with a long roll of white linen, painted on the reverse side. The figures in the crowd were made to move very convincingly by fixing them to wire netting and creating a draught below. Satan's arms moved in a splendid fashion, up and down; wires were put through the arms and controlled from below."[150] Richard Altick provides a lyrical account:

> Through the aperture was seen, first, the "asphaltick lake" with a mountain glowing ruddily in the background; the scrim at the very rear varied in tint and patterns of color as the lights played upon it. The second set—a model of the Palace of Pandaemonium dominated by Satan—rose in front of the former one (which could still be seen through the columns of the palace) and deployed in it were some fifty or sixty small figures representing the satanic army. These were mounted on a kind of grilled platform, and gave the appearance of movement because of their intentionally loose mounting. During the four-minute presentation, powered by a phase motor, a recorded voice read the relevant passage from *Paradise Lost* to

the accompaniment of tempestuous sound. At the end, the model of the palace sank from view, along with its devils, and the sounds of the Cimmerian wind were replaced by the tape of a harpsichord playing interval music.[151]

This show is notable for its blending of Milton's poetry with the auditory experience of the spectacle (descriptive handbills were also available in Loutherbourg's original performances, though there is no evidence any of these were narrated during the action itself) and for the use of prerecorded music on tape (apparently of a poor quality). Such additions — the extra-diegetic voice-over, the graveled imitation of a harpsichord — seem further removed from Loutherbourg's vision of immersive realism, though they perhaps underscore the frictions between art and nature, and art and art, in his design.

Other reproductions created in recent years exploit some of the technological advantages of modern virtual reality systems while still paying homage to Loutherbourg's innovations. In 2005, one Eidophusikon was constructed as part of a joint venture between the Yale Center for British Art and Huntington Library for their exhibit "Sensation and Sensibility," also modeling the Pandaemonium scene, and that same year another replica was installed at the Australian National University. The latter merged Loutherbourg's eighteenth century conception with twenty-first century technologies, including an LCD screen to replace the scrolling canvas backdrop, as it depicted the famed Shipwreck of the Halsewell.[152]

THE "INFERNAL REGIONS"

Decades after Loutherbourg's Eidophusikon, a similar Miltonic entertainment sprang up, this time in Cincinnati, Ohio. In 1829, the Western Museum of Cincinnati developed a complex waxworks exhibit called the "Infernal Regions," based primarily on Dante's *Divine Comedy* but with an interesting repression of *Paradise Lost*. The museum proprietor, Joseph Dorfeuille, had just hired a skilled young artist to repair wax figures that were being damaged en route. The artist, Hiram Powers, would eventually go on to become one of more famous nineteenth century American sculptors while living as an expatriate in Florence, Italy. His ability to create lifelike wax effigies soon evolved from simple repair (he reportedly took some liberties with the more badly damaged specimens, creating grotesques that Dorfeuille thought could be profitable in other milieus) to an entirely new exhibit.[153] In a small upstairs space of the museum, probably little more than 300 square feet, Powers concocted a mesmerizing and frequented rendering of hell, populated with "upwards of thirty wax figures, (size of life) consisting of phantoms, imps, monsters, devils, among which BELZEBUB and LUCIFER are conspicuous, with a variety of human sufferers, in every stage of mental and bodily torment," as well as all manner of moving contraptions and horrid sound and light effects.[154] The show became one of the most popular tourist attractions in the city, and long outlasted its initial purveyors, running for nearly three decades.[155]

In *Weird and Wonderful: The Dime Museum in America,* Andrea Stulman Dennett calls the "Infernal Regions" a "fascinating and frightening multimedia spectacle" based on both Dante and Milton.[156] Those attending found, for instance, the entrance to be a kind of hell's gate, with the standard gloss from Dante above: "Whoever Enters Here Leaves Hope Behind." And in contemporary advertisements for the show, "Dante's Hell" receives top billing as the source.[157] Dennett's claim for Milton is more difficult to piece together. The idea for the show came originally from Frances M. Trollope ("Milton" was, literally, her middle name), who had recently moved from England to Cincinnati and had been involved almost upon arrival in other creative aspects of the museum's development into a "for-profit" enterprise. Her son, recalling the show and his association with the museum years later, copied in his reminiscence one of the vivid contemporary playbills:

> The World to come, as described by Dante, and comprising, Hell, Purgatory, and Paradise, will be exhibited in a room adjoining the Western Museum on the 4th of July, and days following. Admittance, twenty-five cents. In the centre is seen a grand colossal figure of Minos, the Judge of Hell. He is seated at the entrance of the INFERNAL REGIONS [enormous capitals]. His right hand is raised as in the act to pronounce sentence, his left holding a two-pronged sceptre.... On the edge of the opposite side of the frozen

Fig. 1.3. The "Infernal Regions." *Courtesy of the Cincinnati Museum Center—Cincinnati Historical Society Library.*

lake stands a spirit, who is just about to endure the frozen torment; and his attitude and countenance express the agony of extreme cold. Behind him opens the fiery gulf, the reflection of whose lurid glare is seen on his half-frozen body. At his feet a female head, fixed in the ice, looks up to the flames, as longing for their warmth; while a little way within the lake of fire another head is seen gazing with longing eyes upon the ice. A brilliant fountain of flame is in the midst of the lake, and around it crowds of condemned spirits in all varieties of suffering.[158]

In the language of the advertisement, the scene is almost all Dante: in addition to the sign, there is Minos, the frozen lake, and later there are details of the figures of Ugolino, Beatrice, and even as backdrop transparencies of the Mount of Purgatory and a vision of heaven. Trollope himself remembers it as "a representation of some of the more striking scenes of Dante's *Divina Comme-dia*," and makes no mention of *Paradise Lost* (though earlier in the essay he does quote *Lycidas,* supposing that Defeuille, had he not met Hiram Powers, "must have packed up his museum and sought 'fresh woods and pastures new'").[159] Frances Trollope's own account is more general—she does not even take credit for the idea—but does at least allude to the Miltonic: Dorfeuille, she writes, "has constructed a pandaemonium in an upper story of his museum, in which he has congregated all the images of horror that his fertile fancy could devise; dwarfs that by machinery grow into giants before the eyes of the spectator; imps of ebony with eyes of flame; monstrous reptiles devouring youth and beauty; lakes of fire, and mountains of ice; in short, wax, paint and springs have done wonders."[160] It is strikingly difficult to imagine such a scene enclosed in a room of such a small size, considering especially the emphasis the display placed on the *movement* of its mechanical con-traptions. (Moreover, the heat of the space had the effect of slick-ening the wax figures, so that some appeared as "heated, glowing, sweating sinners, of every sex, habit, and character.")[161] Eventu-ally, because of the close proximity between scene and spectator, and the temptation to touch these sweating sinners, the museum encaged the exhibit behind electrical fencing. The mild shocks (and ensuing shrieks) apparently accentuated the feeling of being tormented in a lifelike hell and provided a brief mortification of the flesh for those who succumbed to the prurience of the moment. One reviewer believed that "the host of devils of all grades of iniquity" who were "grinning and gibbering around in all directions" put to shame "Milton's fiends."[162] But the exhibit's devotion to the details of physical torture seems to locate it more readily as an adaptation of Dante. Nonetheless, Trollope's conception of the place as a Pandaemonium asserts Milton as a kind of silent partner.

The assemblage of "wax, paint and springs" that Trollope unfolds offers a few reminders of Milton beyond the reference to Satan's capitol: the "dwarfs that by machinery grow into giants" recall the entrance of the fallen angels into Pandaemonium: "They but now who seem'd / In bigness to surpass Earth's Giant Sons / Now less than smallest Dwarfs, in narrow room / Throng numberless" (*PL* 1.777–80). As with the magic lantern shows that could shrink and magnify images to give the illusion of menacing movement, the "Infernal Regions" depended on a derangement of senses and perspective: figures rose, leapt out from hidden caves, all in a darkened and by all accounts cacophonous chamber. The exhibit was enveloped with screams and cries, thunders and crackles, hisses and roars. Milton's note of congestion—the numberless spirits confined in a "narrow room"—seems doubly appropriate here. One can easily imagine a sense of claustrophobia contributing strongly to the fearsomeness of the exhibit. The reference to the "lake of fire" also points to Milton, an allusion even more strongly felt in the playbill's description of alternating punishments.

In the description of hell in book 2 of *Paradise Lost*, Milton observes that the punishments of future sinners will depend not on a Dantesque hierarchy of fire and ice but on their immediate contrast:

> At certain revolutions all the damn'd
> Are brought: and feel by turns the bitter change
> Of fierce extremes, extremes by change more fierce,
> From Beds of raging Fire to starve in Ice
> Thir soft Ethereal warmth, and there to pine
> Immovable, infixt, and frozen round,
> Periods of time, thence hurried back to fire.   (2.597–603)

In the "Infernal Regions," this becomes the defining template. Spectators, in fact, walked between the two realms, fire on one side and ice on the other, reenacting the ferrying over "*Lethean Sound*" (*PL* 2.604) Milton describes. In the playbill, one spirit about to "endure the frozen torment" is still lit by the reddish glow of fire, giving the appearance of one simultaneously half-frozen and half in flames. The frozen female head at his feet meanwhile looks longingly back at the fire, while within the lake of fire her counterpart looks longingly at the coolness of the ice. This is an imperfect analogue for Milton's punishments, since the sinners seem to experience some hope of relief from their punishments rather than an intensification, as if walking from a heated spa into the cold outdoors. But the description also makes clear that this longing is a kind of intensification—they are not only tortured by the pains of extremes but also tantalized by the false hope that a change of state will bring any remedy.

In later revised productions, there were three major figures to spook the audience: Minos, serving as the judge of hell at the gate, and mechanized so that his right hand would move "at intervals, as in the act to pronounce sentence"; Lucifer, surrounded by skeletons "transformed into Demons and Monsters"; and finally "Belzebub," who was flanked by the two most sophisticated mechanical figures, "Cerberus and Python," both of whom moved "in such a surprising manner, as to inspire the beholder with a belief that they are living."[163] As one reviewer recalled, "Half stupified [*sic*] with the strange influence of the place, I was roused by some soft, smooth body touching my neck and shoulders, and turning quickly I found a huge serpent, with its venomous jaws widely extended, writhing in terrific convulsions, apparently self-supported in the air, close by my side—at the same moment a chained animal at my feet, which I had not before noticed, sprang towards me, gnashing its iron teeth in impotent rage."[164] The placement of Beelzebub amid this trio hearkens back to Milton, as does the incorporation of the serpent, "Python," whom Milton refers to twice: once after the Stygian council in book 2, and the fallen host leave Pandaemonium to play at their "Olympian Games or *Pythian* fields" (*PL* 2.530), alluding to the games that celebrated Apollo's defeat of Python, and again to characterize the transformation of Satan in book 10 ("Now Dragon grown, larger then whom the Sun / Ingenderd in the Pythian Vale on slime, / Huge Python" [10.529–31]). One of the fuller contemporary accounts situates the "terrific gigantic figure representing Belzebub" as "fearfully conspicuous" upon the "burning lake," enabled by machinery to "roll its great eyes, and gnash its teeth."[165] The depiction again evokes Milton, and even the subtle histrionics of the waxwork "rolling its eyes" seems patterned on that first act of Satan in hell, when "round he throws his baleful eyes" (1.56).

In other ways, the representation of Satan in this version of hell hardly resembles either Dante's or Milton's. "In the center of 'The Infernal Regions,'" writes Dennett, "sat the 'King of Terrors.' Costumed in red tights, with red horns and a forked tail, the king welcomed visitors with a wave of his pitchfork while ominous smoke swirled about him. Powers himself played the role of the devil, but he soon tired of the task and constructed an automated devil to take his place."[166] This is plainly the rubicund devil of medieval folklore, made more theatrical with the addition of smoke and a running patter with the audience. Even in its tenebrous surroundings it borders on the burlesque. Another account describes a darker version—a king in sable robes overlooking the vast abyss while seated on an ebon throne, with pitchfork, cloven hoof, and even a "hoary beard, made of horses tails"—that still bears little resemblance to anything in Dante or Milton.[167]

The "Infernal Regions" evolved as time went on, accreting new horrors with added mechanizations, figures, and at various times the substitution of live actors for mechanical ones. It does seem that Milton was an (unacknowledged) influence on the early form; in later incarnations, at least, the exhibit also included a version of Sin. One local visitor remembered the vision as a traumatic one: "I was a small boy, and I recall even yet the feeling of terror with which I beheld the glaring eyes of the frightful female named Sin, who sat hard by the infernal gates, and who jumped at me with a horrid cry."[168] By 1839, Dorfeuille had grown restless, and, wearying of the museum business in Cincinnati, he instead took the original wax figures designed by Powers all the way to Broadway.

There he tried to remount a comparable exhibit, this time called "The Satanic Dominions," but the results were unsuccessful. Dorfeuille died just one year later. In 1840, to the thrill of ironic newspaper headline writers everywhere, some of the last leavings of the "Infernal Regions" that had been sold to another Cincinnati museum were destroyed in a fire. Tattered vestiges of the Western Museum exhibit were still being displayed as late as 1861, though by that time the exhibit had become a ludicrous caricature of its earlier glorious terrors.[169]

Each of these attempts to spectacularize *Paradise Lost* follows a similar, and familiar, narrative: Milton's epic possesses a particular key for the pursuit of "things unattempted yet" in prose, rhyme, or any other genre. The poem becomes a guide to visualizing "things invisible to mortal sight," and a device for exploding the limits of theatrical representation. And yet the disconnect between the material means of production and the depths of Milton's verse return again and again to bedevil such efforts. Dryden became caught in a contradiction he was unable to resolve: how to merge the *seeming* of poetry, upon which the power of the imagination feeds, with the immanence of the spectacular, which has as its end the defiance of imagination.

Servandoni aimed for a grand unification of visual arts in his trompe l'oeil *Paradise Lost*, visions of heaven and hell that were not merely visions but altered realities, and wound up concocting unreasonable facsimiles. D'Ennery and Dugué, with somewhat greater adaptive sophistication, crafted an aptly bizarre Pandaemonium but swept away most of Milton's other representational challenges in the final overflow of the Deluge. Such flooding of the senses, "horrible and real" in Dickens's words, seemed to have achieved something of the resolution Dryden sought between the endless, dizzying inner sensorium and its practical application.

The same scene's mishandling in the Kiralfy production, however, affirms the underwhelming limits of even the most torrential natural effects. The "Infernal Regions" dioramas, like so many gothic trappings, offer a culmination of effects that seem to move inevitably from self-serious to self-parodic. Perhaps most effective, Loutherbourg sought to create infinity in grains of sand

and eternity in the supremely lit moving image. The blueprints of Pandaemonium offered him a guide for conjuring the supernatural into the everyday, for raising art to the level of nature, for dramatizing the tensions of divine workmanship and devilish illusion. But once the novelty had worn off—once an audience's expectations caught up with the technical legerdemain—even this innovative spectacle sunk back into the recesses of the popular imagination.

These productions anticipate similar expansions on artificiality in the technologies of other, pre-cinematic entertainments detailed in the next chapter, including the panorama, phantasmagoria, and magic lantern shows. The problems of representing the Miltonic sublime were not solved by them, nor by the advent of motion pictures, which suffered the same kinds of critique, all around the exploitation of a text more inescapably imaginative than its derivations. The ambitions of pre-cinematic entertainment to fulfill Milton's epic reach, however, were fueled by this very challenge.

Pre-Cinematic Entertainment

THE PANORAMA

On June 19, 1787, Robert Barker patented a device "for the Purpose of displaying Views of nature at large, by Oil-Painting, Fresco, Water-Colours, Crayons, or any other Mode of painting or drawing."[1] In a few years Barker's invention would come to be called the Panorama (a more economical coinage than Barker's original term, *La nature à coup d'oeil*): an immersive visual experience that sought to produce a virtual realism by offering spectators "an entire view of any country or situation, as it appears to an observer turning quite around." In Barker's original design, this virtual reality was to be accomplished by displaying a painted canvas around a circular building while viewers occupied an interior frame, also circular, that provided the perfect distance and perspective to maintain the illusion that the viewer had entered the world of the picture. This effect was further maintained by a "shade or roof" projecting over the interior frame so as to disappear the top of the painting (as well as ceiling skylights); similar construction was employed over the bottom of the painting, such

93

that "observers, on whatever situation [the artist] may wish they should imagine themselves, feel as if really on the very spot."[2]

While the word "panorama" has evolved to mean a sweeping, natural vista, in its origins in the late eighteenth century its meaning was almost the opposite: an artificial representation of a frozen moment, an encompassing rather than liberating visual experience. The Panorama promised access to new visual realities—the kinds of radical perspectival shifts also emerging in the growth of the Romantic sublime, and in concurrent social and technological developments, from mountain climbing to hot-air balloon rides to Jeremy Bentham's infamous Panopticon.[3] But the panorama was also regarded most skeptically by artistes of the old guard, who saw the rapidly rising mass appeal of the new form as not only a dilution of high art but also a vulgarization of nature into its derivative, mechanical components.

Barker set up the first large-scale Panorama at Leicester Square in 1792: *A View of London from Albion Mills, Southwerk*.[4] As Stephan Oettermann points out, the early panoramas were heavily freighted with nationalist and imperialist symbolism: "Barker presented the British with the view of London, the capital of their empire and largest city in the Western world, from the roof of a modern factory. Apart from great national monuments such as the Houses of Parliament and St. Paul's Cathedral, what struck the eye was the smoke rising from factory chimneys and the great number of ships on the Thames, symbols of Britain's supremacy in industry, trade, and naval power."[5] Consequently, the most popular panoramas in the early nineteenth century depicted battles, particularly naval encounters, the verisimilitude of which was painstakingly effected. Still, the lack of movement *within* the early panorama paintings led some viewers to critique the illusions and, compared with some of the detailed, mechanical epicycles in Loutherbourg's work, the relatively static quality of the panorama painting becomes even more apparent. This was partly overcome by the eventual introduction of the revolving "moving panorama" and the concurrent popularity of the more theatrical dioramas of Daguerre and Bouton, which included dynamic lighting effects and the illusion of a scene—cathedral interiors, Alpine retreats—unfolding in time, typically between day and night.[6]

As Anne Friedberg notes, this drift away from the original panorama design had a corollary effect: "as the 'mobility' of the gaze became more 'virtual'—as techniques were developed to paint (and then to photograph) realistic images, as mobility was implied by changes in lighting (and then cinematography)—the observer became more immobile, passive, ready to receive the constructions of a virtual reality placed in front of his or her unmoving body."[7] In this way, the first panoramas seem less preparatory for the kinds of IMAX cinematic experiences of modern times to which they are often compared than an appeal to broader romantic sensibilities.[8] Indeed, the panorama was at first an energetic walkabout—even requiring patrons to enter through a subterranean tunnel and access the panoramic chamber above by means of a dizzying spiral staircase. And in their ability to transport viewers almost magically beyond their political borders, the perambulations of panorama observers came to stand for much longer marches. Altick percep- tively remarks that "the topographical panoramas as a group were a bourgeois public's substitute for the Grand Tour," especially during the war-ravaged years 1793–1815.[9] As one contemporary contributor to *Blackwood's Magazine* put it in 1824, "What cost a couple of hundred pounds and half a year half a century ago, now costs a shilling and quarter of an hour," and saves, moreover, "the innumerable miseries of travel."[10]

If attaining the majestic heights of Mont Blanc seemed imprac- tical, panoramas offered their own version of the sublime for the masses. And like Loutherbourg's Eidophusikon, this new form of visual consumption was invested with secondary effects of sound and sensation: Barker's patented design, for instance, insisted on the circulation of air within the building to reduce the feeling of being indoors. While both the Eidophusikon and panorama depended on moving pictures, the 360-degree Panorama exploded the illu- sion to the point that viewers were now located within rather than beyond the work. The careful framing of the Eidophusikon thus gave way to the panorama's illusion of a borderless spectacle. Both made use of the combination of two- and three-dimensional fig- ures to further blur the borders of realism—the panorama typi- cally disguised its bottom border with seamless, three-dimensional terrain features much as the Eidophusikon incorporated moss and pebbles to stand in for trees and boulders. Altick argues, moreover, that "panoramas of romantic locales—an Alpine pass, Roman ruins, a Niagara cataract, an Irish lake, a medieval French town, a Levantine city—appealed to the same tastes that were drawn to the poetry of Wordsworth, Scott, Byron, and Moore."[11] The panorama could cater to those tastes in a much broader form and had the added benefit of seeming to represent the natural in an unmediated space that could not only imitate but also duplicate the sublime effects of those Romantic locales.

From the earliest reviews, critics asserted the sublimity of the Panorama, an observance that has become a critical commonplace: as the London *Times* reported in 1789, "the vast gratification with which this idea is pregnant, and which we hear that Artist [Barker] means to pursue, must give us real cause for joyful expectancy to every Amateur of an Art which may now, nearly, be called Sublime; it seems surely not far from the summit of perfection."[12] Even the conservative Joshua Reynolds, president of the Royal Academy of Arts, reportedly allowed that the panorama was "capable of producing effects and representing nature in a manner far superior to the limited scale of pictures in general."[13] In *The Prelude* of 1805, Wordsworth himself affirmed of the panorama (with its "whole horizon on all sides") that it provides "every tree / Through all the landscape, tuft, stone, scratch minute, / And every cottage, lurking in the rocks—/ All that the traveller sees when he is there."[14] But Wordsworth does not fully endorse his contemporaries' enthusiastic claims in this passage of *The Prelude,* calling such "ap[ing]" of the "absolute presence of reality" an imitation "fondly made in plain / Confession of man's weakness and his loves" (7.248–49, 254–55). His awe at these indoor spectacles seems at once uncomplicated and unconvinced: the panorama, he writes,

> with power,
> Like that of angels or commissioned spirits,
> Plant[s] us upon some lofty pinnacle,
> Or in a ship on waters, with a world
> Of life, and life-like mockery, to east,
> To west, beneath, behind us, and before.   (7.259–64)

It is that "life-like mockery" upon which critics have fixed as expressing Wordsworth's clear reservation over the imaginative heights staked by the panorama. Gillen D'Arcy Wood, for instance, observes of *The Prelude*, "In Book Thirteen, Mt. Snowdon's misty chasms and abyssal depths give rise to 'circumstance most awful and sublime.' The panorama, by contrast, offers merely a 'lifelike mockery' of *visible* nature" rather than "a more 'elevated mood' inspired by actual nature."[15] Still, Wordsworth's lines evoke the imaginative potency offered by these early displays (they include "life" and its mockery at once), and if they were ultimately unable to compete with his excursions out-of-doors, they nevertheless served him as training grounds. In Wordsworth's experience, the recurring effect is one of transport, and though its concomitant requirement is a suspension of disbelief, it nevertheless provides a fair if imperfect substitution for sublimity: to lose the self in limitless space, or in uncanny detail. Because the supposed sublimity of the panorama was tuned to the middle-class patrons, elite artists tended to downplay its powers. Its status as a vulgar art form persisted: a facsimile of nature at once mechanical, solely imitative, and uninspired (criticisms later launched at photography and film).

Wood also hears in Wordsworth's reflections an allusion to John Milton and *Paradise Regained*, specifically Satan's panoramic presentation of Rome, achieved through "strange Parallax or Optic skill / Of vision multiplied through air, or glass / of Telescope."[16] Richard Reinagle's panorama of Rome had been a popular attraction at the Strand in 1803, and Wood argues that "Milton's reference to the technological wizardry at work in the Satanic vision" is "uncannily prescient of the panorama's self-conscious technological modernity. Milton's 'Rome,' like Reinagle's, invites the awe of the beholder not only at the content of image itself, but at the sheer wonder of its production."[17] If Wordsworth is not mixing metaphors, his placement by angels "upon some lofty pinnacle" might recall the dangerous deceptions implied in the highly technical panorama Satan presents to Jesus. Likelier still is that Wordsworth's attempt to convey the experience of the panorama inevitably merged with a description drawn from Milton's imagination because Milton himself generated so many panoramic scenes throughout his work. Anne-Julia Zwierlein locates a series of panoramic surveys in *Paradise Lost*, such as when Raphael describes the courts of heaven as "wider far / Than all this globous earth in plain outspread" (*PL* 5.648–49) or when Satan gains his "goodly prospect" of Eden (3.549). She argues persuasively that eighteenth and nineteenth century commentary on what were for Milton "Visions of God" tended to transform them into "worldly imperial visions."[18] Further expressing the panoramic qualities of *Paradise Lost,* though emphasizing the experience of the reader rather than the poem's subjects, John Demaray finds that the "grand visual panorama of Hell, Chaos, Earth, and most of Heaven draws one into its enveloping depths like a gigantic, three-dimensional Renaissance setting that leads the eye into infinity."[19] Similarly, Michael's visualization of biblical history, an awesome spectacle that finally overwhelms Adam, anticipates the surmounting views and vanishing horizons of the panorama. It may have been such sweeping moments in Milton, or as Zwierlein supposes, the ready appropriation of his global vision for national-ist purposes, that led to an unusual appropriation of his work at the Leicester Square Panorama.

With the death of Robert Barker in 1806, operation of the Panorama passed to his son, Henry Aston Barker, who main-tained the vogue for epic military scenes, culminating in the most famous of Barker's panoramas, *The Battle of Waterloo* (1816). After Henry retired from the business in 1826, the direction of the Panorama was taken up briefly by John Burford, who died that same year, and then by his son Robert Burford. Under Robert, the Leicester Square Panorama continued showings until 1861, but it is his innovative panorama of 1829 that most distinguishes his directorship from that of his predecessors. In April of that year, Burford departed from the trusted formula of historical battles and romantic landscapes. For the first time, the panorama would ren-der a scene taken not from nature but from literature: Milton's Pandaemonium.

Already discursively entwined by this time, the Miltonic and panoramic sublime would seem to have been natural fits to share at some point the same space. In 1830, John Wilson could write in *Blackwood's* (with just a touch of hesitation) how Milton "sweeps the earth with an angel's wing from the regions of the rising to the regions of the setting sun—shewing you in one panorama, it may almost be said, the whole habitable globe."[20] Painted with the assistance of Henry Courtney Slous, who excelled in figures, Burford's Milton panorama was based largely on the 1825 mezzotint engravings of John Martin. The choice of Martin suggests the sublimity Burford hoped to capture: as Meisel argues, "the materiality of Martin's sublime chiefly lay in the features that excited most wonder: his rendering of space, multitudes, and perhaps above all architecture; his manipulation of perspective and scale."[21] Oettermann recounts that the Milton panorama was, however, almost instantly unpopular, "a fiasco," partly because "Burford probably overestimated his customers, who needed to be familiar with Milton's poetry to enjoy the finer points of the painting."[22] This is a rather loaded claim. It is not clear (or substantiated), for example, that most panorama patrons were insufficiently familiar with Milton, especially with what was easily becoming the most oft-reproduced scene, Pandaemonium. Moreover, it is questionable whether such familiarity would necessarily inform an enjoyment of the painting itself. Was the panorama in service of Milton, or vice versa? As to the objection that panorama patrons might not be "familiar with Milton's poetry," the panorama was often driven by transporting spectators to places of which they had no prior knowledge or experience; in this sense, the Pandaemonium display was clearly breaking new ground, whisking patrons not only across political territories but also into the land of make-believe. But Burton might have rightly wondered, why should a knowledge of literary topography or narrative be different from a fluency in the historical conditions of a Napoleonic battle or architectural nuances of Rome? Why should patrons of the panorama have any direct experience with the Pandaemonium of *poetry* at all? Burford would go on to assert that Milton made his hell "not less local than the habitations of man," and Ralph O'Connor argues persuasively that Burford "treated Pandemonium with the same topographical precision as if it were another earthly city."[23] But Burford also saw the Milton panorama as pushing further the debates over the power of its art and its place in the hierarchy of artistic media, including traditional painting and poetry.

Beyond probably feeling some irresistible synergy in offering a "panorama" of "pandemonium," creating a panorama to rival the extremes of poetic imagination would address a central question: had the panorama evolved, as Griffith was later to believe of the cinema, into a *singularly* expressive form, the only medium grand enough to capture Milton's epic vision? Burford's key to the painting—a standard accompaniment to all panorama programs—offers a preamble that makes plain he was anticipating some objections to his choice of subject:

> In offering the present PANORAMA (which is of so distinct a character to those usually exhibited at this establishment) to the inspection of his Friends and the Public, R. BURFORD thinks it necessary to make a few preliminary observations, in order to obviate any misconstruction which might be attached to the production of what, at first sight, appears so startling and irreverent a subject. During the forty years that this species of painting has been so liberally patronized, the Views have consisted of cities, remarkable for the magnificence of their public buildings, the beauty of their situation, or circumstances connected with their history, which rendered them objects of general attention, varied occasionally by the most striking and interesting events of the day....It having been long and generally admitted that no style of painting could portray these subjects with so much interest and appearance of reality, it occurred to him that it might be adapted to the higher branches of the art with increased effect, and embody, with unrivalled boldness and grandeur, the most sublime and stupendous imagery. With this view he was induced to seek in works of imagination for a subject like the present, for which the Panorama is peculiarly adapted, offering a field of sufficient magnitude to do ample justice to the most vivid and splendid conceptions.[24]

Burford is initially sensitive to the idea that his choice of Milton might seem "irreverent," that this combination of the illustrious with the merely illustrative would seem an act of over-reaching. In affirming the decision, he employs much of the same rhetoric used in the twentieth century to argue why Milton's work would make a great film: the panorama could be "adapted to the higher branches of the art with increased effect," to "embody...the most sublime and stupendous imagery," whereas traditional media had repeatedly failed to convey the world of the imagination. The panorama is thus "peculiarly adapted, offering a field of sufficient magnitude, to do ample justice to the most vivid and splendid conceptions."

All that remains for Burford is to discover in the canons of literature an instance of imaginative flight that would, in effect, justify the panorama.

> The subject has been chosen from MILTON, one of the earliest and the most prominent of the British poets, whose fervid and active imagination, and lofty and elevated mind, disdaining reality, soared to the wild regions of possibility, a height never before reached by poet; and whose wildness of fancy, rich description, and sublime and beautiful imagery, opened a wide field for the talents of the votaries of the sister art, very generally and most successfully taken advantage of, but never before attempted on a scale worthy the elevation of soul and terrific conceptions of the Poet. The Panorama is an attempt to illustrate part of the first book of Paradise Lost: "a poem," says Dr. Johnson, "which considered with respect to design, may claim the first place, and with respect to performance the second, amongst the productions of the human mind"; which has gained admiration unlimited by age or country, and is duly estimated and fully understood by all who have a true relish for English poetry.[25]

Here, the choice is aesthetic, and a political one as well. Milton, on the recommendation of Samuel Johnson, holds the "first place" in that panoramic arena of lofty design, with a "wildness of fancy" disdainful of reality—so disdainful that the soaring wildness has never been satisfied fully by any previous artistic adaptation. Though it has also inevitably provoked the attempt, having "opened a wide field for the talents of the votaries of the sister art," Milton's poem remains the desiring subject, only "very generally" (if also "most successfully") "taken advantage of." It is, finally, the *scale* of the panorama that makes it so suitable to render the "elevation of soul" in Milton. But Burford also evidently wants to align Milton, "one of the most prominent of the British poets," with the "most splendid and honorable achievements" of "British valor" lionized in earlier displays. It is an imperial gesture, whose comprehensive energies are fully explicit in Burford's conclusion: *Paradise Lost* has at once "gained admiration unlimited by age or country" and remained the fulfillment of an exclusively English poetic appetite, making universality and Britishness virtually indistinguishable. Zwierlein situates the decision in a broader appropriation and reshaping of Milton's work, arguing that "the design of

the Pandemonium panorama differs only minimally from the panoramas in the collection which show British colonial possessions
like the city of Calcutta," and that, "like Loutherbourg, Burford
translated Milton's Pandemonium, epitome of the fallen empire,
into a sublime imperial vision."[26] But even if the symbolic codes
exploited by Burford were consistent with the kind of jingoistic
displays to which the panorama was prone, contemporary reactions to the new "literary" panorama ranged from mild surprise to
outright condemnation.[27]

Burford is, on the one hand, conscientious of the scene's poetic
context, placing the panoramic moment explicitly in the spatio-
temporal world of its originating source: "The exact period of
time represented is when Satan, having awakened from the general trance after his nine days' fall from heaven, extricated himself from the 'burning lake,' and summoned his principal chiefs
around him, gives vent to his pride, despair, and impenitence."
Burford than reproduces in the full Satan's speech beginning,
"O myriads of immortal spirits" (*PL* 1.622–62), and concludes
that "Pandemonium, the 'high capital of Satan and his peers,'
may be supposed to have just risen, 'Like an exhalation with the
sound / Of dulcet symphonies and voices sweet.'"[28] On the other
hand, and immediately apparent to anyone who actually *was* familiar with the poem, Burford has condensed rather than expanded
the poetic narrative here since Milton sequences the speech and
the rising of Pandaemonium not as simultaneous but as successive.
In the poem, Satan's lines unfold in a narrative time in which all
other action has been suspended; only after he has spoken does
action resume: the fallen angels bring out their "millions of flaming swords" and "clashed on their sounding shields the din of
war" (1.664, 668). This, in fact, is a wonderfully dilated dramatic
moment in Milton—for how long do the "mighty cherubim"
hurl defiance at the vault of heaven? The force of Satan's speech
demands some prolonged duration, though it is only a half-dozen
lines in the poem itself. Whenever they give this up, the pace of
dramatic action picks up, as toward the "Hill not far whose grisly
top / Belch'd fire and rolling smoke" (1.670–71), "wing'd with
speed / A numerous Brigad hasten'd" (1.674–75).

Meanwhile, the pace of the poem itself unfolds more languidly, in lines attentive to every detail of the volcanic terrain that will supply the materials for the new satanic palace. Milton notes the skewing of time here in comparing those laboring to build Pandaemonium with those mortals who erected the tower of Babel and pyramids of Egypt: "And Strength and Art are easily outdone / By Spirits reprobate, and in an hour / What in an age they with incessant toil / And hands innumerable scarce perform" (*PL* 1.696–99). The climax of this dual time frame is the almost instantaneous manifestation of Pandaemonium itself: "Anon out of the earth a Fabric huge / Rose like an Exhalation" (1.710–11). Again, how long does this take, if time applies at all to these images of eternity? The poet tells us an hour, and we read it across the poem in fewer lines than Milton gives to the ornate description of all Pandaemonium's accoutrements. The sense of successive action, at any rate, is unremitting. And here is where the panorama as an adapting subject cannot fully accommodate Milton's poetics. Because the panorama at this point did not convey movement, Burford had to somehow wrangle all of Milton's temporal oscillations into one frozen field. In this transmediation he has necessarily moved already away from the very infinitude of action, the elevation of soul, with which the sublime distances and endless times of the poem are occupied.

Critics were not oblivious to the paradoxes produced by such arrangements in the panorama. Milton's scene contains multitudes—millions of angels, at the least. In trying to manage this into the panorama, Burford gave prominence to Satan, setting him in a group in the foreground alongside Beelzebub, Moloch, Azazel, and others, noting how "the most exalted and depraved of the fallen, proudly eminent" is "still retaining some of his original angelic brightness, and foaming with haughtiness, malignity, envy, and revenge, as he directs the attention of his surrounding chiefs to the newly arisen Hall of Council."[29] And yet Burford also waxes apologetic for the presentation of the figures: "It may be necessary here to remark, that the figures are on a reduced scale, in order to give effect to the painting. Milton supposes them to have been of colossean [*sic*] dimensions. If they were twenty feet in height, a comparison with the surrounding building will give an idea of the stupendous magnitude of the whole."[30]

In effect, spectators were once more required to resort to their imaginations, to cram within this wooden *O* all the magnitude and multitude of Milton's vision. Rather than the vast scale of the panorama accommodating those lofty heights, it in fact must call attention to its own shortcomings. The London *Times* reviewer complained that the figures were "on too small a scale to admit examination," while another critic objected similarly (and more volubly):

> The principal fault we have to find is the want of prominence in the principal figure: a picture should always tell its own story; while here, it was some time before, even with the assistance of our guide book, we could identify the "Archangel ruined," whom the Poet represents as far "Above the rest / In shape and gesture proudly eminent," — or distinguish him from his compeers. This may partly have arisen from the necessarily reduced scale on which the figures are given, and the shadowy indistinctness thrown around some of them; still, the hero of the piece should certainly be the most prominent personage — whereas he is so minced up with the cohort at his heels, that it is difficult to distinguish him among them, and Beelzebub especially is, to say the least, equally conspicuous.[31]

Which is to say, none of Satan's "original angelic brightness," or his "foaming" assortment of affective disorders was apparent anywhere in the panorama except in the text of the program. There may be no end to the number of angels who can dance on the head of a pin, but Burford quickly found the limits on a panoramic canvas.

The panorama included not just Satan and his council, but the false gods of Scripture, "invested...with form and matter"; the Greek and Roman deities, "heading their different legions"; the fiery lake and "tributary streams"; the "firm ground impregnated with fire"; and other legions of angels, both in chariots and on horse, thronging the palace. To the left of Satan and his group, "Mammon and his numerous brigade, having finished their labour, are seen returning from the 'spacious wound,'" while "Mulciber, the architect, from an elevated spot, views with satisfaction his noble work."[32] Apparent here is that Burford has built into his panorama a kind of self-referentiality, as Mulciber, the infernal architect, stands "from an elevated spot" to take in all of "his noble work." Burford thus guides his patrons to sympathize not with Satan—not only because his ostensible prominence has been subsumed into the overall effect—but with the artist, the creator of the wonderful panorama that is Milton's and now Burford's Pandaemonium. Burford's program glosses all these demonic and mythological figures and more—some 40 specific elements of interest, each with accompanying text from Milton's poem. The influence of Martin's engraving over Milton's poem is apparent in the incorporation into Pandaemonium of elephants and serpents, which Burford interprets as "symbolic of the various idols, &c. worshipped by the ancients; the serpents, supporting the 'starry lamps and blazing cressets,' are symbolic of Satan."[33]

The most substantial departure from Milton's poetic Pandaemonium, however, is Burford's inclusion of a snarling, twisting dragon, which by a considerable margin also happens to be the largest single figure in the panorama. As one critic notes, the array of sometimes indistinguishable figures—those Burford wishes the observer to imbue with colossal dimensions only by imagining them so—"has been in some measure defeated by the enormous size, and conspicuous prominence, and powerful colouring of the great dragon."[34] That the most conspicuous figure should also be the only non-Miltonic (Burford cites only Revelation as its source—this is the only entry without an accompanying extract from Milton's poem) might well suggest that the panorama artists have missed the point. As Milton's Satan blends away, an extratextual marker dominates the attention of the observer, distracting not only from the reportedly most important figure on Burford's canvas but also from the poetry behind it.[35] But the dragon also suggests Satan's final form in *Paradise Lost*—"Now Dragon grown, larger than whom the Sun / Ingenderd in the Pythian Vale on slime" (10.529–30)—and its placement here serves not only as a reminder of the scriptural analogues for Milton's serpent but also as a kind of prolepsis, or an attempt to bring onto the canvas a diachronic narrative element so that we see the alpha and omega of (Milton's) Satan's form, even as the panorama wraps around

Fig. 2.1. Detail from Burford's Pandemonium Panorama. *Courtesy of Houghton Library, Harvard University, call number 14487.16.15.*

upon itself. It unbalances the panorama spatially but activates a temporal motion not unlike Milton's own expansions and contractions in the Pandaemonium sequence. It serves as a reminder, too, of the contractible dimensions of Milton's angels, who may "surpass Earth's Giant Sons" one moment, be "less than smallest Dwarfs" (*PL* 1.779–80) the next, and perhaps sometimes seem both at once. While the public may have missed the subtleties of the display, this seemed ironically a consequence more of the scale of the piece than any lack of familiarity with (or sensitivity over) Milton's poem.

Contemporary responses to the Pandaemonium panorama were not entirely negative, and Oettermann overstates the case in calling the show a "fiasco." The panorama even makes its way into the satirical poem *The Real Devil's Walk*, where the devil, taking a tour of London, praises the numbers in attendance:

> He then went to see Pandemonium,
> As BURFORD portrays it on earth;
> And it pleas'd him to see the thousands come,
> As packet passengers are known to run,
> To examine, before-hand, their berth.[36]

In the *Examiner*, the panorama is praised as a "grand and novel exhibition, which will doubtless be very attractive to all good Christians, as soon as the termination of the Easter festivities will allow them to turn to *serious* enjoyments." This reviewer disregards the fantastic qualities of the piece—calling the figures "beings of other times...in all their fallen greatness. The diabolical Hierarchy is there beheld engaged in full activity....Here is a sight for one shilling!" In other words, this is also an historical display—insofar as Milton was channeling and not inventing the depiction of Satan and his compeers. The reviewer continues,

> The painting, certainly a most extraordinary one, is of the Martin School, and the spectator is at once struck most forcibly by its general resemblance to the style of that artist. We say not this, however, in the slightest disparagement of its merits, as, where the vast, the shadowy, and the mystic is to be portrayed, we know none more appropriate. The building itself is extremely well conceived, while the fiery light and "darkness visible" of the other parts of the picture produce by their contrast a most powerful and even awful effect.... Every patron and admirer of the Fine Arts will of course visit this splendid specimen.

The review also notes that the complaints mounted against the scale of Satan had been addressed: "On re-visiting the painting this morning, (Tuesday) we find that a great improvement has taken place with respect to the principal figure, which is now brought forwarder on the canvas, and the general effect is proportionately increased."[37]

Richard Altick also asserts that the show was a failure and that the *Times* "dismissed the show in a paragraph."[38] However, the *Times* in fact gave the same space to the Pandaemonium review as every other panorama review of that year and the following (and was far more critical of Burford's panoramas of Constantinople and Calcutta, for example). The reviewer does struggle to find a critical standard against which to measure the novelty of the "extraordinary subject," since it does not fall into the familiar categories of "cities, scenery, &c., remarkable either for picturesque beauty or extrinsic interest": "The difference between productions purely artificial and fanciful, and those which are 'built upon the rock of nature,' is very wide, and in proportion as works of art recede from the sublime model, does the judgment concerning them become bewildered and uncertain." Nevertheless, the *Times* grants that Burford "has succeeded in producing a striking and all-engrossing effect, and in so far painting up to his original. The idea of gloom and terror is preserved throughout in the happiest manner; and the colossal palace, as it recedes into indefinite space, overpowers the mind by its immensity and massive grandeur."[39] The few reservations about the panorama center upon the movement away from a representation of nature to a fanciful conjuration of something unnatural (Milton's "darkness visible"). As a *representation*, then, there are no measuring sticks, since there was never anything (or any single thing) presented in the first place. According to this review, if panoramas were meant to produce, above all, verisimilitude of their subject, then pure fantasy—presented however much under the auspices of realism—must necessarily compromise the medium.

The fullest meditation on the Pandaemonium panorama appeared in *Athenaeum,* which discussed not only the departure in subject matter but also the limits of panoramic adaptation in general. It repeats the conventional astonishment at the choice: "Timely announcement had fully prepared the public for some grand and wonderful novelty the Panorama, in Leicester fields; yet there are few, we imagine, who take an interest in matters of this nature, who did not exclaim with surprise on learning that the promised exhibition was to an illustration of Pandemonium. The approvers and admirers of Panoramas in general, held their opinion in suspense as to the probability of success in the bold and heterodox experiment."[40] This panorama would not offer celebrated scenes from nature, the kind of virtual tourism on which the panorama was founded, where an observer could visit "sites and scenes" of "transcendent picturesque beauty" that had "become the objects of interest and curiosity of civilized man in general," and yet existed beyond their normal "locomotive power" to reach. The reviewer nonetheless allows that, as Burford supposes in his *Description,* the "panorama afforded advantages which might be made available for giving effect to efforts in the 'higher branch of the art,' and which might be employed 'to embody with boldness and grandeur the most sublime imagery.'"[41] Indeed, the panorama had become "the best substitute till now devised for actual observation," though it still left much to be desired in imitating the pleasures of the living, breathing real: "Not that a panoramic painting the most perfect that ever was strained around its ample circumference can do more than approach identity of character with the scene which it pretends to represent."[42] And in the question of perfection lies the particular problem in adapting Milton's sublime imagination,

> Who is to design this "sublime imagery?" Exists there the hardy pencil that dares aspire to pourtray Hell's dread Emperor and his millions of subject-spirits as depicted by Milton? The magic hand that traced the "Last Judgment" must have failed in the attempt to embody, to the satisfaction of the readers of the "Paradise Lost," the sublime conceptions of the author, the tower like form, the face, entrenched by thunder scars, of the apostate angel as he stood above the rest, and moved the mighty cherubim to brandish their flaming swords, illumining all hell around, and to hurl defiance towards the vault of heaven.
>
> The attempt, in fact, has not been made, and Mr. Burford, although he has opened a panoramic view of Pandemonium after the design of Mr. Slous, has not essayed to represent the Pandemonium of Milton. Between the two there is this difference: Milton's painting is historical, the panorama is landscape; in the former, the animate objects are principal; the scenery and architecture are accessory; in the latter, the view of the infernal abyss forms the picture, its inmates act a subordinate part.... The outline is grand, and the colouring, where it is not intended to be mysterious, is powerful.... The masses of architecture on the left hand of the dragon, and the vale through which Lethe winds its "slow and silent stream," seemed to us the best parts of the picture. The exhibition, we conclude, will be highly popular for a season; but, loving panoramas, we cannot help indulging a hope that the experiment may not be repeated.[43]

In this criticism of the panorama, it is not Milton's Pandaemonium at all. The reviewer maintains that it may be an adequate stylistic imitation of Martin and may perhaps offer a kind of outline for Milton's design, but because the poem sets in motion, even with "animate figures," while the panorama can only settle for an unchanging immobility, there can be no fruitful comparison between the two works—a position that fails to address the myriad ways in which such appropriations are fruitful even when falling short.

For this reviewer, whereas the panorama privileges the topography and architectural firmness of hell, the poem foregrounds the *details* of character (the scars on Satan's face), dramatic movement (the angels hurling their defiance), and the various perorations (Satan moving the mighty cherubim) that encompass the building of the infernal temple. The reviewer unveils at the end a love for panoramas, and if Burford's made for an unfulfilling and "heterodox experiment," it seems largely because of the transmediation of such generic qualities. A poem can be graced by a million angels in a single line, a painting—even one as accommodating as a panorama—only with a million brushstrokes. And certainly the panoramas were no more successful than the poem at presenting to the observer an instantaneous, 360-degree image. I suggested earlier that the composition of the Pandaemonium panorama does complicate the idea of its own temporality, partly because Milton's own narrativity in the Pandaemonium sequence is so self-consciously divided. But the *Athenaeum* write-up seems content to desire the static qualities of the picture: the panorama was not meant for *poetic* sublimity and all its irregular animations but, paradoxically, for the landscapes of the natural world, here constructed as unmoving, untroubled repositories of "transcendent picturesque beauty," "objects of interest and curiosity" for which the panorama could substitute as a convincing—if still inferior—simulacrum. Its inferiority was in degree, at least, and not in kind.

BACHELDER'S PANORAMA

When interest in panoramas was revived in the later nineteenth century, Milton made a sensational return. R. G. Bachelder (or "Batchelder") took a new moving panorama of *Paradise Lost* on a world tour, with illustrations once more drawn from Martin's prints.[44] There are records of shows as early as 1865 in California and the American Northwest; 1866 in Halifax, Nova Scotia.[45] By the time Bachelder brought the panorama to Australia in March

1867, he claimed to have already presented it "in London for 280 consecutive nights, to more than half a million people, and visited by Her Majesty Queen Victoria and the entire court of Bucking-ham-palace."[46] The show was advertised with all the hyperbole of Victorian showmanship: "The Most Extraordinary Exhibition in the World. The Stupendous Drama of PARADISE LOST," "The Wonder of the Nineteenth Century, the Great Miltonian Tableaux of PARADISE LOST." The initial program is quite detailed in the scenes to be viewed, and insistent on the point that the show would be "a complete illustration of this great poem from beginning to end, carrying out Milton's idea of Heaven, Hell, Chaos, and Paradise." In addition to providing a pseudo-Miltonic "argument" for the whole of *Paradise Lost*, elaborating especially on the three days of the war in heaven, the advertisement sketches out the entire presentation, acknowledging the debt to John Martin.

The opening scenes, set in heaven, promise "Lofty grandeur and ethereal beauty" that "surpass all that has yet been produced by man or witnessed by mortal eye, they being, in fact, one perfect blaze of glory. The sublime representations of The Plains of Heaven—The Angels of Heaven—the Rivers of Bliss—The Gathering of Angels round the Almighty's Throne—The Celestial Palace, baffle all description, and defy the power of the imagination." The second section, unfolding the war in heaven, is even more sizzling: "The most sublime and imposing spectacle ever witnessed," with 25 scenes ranging from "Satan in his celestial palace, with his companions, plotting rebellion" to "Satan in his sun-bright chariot" to "The Son of God with thunderbolts and fire of Heaven." The third section, "Creation," includes the "Magnificent scene of the first rising of the sun and moon on the young earth" and genesis of "fishes, fowls, and insects," while the fourth section, "Hell and Chaos," is said to have "created the most intense sensation" during the London exhibition, when "thousands nightly witnessed them with wonder and amazement." This "most extraordinary spectacle of the age" again features Pandaemonium as part of 30 scenes conveying the "awful and impressive idea of the infernal regions." The fifth section, "Paradise," is described most poetically: "Adam and Eve in the garden surrounded by the gorgeous foliage incident to a tropical clime, with Silvio's lakes and groves, silvery cascades, tropical flowers, birds, and fruit." (The advertisement seems to be appealing to the Australian audience's sense of self-identification in making Eden into a pastoral of the South Seas.) Finally, it is "Eve before the Fountain, Seeing Her Reflection in the Water," that serves as the climax, "The most chaste and beautiful scene ever witnessed." It also proved to be the most controversial, leading some critics to regard Bachelder's sublime, stupendous spectacle as little more than an excuse for a peepshow. In *Canvas Documentaries,* Mimi Colligan relates that the first shows, at Melbourne Polytechnic Hall, were reviewed somewhat unevenly: "The *Age* reviewer thought that the 'copies from Martin...were effectively done' but that Milton's poem was badly read, needing 'an accomplished elocutionist.'"[47] *Paradise Lost* closed at the Polytechnic in April, though as Colligan notes, "Bachelder and his imported panoramas were to form an important part in the panorama business in Australia and New Zealand for the next twenty years," and included numerous tours and revivals of *Paradise Lost,* as well as Bachelder's even more popular *American War Panorama* and another on the Apocalypse, with paintings in the latter once more based on Martin.[48]

Subsequent showings of *Paradise Lost* in New Zealand offer some helpful additional details of the reception of Bachelder's presentation. Certainly the most damning account of the panorama appeared in the New Zealand *Herald,* which called the work "a gross caricature" of Milton's "sublime allegory": the human figures "evince a thorough ignorance of anatomy," the nudes in Eden "were simply pabulum for prurient imaginations," and even the music was "some of the most infernal we have ever heard." The paper reports many patrons abandoning the performance "as the scenes, one by one, became more and more offensive to the good taste of the spectators," and concludes, "we unhesitatingly condemn the Diorama of 'Paradise Lost.' As to Milton's blank verse, could the blind poet have arisen from his grave, he would not have been able to recognize his own production."[49] It is difficult to say in what ways anatomically incorrect figures would feed prurient imaginations—or what patrons otherwise expected Adam and Eve (particularly Milton's sexually active version) to be appareled in. The critique of the music and verse readings seems to be merely piling on to the fundamental objection of offense to good taste—that is, what promised to be sublime and instructive had become not only ridiculous but also pornographic.

The next day, the *Daily Southern Cross* describes "moderately numerous attendance at the Prince of Wales Theatre last evening to witness Batchelder's Diorama of 'Paradise Lost.'" This review, following hard on the ruthless treatment in the New Zealand *Herald* (and probably influenced by it), is also not favorable: "when we say that the landscape painting is excellent, we have perhaps said all that we can in favour of the diorama," and again, "the only part of the entertainment, if we are justified in using such a term, which appeared to be thoroughly appreciated was the distribution of the prizes" (referring to the door prizes almost always advertised alongside the entertainment itself). The chief objection appears to be the lack of "tact" in presenting a larger-than-life piece of nakedness, presumably Eve at the fountain, which the reviewer regards as a kind of colossal centerfold: "Though much artistic effect has been bestowed in giving shape to Milton's grand realizations, the painter has in some parts failed to display that tact and practical foresight which would guard his productions from censure.... The only question is as to the desirability of choosing certain subjects for public representation."[50]

What both reviews share is a subtext of elitist gatekeeping—Milton *the poet* would roll over in his grave at the degradation of his verse, either the manner in which it is being read or the "gross" use to which it has been put in an entertainment aimed at the lowest common denominator: those infantile folk who consume as "pabulum" the superficial spectacles of the body. The second reviewer goes further in asserting that it is the very publicizing of Milton that makes him an unfit subject for consumption. The poetry is condemned to the realm of private pleasures—and let the poet remain sealed and slumbering unobtrusively in the tomb. The transformation of Milton into mass culture, a culture here built around the ultimate in conspicuous display, is constructed by both reviewers as an intrinsic alteration of his value as a signifier for those forms that seem resistant to mass experience (particularly, again, the sublime.) It is not the process of commodification itself—the door prizes are received with appropriate satisfaction—but the misappropriation of the Miltonic commodity that announces the gap between high and low, producer and consumer, the pure and the prurient.

The critique of these "prurient representations" led Bachelder's agent, Harry Eastwood, to issue an immediate defense, trying to re-spin the event by submitting another paper's more positive review:

> I beg to draw the attention of the public to the following criticism given by the *Ballarat Star:* "Mr. Bachelder's entertainment at the Mechanics' was very successful on Saturday night. The hall was crowded in every part. The entertainment itself, as we have before stated, is one of a very superior character, and will well repay a visit....Our space will not permit us to deal with each scene in rotation: we will, however, mention several of the most striking and beautiful. The first represents Satan as prepared for the work which he has determined upon; the next two or three represent Heaven, and the gathering together of the obedient angels after Satan's revolt; the scene next in order is a representation of the plains of Heaven and the celestial encampment. This is one of the most beautiful in the entertainment....The scenes following represent the imitation being given to the rebellious angels that they can no longer abide in heaven, also Satan conferring with his company, and his determination to attempt to regain his former place in heaven. The mustering of the host in heaven, and the battle extending over three days, finishing with the driving of Satan and his host from the battlements of heaven into the burning lake, is a fine piece of representation. Then follows the creation of the world; first, an illustration of chaos, then creation of light and the first rising of the sun. This last is very beautiful, the valleys, lakes, mountains, and rivers forming a landscape of extreme loveliness, and the gradual increase of light, as the sun is rising, leaves nothing to be desired to give it effect. Then follows the creation of trees, plants, birds, beasts, fishes, &c.: and the last scene of this part represents Adam naming the various animals and things which had been created. The second part shows Satan calling up his hosts from the burning lake, the building of Pandemonium; his council, where he explains to his lords that there was yet another world and other beings to ruin....His flight

through the gates of hell, through chaos, and his arrival on earth, are magnificently illustrated, as also is his arrival at Paradise. The views which follow represent the garden of Paradise, with Adam and Eve, yet in purity and innocence, wandering through its flowery vales and by its placid lakes. Then follows the angel warning, the scene showing Eve's surprise at first beholding her image reflected in the lake, the meeting with the tempter in the form of a serpent, and her fall, the whole closing with a very effective representation of the expulsion from the garden....We may add, in concluding this rapid outline, that every scene is explained by Mr. Bachelder in the words of the poet.[51]

As a defense against the earlier critics, this account makes the important move of shepherding Adam and Eve back into the fold of "purity and innocence." There is nothing titillating about these scenes: even the troubling image of Eve at the fountain is reread as a "surprise"—as if Eve is just as shocked at her own naked reflection as the spectators gazing upon the mirror images, but only *at first*. In this narrative, Eve moves on to the dangers of other temptations—those more appropriately channeled through Satan than her own body. There is a decided difference here between the implied glance of Eve's "surprise" and the languorous male gaze in the earlier reviews ascribed to those pabulum-consuming spectators who lingered longingly over the nudes, a gaze further evidenced and repressed by those who left the building entirely. There is also much of value in the details of the performance in this report—one gets a sense absent in the other reviews not only of the pictorial representation but also of the movements and animation, most notably the "gradual increase of light" as the sun rises. The concluding point, passed off as an addendum, may be the most telling: the unanimity of the panoramic presentation with "the words of the poet," seen here not as supplementary but as directing the entire hermeneutic experience. With such guidance—a somewhat ironic privileging of the word at the expense of the picture—any interpretation of sinfulness would surely be preempted.

Other animadversions emphasize less the scandals of Eve and more the mistreatment of literary genius in so popular a medium as the panorama. As another reviewer wrote for an 1870 performance in Odd Fellows Hall, Wellington:

The Panorama itself, however, affords a conclusive proof of the well-known statement, that there is but a step from the sublime to the ridiculous. Paradise Lost is undoubtedly a sublime poem, but the subject is a delicate one to be treated of, and when the treatment is of a pictorial character the result is necessarily to some extent ridiculous. Milton's beautiful language renders the most exaggerated and impossible conceptions grand and impressive, but pictorial representations, although truthful to the poem, strike one as being totally incongruous. Such a poem as Paradise Lost is really desecrated by being made the groundwork of a Panorama, but looking at the matter as a mere exhibition, the pictures are really worth seeing and will well repay a visit.[52]

This is a strong iteration of that discursive tradition that presents Milton as both visually desirable but also beyond the pictorial. Even the most "exaggerated and impossible conceptions"—devices that were part of the panorama discourse from its beginnings—fail rather than fit the infinitudes of Milton's imagination. This is also consonant with a cartoon in the *Ballarat Punch* from October 19, 1867, titled "From the Sublime to the Ridiculous," in which Bachelder's *Paradise Lost* panorama is groaningly misunderstood by a local, who thinks it concerns a bachelor and a "pair o' dice, lost" (see fig. 2.2). It is not entirely clear what is ridiculous in this parody—that *Paradise Lost* should be reduced to so vulgar a thing as a panorama, or that *Paradise Lost* remains sublime, even in a popularized form, and it is the illiterate populace being lampooned.[53]

By 1870, Bachelder's *Paradise Lost* was still being promoted as "the most Instructive Entertainment ever given in Queensland," and had hired a professional Shakespearean, G. W. Carey, to provide the accompanying reading, though ads still made sure to highlight the presentation of Eve before the fountain.[54] The Milton panorama played throughout the 1870s, with Harry Eastwood maintaining showings as late as June 1875 in Dunedin. In December 1878, the *Auckland Star* reported the destruction of "Batchelor's Panorama" in a fire that burned down the Town Hall in Deniliquin.[55] In the end, the popularization of Milton must be said to have persisted despite the strong counterweights of high culture and the ambivalence surrounding the spectacularizing of *Paradise Lost*.

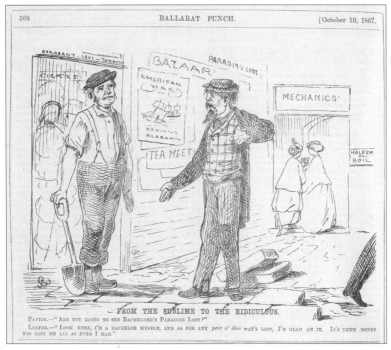

Fig. 2.2. Cartoon of the *Paradise Lost* panorama. *Courtesy of the State Library of Victoria.*

MAGIC LANTERNS

While the panoramas developed Milton as a popular subject for new immersive entertainment and spectacle, their influence upon the cinema is not as great as another technical device that predates considerably the panorama and that led directly to the invention of the moving picture: the magic lantern. Variations on this device can be found centuries before Milton was born, though historian Laurent Mannoni makes a convincing case for the Protestant polymath Christiaan Huygens as the true developer of magic lantern technologies, likely in the late 1650s.[56] These included a series of convex and biconvex lenses seated in a projection tube, stemming from the lantern casing itself (usually a wooden box with chimney), which could project an image with superior focus from a series of glass slides. An especially poignant example of a magic

lantern show in Milton's lifetime is offered by the French physi-
cian and political exile Charles Patin. Sometime between 1670 and
1673, Patin traveled through Nuremberg, visiting there the *Wun-
derkammer* of a famed German, Johann Franz Griendel, an expert
in the manufacture of the most advanced optical instruments of
the day. Griendel dealt in all manner of devices: "opera glasses
and spectacles, *perspectives hollandaises* ('Dutch perspectives,'
paper theatres showing a scene or a landscape with perspective
effects), four-lens terrestrial telescopes and two-lens astronomical
telescopes, binoculars, helioscopes (mirrors for observing the sun
in a camera obscura), triangular glass prisms showing a rainbow
effect, multi-faceted lenses, steel mirrors, anamorphoses."[57] The
real draws for visitors, however, were Griendel's *Laternae Magicae
oder Bilder-Laterne*. Patin describes the show put on by these projection devices as nothing short of miraculous:

> I was apt to believe that there never was in the World a greater
> Magitian than he. For it seem'd to me as if I had a sight of Paradise,
> of Hell and of wand'ring Spirits and Phantoms, so that altho' I
> know myself to be endu'd with some measure of Resoluteness,
> yet at that time I wou'd willingly have given one half to save the
> other. All these Apparitions suddenly disappear'd and gave place to
> Shews of another Nature: For in a moment, I saw the Air fill'd with
> all sorts of Birds, almost after the same manner as they are usually
> painted round about *Orpheus,* and in the twinkling of an Eye, a
> Country-Wedding appear'd to my view, with so natural and lively a
> representation that I imagin'd myself to be one of the Guests at the
> Solemnity. Afterward the *Horizon* of my sight was taken up with
> a Palace so stately, that nothing like it can be produc'd, but in the
> Imagination; before which there were divers Personages running at
> the Ring. These Heroes seem'd to be the Gods that were ador'd by
> antiquity.[58]

The scenes before Patin—gripping visions of heaven and hell,
ghosts called forth from the infernal regions, flocks of birds filling the sky, pastoral retreats, an unimaginable palace of Olympian
gods, playing at war games—were in many ways already standard
fare for the most important precursor of the cinema, the magic
lantern. If the scenes also seem to conjure up images from Milton's

Paradise Lost, this too is not entirely coincidental, since from their inception magical lantern shows shared with Milton a repertoire of fantastic images and visual techniques. Indeed, the history of Milton on film emerges most clearly from the involvement of his work in the history and evolution of the magic lantern.

From its beginnings in the Middle Ages, the art of optical projection was occupied with the ineffable landscapes of paradise and hell, and especially the terrifying spirits inhabiting those realms. The earliest image to capture the idea of a magic lantern dates from Giovanni da Fontana's *Bellicorum instrumentorum liber cum figures delineates et ficticiis literis conscriptus* (c. 1420), and it presents a "nocturnal apparition for frightening viewers," a towering devil with horns, wings, and a particularly nasty looking spear (see fig. 2.3). Within the lantern can be seen the smaller image to be projected, along with a light source and chimney to round out what would have produced, without a lens, a rather indistinct projection. Fontana nonetheless includes it among the rest of his war machines as a device, presumably, for frightening one's enemies off the battlefield.[59] Fontana's sketch, while not presenting a true "magic lantern," the technical qualities of which were not realized until the mid-seventeenth century, nonetheless makes apparent the fantastical power of the device. The robed figure is at once dwarfed by the gigantic scale of the summoned fiend and serenely empowered by his own relative position over the miniature demon seemingly trapped within the lantern. The scene anticipates the genie-from-the-lamp tales of the *Arabian Nights,* while the power of the act is both martial—a huge, menacing, fiercely armed warrior—and mystical: the image floats, detached yet controlled by the lanternist without any visible connection. Fontana does not elaborate on the success of the illusion in battle, but one can imagine its potential dazzle.

The magic lantern, like the magic mirror and camera obscura before it, lent itself to the abuse of charlatans who promoted their illusions as reality. Indeed, the camera obscura, the "dark room" of various dimensions that allowed the reflected light of images outside the room to pass through a small aperture and the images to be thus viewed on a screen within, presented an even more convincing

Fig. 2.3. Fontana's magic lantern with satanic figure. *Courtesy of Bayerische Staatsbibliothek München, Cod.icon. 242, fol. 70r.*

optical illusion since it showed moving images. Around the year 1608, Cornelius Drebbel remarked on a new invention that could create illusions "as if the earth opens and the spirits rise up from it, first in the form of a cloud and then changing themselves into such a shape as I think fit. . . . Nay, I make the giants, such as they existed in former ages, to seem to rise up from the earth, twenty, thirty feet tall, moving and stirring so wonderfull and perfectly as if the parts of their bodies seem to live in a natural way."[60] These magical shows were being debunked as early as 1613, when Francois d'Aguillon published his *Opticorum libri VI* and called out those "certain tricksters" who "attempt to take advantage of unknowing people" and "boast of making the ghosts of the devil appear from Hell itself."[61] D'Aguillon's treatise makes clear the methods used by which a performer outside the camera obscura, costumed in a "devil mask, such that he resembles the images of demons which one is used to see, with a hideous and monstrous face and horns on the forehead, a tail, and a wolf's skin with claws at hands and feet," might "strut" about an exteriorized stage and project in a terrifying manner in front of the beguiled spectators housed within the camera.[62] These disembodied spirits might be augmented by sound effects, including ventriloquism, or alternately by a request for complete silence, capitalizing on the supernatural eeriness of moving pictures that somehow make no accompanying sound. In this they anticipate the first wave of silent films, particularly those phantasmagoric efforts of French filmmaker Georges Méliès, and by the early seventeenth century the depiction of animals and landscapes via the camera obscura were already being proclaimed an artistic mode superior to the static images of painting, since the camera obscura "represents that which the painter has never been able to place in his picture, namely *continuous movement* from place to place."[63] But despite its ability to capture motion, the strict exigencies of the camera obscura's operation—most notably the need for strong solar lighting—led to its virtual obsolescence with the arrival of the magic lantern.

Advanced designs for the camera obscura were treated in Athanasius Kircher's famed volume *Ars magna lucis et umbrae* (1646), which did not yet discuss the lantern, though Kircher has been sometimes credited with its invention.[64] A letter to Huygens dated March 25, 1660, remarks how "the goodman Kirkher is doing a thousand tricks with the magnet in the gallery of the College of Rome here; if he had the invention of the Lantern, he would truly be terrifying the cardinals with ghosts."[65] The remark is notable not only for suggesting Kircher knew nothing of the lantern at this time but also for linking the device once more to Faustian spirit raising. Nor could Huygens resist the lure of the macabre: in 1659 he drew a series of images, based on Holbein's *The Dance of Death,* that serve as the first illustrations of a moving magic lantern slide—an effect accomplished by placing two slides over one another and turning them with a lever or similar mechanism. Still, for a serious scientist like Huygens, the invention of the magical lantern (it was first given this sobriquet in 1668 by the Italian mathematician Francesco Eschinardi) was neither an artistic triumph nor a technological marvel; he seemed to consider it little more than a curiosity for an evening's entertainment, a bit of legerdemain to amuse an audience perhaps already in on the technical innovations of the device.

The levity of the lantern show is supported in the first details of such performances in London. Samuel Pepys describes a meeting with the optician John Reeves on August 19, 1666, in which the lantern figures as little more than a curio: "But by and by comes by agreement Mr. Reeves, and after him Mr. Spong, and all day with them...upon opticke enquiries....He did also bring a lanthorne with pictures in glasse, to make strange things appear on a wall, very pretty."[66] A few days later, on August 22, Pepys mentions purchasing from Reeves "the Lanthorne that shows tricks" along with a telescope and miniature perspective. Reeves, who was a correspondent of Huygens, had been selling lanterns in London since at least 1663, just a few years before the first publication of *Paradise Lost.* For Pepys, the lantern and its "pictures in glass" were still a novelty item. Not only was its presentation "very pretty" but it also "shows tricks"; the combination made it enough of a conversation piece in 1666 to justify its purchase, along with the more complex instrument, the telescope, and a more amateurish one, the miniature perspective. That for Pepys the things appearing on his wall should be "strange" also suggests something of the supernatural effects the lantern shared with the earlier camera obscura, though Pepys does not detail the exact nature of these images. Two years later, in the journal *Philosophical Transactions,* Robert Hooke laid claim to an invention similar to both the magic lantern and the camera obscura, by which one could project seemingly miraculous "Apparitions of Angels, or Devils," in addition to "the vanishing of them in a cloud, and then appearing no more after the cloud is vanisht."[67] Hooke had reportedly been putting on parlor performances such as this for years. The close and continued alliance of the magic lantern with this level of entertainment, particularly of a frightening or unearthly sort, is fully defined by 1690, when the *Dictionnaire Universel* denotes the "Lanterne Magique" as "a small optical machine which makes visible in the darkness on a white wall several ghosts and monsters."[68]

The rise of the lantern show coincides precisely with Milton's publication of *Paradise Lost* in 1667, which in turn, as many critics have noted, displays a growing cultural fascination with optical tricks of all sorts. While Milton's familiarity with Galileo's telescope has often been discussed, the range of other optical innovations with which Milton might have been familiar, including the microscope, has been less observed.[69] The perspectival shifts that Milton employs in *Paradise Lost* certainly seem to sweep the heavens as if through an "optic glass," as when Satan gets his first "close-up" of the planet Earth:

> upon the firm opacous globe
> Of this round World, whose first convex divides
> The luminous inferior Orbs, enclosed
> From Chaos, and the inroad of Darkness old,
> Satan alighted walks. A globe far off
> It seemed; now seems a boundless continent
> Dark, waste, and wild, under the frown of
> Night Starless expos'd.   (*PL* 3.418–25)

Unlike with Galileo's "optic glass" (1.288), there is nothing explicit linking the visual acrobatics of the poem to the innovations of the magic lantern. Still, the same kinds of optical operations for which the lantern was famous can be glimpsed in Milton. The magic lantern, sometimes termed in the 1600s a "megalographic lantern" because of the gigantic magnification of its projected images, could, in the words of one writer, fashion "an elephant out of a fly."[70] Indeed, it was one of the trademark ploys of the lantern shows to move the lamp to manipulate the image, making it seem suddenly either to shrink or grow in scale. A show before the emperor of China in the early 1670s, for instance, featured "pictures … on the wall opposite, smaller or of a prodigious size, according to whether the wall is close or far away."[71] Such effects became a mainstay, in particular, of the later phantasmagorias, when the summoned specters would seem to advance on the audience as the magic lantern was withdrawn on rollers. Milton's description of the fallen angels entering Pandaemonium reads precisely like the patter of one of these performances: "Behold a wonder! They but now who seem'd / In bigness to surpass Earth's Giant Sons / Now less than smallest Dwarfs, in narrow room / Throng numberless" (1.777–80). The shift from giant to pygmy, when "incorporeal Spirits to smallest forms / Reduc'd thir shapes immense" (1.789–90), and back again at the end of book 1, when the focus returns to the "great Seraphic Lords and Cherubim" meeting "in thir own dimensions" (1.794, 793), participates in what Tom Gunning calls an "aesthetics of astonishment" in the beginnings of cinema, when it was not a ghost or ghoul but a train seeming to barrel toward the stunned audience, and in the kinds of strange wonders that Pepys and others witnessed in the first dawning of the magic lantern.

THE PHANTASMAGORIA

Around the time of Loutherbourg's Eidophusikon, magic lantern shows were surging in popularity, and traveling showmen created makeshift home theaters for even the poorest of audiences. But it was in the nineteenth century that the medium reached its zenith. By the 1800s, magic lanterns varied greatly in their effects, lenses, and type of illumination (gas lamp or searing limelight). Many could simulate motion in their pictures—undulating snakes, for instance—with dissolving views, rotating slides, or other manipulations to reproduce simple linear or rotational movement (the most famous of this latter type was "Man Eating Rats"), or even a moving dioramic effect, in which two long slides—one featuring the background, the other the mobile figures, were slid across each other on grooves to show such popular effects as the Israelites crossing the Red Sea or a parade of animals entering Noah's Ark. Multiple lanterns could be employed to make the movement even more dramatic: the "Angel of Peace" slide featured "A beautiful landscape showing a city at night, with the new moon in the sky reflected in the water. The figure of an angel bearing a child appears like a vision in the sky, and then fades away"; the "Magician and Caldron" showed "Cave, and magician with his magic wand, with caldron in corner, out of which appears at various times, ghosts, witches, hobgoblins, etc."[72]

Near the turn of the eighteenth century, some of these innovations in the magic lantern contributed to the emergence of phantasmagorias, ghostly shows that maintained the age-old promise to summon spirits from a lugubrious netherworld. Caught in the tension between rational entertainment and romantic escapism, the phantasmagorias promoted themselves by both rejecting and adopting claims of necromancy. Further capitalizing on and helping to speed along the public's taste for gothicism, the shows utilized multiple lanterns, including new designs like the fantascope and megascope, which could slide about on runners and project opaque objects to give the illusion of animated spirits hovering about a suitably sepulchral chamber.[73] The effects were accentuated by the use of smoke and mirrors, the sound of tempest, and occasionally by the addition of masked actors. The set piece almost always began with the room plunged into complete darkness and a phantom gradually materializing, commencing as a point of light and then growing in size until seeming to advance on the audience, thanks to the manipulation of the hidden projectors. Many shows also favored the accompaniment of a peculiar musical instrument, the glass harmonica, whose spectral tones were produced by some "thirty glass cups mounted horizontally on a rotating axle, driven by a foot pedal," the mystical sounds of which, according to one report, had "such a weakening power on the nervous system of those hearing it, that it is impossible to bear its effect for more than a few minutes, without exposing oneself to going mad."[74] Some phantasmagorias lasted upwards of two hours.

The most accomplished phantasmagorist, Étienne-Gaspard Robert (Robertson), born in Belgium in 1763 and active throughout the late eighteenth and early nineteenth centuries, details in his autobiography how he tried from an early age to discover the

secrets of the occult. In one incident, Robertson recalls seques-
tering himself in his room in order to raise Satan, only to find
that the crudeness of his animal sacrifice failed to produce even
a lesser devil. After hours of plying every machination and psychological bait-and-switch he could to beckon forth an infernal
spirit, he finally gave up the naturalistic approach for the scholastic.
Poring over such tomes as Giambattista della Porta's *Magia natu-
ralis* (1558) and Claude Mydorge's *Examen du livre des récréa-
tions mathématiques* (1630), he learned of the history of optical
techniques by which spirits might seem to be raised, declaring in
his autobiography, "the devil refusing to communicate to me the
science of producing miracles, I began to produce devils, and my
wand had only to move in order to force the whole procession to
the light of day. My dwelling became a veritable Pandemonium."[75]

Robertson's transmogrification of his modest flat into Milton's
demonic palace suggests a number of significations: first that
Robertson's imaginative powers were closer to Milton's Satan
than to Faust, with visions already of designing not a parlor-room
dialogue with a summoned devil but a complete architecture of
hell, inhabited by the demons that he would shape to his will.
Milton's lines on the perspectival shifts in the size of the demons
may be inherent in Robertson's recollection as well, since that was
the defining trait of the phantasmagoria show. Moreover, when
Robertson eventually came to translate his private occultish interests into public performance, he did so in a way again informed
by Milton's Pandaemonium, offering to show "the same methods
which must have been employed by the Witch [of Endor] when
she invoked the spirit of Samuel, the three witches when they
appeared to Macbeth, the priests of Memphis in the mysteries of
their initiation."[76] Robertson sought no less than to dispel and yet
overreach those ancient rituals, which he came to regard as the
enemies of reason but the devoted friends of his own economics.
Like Milton's Pandaemonium, his shows aimed to demonstrate
how "those / Who boast in mortal things, and wond'ring tell / Of
Babel, and the works of *Memphian* Kings, . . . / are easily outdone /
By *Spirits* reprobate" (1.692–97), upending in one hour all their
mystification.

In 1798, Robertson started showing his phantasmagoria in Paris, first to small crowds at the Pavillon de l'Échiquier, and then later at the gloomy Couvent des Capucines, where it was a huge hit. The visions he created were driven by a carefully constructed narrative that often began before the show proper and were punctuated by the Grand Guignol of assorted dramas. After creating his personal Pandaemonium, Robertson seems never to have returned explicitly to the language or imagery of *Paradise Lost*. (His repertoire, a mélange of revolutionary politics, popular gothicism, and other well-traveled sensationalisms, is well preserved in his own writings.) Still, the idea of Milton's hell was never far from such performances. Brewster attended one of Paul De Philipstahl's phantasmagorias which was running in London and Edinburgh in 1802, shows for which Philipstahl had appropriated and popularized much of Robertson's catalogue, and Brewster described the show as if lifted from the opening of Milton's epic: "The small theatre of exhibition was lighted only by one hanging lamp, the flame of which was drawn up into an opaque chimney or shade when the performance began. In this 'darkness visible,' the curtain rose, and displayed a cave, with skeletons and other terrific figures in relief upon its walls."[77] Not only Brewster's application of Milton's famous paradox of "darkness visible" to the lamplight but also the involvement of homologous spaces—the cave with skeletons ("and other terrific figures") as a reinterpretation of Satan and his "Dungeon horrible" (*PL* 1.61)—suggest that in Brewster's imagination the curtain was rising on book 1 of a *Paradise Lost* phantasmagoria. Even more directly, Henry Lemoine memorialized the phantasmagoria craze in "The Phantasmagoria," a light-hearted poem published in 1802 in which he evokes Milton explicitly:

> To these [other ghosts] succeed in wild vindictive rage
> A ghostly group of specters that engage
> Fierce as the knights in chivalry of yore
> Or Milton's fallen spirits long before.
> Appall'd with fear, see killing Death pursue,
> E'en the sad victims of his silent crew,
> 'Till, sinking in a flood of liquid fire,
> The vanquish'd and victorious both retire.[78]

In these viewings of Milton by firelight, the fantasy of *Paradise Lost*'s opening scene persists in the "flood of liquid fire," though it is secondary to Lemoine's more elaborate conflation of the show and the poem: the "ghostly group of specters" who fight first like knights and then like "Milton's fallen spirits." This sounds less like a reference to the war in heaven than to the competitions of the fallen host after the council in hell, when they vie like "Aery Knights" who "Battle in the Clouds" (*PL* 2.530, 536, 535). It approaches a resurrection of Griendel's *Laterna Magica* performance in the 1670s, when Charles Patin witnessed the old gods "running at Ring." Clearly, it was difficult to attend an animation of spirits, particularly in "battalious aspect," and not regard it as a visualization of Milton's design.[79]

LONSDALE'S PHANTASMAGORIC *L'ALLEGRO*

In January 1802, Mark Lonsdale, a songwriter and stage manager at Sadler's Wells who had produced numerous popular pantomimes, offered a novel exhibition in the Scenic Theatre at the Lyceum: an evening entertainment called *Aegyptiana*. The show promised artistic scenes from Egyptian history and culture (drawn from Dominique Vivant Denon's just published *Travels in Upper and Lower Egypt*) as well as intermezzo literary readings, all "illustrated by machinery and painting." The exact nature of the new "machinery" is unclear—Lonsdale's friend John Britton, who provided the scripted commentary for *Aegyptiana*, later termed the show a "moving panorama for the stage."[80] But it is not evident exactly how the images moved—whether, for instance, the paintings were scrolled across a stage on a single canvas with rollers, or whether there was merely a succession of images that was mechanically changed over via transparencies. (The former—the true "moving panorama" of the nineteenth century, not only animated but portable—is unlikely, since Lonsdale's entertainment predates the first recognized instances of such presentations by about 20 years.) Much more clear is Lonsdale's direct competition: Philipstahl's ragingly popular Miltonic Phantasmagoria, with its "Grand CABINET of OPTICAL and MECHANICAL ILLUSIONS" and its production of "Phantoms or Apparitions of the Dead or Absent," which had been playing to sold-out shows in the Lyceum's lower rooms since late in 1801. As Marina Warner writes, "phantasmagorias gave an impression of vitality far more beguiling than even the miniaturized intricacies of panoramas," since their mobile projectors and billowing images, directed against a smoky miasma, "swelled and shrunk, as well as shifting with tricks of light, and so created an illusion that they possessed that quality of conscious life: animation."[81] It seems plausible that Lonsdale was using similar mechanisms to achieve movement in his show, perhaps involving at least one magic lantern; certainly he understood that such sophisticated animation was a crucial part of Philipstahl's success. Indeed, Lonsdale saw an opportunity in *Aegyptiana* to capitalize on the public's taste for phantasmagoria by introducing his own selection of exotic and macabre images. But ultimately Lonsdale misread his public and his appropriations proved *too* tasteful, not least in his somewhat surprising inclusion of Milton's poem *L'Allegro*. Despite constant revisions to the show, it closed with a thud at the end of its first season.

The advance notices for *Aegyptiana* held much promise, offering a tantalizing fusion of "Poetry, Painting, and Spectacle," with "Fact in its most Picturesque Form" to be relieved by "a few Productions of Fancy," including "Fancy-tinted Drawings, and Animated Sketches in Charcoal."[82] The opening day program, "addressed to the Eye and Ear," featured three parts: first, "A Review of the Arts, Manners, and Mythology of Ancient Egypt…including the Catacombs, the Pyramids," with an intermezzo of the strenuously gothic piece "An Elegy under a Gallows"; second, "A Sketch of Modern Egypt, and its most picturesque productions," followed by another intermezzo, this time one of John Gay's fables, the grimly comical "The Hare and Many Friends"; and finally, "A view of the street, scenery, and costume of Egypt," with the conclusion "L'Allegro (from Milton) accompanied by a scenic view of the Imagery of the Poet." There were 32 "scenic pictures" in all, each "upon an extensive scale." A Mr. Dighton provided the "comic readings," while the "Poetic Recitations" were provided by a "young Gentleman, who makes his first attempt before a public audience," the aggregate of which, it was hoped, would result in a "rational Amusement with an Evening Lounge."[83]

The "Embellished recitation of Milton's L'Allegro" included "a Scenic View of the Imagery of the Poet. In Ten Successive Pictures, produced by a system of machinery upon a plan entirely new." Whatever particular innovations Lonsdale's machinery made, the Milton sequence follows the general narrative order of the poem (though commencing with "the Poet's study"): in succession, "A Rural Scene, at Daybreak; Sun-rise — An Open Landscape; A Rustic Noontide Repast; The Upland Hamlet and Holiday Sports; Evening — The Cottage Fireside; A Splendid Tournament; An Ancient Hall, with a Banquet; a Theatre — Scenes from Johnson [Jonson] and Shakespeare; A music Saloon — Opening to a View of the Elysian Fields."[84] Edward Ziter suggests that the entire panorama displayed an "antiquarian fetish for the non-modern," with its concatenation of Egyptian imagery and Gothic locales — including those drawn from the more medieval moments of *L'Allegro* (the "Splendid Tournament" and "Ancient Hall").[85] There is more than a hint, too, of the kinds of manipulations that began with the Eidophusikon and would be advanced in the diorama — the shifts in lighting from sunrise to noon to evening, self-referential involutions of theatricality (Milton framing Jonson and Shakespeare), the synthesis of audiovisual sensation. As a poem, *L'Allegro* was actually an apt choice for such a range of effects, particularly the subtle treatment of light and shade, the incorporation of dreamlike and spectacular entertainments, even the goblins and fairies and "haunted stream" that further conjure something of the Gothic. The verse, likewise, is at once alacritous and musical, full of racing scene shifts and embedded instrumentation (whistling plowmen, merry bells, jocund rebecks), culminating in the allusion to the theater. There, again, it is the musicality that beckons — Shakespeare's warbling notes, a return to the lark that breaks the morning earlier in the poem — while also evoking the competing representational concerns of art ("Jonson's learned sock") and nature (Shakespeare's unstudied "wood notes").

Lonsdale, a veteran of the London musical theater, hoped his new venture would revolutionize the very possibilities of theatricality—even as Milton's poem transformed the drama of Jonson and Shakespeare to pure lyricism. Indeed, there is a strong sense in Lonsdale's show of lyricality—of fanciful vignettes, of choice and evanescent images, and, above all, of momentary transport. But perhaps because these lyrical functions jarred with the grand spectacles Lonsdale promised, or perhaps because Lonsdale simply overloaded and overstimulated his audience, his vision of a multimedia, multigenre hybrid was financially disastrous. Even more disappointing than Burford's Pandaemonium, Lonsdale's show was also more of a hodgepodge; the Miltonic elements failed as popular entertainment, though the use to which Lonsdale put them is compelling and, in their ambition to both entertain and educate, just a few decades before its time. Britton reported with faint praise that the performance made "a pleasing and rational exhibition, but was not sufficiently attractive to draw remunerating houses; indeed the unfortunate adventurer was unable to pay his creditors."[86] In her study of the phantasmagoria, Warner observes that "dioramas and panoramas concentrated on battles, modern cityscapes, or exotic scenery, customs, and people"—conventions Lonsdale was desperately trying to absorb and merge into the spectral forms of Philipstahl's shows.[87] In fact, one of the only existing contemporary reviews applauded especially the presence in the painted Egyptian sequences of mummies and man-eating crocodiles; the latter were seen to advance along a river toward an unsuspecting farmer and his cattle.[88] Lonsdale similarly channeled the lurid appeal of the phantasmagoria into other aspects of the panoramic entertainment—massing together catacombs, pyramids, and chthonic Egyptian mythology, the ghastly "Gallows" elegy, even the sporadic Gothic irruptions of *L'Allegro*.[89]

But the combination of Egyptian edification and gothic phantasmagoria clashed as much in taste as genre. By February, Lonsdale began drifting to the dark side completely, incorporating into *Aegyptiana* his own phantasmagoria sideshow with the "Ghost of Sir Bevis of Lancaster." Moreover, unlike that shady phantasmagoria going on beneath the upper rooms, Lonsdale's version promised "so natural a kind of illusion...that the impression it leaves on the spectator is perfectly divested of the effect of Raree-show representation, and, of course, draws forth the approbation of classical sense, as well as the plaudits of common curiosity."[90] This new phantasmagoria, like the lessons in Egyptology surrounding it, purported to be not simply sensational but also enriching—another rationale for maintaining the cultural capital of Milton's verse as a cornerstone of the show. But it was not long before the phantasms overwhelmed the "approbation of classical sense" like so many Nile crocodiles devouring oxen.

The new "spectrology" appears to have boosted the receipts temporarily—in March, a notice described the "rising celebrity of the EGYPTIANA and its recent *Spectrographic* additions."[91] The increased interest encouraged Lonsdale to commit almost entirely to these elements of phantasmagoria: a "new finale" offered, along with the Sir Bevis, "the ghost of Julius Caeser [*sic*] appearing to Brutus, the murdered Princes appearing to Richard III, the apparition of Sir George Villiers, the spirit before Macbeth," and "a mock spectre in a country churchyard."[92] In addition, Lonsdale maintained in this same sequence the "illustrations from Milton," further suggesting that Lonsdale saw *L'Allegro* not only as a whimsical burst of mirth but also as consonant with the literary gothicism of Shakespearean tragedy. (The ghost of Julius Caesar was a staple of many shows, pressed into service by Brutus's line, "Between the acting of a dreadful thing / And the first motion, all the interim is / Like a phantasma or a hideous dream" [2.1.63–65].) Lonsdale continued, however, to differentiate himself from Philipstahl, pointing out that his apparitions would materialize in full light rather than in a darkened room (also a necessity for maintaining the display of paintings). This illumination seems also to have backfired: the shedding of light on the ghosts (and the mechanisms producing them) was equivalent to a magician revealing the secrets of his tricks before the show begins. Finally, in April 1802, Lonsdale had to proclaim that his show was not a "servile imitation of the phantasmagoria, which is rightly, universally admired and deservedly applauded at the Lyceum."[93] In fact, his show had not been phantasmagoric enough.[94] According to Britton, Lonsdale never recovered from the ruinous *Aegyptiana*. He spent three years in Ireland as a tutor, still unable to pay his debts, and after many "doleful letters" was able to accept a return to Covent Garden

Theatre, but "his heart was broken" and he died shortly thereafter "in the prime of life."[95]

VICTORIAN LANTERN SHOWS

Had Lonsdale arrived on the scene later in the nineteenth century, his gambit might have paid off handsomely. For as the century wound on, magic lanterns increasingly moved from thaumaturgical wonders and unearthly phantasmic displays to instruments of elucidation for church sermons and scientific lectures. For the latter, they were especially successful in supplementing talks concerned with insects and other miniature organisms that could be transformed into super versions of themselves under projection. In *Before the Nickelodeon,* Charles Musser notes that during the 1880s religious-themed sequences were playing in local Pennsylvania Methodist, Episcopal, and Lutheran churches alongside such works as "The Customs and Times of Washington" and "Sights and Scenes in Europe" as part of church efforts "seeking to educate, inspire, and entertain their mostly middle-class congregations."[96] And *Frank Leslie's Illustrated Newspaper* included a sketch in March 1879 proclaiming in Boston "The latest novelty in church music—substitution of the magic-lantern for the hymn book," while explaining that with this innovation, "there is no reason why one who can sing won't sing. The objection of having no book, or of having left the book at home, or of eye-trying fine type, are annihilated."[97] Slideshows also remained popular as virtual travel and as illustrations for all manner of narratives, both comic and melodramatic, with morality tales like "Ten Nights in a Bar Room" among the most common. As Judith Buchanan notes, classic literary adaptations were also well represented: "in addition to the ever-popular Defoe, authors such as Bunyan, Milton, Swift, Dickens, Longfellow and Tennyson were also regularly plundered as a source for slide sequences."[98] And thanks largely to the engravings of John Martin and Gustave Doré, *Paradise Lost* became a favorite subject of Victorian lanternists.

Perhaps the most significant shift in the use of magic lanterns was their widespread domestication. There was an abiding interest in magic lanterns as parlor entertainment—homegrown phantasmagorias were especially popular, as attested to in such guides as *The Magic Lantern: How to Buy and How to Use It,* which included a chapter called "How to Raise a Ghost."[99] Another game encouraged participants to author their own storyline around a succession of disparate images. Showings in the privacy of one's own home also whetted the appetite for more spectacular public shows. Lorenzo J. Marcy, in his compendious *The Sciopticon Manual: Explaining Lantern Projections in General,* explains that "A fine photograph (and what can be finer?) projected upon a large screen, before a thousand spectators, gives, it is safe to say, ten thousand times the satisfaction that one alone with his stereoscope receives from it." Moreover, if one is seeking to draw in the biggest audiences, a correspondingly grand theme must be the attraction. "It is found that some rousing title to a public entertainment helps to popularize it in its advance," advises Marcy, and among his suggested titles—including such showstoppers as "The World, from Chaos to Man," "The Ice-bound Seas of the Frozen North," and "The Wonders of the Star Depths"—he places "Milton's Paradise Lost."[100] Along with Bunyan's *Pilgrim's Progress,* this sequence of slides was certainly among the more popular literary representations, both for its moral instruction and its spectacular (if not still lurid) imagery. Milton's *Paradise Lost* became a popular crossover text, regularly appearing in churches and other public forums. In Dallas, Texas, a magic lantern exhibit of the poem was shown at the local YMCA in 1885 as part of a fundraiser for the building of a new library.[101] Even *Paradise Regained* received some play—that same year, one Pennsylvania newspaper advertised a Milton double feature: a "stereoscopic representation of Milton's 'Paradise Lost' and 'Paradise Regained,'" which may have included the added effect of slides dissolving into one another to cast the poems in 3-D.[102]

Doré's illustrations dominated the magic lantern scene: sets of 230 colored slides for his Bible illustrations and 76 for his *Divine Comedy* were mainstays in the magic lantern catalogues. In 1867, the McAllister lantern slide company of New York began offering a set of 50 *Paradise Lost* slides, also direct copies of pictures by Doré and Martin.[103] These slides, along with an accompanying reading from an abridgement of the poem, covered the epic in its entirety—though the notes to the abridgement recommend that "If the whole of the abridgment of 'Paradise Lost' be considered too long, it is recommended to omit Nos. 29 to 40 (both inclusive), which will then leave the story of the Fall complete."[104] Such excision eliminated the entire visit of Raphael, and all of books 6 and 7, privileging Adam and Eve at the expense of what later adaptations would find the most concertedly interesting sequence, the war in heaven. The abridged text also makes alterations in the verse—elisions and compressions of Milton's language, often cutting first the more allusive or obscure passages—as well as interpolations of Milton's 1674 prefatory additions to fill in story gaps. Thus, the opening of an evening of Milton would have begun with a slide from Doré and this adapted invocation of 1.1–7:

> Of Man's first disobedience, and the fruit
> Of that forbidden tree, whose mortal taste
> Brought Death into the world, and all our woe,
> With loss of Eden, till one greater Man
> Restore us, and regain the blissful seat,
> Sing, heavenly Muse! O Spirit! That dost prefer
> Before all temples th'upright heart and pure.

The final books are largely omitted, cutting all of Michael's visions and even the final punishment of Satan and his host, transformed into serpents in one of Doré's most dynamic scenes. The 50-slide set was also gradually whittled down; beginning in 1880 a new set of 12 slides, manufactured by the slide wholesaler C. W. Briggs, was carried by McAllister and many of the other companies operating at the time. The 12-slide set was also by Doré, but Briggs had the engravings overpainted to improve the projectability. (Doré's images were often so dark that they did not read well when projected; most of them were eventually replaced with overpaintings or reconceptions by Beale.)[105] Other sets offered by Newton and Company in the early twentieth century included a series of 24 painted slides based exclusively on John Martin's mezzotints, 13 slides showing the "Life of Milton," and "John Milton (Citizen of London)," 54 slides "with typed Lecture by the Rev. W. Melville

Harris, M.A." that likely combined Doré, Martin, and the bio-graphical images.[106]

Even as the trend in Milton slides moved steadily toward abridg-ment of both text and image, Milton remained a consistent part of the lanternist repertoire. But the magic lantern shows also disclose other emergent issues about the representation of Milton and his transference into new media. For one, slide sequences for *Paradise Lost* were almost always recombinant, cannibalizing from other Doré engravings, particularly those drawn from the Bible. This exchange may have contributed paradoxically to the elimination from slideshows of those sections of *Paradise Lost* that came closest to the kinds of biblical history an audience could find elsewhere (as with Michael's prophetic visions, above).[107] Like the unannounced excisions and compressions of his poetry in the evening readings, the insertion of images not originally designed for *Paradise Lost* but nonetheless used to accompany, illuminate, or stand in for his poetry also presents a significant challenge in tracing how, exactly, Milton is being represented in the popular imagination. There are the old issues of fidelity—artistic interpretations of Milton's poetry are not the poetry itself. Rather less convincing as the poetry itself are illustrations of texts, biblical or otherwise, not written by Milton at all. These were nonetheless substituted freely for his work, creat-ing a series of discontinuous Miltonic "moments" unmoored from text and context, a pattern that anticipates the many mixed appro-priations of Milton on film: a dependence on the cultural capital of the Milton signifier, and a simultaneous distancing from the "Milton of it all."[108] The depiction of Milton's hell was perhaps the most problematic in this regard. Images from Doré's engravings for Dante's *Inferno* were swapped almost willy-nilly for Milton's hell, presumably to add the sensationalism of graphic torture. Such infusions and confusions make for a potentially strong misrepre-sentation of *Paradise Lost* and an equally strong retextualizing of what Milton's epic had come to signify: a "rousing title," a delivery system for the sublime and the spectacular, a narrative so universal in its scope as to be almost universally accommodating.

A final and related issue was the colorization of magic lantern slides, particularly the black-and-white Doré engravings.[109] The addition of color, like other special effects in the lantern shows, increased the degree of visual information received by a spectator, accenting certain elements while dulling others. For the Milton slides, the colorization exists in an uneasy relationship with the verisimilitude of the images—the trees of Eden are verdant, the waters of creation are Prussian blue. But there is also a drift, once again, from the original artistry of both Milton and Doré, and at times a kind of inauthentic cosmeticism to the overall effect. The scene of the fallen angels' metamorphosis into snakes, for instance (the very scene the *New York Times* argued "begs to be seen in all its computer-animated glory"), shows crimson dragons with wings of burnished gold, masses of coiled sea-green serpents, billows of rusty smoke, and Satan on his golden throne, clad in aqua-blue (see fig. 2.4). A greater number of figures are brought into relief than in the black-and-white original, and a lifelike quality is engendered in some of the lolling red tongues and pale flesh. Satan, on the contrary, seems even more purposefully isolated and chromatically out of place, the only touch of blue at the dead of center of the picture.

CONEY ISLAND

The Milton spectacles culminate in an almost perfect combination of high and low culture with the "The Deluge" attraction on Coney Island in the summer of 1906. Reenactments of great floods had been a popular draw at Coney Island for a number of years, and so in a building already devoted to the Johnstown Flood of 1889, Herbert A. Bradwell decided to go bigger. As one local paper put it, "Daring as have been some of the Herbert A. Bradwell productions 'The Deluge' is the most daring ever."[110] Just how daring? The reviewer continues, "In it Mr. Bradwell undertakes no less a task than to portray in mechanical effect the great imagery of the immortal Milton, when in book XI, 'Paradise Lost,' he describes 'The Deluge.'" The significance of the choice—anchoring the new Flood not only to the biblical tale but also to *Milton's* version—seems at least on the surface an attempt to draw on some of the spectacular Milton adaptations of the nineteenth century,

Fig. 2.4. Magic lanternists tinted black-and-white illustrations like this one by Gustave Doré using pigments such as indigo, gamboge, and crimson lake. The colorized version of this slide appears on the endsheets of this book. *Author's collection.*

including Kiralfy's grand show. "The Deluge" combined live action against a dioramic backdrop—in this case, extracted from Doré's illustrations—and accompanying verse from the poet. The latter added needed resonance to the overall effect—for sonorous flood verse, Milton is difficult to surpass. The *Fulton Times* reviewer, at any rate, feels sure that the upgrade from Johnstown to Milton will be meaningful at the ticket counter:

> Unlike the Johnstown Flood, "The Deluge" will be portrayed by a large cast of actors. The Byzantium Palace outside Constantinople will be the main picture of the five that will be shown. The Siren Girls and soldiery will be discovered catering to the desires of royalty in defiance of the warning and preparations made by Noah when suddenly—again Milton is quoted: "and them, with all their pomp, / Deep under water rolled; sea covered sea." In its electrical effects "The Deluge" promises to be a marvel. The big auditorium will be the same as the Johnstown flood, but the stage will be largely increased. Real water, steam and electric current in great profusion will be used throughout the production and it is safe to say that "The Deluge" will be one of the big talk creators at Coney Island next Summer.[111]

"Safe to say" is probably not the right way of putting it, with the "great profusion" of water, steam, and electrical current, but the show was a success. It opened May 26, 1906, and played into the following season, 1907. There were three acts and a cast of around 50 actors, along with an elocutor reading from Milton's verse. The backdrops were taken from Doré, particularly the design of the temple in the Flood engravings. In a dramatization of Noah's remonstrances and rejections, he first visits the temple-goers, who are behaving in various degrees of badly, and warns them of the coming cataclysm. The sinners at the temple laugh him off, celebrating even more fervidly after he leaves. At last a tempestuous noise of thunder begins the rains and flooding, while the ark appears floating in the distance, embraced by a glowing halo. The audience then saw the ark growing larger in its approach, as the flood sank away to uncover Mt. Ararat, as well as the disembarking of the animals, and Noah's covenant. The final scene depicted angels flanking the stage and floating about in midair to promise the dawn of a new age. As another reviewer succinctly concluded, "If people desire to witness something that is grand, beautiful and sublime, they will find it in The Deluge."[112]

Milton, then, was front and center in the development of all of these pre-cinematic entertainments. The panoramas, like the dramatic spectacles with which they shared a desire for immersive reality, exploited the limitless scale of Milton's visual imagination. Indeed, they seem modeled after his own panoramic aesthetics. Magic lantern shows, with all their optical virtuosity, similarly shared with Milton's poem a pattern of innovative visual exercises. His aesthetics were absorbed by advancing seventeenth century optics even as his sublime creations motivated and impelled the very application of those technologies. In the phantasmagorias of Robertson, Philipstahl, and Lonsdale can be seen the stirrings of the Romantic spirit that came to cherish the dark elements and terrifying spaces of Milton's verses (in the case of Lonsdale, in somewhat unexpected corners), whereas Victorian lantern shows depended primarily on the new illustrators of Milton to convey to the eyes what previously only the mind could contain. Many of these adaptations and appropriations of Milton exhibit the same tensions between the sublime and the ridiculous, high art and low culture, artistic integrity and mass accessibility evident in other popularizations. Yet in almost every case the recontextualizing of Milton produces concomitant appreciation, if not outright celebration, of these new ways of representing the poet. The history of these entertainments, then, serves not only to evince Milton's pervasive presence in the techniques and advances that led to the cinema, but also to tease out the roots of the resistance to the popularizing of Milton. The sublime effects that all of these entertainers hoped to achieve, from Burford to Bachelder to Lonsdale and Marcy, who placed *Paradise Lost* on the same blockbuster level as "Ice-bound Seas" and "Star Depths," were carried over into the cinema proper. It was the cinema itself, however, especially through the epic ambitions of D. W. Griffith, that self-consciously appropriated and codified the romantic sublime as its own raison d'etre. It was not coincidentally also in the early days of the cinema that filmmakers sought most ardently to adapt *Paradise Lost* for the screen.

Early Cinema and the
Cinematic Sublime

The idea that the cinema stands on the shoulders of earlier entertainments, both technologically and aesthetically, was contemporary with its arrival in the late nineteenth century. In *Animated Pictures* (1898), Charles Francis Jenkins remarks that "the moving picture machine is simply a modified stereopticon or lantern," while Henry V. Hopwood, in *Living Pictures* (1899), observes, "a film for projecting a living picture is nothing more, after all, than a multiple lantern slide."[1] Cinema historians have unwound the various threads of influence differently—Raymond Lister sees Loutherbourg's Eidophusikon as "leading to the eventual development of the cinema," while for Oliver Grau the panorama stands out as an "illusionist image space" continuous with modern virtual reality systems, including "Sensorama, Expanded Cinema, 3-D, Omnimax, and IMAX cinema."[2] Echoing Jenkins and Hopwood, Charles Musser argues that the "cinema appears as the continuation and transformation of magic-lantern traditions in which showmen displayed images on a screen, accompanying them with

141

voice, music, and sound effects."[3] And, in fact, early silent films often borrowed the script and patter of magic lantern slideshows in their performance. Still others point to the influence of pantomimes and theatrical spectacle, particularly on such filmmakers as Georges Méliès.[4]

Among the cinema's earliest practitioners, Méliès drew heavily on the phantasmagoric traditions of Robertson and Philipstahl, preferring the fantastic, horrific, and gothic to the ultrarealist "actualities" produced by brothers Auguste and Louis Lumière during the 1890s. The latter strove to capture scenes from real life, purposefully mundane scenarios that demonstrated the camera's ability not just to imitate but seemingly transfer an authentic, recognizable instance of mass experience. While the subjects were literally workmanlike—early efforts included *Demolition of a Wall* (1895) and *Loading a Boiler* (1896)—the most famous Lumière films are not without their own spectacle and shock value. Such brief films as *Workers Leaving the Lumière Factory* (1895), *Drawing Out the Coke* (1896), and especially *Arrival of a Train at a Station* (1895) were prime instances of Gunning's "aesthetics of astonishment" that can be traced to the magic lanternists: the poising of a still image and its sudden animation, giving life to still life. The *actualité* films depend, furthermore, on the same voyeuristic desires evident in many camera obscura, panorama, and realistic magic lantern displays: *Cordeliers Square in Lyon* (dir. Louis Lumière, 1895) presents a straightforward view of a street in motion, but its core subject is people-watching. The surreal fantasies of Méliès, as early as *The Haunted Castle* (1896) and *The House of the Devil* (1896), are more clearly continuous with the transporting effects cultivated by the Romantic imagination, a continuity marked self-referentially in such works as *La lanterne magique* (1903). A number of Méliès's works centered on the devil or diabolical figures in the guise of magicians and other conjurors, suggesting that the illusive effects of the cinema were drawn from Satan's own bag of tricks.

From these two predominant types of visual spectacle—unfiltered realism and strange manipulation—emerged an important reconceptualization of the sublime, an attempt to synthesize the natural and artificial, which formed an important part of the early cinema's self-fashioning.[5] This new "cinematic sublime" fits into a broader movement, what David E. Nye calls the technological sublime, in which technical inventions and innovations, especially under the aegis of American industrialism, contended with both nature and the arts as expressions of the real.[6] The contest is evinced as early as the 1850s, when English scientist Thomas Ewbank, then in the privileged position of U.S. Commissioner of Patents, announced "his preference for the useful to the merely imaginative," and remarked, "in truth it is in such, that the truly beautiful or sublime is to be found. A steamer is a mightier epic than the *Iliad*,—and Whitney, Jacquard and Blanchard might laugh even Virgil, Milton and Tasso to scorn."[7] It is an essentially Platonic model—cultivate the craftsman, banish the poet—but it is the language of sublimity and *epos* explicit in Ewbank's declaration that recurs discursively in the language of the early cinema. As much as cinema shared with such forerunners as the magic lantern, an emerging narrative presented the cinema as radically new, particularly in its ability to convey not only a richer experience of the world than could be found in the daily quiddities of "real" life, but also deeper moral truths as well. The cinema would be a perfect blending of art and invention, a new technology that birthed fantasies of a new and universal language, a unification of the natural and the artificial into a unique sublimity.

In his influential theorization of film's alteration of the nature of art, Walter Benjamin cites the French silent film actor Séverin-Mars on the perception that the early cinema offered a new sacredness: "What art has been granted a dream more poetical and more real at the same time! Approached in this fashion the film might represent an incomparable means of expression. Only the most high-minded persons, in the most perfect and mysterious moments of their lives, should be allowed to enter its ambience."[8] No one promoted this ideal more fervently than the American filmmaker D. W. Griffith. In his widely circulated promotional essay "The Motion Picture and Witch Burners," he lavishes praise on the advances of the cinema while insisting on its particular transcendence:

> I think it is generally agreed that the motion picture is at least on a par with the spoken and written word as a mode of expression. The motion picture has progressed. It is capable of conveying a given message in many ways enormously more effectively than any mode of expression the world has ever possessed. It is already performing

this work. It is softening the hard life of the plain citizen with beauty and sweetness: it keeps men away from saloons and drink, because it gives them a place of recreation in pleasant surroundings: it brings to the poor who are unable to travel away from their own dingy surroundings the beauty and poetry of moving foreign scenes, of flowers, waving grasses, the beauty of uplifted mountain crests, and the wonders of nature. The great outdoors and beauty of dreams have uplifted man slowly and painfully with much torture and aching joints out of the state of beasts. The motion picture will help as no other art has done in this work.[9]

The claims here are for a radical singularity—the motion picture has surpassed "the spoken and written word," it is better "than any mode of expression the world has ever possessed," it will "help as no other art has done." Yet even as Griffith looks to fresh woods and pastures new, there is significant recycling. His idea that the cinema "brings to the poor who are unable to travel away from their own dingy surroundings the beauty and poetry of moving foreign scenes" repeats almost verbatim the kind of advances attributed to the stage spectacles and panoramas by numerous writers in the preceding centuries, shortcutting those "innumerable miseries of travel."

The double duty of film as morality play also had a parallel tradition in the temperance magic lantern slideshows. Griffith's alliance of the revolutionary expressiveness of the cinema and the sublimity of the natural world nevertheless manages to sound progressive. In particular, Griffith's examples of the "wonders of nature" are full of motion: the grasses wave and even the mountains seem to raise themselves up. This movement then gets transferred onto the human subject so that experiencing a soaring mountain peak has a corresponding effect on the soul. It is a *poetic* quality (the "beauty and poetry of moving foreign scenes") but it has been subsumed and refined into the "beauty of dreams" so that it is also an antipoetic quality, a barely contained reverie of symbolic language beyond the spoken and written word. And so the motion picture is somehow at one with the "great outdoors" and largely interiorized, the very model for the sublime as a cinematic experience.

If the essential quality of cinema is the moving image, its version of the sublime depends on this motion, partly because the sublime itself is a transitive state; it cannot be had without reciprocation and difference. In almost any form it is both strongly mediated and strongly resistant to mediation. For Kant, the sublime was the mediation of the imagination by reason. Mediation allows one to withdraw and return, to stand on a precipice and not in a void; it is the constitutive parts of painting, poem, or the matrices of nature that enable the sublime experience. And yet as an experience of the infinite, of limitlessness, it is unbounded, or must *seem* unbounded. For Benjamin, the camera provides a similar mediation, a flux between hyperrealities invisible to the momentary gaze and an explosive expansiveness that transports the viewer beyond the "prison-world" of concrete experience: "By close-ups of the things around us, by focusing on hidden details of familiar objects, by exploring common place milieus under the ingenious guidance of the camera, the film, on the one hand, extends our comprehension of the necessities which rule our lives; on the other hand, it manages to assure us of an immense and unexpected field of action."[10] Or, to put it another way, the sublime is "the effect of immeasurable emotion which can only be conveyed through a failure of the text; it is, in writing, the accounts of experiences where characters are 'lost for words'; or in visual representation it is where some aspects of the optical cannot be figured."[11] For Griffith, the cinema managed this dialectic perfectly. Its compressions of time, for instance, contributed to its transcendent effects: the pontifications of Woodrow Wilson, the stories of Rudyard Kipling, works that might take "years to write and days to be read," could be managed in three (short) hours.[12] The cinema—even as it depended on a calibrated arrangement of performance space: screens, projectors, seats, all regulated in distance and timing to maintain focus and the persistence of vision of a film reel passing at 16 frames per second—made manifest the unimaginable in time and space.[13]

John Milton's own sublimity helped to give shape to some of this early film discourse. As F. T. Prince noticed long ago, Milton's sublimity derives from "the conscious lavishness, the emphatic completeness of the picture and the action—the enactment of the picture."[14] Similarly, Joseph Wittreich shows how *Paradise Lost* is "pictorially energized," the demands of a prophetic, spiritual epic producing "the imitation of visual processes" and "visual impressions, or images, in order to render visual experiences." Milton, Wittreich contends, "is intent upon transcending the limitations of his medium by devising for literature a new optical system, an intention he accomplishes by spurning the boundaries of any single form, achieving an interpenetration of the arts, and in the process literalizing Sidney's metaphor, which portrays poetry as a speaking picture."[15] For a cinema aiming to produce not just visible representations but also visionary experiences — affective states beyond reason, or the adopting of what Wittreich calls the "gross matter of the senses" for the purpose of a refined and enlightened understanding — Milton made an impeccable model. In *Paradise Lost,* it is the transition Michael urges upon Adam in the panoramas of human history, when mortal eyesight fails and Adam's revelations must be related in purely poetical terms by the archangel.[16] In book 12, these speaking pictures arrive at just the point where universal language splinters and fails, at the building of Babel. In adapting Milton, early cinema sought to recuperate that loss through the sublimity of moving pictures without words.

The earliest effort at incorporating Milton into this agenda is that of the Vitagraph Company. Founded in Brooklyn in 1897, Vitagraph was soon the most prolific of American studios, and especially active in producing Shakespearean shorts — *Romeo and Juliet, Macbeth,* and *Richard III* in 1908, *King Lear* and *A Midsummer Night's Dream* in 1909 — under what Anthony Slide calls an institutionalized "policy of filming the classics."[17] In a 1910 promotional piece, the company described their efforts as "more than motion pictures," having instead "the vital spark of life itself."[18] By late 1911, Vitagraph had begun making three-reel features of such works as *Vanity Fair* and *David Copperfield.* But Vitagraph's Holy Grail was a feature-length adaptation of *Paradise Lost.* As the influential trade weekly *Moving Picture World* reported, "This last stupendous undertaking will not only eclipse all their previous efforts but it is their intention to make it a world beater."[19] A week later, the rhetoric and scope had both intensified, now encompassing not only *Paradise Lost* but its sequel as well: "They have in course of preparation two classics from the pen of John Milton, which will be given animated interpretations, both masterpieces of this great mind, 'Paradise Lost' and 'Paradise Regained.' The Vitagraph aim is to make these productions even more wonderful than anything they have ever evolved, meeting the high standard of quality and the cultured tasted which the Vitagraph life portrayals have established."[20] The company had hired a prolific scenarist, Eugene Mullin, to head up these efforts at producing not just motion pictures but the "vital spark of life." Mullin had earlier in the year completed a three-reel adaptation of Charles Dickens's *A Tale of Two Cities* to rave reviews. And it was Mullin who adapted *Vanity Fair* (released December 19, 1911) and later Scott's *Lady of the Lake* (May 27, 1912), among numerous other works. But despite the enthusiastic advance copy on *Paradise Lost,* no Milton world-beater ever turned up. Neither of Milton's epics was ever produced by Vitagraph.[21] Other failed attempts followed: in the early 1920s, Max Reinhardt was hired by the European Film Alliance to produce *Paradise Lost.* And in 1927, Henry Otto, who had already adapted *Dante's Inferno* and *The Ancient Mariner,* announced he would make *Paradise Lost.*[22] Neither ever did.

In 1912, another production company, Eclipse, released a film by George Kleine without quite the vaulting ambition of Vitagraph. *John Milton: The Blind Poet* debuted on April 24, 1912, to a decidedly mixed reception. Milton had already been the subject of an earlier Italian biographical short, *Giovanni Milton,* produced in February 1911 by Itala Film. It was said that this film "somehow seems to bring the man before one and show him as he was, something which is impossible in reading."[23] No such claims of virtual resurrection were made, however, for *The Blind Poet,* which seemed, rather, to enforce a distance between its historical and cinematic subjects. The film takes broad liberties with the life of Milton after the Restoration, imagining him "decreed an outlaw" and ordered into exile because of "religious differences."[24] With overtones of Lear and Edgar, the film dramatizes Milton's attempt to leave England with the assistance of his daughter Deborah. Her rather surprising lover, Lord Davenant, also lends assistance in the

form of a letter urging safe conduct, but as Deborah is guiding
her blind father through the countryside to make their escape,
the Miltons are captured by royalist soldiers. The soldiers arrest
Milton and hurry him off to prison, where later, in a shocking
denouement, King Charles II arrives at Milton's cell to "comfort
the poet in his distress by reading from the famous epic poem,
'Paradise Lost.'"

The film, which ran on a double reel with the "Exhibition
Drill of the H. M. S. 'Excellent' Prize Gun Crew," did receive
at first some tepid praise. One reviewer called it a "simple, digni-
fied picture, not very accurate, but pleasingly conducted and photographed. The best scene in it shows a faint foot-path leading
through the green twilight of a forest."[25] But a more intriguing
(and less forgiving) commentary appeared months later in *Moving
Picture World:*

> Recently we have seen an attempt to pay a cinematographic trib-
> ute to the memory of John Milton. It was worse than a failure; it
> was a travesty. It is difficult to overestimate the harm done by such
> pictures. The number of intelligent and educated patrons of the
> motion picture is steadily increasing. Nothing is more calculated to
> alienate their loyalty to the picture and make them turn with disgust
> from the motion picture theatre than the production of shockingly
> false and preposterous so-called historic pictures, especially when
> they offend against the traditions and the common knowledge of a
> race or nation. The name of John Milton is sacred to the ears of the
> English-speaking race. It is quite fair to assume that ten per cent. at
> least of the average audience to-day have a good and even accurate
> knowledge of his life and his character. Now, in this picture the
> great poet is represented as an insufferable ranter, theatrical in the
> extreme, full of furious gesticulation. The Milton of English history
> is an entirely different personage. We know him for his lofty faith,
> his noble resignation, his sublime calm in the midst of reverses and
> afflictions. We think of him clothed with dignity as with a garment.
> It hurts us to see him parodied, even when we know that there is no
> intention to do so. We say nothing of the fact that the plot of the
> story is not only pure invention, but clumsy and improbable as well,
> or that the costuming in parts is absolutely wrong. These objections
> alone would be enough to condemn the picture, but they might
> have been forgiven more easily than the burlesque on the character

of one of the greatest of all Englishmen. [We believe] it to be an unavoidable duty to take exception to this kind of historic pictures. They make the art of cinematography ridiculous. Better far to keep away from historic subjects altogether than mangle and tear them into tatters.[26]

The review is notable for its designation of Milton himself as a sacred and sublime subject, a parody of whom would be a particularly depraved form of desecration, and for its registering of these divine attributes as potential box-office draws. Milton the man might potentially encourage an increasingly "intelligent and educated" audience to embrace a cinematic experience they might otherwise consider beneath them. Indeed, this review maintains as its premise the earlier approbation of *Giovanni Milton:* that an authentic experience of the man himself cannot be had by reading. Under the effects of a properly cinematized "Milton of English history," that desirable demographic of an educated audience would presumably be carried away by contemplation of Milton's sublimity: the soaring peaks of his "lofty faith," the bottomless depths of his "noble resignation," his equanimity and his endless calm. And in short, the audience would be led to these heights by a kind of insistent wordlessness, if not an outright denial of affect. That *John Milton: The Blind Poet* fails at this sublimity can be directly traced not to the "improbable" plot elements—Deborah's clandestine turn with Davenant, the conciliatory encounter between Milton and Charles, not even the kingly recitation of *Paradise Lost*—but to the presentation of Milton as a "ranter." It is his corrupt theatricality, his boundedness to gesture and blather and other inferior acts of signification, to which the reviewer so vehemently objects, because such effects deny the ends of the cinema as a medium purposed for transcendence.

A striking, and highly parodic, adaptation of Milton's *Paradise Lost* occurs in *The Perils of Pauline* (dir. Louis J. Gasnier and Donald MacKenzie, 1914), among the most famous serialized films of the silent era and popularizer of the dramatic cliffhanger. Divided into 20 films, the series follows its irrepressible but very much distressed heroine Pauline (Pearl White) through umpteen near-fatal, around-the-world adventures. The series begins with Pauline as the ward of a wealthy, adoptive father (Edward José), who urges a

marriage with his own son, Harry (Crane Wilbur), who happens to be madly in love with Pauline. While Pauline shows interest, she also reveals her ambitions to be a writer, and her father promises her a year to travel and see the world before marrying Harry. Quite soon thereafter, her father dies after a strange encounter in his study with a mummy. Pauline and Harry each receive half of the rich inheritance, with one crucial contingency: should Pauline die before marrying Harry, her portion will go instead to her father's nefarious assistant, Raymond Owen (Paul Panzer). The premise for the remaining 19 films then becomes the assorted attempts by Owen to kill off Pauline, with a loyal but exasperated Harry repeatedly coming to the rescue.

Pauline runs through virtually every sensationalized adventure of the day imaginable: she has scrapes with villainous pirates, cowboys, Indians, smugglers, spies, and gypsies, speeding planes and automobiles, not to mention vicious lions, rats, rattlesnakes, and, anticipating *King Kong*, some prolonged peril at the hands of an enormous, possessive gorilla. Amid all of this standard fare, there is a fascinating metadramatic episode in which *Paradise Lost* figures prominently. In episode 9 ("A Just Retribution"), Pauline has just escaped from Indians and is looking for a less harrowing trip. She decides to pursue acting in silent films, and so meets with the real-life production company of *The Perils of Pauline* (Pathé Freres) and the director Louis J. Gasnier, also playing himself as director of a feature film adaptation of Milton's *Paradise Lost*. Pauline is successfully cast as one of the good angels, while the evil Owen accompanies her, cast in the film as a carnivalesque devil. The filming location is the remote "Devil's Island." Unfortunately, the entire episode has been lost.[27] The plot, at any rate, quickly moves from the Miltonic film-in-progress to the elimination of Pauline. Owen, the tempting Satan, convinces another actor, already infatuated with Pauline, to kidnap her. As usual, Harry comes to the rescue at the last minute, though the film ends with Pauline saving herself from a burning plane after the pilot abandons her.[28]

From the few summaries and stills available, it seems that *Paradise Lost* fits here mostly as an excuse to costume Owen as diabolically as possible, Pauline as divinely.[29] But it is certainly among the most interesting early renderings of Milton's epic, particularly as a tale of adventure and intrigue both interchangeable with stock cinematic narratives like the Western and so distinct from them that it can only be represented obliquely, a film-within-a-film, an escape from escapism. In short, *The Perils of Pauline* presents Milton's *Paradise Lost* as assimilable into film—a work that can be freely appropriated for the most conventional of generic ends, a black-and-white case study in good versus evil—while also underscoring that the incorporation of Milton seems particularly disruptive of conventional filmic representation. *Paradise Lost* in this reading works in film only via some mediating frame, a frame that can contain rather than release exponentially its sublime scope and energies—here is not Milton but the making of Milton—allowing an audience to approach from behind the scenes, to observe the heat of Satan's hell without being burned in the same way they might uncover buried treasure without any danger of having to walk the plank.

MAGGI'S *SATANA*

As ambitious as any film of the era to lay claim to the superiority of the cinematic sublime, Luigi Maggi's 1912 *Satana, ovvero*

Il Dramma dell'Umanita (*Satan; or, The Drama of Humanity*) stands as a landmark in the history of Milton on film. It is the first successful attempt to adapt elements of *Paradise Lost* for the cinema on an epic scale, and its inclusion of the war in heaven as a prelude to the story of Adam and Eve also serves as a template for numerous other efforts to film the poem, including the most recent Hollywood adaptation. Maggi (1867–1946) had previously directed other epic tales—including the films for which he remains most famous, *The Last Days of Pompeii* (1908) and *Nero; or, The Burning of Rome* (1909), produced in Turin by Arturo Ambrosio's Società Anonima Ambrosio. Jon Solomon proclaims this period in Italian filmmaking "the virtual birth …of the epic cinema."[30] Maggi's *Satana* reportedly cost some $200,000 and took four months to film, the largest budget yet for an Ambrosio epic, and when it came to America in 1913 it signaled the shift to feature films that was already well underway in Europe but still gaining traction in the United States.[31] The film was a hit at the box office (with a running time well over an hour), beginning with a capacity showing at the New York Hippodrome in January and was widely advertised as "The Biggest Money Getter That Ever Came across the Atlantic."[32] At times accompanied by edifying lectures and an extensive musical accompaniment, it was also trumpeted as "The Greatest Morality Picture Ever Produced," "Suitable for Schools, Churches, or Theater."[33] W. Stephen Bush, reviewing the film for *Moving Picture World*, writes enthusiastically that "too much praise cannot be given to pictures of this kind. They justify the faith and hope in the higher possibilities of the moving picture."[34]

Certainly the press booklet for *Satana* advances the claim that the era of epic film had not merely arrived but was in the process of supplanting both the short film and epic poem:

> The major literary works of every nation have by now been con-
> quered by cinematography and transported from the gleaming
> domain of words to the more concrete and amusing one of screen
> and spectacle. Faithful to this tradition of popularizing the great-
> est sources of beauty and thought, we have reduced to a cinematic
> drama the unsurpassed masterpiece of English poetry, the immense
> and formidable vision of Britain's own blind and wretched Homer,

in a word, John Milton's "Paradise Lost." Certainly, it requires undeniable boldness to set oneself to such a task, to attempt to measure up to Milton, but cinematography has made such enormous progress in recent times as to allow even this audacity, and we come out of this trial convinced of our victory, convinced of making the spectator feel as if he were present at the titanic battles between heaven and earth, which the minds of poets have seen and translated into impassioned words and immortal verse.[35]

The relationship unfolding here between the literary and cinematic is a curious one. It is primarily combative, as cinema "conquers" the "works of every nation," and the rhetoric sounds more than a little like that of Milton's Satan himself. This new cinema possesses the "undeniable boldness" to challenge the "immense and formidable vision" of its literary progenitor. It transports the literary work from a "gleaming domain"—the domain of words as the Word—to one of popular spectacle, a concrete world that substitutes, and imposes a difference between, visions on the page and the screen. In depicting the "titanic battles between heaven and earth," Maggi's film fights as one of those titans, stealing fire from the invisible minds of poets and their immortal verse. Further, the challenge is conceived through a series of displacements, observing Milton's own movement with and against the Greek epic. But the relationship also remains at times a playful one; film is still a reductive force working to amuse. Also evident is the film's attachment to Milton as a source of authenticity—the mind of the poet has *seen* the real, an irreducible original that has been transferred into words. The film seeks not merely to transpose those words but to overleap them to their numinous source.

According to one report (probably a review prepared by the production company), the decision to put Milton on film was nothing less than a second Judgment of Paris:

> Some two years ago the directors of the Ambrosio Company, long famous for their feature subjects, conceived the idea of producing a picture which would surpass anything yet produced in the moving picture world. To this end they immediately secured the services of noted authors of Europe and offered a handsome prize for the one selecting the best title. All the leading libraries were searched and

almost every classic in literature was submitted for consideration but none were thought to be worthy of such a magnificent production. Just when the directors were giving up in despair of ever attaining their ambitions, a noted author submitted Milton's "Paradise Lost" and another Klopstock's "Messiah." Both were excellent classics from which the picture could be taken but the directors saw greater possibilities in the two combined into one subject. One of Europe's greatest playwrights was then engaged to dramatize the two works and to add to the two parts two other parts bringing the story of the drama up to the present day. After the manuscript was completed, work was then started on engaging the artists to portray the many characters. All the leading actors and actresses of France, Germany, Italy, and other European countries were engaged and rehearsals were commenced. After many hard, trying months of changing, rewriting, and rehearsing; the director pronounced the production finished and the final performance was given before the camera. Upon its first presentation to the public "Satan" was pronounced to be the greatest educational and instructive film ever produced. It was shown throughout Europe with phenomenal success and is duplicating the sensation in America.[36]

Beyond the expected hyperbole of these sorts of pieces—the worldwide search in all the best libraries, the recruitment of the best writers to ferret out a worthy title, the surprising failure of this all-star research team to come up with a single work of classic literature that could live up to the standards of the producer—the account makes the coming of Milton and Klopstock virtually messianic.

The subject matter, *Paradise Lost* intermixed with the life of Christ, only serves to reinforce this larger narrative: the film will do for literature what the Savior did for a fallen world. In redeeming the shortcomings of all previous literary art, and "surpassing anything yet produced in the moving picture world," this Ambrosio production will inaugurate a new age, an age not of authors but actors, a revelation made all the more poignant by the claim at the end that this work is the "greatest educational and instructive film ever produced." Thus, *Satana* truly expresses the "higher possibilities" of film. Of course, these claims are full of anxiety about the place of film as an art form, the writer trying with effort to present the medium's superior ability to educate and inform the public. Meanwhile, not much is really done with the sources, Milton and Klopstock. They are essentially interchangeable, certainly presented as equivalent in their excellence; what makes them stand out from other works is apparently the very simple idea that a "picture can be taken from them." Beyond that, there is no desire to explicate the material or to offer a rationale for their combined salvation of the cinema.

While most of *Satana* has been lost, much of the plot can be reconstructed through surviving stills and promotional materials. The premise throughout is the malefic influence of Satan upon human life over the course of four distinct historical movements. The first two acts of the film develop the idea of Satan as the "Great Rebel," first showing *Satana contro il Creatore* and then *Satana contro il Salvatore*. The first of these, Satan pitting himself against the Creator, is modeled after Milton (with Satan played throughout and to great acclaim by Mario Bonnard). Yet for all the talk of "reduc[ing] to a cinematic tragedy the unsurpassed masterpiece of English poetry," very little of Milton's poem actually makes its way directly into the film. The action begins in "heaven's endless fields," with Satan brooding over God's goodness, and quickly moves through the war in heaven until "the battle between good and evil angels has finished; the rebel phalanxes lie exhausted and devastated on the ground. And here is Satan, wounded and overturned, who rises again, burning with inextinguishable hate, with an abiding thirst for vengeance."[37]

A surviving still shows Satan fiercely intent but huddled at the bottom of the frame, his back turned to the celestial powers looming over him on the painted backdrop (see fig. 3.1). In his scaled armor he appears already reptilian, a visual foreshadowing of his imminent transformation into the serpent. Maggi makes a great show of Satan's change, using a clever double exposure such that Satan seems to morph into the serpentine form. In this battle scene (that is also not a battle, but a kind of suspended moment), he already bears the marks of the fall: horned wings, scaled armor. One London critic observed of Satan's early appearance in the film that he had "claws and scales," though these were "only obvious

at the outset"—as history marches on, he will take on an increasingly civilized attire.[38] But Bonnard's weighty pose articulates an
inner conflict: one hand wrapped around the long spear of war,
the other still clinging firmly to the bedrock of heaven. In laying
claim to Milton as its forefather, this first act of the film seems to
show one of the few instances when a sympathetic Satan still seems
a possibility in the film's greater narrative. For most of the remaining acts, he is ruthlessly cold-blooded, infecting the world with
every evil in Pandora's box. Here, Bonnard projects at least some
undercurrent of ambivalence. It is also suggested in his Roman
legionnaire attire and that of his troops, who are waging an uphill
battle against the angelic host. He prefigures the soldiers who will
torture and torment Christ in the film's second act, even as he
recalls the classical virtuosity of Italy's heroic age. Finally, in this
moment, at least, the living, breathing, human signifier is Satan.
The angelic beings reign over the rebel angels, but they also do so
in the background as figures supremely two-dimensional.

Fig. 3.2. Earliest image of Milton on film: Maggi's *Satana* (1912).
Courtesy of Museo Nazionale del Cinema, Torino.

According to Bush, the opening of the film offered only "a glimpse—all too brief—of the warring angels 'on the plains of Heaven.' We see Lucifer's last onslaught on the 'impregnable towers' and his utter rout and expulsion." He adds, "There is something at least of the Miltonic splendor in the following scenes, pleasing and impressive."[39] There does not appear, however, to be anything specifically Miltonic in the action of this war. The language of the press booklet picks up on the romantic Miltonic Satan here, but in a rather un-Miltonic description of events: "He wishes still to throw himself against heaven, wishes still to fight. His hubris will not allow him to bow down, to admit defeat. But God's flaming sword flashes before his eyes; he falls from heaven's height, tumbling through the ether."[40] The chariot of the Son has been replaced with the sword of God, and Satan's attitude of Promethean defiance, his unwillingness to admit defeat, is scarcely evident in the comparable scene in *Paradise Lost*. Bush's calling it an "utter rout and expulsion" may better reflect Milton's account, though it is equally possible that Bush is reading Milton into the scene. His quotation of the "impregnable towers" is really a misquotation of *Paradise Lost,* book 2, when Belial speaks of the "Tow'rs of Heav'n" that "are fill'd / With Armed watch" and "that render all access / Impregnable" (2.128–31). Is Bush misremembering the poem, or citing a Milton paraphrase that might have been used in the film itself as an intertitle? In leaving behind the "gleaming domain of words," does Maggi's adaptation maintain any connection with the language of Milton? In any case, whatever heroic splendor emerges is contrasted almost completely with the depraved Satan that follows, and it is at the point of the fall from heaven—likely no more than a minute or two into the film—that the opening act breaks with its Miltonic source. Instead of plummeting into hell, Satan descends to earth, where he lands "at the foot of a harsh and rugged mountain." There, still "grasping for heaven," he "clings to the mountain and attempts to climb it, to rise again. But when, after immense effort, frothing from exertion and rage, he reaches the summit, he sees that heaven is still too far, and turns his gaze to the plain." Once these last throes of desperate (revenge? regret? rage alone?) pass over him, Satan settles into a more generic characterization. From this point on, there is little semblance of anything in Milton's narrative beyond the core elements of the Fall and an acceleration through biblical history.[41]

From the heaven he forswears, Satan shifts his gaze to the stretch of Eden beneath him: "The fresh beauty of the young earth seduces him. He swears to conquer it, become its master. He begins to fly and reaches the edges of a forest. There appear to him the first humans, and he seduces them, taking the form of a serpent. When, innocence lost, they are wracked with despair, Satan introduces himself to them and offers himself as a guide."[42] A long and inventive sequence follows depicting the first murder, with Cain, Abel, and their tribe appearing as prehistoric man, living in huts but looking suspiciously like Neanderthals. The wolf skins worn by the sons of Cain catch Satan's eye and, seemingly inspired by these signs of death, he instigates the killing of Abel. Satan also incites the sons of Cain against the daughter of Abel. He teaches the art of metallurgy, overseeing the molding of the first blade, and convinces the tribes to worship Moloch. Another borrowing from *Paradise Lost* may be happening here, when one of the sons of Cain first forges metal and "the liquid Ore he drain'd / Into fit moulds prepar'd" (*PL* 11.570–71). There is a poetic revenge in the design of this weapon: the arms of his oppressor, a perversion of the "flaming sword" that drove him from heaven. At the base of the Moloch idol, the sword is employed in the first human sacrifice—Abel's daughter, who has rejected the advances of Cain's son Nimrod. In the grand finale of the first act, Satan oversees the rise and fall of the Tower of Babel, a catastrophe that kills thousands, and one that will be echoed in the film's final explosive scene.

The lone surviving piece of the film, held by the British Film Institute, is an imperfect eight-minute fragment from the second act, "Satan against the Savior," which turns from Milton to take its inspiration from Klopstock's *Messias*. Several sequences in the fragment are out of order, others are repeated and looped, and the quality of the print is only fair. Still, the fragment includes such scenes as Christ's baptism, his presentation to the crowd by Pontius

Pilate, and his Passion and Crucifixion. Among the more visually arresting images is the whipping of Christ, portrayed as a kind of shadow show against a wall, as leering Roman soldiers watch excitedly. It is a striking and imaginative staging, and one that elegantly implicates the audience as well: like the soldiers, the theatergoers are watching a play of shadows, seemingly safely distanced but, the film would suggest, wiser to meditate on the immediacy of the image. The film fragment also provides a few seconds of Bonnard's Satan, an even more voyeuristic presence, kept offscreen entirely or presented as an observer, watching the calamities around him. In one scene he is shown viewing the Crucifixion with Judas, who deserts him, and in the following shot Satan rolls about in either torment or ecstasy. The reel ends with the Resurrection, Satan baffled and writhing beneath the broken portal of the tomb as Jesus ascends into heaven.

The final two acts, *Il Demone verde, ossia Satana nel Medioevo* and *Il Demone rosso, ossia Satana nella vita moderna,* present Satan in his manifestation as "The Destroyer." The third act shifts to the Middle Ages, where Satan finds a monk named Gerbert who is drawn to the arts of alchemy. Satan teaches him how to concoct absinthe (whence the "Green Demon" of the subtitle), and all manner of evil springs from the alcohol. The entire monastery is eventually corrupted by drink, and Gerbert's inhibitions go up in smoke as he is driven mad for a courtesan, Fiammeta, and eventually kills her lover and himself. This cataclysm is topped off by Satan toasting to the destruction of all humankind. The final act, set in the present day, sees Satan set a humble factory worker named Furio and an equally mild florist named Maria down a fatal path. In this melodramatic conclusion, an allegory for the tyranny of industrialism, Satan demonstrates the exploitation even unto death of the labor on which modern society depends. Satan simultaneously manages to stir up the entire factory against their overseers and convinces Furio to murder his domineering boss. After further persuading Maria to deceive Furio to have him arrested, Furio finds himself surrounded on all sides by the police. At last, Satan urges the man to blow up the entire factory, causing the death of Maria, the police and himself. The film's final image is of Satan in top hat, coat and tails, lighting a cigarette from the embers of the fallen pile. It is a return to the implosion of Babel and intended as a haunting triumph of his will over that of the God who cast him out: Satan seems at last to have succeeded in remaking earth into a parody of hell.[43]

BERTRAM BRACKEN'S *CONSCIENCE*

Bertram Bracken's little-known film *Conscience* (1917) is one of the more extensive silent era dramatizations of Milton, employing the man himself, along with his daughters. The Hungarian artist Mihály Munkácsy's famous painting of "Blind Milton Dictating 'Paradise Lost' to His Daughters" (1877) serves as the inspiration and model for the opening prologue, a dramatization not only of Milton's domestic dictation but of a war in heaven redux. The film's main story is a highly allegorical morality play starring Gladys Brockwell as Ruth Somers, a "fashionable heiress" and serial seducer who has callously thrown over a string of doting paramours.[44] Not an especially well-received work—it was regarded as a "lurid melodrama, rather too lurid and distasteful, perhaps, for a sensitively refined audience"—*Conscience* nonetheless was celebrated for its technical achievements and for the virtuoso performance of Brockwell.[45] The story begins with Ruth on her wedding day (she has settled for the rich bachelor Cecil Brooke, "the prize that no one thought would ever marry"), admiring herself and her gown in a mirror. She receives a desperate note from one of her recent lovers, Ned Langley, begging her to take him back. (In a later scene, the film shows Ned's fiancée killing herself after witnessing him professing his love to Somers, whom he has only known for a day.) At this point, Conscience appears and draws Ruth into a mystical court, where she is subjected to flashbacks of her past sins. Ruth is tormented in turn by Avarice, Lust, Ambition, Vanity, each of whom is also being played by Brockwell.[46] A novel visual effect, achieved with a quintuple exposure, allowed all these roles to be presented simultaneously, as the allegorical characters personated by Brockwell compass around Ruth during the trial. Throughout the film a natty devil, "Dr. Norton" (Bertram Grassby), keeps her company as her "strange and complicated" guardian, delighting in the evils she perpetrates on men (including inviting them for trysts aboard her fiancé's yacht, where much of the film's action is set, and murdering one of them). Despite Conscience's best efforts, the trial fails to move her, and she returns to the scene of her wedding. However, Ned then arrives in the flesh, breaking in upon the marriage ceremony at the same moment every melodramatic ex-lover must break in ("if anyone here present…"); Ruth once more scorns him, however, and he is taken from the wedding, only to shoot himself in an adjoining room. This, at last, convinces the cuckolded groom to leave Ruth at the altar, and only then does she see the error of her ways. She ends the film by banishing the devil and falling to her knees, pleading with heaven for forgiveness.

The prologue ushering forth all this action begins promptly with Milton, the title card a paraphrase of Munkácsy's painting: "Milton, the blind poet, immortally inspired, dictates to his daughters that epic of all ages, 'Paradise Lost'" (see fig. 3.3). Then there is a long shot of Milton's room as the film fades in to reveal the painter's tableau: "Milton seated dictating to his daughters—Daughters looking at the Inspired Blind Poet-father with impressive awe," and finally, importantly, "Milton slowly opens his lips and begins speaking." A close-up on Milton, then, as the title card displays his sonorous, but only quasi-Miltonic, oration: "And Michael, bright archangel, drives from a paradise eternal the host of fallen angels who conspired against the divine power of almighty god." The appropriation of Milton here is a curious one: his presence inaugurates the puritanical allegory, to be sure, but the tension between his divine inspiration—the words themselves—and the silent medium is provocative. The insufficiency of the title card conveys some of this: as we build to Milton speaking "that epic of all ages," it is counterpointed by the impression upon his taciturn daughters: awed scribbling. The film then implies that the ensuing gloss on Michael's conquest of the fallen angels is Milton's, though these words are neither lines from *Paradise Lost* nor an accurate digest of the action in the poem. While the cultural capital of Milton here is meant to compound the gravity and power of the morality tale to follow—and to awe his spectators, like his daughters, into submission—the fracture with the poem highlights not only the typical path of Miltonic adaptations—skewing from the text at every possible turn—but also the inherent disturbance in the silent film medium as it grapples with the weight of the word.

The shot returns to Milton, "speaking as before," until he lifts his face in an "ecstatic, inspired manner as if he were visualizing the scene that follows." At this point, as the scene dissolves to the gates of heaven, a cinematic coup has been launched. Milton's ecstasy begins to drift beyond the powers of orality and into the purely visual, the visionary experience that only film can properly mediate. Thus, when the gates materialize in the subsequent long shot, the filmmakers turn not to the poem for their descriptive language or visual imagery but to another film, Lois Weber's *Where Are My Children?* from the previous year: "I would advise the Director to see a print.... Fine local color may be obtained from this story, as Mrs. Smalley has a Gate such as this exact—incidentally, it made

Fig. 3.3. The blind Milton dictating *Paradise Lost* in *Conscience*. *Courtesy of Museum of Modern Art.*

a very fine effect." The Weber film, a lurid melodrama in its own right, and better known to modern audiences for its propagandistic treatment of the prolife movement than for its heavenly gates, provides an important intervention here. It breaks the intertextual pull toward Milton, replacing it instead with an exclusively cinematic image to substitute as Milton's first view *of his own verse*. Where Milton was blind, now he, and the audience, can see:

> Large, white gates—the top part of the scene is illumined by a flood of light, a pair of steps lead down apparently into nothingness—from the bottom of these steps, thin, spiral shafts of smoke blow up from time to time....At the top of steps is seen Michael, Archangel, surrounded by a halo of light—flaming sword—driving down this stairway a host of spirits—spirits are crouching, pleading, tumbling down—Fine, red Night tint to lower part of scene—a vague suggestion of the flames of Hell working their relentless way up to the very Gates of Heaven.

The scene offers a collapsed cosmic view, the bright illumination at the top of the screen balanced by the tinted glow at the bottom, the gates of heaven embroiled with the flames of hell, and Michael dominating the top half of the frame as the fallen angels cower and tumble down the lower half. But this is not Milton's cosmos, nor a scene from the poem. Of course, the film is not interested in the poem for its own sake—it is interested in the idea of Milton and the idea of a divine, cosmic battle, one begun between Michael and Lucifer and continued into the later narrative of the film as an unending contest between Conscience and Sin. There is a sense, then, in which the impending scene here supplants the poem—the film leads us to see what Milton sees. How he renders, in words inadequate for the task (as the poet repeatedly insists), is secondary and derivative of this greater, filmic vision.

Following the shot of the gates and the triumphant archangel, the film cuts back to Milton's room, where the scene that began as a precise replication of Munkácsy's painting now comes fully to life. Milton, at first "seated dictating as before—daughters writing," rises from his seat, his eyes closed, as he "raises his hands inspired," and dictates with increasing animation. He has become even more an "impressive, awe-inspiring figure," something the seated Milton of the painting can only imply. As Milton begins to move, the scene shifts back again to the gates of heaven, which matches the increased agitation of the poet with continued action along the stairs: "spirits still tumbling down—crouching, pleading, praying—distorted faces," Michael still brandishing his flaming sword, and then a climactic "burst of flame" erupts into the scene, and the view shifts to a close-up of the gates. Lucifer has arrived and he has brought a friend. Brockwell also plays the part here of Serama, one of the fallen angels and, like Milton's Sin, both daughter and consort to Lucifer:

> Michael standing and looking off sadly down steps—majestically—trifle sadly—he turns—elevates flaming sword—gates slowly open and a flood of light shoots out—beautiful vista background—exterior vista—few girls dancing in diaphanous garments by side of brook or something allegorical—Lucifer—dressed in long black cloak and Serama "Theda Bara" appear and the gates slowly close behind them—Serama dressed in white robe—her expression is pleading—the countenance of Lucifer is dark and saturnine—no horns nor hoofs—not the popular conception of the Devil—They stand near the gates looking at the Archangel—all with statuesque poses.

Resorting to a panoramic view of heaven, and also the scantily clad dancing girls, the scene recalls those nineteenth century spectaculars even as the film appropriates them for its own conservative moralism. Indeed, the massive spectacle here, of heaven in all its dimensions (and with some questionable embroidery to boot), dwarfs Lucifer and Serama both. As the camera closes on Lucifer, he lowers his gaze—"he cannot bear the brightness of the Archangel's eye." But the archangel's eye only stands in for the camera's. A title card tells us that he has "fallen from his high estate"—a quote not from *Paradise Lost* but Dryden's *Alexander's Feast,* another veering off from Milton's poem, though not this time from poetry itself. Satan's inability to regard the spectacle of heaven marks his fall as a new kind of collapse, a cinematic failure to maintain his gaze. While the blind Milton rises above the limitations of the page into these overwhelmingly illuminated visions, the dark and brooding Lucifer has lost his light completely. Serama's close-up reveals that she continues to bear this light: "Serama—in white—beautiful—looking off towards the Archangel—supplicating light in her eyes." The film ultimately rewards such vision—the cinema has allegorized itself, correcting and emending the morality of its observers, and rejecting those who cannot stand to watch.

As Michael advances wordlessly on the pair, pointing his flaming sword down the stairs, Lucifer is resigned to accept his banishment. Serama, however, drops to her knees, and the camera frames her in a position of supplication, an orant figure out of medieval art. There is "wild fright and terror" in her appearance, and then the film cuts back to Milton once more, who is also "working himself up to an impressive but suppressed poetic pitch." The film wants to align Milton not with Satan, but with Serama. There is no sympathy for the devil, only his feminine right hand. A similar identification happens with Milton's daughters, who begin as recorders but are gradually removed offscreen, put in the place of the implied observer, so that the film makes clear its aims of redeeming the failings not of men, who like Lucifer are ancillary to this tale, "defeated but defiant," but of women.

When the scene cuts back to heaven, Michael remains intractable despite Serama's continued pleas. Yet when he relents to speak, the words offer a chance: "Go forth to the perdition prepared for thee and in pain and torment work out thy salvation; that once again thou may'st sit in that bright heaven thou hast forfeited by thy rebellion." The vague pelagianism of Michael's command is a syncretic blend of Milton's theology. His pronouncement transfers onto Serama the same hope God offers Eve but never Satan—though Lucifer also appears excluded from the offer in Bracken's film. Indeed, Serama's ensuing cry, "Have mercy, O Michael! The fault was not mine. 'Twas the proud and rebellious Lucifer who urged me on," is a paraphrase of Eve's plea after the Fall ("The Serpent me beguil'd and I did eat" [*PL* 10.162]). Serama, then, who owes something to Milton's Sin, is also the fallen woman. This is followed by yet another cut back to Milton's room, this time including his daughters, still writing, while Milton's own "poetic fervor" is keeping pace with the intensity of Serama's pleas. There may be a slip in the identification between Milton and Serama here, though, and a transference onto Michael, who has clearly been repressing the full power of his majesty but loses control a bit at the repeated appeals of Serama: "Begone! Resist the counsels of Lucifer, who shall be called Satan. Obey him, and thousands of years shall be added unto thy punishment." This pronouncement, finally, gets under Lucifer's skin, who until this point has remained "calm and quiet," "cynical" and "saturnine." Now with his first words, he fires back at Michael, "Far down in that burning chaos, Lucifer shall create a kingdom of his own and his subjects shall be men and Serama shall be his queen." This is at once the closest and farthest *Conscience* comes to Milton's original, as Lucifer promises here to "make a heaven of hell," but to do so with a new queen of the damned. This is defiance, certainly, if not exactly irrepressible heroism. It underscores Serama's essential goodness, or at least capacity for reform, since she seems an unwilling accomplice, a victim of Satan's imperial designs.

When Lucifer finishes, Michael once again directs him and Serama to the abyss: "They are looking off towards the Archangel—they turn—burst of flame—Serama shrinks—Lucifer raises his finger—long and talon like—points below—Serama looks at him a moment—slowly descends the steps and out of scene—Lucifer casts one look back and slowly follows her—black cloak wrapped about him—he disappears—burst of flame after he has gone." The characterization of Lucifer in this sequence tends away from the bestial—no horns or hooves, though he seems to have talons—and toward an urbane, dapper, Victorian devil. He is adorned with a black cape instead of bat wings. This is the turning point, and for the last few shots the film anticipates the larger action of the Ruth Somers plot.

Immediately after the disappearance of Serama and Lucifer, the film cuts back to Milton, this time for a wonderfully discontinuous interjection. He is still narrating, as before, with his daughters transcribing, but now pauses to offer the basic tagline for the film: "In every human soul will I place conscience; and this, not I, will be their judge and punish them." Who or what is the "I" in this statement? At first glance it seems to be the word of God, though there has been no mention or glimpse of the godhead yet in the script (and in fact a displacement of the Son by Michael). It is unquestionably Milton speaking, and the film has been driving the passions and divine inspiration of Milton along at so awesome a rate that this moment becomes a kind of apotheosis for the poet. Milton, as the appearance of his daughters affirms, has become fully the Father. But while the film develops Milton in this way, still the lines he speaks are not those of *Paradise Lost*. They are, however, a very close approximation of the passage in book 3 of the poem when God unfolds to his Son his full plans for the redemption of human beings. He declares that his project of "Prayer, repentance, and obedience" (*PL* 3.191) will be complemented by "a guide": "And I will place within them as a guide / My Umpire *Conscience*, whom if they will hear, / Light after light well us'd they shall attain, / And to the end persisting, safe arrive" (*PL* 3.194–97). Knowledge of the film's "I," then, depends on an implicit sense of intertextuality between the title card and the poem, a recognition in the echoes of "place" and "conscience" that the film has turned to *Paradise Lost* to authorize its interpretation of the central role of Conscience in human affairs. Without this tissue of familiarity between the two works, the film's segue from the vanishing Satan to Milton speaking becomes nonsensical. Moreover, the film resorts here to the poem to complete the absence in its own representational scheme: just as it removes the Son, so too the film makes no attempt to indicate the godhead. The closest it comes is Milton himself, acting as the guiding moral compass for all human souls.[47] And this is, in fact, our last view of him in the film.

The scene shifts for a last time back to the gates of heaven, where Michael stands "looking sadly down the steps." The gates then reopen, and a veiled figure emerges, the personification of Conscience, "its hands upon its bosom waiting for his command." Instead of cutting back to Milton's room, the shot now moves to the "desolate" and "terrible region" being traversed by Lucifer and Serama: first a "Blasted Pathway" with "stunted vegetation" and a large snake that "wriggle[s] across the foreground," then the "Brow of [a] Mountain—with Valley Beyond." But the desolate regions are not those of hell but earth. Lucifer takes another panoramic sweep of the valley, in which can be seen the lights of human habitation, while he himself is "outlined against the flaming sky" (the shot was directed to be photographed "against flaming sunset"). He tells his consort, "Yonder lie the kingdoms of Earth and they shall be mine and thine, Serama," and the film shifts its register from *Paradise Lost* to *Paradise Regained,* as the moment reenacts Satan's panoramic presentation of the kingdoms of earth to the Son. Indeed, this is the trajectory for the film in general. The prologue ends with Michael speaking to Conscience and directing her to the world below: "Go forth, Conscience, and implant thyself into the souls of men and women, as God hath commanded thee." The scene dissolves to "The Wedding Day of Ruth Somers, courted society girl, who, through the ages, has become the reincarnation of the fallen spirit, Serama." The rest of the film works through its allegorical schemes to restore Serama to heaven, shifting her from a fallen Eve-Sin hybrid (in one place the script calls her expression that of a "serpent considering its victim") to a redeemed daughter of God, ready to stand against Satan's temptations as Milton's messiah had rejected his offers of worldly dominion.[48]

There was some praise for the Milton sequence. R. M. Johnson enthuses that these scenes "are clever reproductions of the most vivid of Gustave Doré's pictures of the entrance to the place of eternal torment. The spirits are driven down, down by the devil himself. The blazing fires, the fiery wand in the hand of the Archangel Michael, the unrest of the condemned, the whole artistry of the picture compares favorably with the screen masterpieces."[49] But the use of Milton in the film also led to a harsh review by Edward Weitzel in *Moving Picture World:*

> The story attempts to disguise its true character by pretending to teach a moral lesson with the aid of allegory, but, stripped of its thin veneer of being inspired by Milton's "Paradise Lost," it is revealed as a sordid tale of the physical wrong doing of a fair but frail young woman whose promiscuity threatens to embrace every man in the case. The manner of making this clear to the spectator is accomplished with the delicacy of touch that characterizes a sledge hammer when swung by a husky son of Italy. The fact that the lady is supposed to be the reincarnation of Serama, the consort of Lucifer, and that she is under his dominance all through the play: also, that

she repents and is seen, at the finish, climbing up to the heaven
from which she was driven, does not excuse the bald suggestion
with which her frequent falls from virtue are shown. To prostitute
Milton's noble work in such a way is an artistic crime.[50]

The "veneer" of Miltonic inspiration is certifiably thin at
times — Ned pleads with Ruth in his note, "Do not cast me
headlong into that hell created by a broken heart," enfolding
the poet's epic account of Satan being "Hurled headlong flaming from th'Ethereal sky" (*PL* 1.45) into the plaintive clichés of a
failed troubadour. And perhaps because the links to Milton are not
stronger, other contemporary reviews leave out the Milton prologue entirely, only implying the Serama reincarnation by referring to the heroine's "fiendish pleasure" and "devilish delight"
in discarding the men she has seduced.[51] Weitzel's disgust that
Milton should be "prostituted in this way" turns the poet into
the promiscuous heroine of the film, coquettishly inviting everyone in but failing to deliver anything of substance. And yet, rather
than justifying the bathos of the "lurid" allegory that follows, the
Milton prologue seems to be an attempt to bring his poem to the
screen and to master it, to cinematize it, to translate, or perhaps
vampirize, the poetic powers of *Paradise Lost* into the sublimities
of film, even while casting it headlong into the infernal realms of
melodrama.

D. W. GRIFFITH

During the years 1908–31, David Wark Griffith directed nearly
500 films, the majority for the American Mutoscope and Biograph
Company between 1908 and 1913. Critics have generally regarded
these early films, mostly one- and two-reel shorts, as essential sub-
strate for the famed pictures that followed, all of which Griffith
directed with other production companies. Robert M. Henderson
argues that "the golden age of *The Birth of a Nation* (1916), *Intolerance* (1916), *Broken Blossoms* (1919), *Way Down East* (1920),
and *Orphans of the Storm* (1921) was possible only as a result of
the mastery of the medium Griffith achieved at Biograph."[52] As
Griffith was becoming increasingly interested in and ambitious

about the length of his films—the shorts Griffith churned out for Biograph culminated in the four-reel *Judith of Bethulia* (1914), his final picture with them, and the ten-reel epics of his "golden age"—he was also concerned with finding enough sources to supply the demand for new stories. In addition to scenarios, short stories, plays, and novels, Griffith freely adapted poetic works by Browning, Tennyson, Poe, and Kingsley (though these generally can be traced through intermedial dramatic works—for example, his adaptation of Browning's *Pippa Passes* depends on a 1906 playlet by Henry Miller).[53] Mikhail Iampolski suggests that these Biograph films, particularly Griffith's various adaptations of Tennyson's *Enoch Arden,* were also "Griffith's first efforts at applying the poetics of transcendentalism to film."[54] This was a steady and earnest enterprise: to turn, as it were, poetry into film and film into a new poetic language. Griffith later reflected on his literary adaptations by trumpeting that "we made *Macbeth, Don Quixote,* Poe's *Tell-Tale Heart,* Kingsley's *Sands of Dee,*" and "we even had poetry in the screen titles."[55] Later, a line from Whitman's *Leaves of Grass* would figure as a structural device in *Intolerance* (1916). And Griffith, to his delight, even published one poem, "The Wild Duck," and reportedly carried about in his predirectorial days notebooks of unpublished verse.[56]

Biograph produced pictures with a strong moral imperative, a movement to reform film from its sallow nickelodeon-hall past. Griffith had worked on stage to modest acclaim for a decade in some of those halls before turning to film as a financial last resort. He came to Biograph first as a writer and sometime actor who fell into direction when it was still seen as no more than tertiary to the cameraman and actors. But his conservative worldview and Victorian sensibilities soon made him the ideal crusader for Biograph. His pioneering films had an "explicitly Protestant tone" and "dramatized every major concern of the day: labor-management conflict, white slavery, eugenics, prohibition, women's emancipation, and civic corruption."[57] In all of which, wrote Griffith, "the ordinary virtues of American life triumph. No Toryism. No Socialism."[58] Griffith's success at Biograph, especially his success in adapting works of high art, led the *New York Times* in October 1909 to proclaim "a reformed motion picture industry" (this, after the mayor of New York had shut down the nickelodeons citywide on Christmas Eve a year earlier).[59] Griffith took up the torch, declaring in the notes for his autobiography, "Reform was sweeping the country, newspapers were laying down a barrage against gambling, rum and light ladies, particularly light ladies. There were complaints against everything, so I decided to reform the motion picture industry."[60] As part of this reform, Griffith strove to legitimize film as a revolutionary art. Iampolski convincingly sees Griffith as aspiring at once to appropriate and repress the poetry he revered in exchange for the cinema in which he prospered: "Griffith wanted to effect a kind of illusory metamorphosis, transforming his films into works made in some other artistic medium."[61] As Griffith became more deeply immersed in cinema, he distanced himself from the stage as well: "Picture entertainment is far ahead of the stage play. Poetry is apparently a lost art in the regular theater, but it is the very life and essence of the motion playhouse."[62]

If movies had at one time seemed transient curiosities, second fiddle at best to the stage, Griffith would eventually come to see them as prophetic of a new universal language. As Russell Merritt summarizes, "Cinema ... meant liberation from theatrical acting (exaggerated gesture), from theatrical décor (false scenery), from the theatrical proscenium (the fixed view of the spectator in his seat), and from theatrical time (scenes arranged in fixed chronological order)."[63] These liberations set Griffith on a course to imagine an epic cinema, one unbound by the conventions of theater or, for that matter, the limits of space and time. "The Motion Picture," Griffith opines, "is epic rather than dramatic."[64] Moreover, he believed it an epic for all humanity, an extralinguistic system that crossed class, culture, and continent. It was this push to expand into new dimensions that eventually led to Griffith's break with Biograph—his desire for longer feature-length films was tied partly to economics but was at its heart an ideological compulsion to reconstitute the new medium as a transcendent genre.[65]

For Griffith, John Milton figured prominently in this project. In 1914, the newly independent director was asked to weigh in on the relative artistry of the stage versus the motion picture, and

Griffith responded with his increasingly characteristic disdain for the "old stage." He immediately and unequivocally proclaimed the supremacy of the cinema and its rightful displacement of theater as the new high art. And though he had not yet adapted him, his touchstone for this superiority was Milton. He imagined the woeful state of a playwright trying to pitch a new adaptation of *Paradise Lost:* "In your natural enthusiasm after the completion of a great work, to whom would you go and even expect a production? Can you imagine your reception in the average manager's office with a manuscript of a classic under your arm? Or, supposing the impossible, that you had secured a production, of what manager would you expect a performance that would contain any of the poetry, any of the soul of your work?"[66] Two issues are interwoven in this scenario: the failure of producers to comprehend the mass appeal of a work like *Paradise Lost,* and the failure of the dramatic medium to articulate the greatness of the work. Griffith does not criticize the playwright, even commending the act of adaptation itself. Rather, Griffith supposes that the "poetry," the "soul" of the original work, has been preserved in the transference of the written word. The problem of the stage is the stage.

The interviewer here pauses to admit that "the prospect of peddling 'Paradise Lost' along Broadway is not alluring." (He was apparently unaware of the nineteenth century spectacles that had already brought *Paradise Lost* to Broadway, an obliviousness itself suggestive of the limited success of such shows.) In agreement, Griffith shifts to a panegyric on the cinema, championing the "big idea," even at the expense of the "artistic," as noted earlier in my introduction. He continues, "The motion picture is doing daily more than the stage of to-day can think of doing. Before the stage attempts to criticise the photoplay let it do one part of what the motion picture is doing for the enjoyment, uplift and education of the people."[67] Griffith's protestations evince the tensions between high art and popular culture, here located as a struggle to channel and represent the specifically poetic transcendence of the past. But the use of Milton is remarkable foremost as a placeholder for art *in extremis.* Griffith did not offer up Shakespeare (allied with the stage and its limitations) since, he implies, any two-bit fleapit might manage a tragedy—particularly one full of stylized acting and histrionics. Only film, Griffith argues, can attain something epic, the really "big idea." Milton, and specifically here *Paradise Lost,* represents an ineffable magnitude, a movement forward in the cognitive evolution of humankind only fully able to manifest with the arrival of cinema.

The advance is driven narratively, as well: an epic whose form cannot be managed on stage even if every classical unity were shattered can now be experienced off the page. The cinema and not the theater is the place for "poetry," for "the soul" of the work, not least because, as Griffith goes on to argue, film has inaugurated the age of close-ups, of interiority, subtlety, and nuance—a "faithful picture of life" rather than the overwrought techniques of the stage player.[68] Griffith likely had, as well, an affinity for Milton's reforming spirit, his purposeful intentions to edify and instruct his readers, and his visionary proclamation to pursue "Things unattempted yet in Prose or Rhime." In Griffith's eyes, the cinematic medium *was* Milton's poem, soaring above the Aeonian mount and calling into being an energy, a "big idea," the likes of which the world had never seen.

A year later, in 1915, Griffith prophesied that movies would "keep boys and girls along the right lines of conduct. No one need fear it will deviate from the Puritan plane."[69] By 1921, Griffith had come to see film as an eschatological deliverance. In his essay "Cinema: Miracle of Modern Photography," he begins by quoting an "eminent historian" who had just seen one of Griffith's war movies: "History must hereafter be divided into four epochs: The Stone Age, The Bronze Age, the Age of the Printed Page—and the Film Age."[70] The movies were guiding the way to a new, puritanical order and the promise of final redemption. But there was as much tension as ever over film and high art in the early days of the motion picture—Griffith's protestations signal the very anxieties he is attempting to dismiss—and a number of counterexamples to the idea of a reformed film might be given. The British writer Walter Lionel George also uses Milton as his exemplar. While allowing that the cinema "is destined to play a still larger part in the amusement of the people," and that directors like Griffith are "of some slight culture" and "not entirely devoid of taste," he hates movies for their hijinks and horseplay, their silly physicality—"people falling out of windows" and "the rush of flying crockery." He observes how "we should remember that the pioneers of the cinema were Americans of the travelling-showman type...and that type of man could not be expected to like, and therefore to put forward, a dramatic version of *Paradise Lost*. Briefly, the cinema was put forward by the vulgar, for the vulgar."[71]

· Even in 1914 Griffith was overplaying his hand. While it is true that by that time Griffith and others had brought poetry and other "highbrowed" works to film, these were by and large in the minority of the material being adapted, not to mention, as Griffith himself notes, not always artistically successful. The "big idea," then, seems to be meant in a rather literal sense—the poems have become amplified, turned into larger-than-life, big-screen feasts for the eyes. Moreover, since neither Griffith nor any of his American contemporaries had yet attempted *Paradise Lost* (he may have Luigi Maggi's *Satana* in mind here), or for that matter any other epic, Griffith's idealizations fall short of what was actually being produced. Griffith by this time already had plans for his own film epics like *Birth of a Nation,* but even in his later career Griffith was forced to reflect on his general failure in pursuing the epic scope he proposed in the interview. In an essay published in 1927, Griffith revisited more than a little wistfully his plans for an epic cinema:

> There were better stories in the early days, like *Pippa Passes* and the works of Shakespeare, but exhibitors would not buy them today. It is above the taste of the masses....Pictures are the only medium that can carry big stories, epochal poetry and events—that is what I would like to see, but who knows! If I had my way, I would do Homer's *Iliad, Antony and Cleopatra, The Life of Napoleon, Medea*—things that can never be done as effectively on the speaking stage, stories in which all the illusion of a spectacle and authenticity might be introduced.[72]

He sounds desperately reiterative here, still clamoring that film can do all of these things but agonizingly exhausted by what he perceives as the "taste of the masses." In fact, he seems to be cleaving closer to George's cantankerous diatribe on the irrepressible vulgarity of films.

Eisenstein famously appointed Charles Dickens the proper fore-runner of Griffith, particularly in the breaking of narrative continu-ities, the use of flashbacks, a point that Griffith affirms in his essay "What I Demand of Film Actors" (1917). Merritt supposes that the techniques of narrative form were more readily available from Ibsen and Sudermann; certainly poetry was heavily influential in suggesting these techniques as well, as Iampolski and others have shown.[73] An epic like *Paradise Lost* is obviously particularly instruc-tive as well in the use of flashbacks and other narrative breaks, a link implied by Griffith's contemporary, Vachel Lindsay, who called *Intolerance* "good Epic Poetry."[74] But Milton does make his way into Griffith's work in other ways. A number of his films, both at Biograph and beyond, adapt elements of Milton, supporting Griffith's plan to craft a new poetics of film even as they call atten-tion to the ongoing resistance of *Paradise Lost* to feature-length adaptation.

Paradise Lost and *Home, Sweet Home*

In 1912, the same year as Maggi's *Satana*, D. W. Griffith directed a short film called *Paradise Lost*, subtitled "A New Cure for the Sin of Intemperance," one of a number of such temperance shorts Griffith directed for Biograph—others include *A Drunkard's Reformation* (1909), *What Drink Did* (1909), and *The Lesson* (1910). The story begins with a poor and besotted ne'er-do-well, Pete (played with broad comic turns by Mack Sennett), drinking and loafing about while his desperate wife and scolding young daughter labor at chopping wood. When the local parson comes by, Pete attempts to hide his bottle but is confounded when the parson takes it away and empties it. Pete follows the parson past a local bar, where he snatches a bottle of wine from the barkeep and absconds with it to a roadside picket fence, where he drinks and promptly passes out.

The rest of the film works through a Christopher Sly tale, in which unconscious Pete is relocated by the parson and his wealthy friends to a comfortable four-poster bed in one of their upscale homes so that he will "believe he is in Paradise."[75] Sure enough, when Pete awakens he sees the ornate bedposts, which seem to signal to him the gates of heaven, and is suitably terrified. His suspicions are confirmed—he has died and gone to heaven—when he sees the two housemaids, whom the men have dressed as angels, adorning them with white linen robes and pure white butterfly wings. Pete is frightened, pleading on his knees before them, until one of the angels waves her arms and the second ministering spirit comes in with a bottle of celestial liquor. This seems to change his opinion of the place, while Griffith intercuts the scene with the parson and his men laughing in the next room. Before long, two more bottles are brought in.

A flirty Pete is particularly amazed when one of the angels shaves his face—even such scruff must be purified—by lathering cream on his face and then simply blowing on the foam. The whiskers and lather both disappear in an instant. The angels continue to truck in bottles until Pete is overwhelmed and once more passes out. The men then remove him back to his original location, where he awakes to find a donkey staring him down. He jumps up and runs off, encountering two little girls in white dresses and ribbons whom he at first links with the angels he has just seen. He races about the countryside, attempting to tell anyone who will listen the story of his heavenly trip (this is conveyed by flapping his arms like a chicken to denote the angels, and miming the shaving-cream special effect to strike home the miracle of it all), but he is generally ignored as a raving lunatic. Finally, he returns to his wife, and the parson arrives to test him. Miraculously, Pete has given up alcohol for good, duly chastened by his experience of death, and to everyone's delight he begins to help his wife with her work by sawing a plank of wood. The Biograph catalogue declares happily that "the scheme worked to perfection and it looks as if the village saloon will get no more of Pete's money for drink."

The film's Miltonic title seems motivated partly by the ruse of the ministering angels, partly by the puritanical message of temperance, and partly by Pete's vaguely satanic character. In its immediate context, it is also an oddly ironic title: the paradise lost by Pete is either his former life of lazy sin or his vision of a besotted heaven. Continuing the Miltonic theme, the central conflict between Pete and the parson begins as a kind of inversion of divine rebellion, the parson swiping his bottle and Pete in pursuit. When this tack fails, the parson cures Pete's malady by getting him to surfeit on liquor until he sickens of it—by giving him freedom to fall rather than confining him with strict rule. But the film is also a narrative of domestic discord, a fallen world of labor and sweating brows. Pete may have lost heaven, but it was a heaven of which he ultimately wanted no part. (And in a reaffirmation of the film's class tensions, an affluent heaven from which he must be excluded.) Instead, Pete has gained a more satisfying paradise within as his family unites in the finale.

Griffith left Biograph in 1913, going on to create his most lasting and controversial films in the years following. Some critics have seen the four-part structure of *Intolerance* as fashioned after Luigi Maggi's *Satana,* and in many of Griffith's films from this time he seems to be working through the dramatic devices of Milton, though not always with success. Scott Simmon, for instance, finds that "his most literal religious imagery plays quite inauthentically. He could seldom resist flying in angels on wires or Christ himself to beatify grand finales, as in *Home, Sweet Home, Birth of a Nation,* and *Intolerance.*"[76] The end of *Home, Sweet Home* features a stark epilogue, the "vain fight to rise from the pit of evil," in which the hero, a poet named John Payne, finds himself in a hellish quarry, struggling to claw and clamber his way out. An angel (his beloved transformed) appears and with her assistance he is ushered into heaven. An earlier work, *The Avenging Conscience* (1914), also was to feature a host of angels. The film is a kind of Poe medley (featuring his poems "Annabel Lee," "To One in Paradise," and "The Bells") with a scenario derived from *The Tell-Tale Heart.* Griffith wanted angels in the finale, "played by as many pretty young girls as could be found in the neighborhood" and "swung from heavy piano wires from overhead rigging."[77] Karl Brown, who was assistant cameraman, reports that the metamorphosis of angels from neighborhood nymphs was not a smooth one:

> The girls were assembled, fitted with harnesses to which the wings could be attached, dressed in angel robes, and crowned with identical long-flowing blond wigs. They were then hoisted, one by one, until their feet were about fifteen feet above the floor. This took time, and by the time the ninth or tenth girl had been hauled up

into position, angels numbers one and two began to be very sick indeed. They were lowered and made to lie down and sniff smelling salts. During this, the other girls who had been hauled up decided to join the act, so they too got rid of whatever breakfast they had aboard. Pretty soon all we had was a lot of sick angels lying around the edges of the stage.[78]

Problems continued when the angels were hoisted and began to turn about eradically, requiring that they be tethered by black thread to individuals on the ground who would steer them correctly. The sequence was shot as a double exposure to blend with heavenly clouds, but had to be rushed because of the delays on set. Griffith, in fact, screened the newly cut film for a test audience that very night without having viewed it himself first, and was humiliated to discover that the angels on screen "were not serenely happy and joyous as angels are supposed to be. They were the sickest, most woebegone angels anyone could imagine.... They should have been flying like birds, with heads forward and bodies back, with flowing draperies and gracefully moving wings, and not like so many white socks hung out on a washline to dry."[79] The scene was eventually cut from the film entirely.

The Sorrows of Satan

By 1926, Griffith was in the midst of one of the more uneven stretches of his career. Directing now for Famous Players, his most recent films were two W. C. Fields–Carol Dempster comedies: the well-received *Sally of the Sawdust* (1925) and the box-office bomb *That Royle Girl* (1925). Around this time he was offered the chance at one of the studio's prized projects: an adaptation of Marie Corelli's popular novel *The Sorrows of Satan* (1895). One of the best-selling works of its day, Corelli's novel tells the Faustian story of Geoffrey Tempest, a struggling and impoverished writer who bargains his soul for a fortune. He is guided through the upper caste of European society by Lucio, the devil incarnate, who arranges a marriage with Lady Sibyl Elton, a wicked English heiress. Midway through the novel, Tempest meets Mavis Clare, a kindred soul and fellow writer, whose guileless charm and simple faith prompt him to redeem his life of decadence for spiritual riches.

There are several allusions to Milton in the text, the most notable of which becomes the informing model for redemption in Griffith's adaptation. It is not from *Paradise Lost* but *Comus,* the Elder Brother's magisterial defense of chastity at lines 453–63. In the novel, it is the diabolical Lucio who quotes the passage at length, describing Geoffrey's attraction to Mavis:

> You know what Milton says: "So dear to Heaven is saintly chastity /
> That when a soul is found sincerely so, / A thousand liveried angels
> lacquey her, / Driving far off each thing of sin and guilt, / And in
> clear dream and solemn vision / Tell her of things which no gross
> ear can hear, / Till oft converse with heavenly habitants / Begin to
> cast a beam on th'outward shape / The unpolluted temple of the
> mind, / And turns it by degrees to the soul's essence / Till all be
> made immortal!" He quoted the lines softly and with an exquisite
> gravity. "That is what you see in Mavis Clare," he continued—"that
> 'beam on the outward shape' which 'turns it by degrees to the
> soul's essence,'—and which makes her beautiful without what is
> called beauty by lustful men."[80]

The power of chastity was a potent lure for Griffith, as well. Lary May argues that Griffith "used film to make his idea of saintly womanhood come alive."[81] Indeed, one of his most famous techniques for showing saintly womanhood—the "hazy photography" that seemed to imbue women with a divine luminescence—could be drawn from Milton's own lines. Griffith said he wanted "a face where the skin radiated a smooth soft outline," and noted that moving back and forth "between characters lighted 'like archangels or devils'" helped clarify the allegories at work.[82] Certainly the exalting of chastity is a central device of Griffith's film adaptation, although it never invokes Milton as explicitly as Corelli, and when it does, it prefers *Paradise Lost* to *Comus.* The book is full of unambiguous moralizing—Mavis the angel, Sibyl the fiend—and quaint sensibilities, elements that would have been perfect fits at Biograph 10 or 15 years prior but which resonated far less resoundingly by the mid-1920s. The film had suffered through numerous delays, and it was rumored that Cecil B. De Mille had his heart set on the project as well (Schickel relates that he left Paramount after being refused as director).[83] When Griffith went forward with it, he had in mind this film serving for his *Paradise Lost*, a war in heaven that spills over onto earth in imagery no less lavish than the lushest of Milton's epic.

While the film's prologue appropriates Milton most directly—drawing from Doré a dramatization of the war in heaven and Satan's expulsion—the whole of *The Sorrows of Satan*, as Schickel puts it, "gave Griffith splendid opportunities for those symbolic representations of heaven and hellishness, that he favored."[84] Though Griffith had also complained that Corelli's work was not more highbrow—calling the production of such a novel a "pitiful waste of time" when literary gems like Conrad's *Heart of Darkness* remained unfilmed—he nonetheless pushed for the final film to embrace whatever "astonishing visions of the struggle between the forces of light and darkness" could be extracted and brought to the screen.[85] *Paradise Lost* informed not only the scope of these "astonishing visions," but the revolutionary dynamics of the film itself. Griffith spoke of the project in a glowing expectation of the Miltonic, effectively at the expense of the novel's actual author: "'But why Marie Corelli?' my friends ask. Greater writers than she have taken the Evil One as their theme. True—quite true! Dante and Milton immediately come to mind.... But to my mind, justice hasn't been done him in the movies."[86] Schickel concludes that Griffith was "seeking transcendence, a film that would rise above its silly source to achieve the visionary," including a climactic apotheosis in which the devil returns to the heavenly gates for a breath of paradise.[87]

Recognizing the imaginative appeal of such a scene, Paramount promoted the sequence in its press sheets, describing how "The pearly gates of the Elysian Fields were opened not long ago at Astoria, L.I., and a thousand souls marched into the Kingdom of Heaven," and calling the scene "one of the most difficult, technically, ever filmed." The scene reportedly took an entire day of filming and used six exposures to bring out "the eerie transparency and ethereal quality necessary in such highly imaginative film art."[88] It would have made a breathtaking conclusion, stretching the boundaries of film as conceptual art and realizing Griffith's vision of the *Sorrows of Satan* as a transcendent cinematic work. As the repeated exposures effect the ethereality of Elysium, they also seem to be an attempt to scour the film of its very materiality, to diffuse the substance of image and work until they reach a point of sublimation. Alas, this transcendent scene never made the final cut. The film had become a battleground of another sort, pitched between Griffith and the producers at Paramount, and many of Griffith's idealized plans died in the encounter.

Film historians have come to regard the ultimate failings of *Sorrows* as the beginning of the end for Griffith as a director. Robert M. Henderson writes that "*The Sorrows of Satan* had been budgeted as a major motion picture, and the initial planning had called for considerable spectacle. It has been said that [producer, Adolph] Zukor insisted on Griffith's concentrating on the love story and spending more screen time in dull, vapid close-ups of Carol Dempster and Ricardo Cortez.... After the first cut, Griffith was taken off the picture by Lasky and, with Zukor's approval, Julian Johnson re-edited the film."[89] The artistic differences resulted in a significant loss of the visionary and astonishing—Griffith's plan for the final climax was scrapped—but also serendipitously led to the most Miltonic sequence yet filmed.

The Sorrows of Satan gets to Milton immediately. The title card is set over an ominous image of Satan, copied unmistakably from Doré, looking suitably sorrowful, hand on chin, as he gazes over a glowing cityscape (the story is set in London).[90] In the poem, Doré's image corresponds with that moment in book 6 when Satan has suffered his first defeat and retires under the "Cloudie covert" of darkness. Doré portrays a moment not explicitly presented by Milton: a sullen, perhaps fuming, Satan gazing alone into the chasms of heaven, apparently to capture his contemplation and revelation that "Deep under ground, materials dark and crude" may yield "weapons more violent" (*PL* 6.478, 439). If it is the governing image of the film, it places the "materials dark and crude" squarely in the urban sprawl below. And indeed, the plot suggests that humanity is relentlessly fallen: Satan's plight is that he cannot find anyone able to resist his temptations. This initial tableau of Milton's Satan, struck down but intent on recovering himself, mining the subterranean slums and alleys of earth to find one refined soul, does govern much of the film's movement. Griffith's devil is too charming for his own good.

The titles employ the understated vernacular of the day to announce that the story was "suggested by Marie Corelli," and the film adapts the novel freely. Mavis, for instance, appears almost immediately and the film is generally focalized through her, whereas in the novel, narrated by Tempest, Mavis appears much later and is already a successful "literary woman." The war in heaven prologue is the first major departure. Longtime screenwriter Forrest Halsey, adapting a treatment by John Russell, proposed "open[ing] with an allegory based on Milton's *Paradise Lost,* showing Lucifer, most radiant of all the angels whose envy of man has caused his fall."[91] Halsey writes approvingly of Russell's initial recommendation that "the Doré pictures of *Paradise Lost* may have some suggestions," and goes on to describe "a few big tableaux" of Satan triumphing over earth, culminating in a confrontation with Christ, before whom he "quail[s]...as before his great enemy."[92] In the later continuity script, this sequence has been moved from an opening prologue to a slightly later imaginative sequence, prompted by Tempest opening an "old book" containing the story of Satan's fall. The first long shot of heaven is linked with *Paradise Lost:* "At first the screen is filled with a tumultuous mass of clouds, which may be from what Milton is pleased to term: 'The thunderous artillery of Heaven.' They roll and seethe."[93] Milton was not quite so pleased: this is an apparently misremembered Miltonism, perhaps from Satan's confrontation with Death in book 2, when "Each cast at th' other, as when two black Clouds / With Heav'ns Artillery fraught, come rattling on" (*PL* 2.714–15).

As the scene in the script goes on, "we see ranked the angels of the Lord of Hosts, armed and helmed, their outspread wings flashing in the heavenly radiance." Opposing them is Lucifer, armor agleam, and a "great curve of dark, twisting figures." But the appearance of active opposition is deceiving—the scene actually picks up at the conclusion of the war, with Lucifer awaiting (still defiantly) his punishment. Michael appears with his flaming sword to banish Lucifer: "thou shalt be forever bound to the pits of thine own damnation." Lucifer questions God's mercifulness, and the punishment is mitigated: should any souls resist his temptations, he will be permitted to return to heaven for a single hour. With that, Lucifer and his cowardly lot are transformed as the archangel "seizes him and casts him downward. Clouds rush over the screen." There follows a single shot of the fall through space — "tiny worlds seem flaming and falling. The dark masses of the falling angels, like thunder clouds descending upon the earth. . . . Again the clouds cover the screen, then part and we see rising toward us the curve of the sun-lit earth. The shadow of Lucifer falls upon it. Again there are storms, tempests, explosions."[94] The sequence ends with Satan standing atop a mountain peak, then turning and striding into the camera.

From Halsey's first version, the most significant cut is Christ. In a move made frequently in adaptations of Milton's war, Michael stands in for the Son. The war itself exists only in these shuddering aftershocks, and the fall is a pleasure trip compared to Milton's rendering: Satan plummets not to hell but earth, and his eternal damnation becomes a series of long and laborious tortures punctuated by some refreshing time off back in heaven. The "allegorical" nature of the sequence seems to send a powerfully mixed message: forgiveness and mercy make for weak deterrents, while the final image seems intended mostly to scare a moviegoer straight. Meanwhile, the ultimate message — that the goodness of humankind has the incidental effect of succoring its greatest adversary — seems patently unfair. Perhaps for such reasons Griffith struggled with how best to render the scene and also where to place the sequence in the script. At some point near the close of filming it moved from prologue to a climactic sequence, and around this same time two versions of the heaven scenes were filmed.

Griffith's producers, Jesse Lasky and Walter Wanger, had wearied of Griffith's frustrations with the sequence and brought in the famed stage designer Norman Bel Geddes to assist. According to Bel Geddes, Griffith had been "floundering for a month or more."[95] Elaborating significantly on the Halsey script, Bel Geddes drew up his own scenario just 36 hours later (the rough draft in his papers runs for four pages, though he claims it was ten pages long in his autobiography). He also put together 13 charcoal drawings (he recalls only 12 in the autobiography), and reports that the "delighted" producers immediately asked him to film the sequence, unbeknownst to Griffith. He agreed, ironically, because what he saw of Griffith's own final scene seemed so incongruent with the rest of the film: "[Fred] Waller [Bel Geddes's camera-man] ran off the latest Griffith rushes for me. They were as close to the drawings of Gustave Doré for *Paradise Lost* as scenery and camera could get, and, as far as I was concerned, totally unrelated to the earlier, or earthly, part of the film. Almost any change would have been an improvement." As Bel Geddes recalls, his sequence unfolded from the central conflict between Michael and Lucifer:

> The central issue of the final sequence was the expulsion of Lucifer from Heaven by Michael the Archangel, after the former had, as it were, crashed the gates to protest God's having made him in man's image. I began the sequence in total darkness. Lucifer's advent was announced by a dazzling flash of light splitting the darkness, and pushing it back slowly as though two gigantic doors had opened over the Stygian blackness. As one's eyes became used to the bright light, a group of figures with Lucifer in the lead could be discerned making its way up an immense staircase, which took form gradually out of the horizontal light rays. In the next moment Michael the Archangel, his sword a shimmering flame, appeared with his attendant angels at the top of the stairs. Immediately Lucifer and company took the form of devils, and the battle was joined. Naturally Michael and his cohorts prevailed and dropped Lucifer and his followers back into the impenetrable pit.[96]

Though Griffith went back and reshot Bel Geddes's sequence himself, eventually reverting to using it as the film's prologue, Bel Geddes said that "in the finished product about half of the film Waller and I had shot was used, as was ninety per cent of my scenario."[97] Still, Bel Geddes's recollection is a substantially accurate transcription of the sequence as it appears in the final film. The war in heaven is striking, as dazzling as Bel Geddes remembers it, but brief (see fig. 3.4).

After an opening title that sets the scene with a bit of quasi-Miltonic lyricism—"Because God created man in His divine image, Lucifer—mightiest of the Archangels—rose in rebellion, and with all his bright host was hurled from the gates of Heaven"—Lucifer leads his phalanx up the steps of heaven, a steady climb toward gleaming light. The shot changes then, the camera beginning to corner the troop in the lower left quadrant of the frame, while a broad expanse of screen remains for the host of angels led by Michael to zoom across. The effect emends whatever awkwardness Griffith sunk to in *Avenging Conscience*—these angels are brazen and full of intent, bearing gleaming armor and sunburst shields, firing like javelins from the light of the heavenly gate. There is not a single sick or woebegone white-sock-on-a-washline among them. The entire panoply, as Bel Geddes indicated, derives from Doré's engraving of the fallen host "Hurl'd headlong flaming from th' Ethereal sky" (*PL* 1.45). Ripples of pulsating light follow the angelic host across the screen, washing over the rebel angels. Michael and the rest hover menacingly over their pedestrian brethren, who seem to cringe and cower beneath them. There is, however, more sabre rattling than clash of arms in this scene. In fact, there is no clash of arms whatsoever—no stampeding warhorses or fiery chariots or thundering cannons, only a confrontation at the threshold. Bel Geddes's account of a "battle joined" overstates the violence considerably. In his draft of the scenario, the archangel "advances towards Lucifer. His Knights follow him. All swords are held point upward. Lucifer remains immovable, fearless, though his followers have retreated some distance away from him and would run if they knew where."[98] The ensuing transformation of Lucifer is more grotesque and painful than the final film—"their skins become thick and fold in heavy plaits like a rhinoceros but looking more like the shelled body of a crayfish"—but the attack is never resisted (see fig. 3.5).

While the solar sigils on the shields may allude to the Son, he too is notably absent. The film also remotivates Satan's rebellion, ascribing it to his resentment of the elevation of humanity rather than the Son. Michael himself, backed by his sword-brandishing fellows, condemns and banishes Satan: "Lucifer thou shalt be called no more! Satan shall be thy name—and forever thou shalt tempt the sons of men to sin against the God who made you both!" Still Satan, despite his relegation to the lower corner

Fig. 3.4. The war in heaven, from Griffith's *The Sorrows of Satan* (1926). *Courtesy of Museum of Modern Art.*

Fig. 3.5. Norman Bel Geddes sketch for the opening sequence of *The Sorrows of Satan. Harry Ransom Center, The University of Texas at Austin. Image courtesy of the Edith Lutyens and Norman Bel Geddes Foundation.*

of the shot, nonetheless gets all the close-ups. We see him first as golden haired, armored and plumed like his fellow angels. Then as Satan bows down we see him and his troop transformed into the devils of Doré: bat-winged, ebon haired, goat horned, with black capes and armor. The essential plot device is then set in motion, as Michael declares "Only when all men turn from thee, canst thou resume thy glorious place at God's right hand—yet for every soul that resists thee, thou shalt have one hour at the gates of Paradise!" In a final compelling cinematic stroke, Satan and his fellows seem to fall and tumble rapidly down the screen, as if sucked into some offscreen vortex.

At this point most of Bel Geddes's particular vision seems to have been cut. He had extended the fall of Satan into a series of elongated movements through space, ending with a pitch into darkness visible. Satan streaks like a comet while "the spectacle of the heavens rushes by like streaks of fire as they pass the various strata of atmosphere, air currents, milky way, nebulae, stars, clouds, and suggestion of a recognizable planet such as Saturn." Unlike in the Halsey script, the angels fall into the bowels of the earth and a largely Miltonic hell, "rush[ing] past the camera, through the clouds, falling away at a terrifying pace toward their own shadows" (see fig. 3.6). When they land, there is complete blackness. Gradually, this becomes a "semi-darkness," around which can be seen the topography of hell, "not unlike the crater of a volcano." Pools of molten metal serve as a lake of fire. The fallen are "terror stricken" and "behave like whining curs until suddenly Lucifer jumps into the midst." But after this Miltonic scene, Bel Geddes concludes with Halsey's device, albeit displaced into the "foul-sired entrails of the material earth": "Standing on a slight eminence, steam rising around him, his figure lit by a molten glow, Lucifer strides toward the camera until the horror of his presence fills the whole screen."[99] The imagery of Milton's opening book pervades the sequence, and it is interesting that—with all the oblique Milton indicators—this most literal adaptation of *Paradise Lost* should be excised. Part of this must be due to Griffith's repossession of the film's tenor and scope, at the expense of whatever Bel Geddes filmed, and it does seem that artistically the vision of space and hell so close to a Miltonic sublime overwhelms the quiet, quotidian treatment of impoverishment (or, for that matter, the bland decadence) that Griffith occupies himself with throughout much of the film. The heaven prologue, meanwhile, perhaps because it is relatively so tame and contained (Bel Geddes had a grander vision of the Elysian fields that was also cut), did not in the end provide such an abrupt, or overshadowing, addition to the film as a whole. In this ambivalent attitude toward Milton, this strong desire complicating an inferiority complex, an anxiety of influence, can be seen the template for a number of later treatments.

In the remainder of the film, Satan's redemption depends on a kind of universal chastity, and his paradoxical hope that humankind

Fig. 3.6. Norman Bel Geddes sketch, scene for the fall of Satan (cut from the final film). *Harry Ransom Center, The University of Texas at Austin. Image courtesy of the Edith Lutyens and Norman Bel Geddes Foundation.*

will resist his irresistible charms. His reward, too, recalls Milton's lines on chastity in Corelli's novel: an hour of potential "converse with heavenly habitants" for each soul that sincerely denies him. The main narrative is as Faustian as Miltonic, though it offers at least one speech that hearkens back to Satan's lines in *Paradise Lost*. Tempest (Ricardo Cortez), like Griffith in his youth, is a struggling poet. Across the hall of his boardinghouse is another struggling writer, Mavis Clare (Carol Dempster). They fall in love over their shared artistic leanings and common misfortunes, and plan to marry. There is considerable distress at the start over Tempest's aggressive courting of Mavis—she wants to maintain her principles even while she loves him passionately but can hardly resist crossing the corridor to his room. They finally do spend a night together (chastely) in Tempest's apartment, an act that nevertheless registers as a fall. Though there has been no sex, Mavis is abashed when the conservative landlady observes her leaving Tempest's room. Afraid of suffering some postlapsarian punishment (even without a crime), Mavis is troubled until Tempest surprises her with a marriage proposal. Happy but penurious, the couple pawns a watch to raise the money for a marriage license, and all seems well until Tempest loses his job as a hack reviewer, even as Mavis's literary fortunes reverse with the paid acceptance of a short story.

At this point, Tempest breaks down, as the film makes an explicit connection between his misery and that of Satan in heaven: "Bitter rebellion was all that Tempest got from his reverses." His fulfillment of that figure continues as Tempest rails against the Almighty, "God's love! God's justice! I could run things better than He does!" This and Tempest's ensuing promise to sell his soul for money cues the entrance of the devil himself, the spiffy and urbane Prince Lucio Riminez (Adolphe Menjou). His appearance echoes the poetic epigraph that begins the entire film, a bit of verse from Heinrich Heine: "I called the Devil and he came, / And with wonder his form did I scan; / He is not ugly, and is not lame, / But really a handsome and charming man." The merging of two devilish discourses here—the tempting trader in souls and the divine rebel—has its source in the source, as it were, and derives as much from Milton as Heine. In Corelli's novel, Mavis remarks on the suave appeal of Milton's Satan: "'I never picture

him as the possessor of hoofs and a tail,—common sense assures
me that no creature presenting himself under such an aspect would
have the slightest power to attract. Milton's conception of Satan
is the finest,'—and her eyes darkened swiftly with the intensity of
her thoughts—'A mighty Angel fallen!'" The moment highlights
a general fusion in the film of romanticized Milton with a conventional deal-with-the-devil morality tale. It is Tempest's Miltonic
desires, however, that are clearly unanswered; he never gets to rule
in heaven, to "run things better than He does." Instead, the prince
appears at the crash of thunder to reveal a miracle: Tempest has
inherited a fortune from a forgotten uncle that will make him one
of the richest men in the world. The film seems wary of embracing the sympathetic Satan (eventually disclosing his monstrosities)
even as it depends on that very evocation. As the story heads toward
its climax, Tempest follows the prince's every bidding, abandoning Mavis and her modest success and marrying instead a Russian
princess, Olga Godovsky (Lya de Putti). It is a Faustian triangle,
with Lucio his Mephistopheles, Olga his Helen; it is probably not
a coincidence that F. W. Murnau's masterful *Faust* appeared this
same year. Olga also exudes qualities of Milton's Sin: Lucio is
both her undoer and her beloved, an antitype to the "unconquerable soul" of Mavis, just as Sin serves as a type and foil for Eve in
Paradise Lost. Olga kills herself after being rejected by Lucio and
Tempest flees back to Mavis after Lucio reveals his true, monstrous
form. Mavis's true heart saves them both.

Despite Henderson's view that "the production of *The Sorrows
of Satan* was a descent into disaster," contemporary reviews were
generally positive. Mordaunt Hall, reviewing the picture for the
New York Times, saw it as a triumph: "a photodrama that excels
anything he has done in recent years" and "a marvelously beautiful
film." He notes too the film's chiaroscuro, the "soft shadows" and
"bright lights" that body forth the classic Griffith binaries: poverty
and decadence, desperation and faith, relentless ambition and quiet
sacrifice. What has become the iconic image from the film—the
shadow of a metamorphosed devil, all wings and loathing, projected over a terrified Tempest—was for Hall the only false note
(though he admits the first half of the film was "far more absorbing

than the latter").[100] In confronting the unmasked prince, Cortez seemed "overdone," unnatural—easily recognizable to a modern viewer as a bit of B-movie mugging for the monster—in an otherwise satisfying dramatization of the hellish and the heavenly.

While not a popular film, in Hall's review *The Sorrows of Satan* achieves its considerable artistic success in those moments when Griffith came closest to transforming it into the Miltonic. Griffith never did direct a feature-length adaptation of *Paradise Lost,* but from the spectacle of the war in heaven to the handsome charms of Satan, and even the latent sermonizing of *Comus, The Sorrows of Satan* did begin the trailblazing for adaptations of Milton in later twentieth century filmmaking. Whether early cinema ever realized its aim at producing a new sublimity, an emerging discourse on the power of film to subsume the energies of the epic gained significant force. Even as adapting *Paradise Lost* sometimes signified all that was *wrong* with the appropriation of classics and high art by Hollywood, directors like Maggi, Bracken, and Griffith—and all the others who saw the potential in the poem for the greatest picture ever made—established just how desirable Milton could be.

The Ambivalence of
the Miltonic Film

After the silent era, the drive to adapt *Paradise Lost* into a feature film has a decidedly ambivalent history. The most ambitious attempt in the twentieth century was John Collier's, but this film project suffered one serious setback after another, eventually coming to fruition only as a stand-alone screenplay hybrid. However, in the absence of a direct adaptation, one finds instead a far-reaching field of quotations, citations, allusions, reminders, borrowings, and outright poachings of John Milton's works in multiple films and genres. At the same time, the presence of Milton on film is often marked by his absence: negations, excisions, denials, and other acts of unmaking that leave him on the cutting-room floor. Many of these forms of resistance are in direct keeping with Addison's succinct rebuttal regarding the "too seriousness" of the poet for popular entertainment. This chapter charts these acts of appropriation—for even the films that seize upon Milton only to reject him are dynamic engagements—in films throughout the modern era, culminating in Collier's sustained but ultimately frustrated effort.

One unifying impression is that attention to the spectacular in Milton has given way, in many films, to Milton as a preeminent poet of the establishment. While Griffith saw Milton's sublimity as complicit with a new poetics of the cinema, contemporary films tend to foreground Milton as a poet in order to enact some distance between the poetic and cinematic modes. While still keyed to spectacle—Milton is routinely credited with opening up for the cinema the endless vistas of outer space—the poet's works are also put to broader use, with greater borrowing from texts beyond *Paradise Lost*—especially *Comus, Samson Agonistes,* and his lyrical poetry.

In the most telling mainstream instance of Milton on film, John Landis's *Animal House* (1978), the English professor Dave Jennings, played craftily by Donald Sutherland, attempts to teach the epic to a group of uninterested and unresponsive undergraduates. The film shares much with *Paradise Lost*—even the title *Animal House* is evocative of Satan's palace, with demonic fallen angels transferred to a bestial fraternity—and at various times references the temptation of Eve, debates on free will, antiauthoritarian rebellion, and other strains of Milton's epic. Yet in perpetuating a general ambivalence about Milton, its lasting portrayal of *Paradise Lost* is as a text devoid of interest.

The classroom scene begins *in medias res*—in fact, the Milton "lecture" lasts less than two minutes before a bell rings for dismissal, so presumably the students have been covering some other material for the bulk of their time. It is worth pointing out that the class, then, is already terminally bored before Jennings introduces *Paradise Lost,* though the poem does nothing to raise student enthusiasm or rouse those already asleep. Jennings himself begins a bit listlessly, "Now...what can we say of John Milton's *Paradise Lost?* Well, it's a very long poem, it was written a long time ago, and I'm sure a lot of you have difficulty understanding exactly what Milton was trying to say. Certainly we know that he was trying to describe the struggle between good and evil, right?" At this point Jennings swipes an apple from off his desk before continuing: "Okay. The most intriguing character, as we all know from our reading, was Satan. Now, was Milton trying to tell us that being bad was more fun than being good?" Cue the biting of the apple. There is a pregnant pause as he chews, but not a single student takes him up on the question. (Jennings has timed this question somewhat inelegantly, however, asking with only seconds left in the class period, the graveyard shift for a professor wanting students to take up such a problem.) Furthermore, if Jennings intends the apple-eating dramatization as a kind of joke, this too fails—not even a snicker from his audience. The silence leads Jennings to break character, as he moves to align himself with his young readers—not to seem sympathetic to Satan but hip to the tedium of Milton the man: "Okay...don't write this down, but I find Milton probably as boring as you find Milton. Mrs. Milton found him boring, too. He, uh, he's a little bit long-winded, he doesn't translate very well into our generation, and his jokes are terrible."

That Jennings wants to be counted as part of the students' own generation is clear, and elaborated further in the film when he hosts several of them at his house and invites them to smoke weed. (That scene, along with the later revelation that he is sleeping with at least one of his students, helps mark him further as tempter.) That he is failing at being included is also clear, since his own jokes seem to flop as terribly as Milton's. When the bell rings, the students jump up and disperse, while Jennings tries feebly to make his final point: "But that does not relieve you from your responsibility for this material! Now, I'm waiting for reports from some of you! Listen, I'm not joking! This is my job!"

Not usually noted about this scene is that Jennings here, and later, fashions himself as Satan against Milton with unhappy results for both. Which is to say, he eats the apple not as Adam (or Eve) but as the devil. His attempt to revive the spiritless students into an engagement with "the struggle between good and evil" recalls Satan's opening oration to the fallen angels, whom he finds "slumber[ing]" on the lake (*PL* 1.321). Milton underscores that they languish in their fiery prison more from lassitude than divine constraint, even with the first imperative, "Awake," of Satan's exhortation: "Awake, arise, or be for ever fall'n" (1.330), and the ensuing epic simile develops the same somnolent image:

"They heard, and were abasht, and up they sprung / Upon the wing, as when men wont to watch / On duty, sleeping found by whom they dread, / Rouse and bestir themselves ere well awake" (1.331–34). In *Animal House,* even Satan, whom Jennings both wants to be and wants to be intriguing, fails to rouse: it is the sonorous bell that sends the students rushing out and about like a swarm of locusts, while Jennings struggles to be heard over the din. The students will not only not speak about the poem, they will not write about it. One is led to conclude they are not reading it at all. In fact, the film seems to argue that they may not be reading it because they are already living it. The scene that leads into the classroom sequence is a satanic-looking fraternity hazing, to "consecrate the bond of obedience," complete with black robes, occult symbols, rows of candles, and sadomasochistic ritual spanking. The pledge (Kevin Bacon) paddled during the ceremony is also the first exhausted undergraduate shown in close-up in the lecture hall, visibly oblivious to any connection between his previous night's activities and the assigned poem.[1]

What this sequence impressed upon generations of filmgoers was a Milton not only serious but tedious, uncool, and unfunny—and, if "Mrs. Milton" is any indication, unsexy to boot. As Douglas L. Howard remarks, the classroom scene advances the "moral of the film that 'being bad is more fun than being good,'" with Satan signifying the film's social and political "challenge to authority."[2] But the film ultimately rejects Milton's Satan for other, less sententious kinds of misrule. Even as the film maintains the old Johnsonian allowance that, despite the hindrances of *Paradise Lost,* one is still "responsible for this material," nothing in the film provides incentive to pay such attention. In the carnival, carnal energies of *Animal House,* general disobedience prevails at Milton's expense rather than with his backing. The war in heaven becomes a food fight in the cafeteria, or a doodle of fighter jets, one crashing into flames as the other opens fire, as one student scribbles during the *Paradise Lost* lecture. Or it becomes a morality-play debate between a lascivious devil and puritanical angel over whether a passed-out date should be molested. Such ambivalence over the use of Milton can be seen in a number of films that follow—many of which are virtual reenactments of the Jennings classroom scene.[3]

In the case of *Paradise Lost,* few films sharing that title have any significant debt to Milton beyond as a common catchphrase. A long line of such films stretches back at least 80 years: F. W. Murnau's film *Tabu* (1931), a drama set in the South Pacific, was also known as *Paradise Lost.* The 1948 Italian short *Il paradiso perduto,* directed by Luciano Emmer and Enrico Grass, is based on the paintings of Hieronymus Bosch. Those with an environmental bent include the Canadian antipollution short *Paradise Lost* (dir. Evelyn Lambart, 1970) and Herb Freed's *Paradise Lost* (1999), concerned with the destruction of rain forests. The Japanese film *Shitsurakuen* (*Paradise Lost*), directed in 1997 by Yoshimitsu Morina, covers sex and infidelity. There is the schlocky thriller *Paradise Lost* (dir. John Stockwell, 2006, released as *Turistas* in the United States), where unwitting backpackers stumble into an organ-harvesting operation in the middle of the Brazilian jungle. Benicio del Toro stars as drug lord Pablo Escobar in the biopic *Paradise Lost* (dir. Andrea Di Stefano, 2014), set in Colombia. And most prominently, as representations of fallen innocence, there are the HBO *Paradise Lost* documentaries treating crimes against children, beginning with *The Child Murders at Robin Hood Hills* (dir. Joe Berlinger and Bruce Sinofsky, 1996). Undoubtedly the most unexpected mash-up of Milton's title and moving pictures comes from an episode of the animated children's television show *The Smurfs,* called simply *Paradise Smurfed.*[4] Three of the small blue beings—Lazy, Brainy, and Greedy—enter a kind of Land of Cockaigne, governed by Bacchus, where their every need is met. Once satiated, the Smurfs are hunted by Bacchus, who tries to capture and eat them as the garden transforms into a hazardous land of giant carnivorous plants and frozen waterfalls.

However, as these rampant appropriations of the title "Paradise Lost" imply, there is cultural capital to be gained even with the most superficial alignments with Milton's work. One recurring device is the insertion of some volume of Milton into a film's mise-en-scène. At times this amounts to little more than a materialized name-dropping, a "book dropping" that displays prominently but often vacuously the tome or the name "John Milton" on the cover, with little concern for what lies within. This is epitomized in Kevin Costner's futuristic *Waterworld* (dir. Kevin Reynolds, 1995), when

Costner's character, Mariner, uncovers an old *National Geographic* with dry land and palm trees on the cover, titled "Paradise Lost." The value of the book *qua* book is exhibited in the comical 1939 murder mystery *Fast and Loose* (dir. Edwin L. Marin), when a stolen first edition of *Paradise Lost* is lovingly pawed over. Though the plot focuses primarily on a forged Shakespeare manuscript, the Milton book comes in a close second: "Here's a first edition of *Paradise Lost*. I don't have to tell you how rare or how valuable it is." And in *Sunday Bloody Sunday* (dir. John Schlesinger, 1971), about triangulating sexual affairs, a short attempt to render *Paradise Lost* during a game of charades suffices to convey the intellectuality of the partygoers ("Two words. A book").

With only slightly greater elaboration, the difficult-to-characterize *Henry Fool* (dir. Hal Hartley, 1998) sketches the implausible rise of a downtrodden garbage man, Simon Grim (James Urbaniak), into a Nobel Prize–winning poet. His guide is Henry Fool (Thomas Jay Ryan), alternately satanic scoundrel and Virgilian pedagogue, guiding Simon by the scruff of his neck up from an underworld of illiteracy. Over the course of the bildungsroman, Simon learns to appreciate the work of other poets. Henry has Simon check out *Paradise Lost* from the local library ("Milton. Seventeenth Century. English"). In the shooting script, Simon stumbles upon a quote — "Whereto with speedy words th' Arch-fiend repli'd. / Fall'n Cherub, to be weak is miserable" (*PL* 1.156–57) — that seems to double as a message from his fiendish guru for Simon to embolden himself, particularly around girls. In the film, the Milton quote is cut and Simon simply wanders the library stacks, *Paradise Lost* in hand, scaring away the women he bumps into.

As with *The Wrath of Khan,* however, the egregious presence of a Milton book can work effectively as an amplified "phraseological adaptation" and extend deeply into other narrative and thematic elements of a film. An especially attractive copy of *Paradise Lost,* for instance, looms large in the 1941 adaptation of Jack London's novel *The Sea-Wolf.* In London's tale, a writer and sensitive intellectual, Humphrey Van Weyden, must survive being dragged into a brutal life on board a Pacific sealing ship, captained by the domineering sociopath Wolf Larsen. The Michael Curtiz film conflates two scenes in the book that establish and develop Larsen's surprising literacy. While cleaning Larsen's state-room for the first time, Van Weyden discovers a shelf of books that seem to contrast with the uncivilized barbarity he has witnessed in the captain: "I glanced over them, noting with astonishment such names as Shakespeare, Tennyson, Poe, and De Quincey."[5] While he does not mention Milton, later in the novel Larsen shows his fluency by expounding at length on *Paradise Lost* and its heroic rebel: "he was preaching the passion of revolt. It was inevitable that Milton's Lucifer should be instanced, and the keenness with which Wolf Larsen analyzed and depicted the character was a revelation of his stifled genius."[6] After expatiating on Satan's defiance and resilience, his strong will and individuality, Larsen recites several lines from the "Here at least / We shall be free" speech (*PL* 1.258–59).

Curtiz combines these elements so that when Van Weyden is sorting through Larsen's cabin, he discovers the bookshelf with such literary titles in close-up as *The Works of Edgar Allan Poe* and De Quincey's *Confessions of an English Opium Eater*. He then notices, opened on a desk beneath him, a lavish Victorian folio edition of *Paradise Lost* with illustrations by Gustave Doré. He picks it up as the camera closes on the front cover, which announces in gilt lettering, "Milton's *Paradise Lost*." There is a cut to an insert of the bookmarked page itself; the same speech given in the novel is here underlined in pencil. Portions of the surrounding text are also visible—the frame first stretches from, roughly, "What matter where" until "Him followed his next mate," before closing for a few readable seconds on the lines from "We shall be free" to "Better to reign in Hell than serve in Heaven." When Larsen (Edward G. Robinson) abruptly enters to find Van Weyden with book in hand, the "literary cabin-boy" tries nervously to explain himself to the Captain—"I happened to find this lying open...and"—before Larsen sits and remarks coolly, "That's a great poem isn't it?" Van Weyden replies simply, "Yes, it's a great poem." Larsen commands him, "Read me some of it," and Van Weyden complies by reading aloud from the underscored lines: "Here at least we shall be free, here we may reign secure, and in my choice to reign is worth ambition though in hell." Larsen then interrupts and finishes the speech: "Better to reign in hell than serve in heaven." "That's a great line," he concludes. "Milton really understood the devil."[7]

A comparable effect is achieved in the HBO film *Cheaters* (dir. John Stockwell, 2000), based on the scandalous 1995 U.S. Academic Decathlon competition in Chicago, when high school English teacher Dr. Jerry Plecki guided his working-class team from Steinmetz High to an unexpected victory against perennial power magnet school, Whitney Young. The team from Steinmetz had managed to obtain a copy of the written exam in advance of the competition, and with Plecki's backing used the exam to upset Whitney Young; when accusations of cheating became public, the students from Steinmetz, and Plecki himself, stridently maintained their innocence, while the controversy over the accusations themselves, and the revelations that followed, sparked a firestorm of national media attention. Plecki is played in the film by Jeff Daniels, his team depicted as a group of gifted but underachieving students whom fortune has placed in a school where they have no chance to succeed. While they manage to place high enough in a regional meet to advance to the state competition, the film makes clear they have no legitimate chance to defeat their nearly omniscient opponents from Whitney Young, the nine-year reigning champions with all the privilege, pomposity, and "unlimited budget" Steinmetz lacks. The basic moral dilemma of the film arrives when the hardworking rebels come upon the contraband copy of the state test and have to decide whether to cheat their way to victory or lose with integrity. In making this choice, they are guided by their teacher and the lessons of *Paradise Lost,* the text which bookends the entire film: when the deck has been so unfairly stacked as to leave no choice, and submission is not an option, they effectively determine to dethrone their opponents by working "in close design, by fraud or guile" (*PL* 1.646).

The film begins with a montage of hellacious scenes in and around the high school—police attempting to keep control in the halls, students passing through metal detectors into the "Gun Free Zone"—before settling on a classroom in which students are reading from *Paradise Lost*. One of the students, Aisa (Aisa Soloduszkiewicz), is doing her best with Satan's lines from book 1:

> What matter where, if I be still the same,
> And what I should be, all but less than hee

Whom Thunder hath made greater? Here at least
We shall be free; th' Almighty hath not built
Here for his envy, will not drive us hence:
Here we may reign secure, and in my choice
To reign is worth ambition though in Hell:
Better to reign in Hell, than serve in Heav'n.[8]   (*PL* 1.256–63)

The lines are meant both to ironize (these students are anything but free as they are searched and scanned on their way into the pandemonium of school) and to anticipate the central dilemma: is it better to be the best of the worst than the worst of the best?

The entire scene recalls the classroom scene in *Animal House,* when Professor Jennings stands before his inattentive and uninterested collection of undergraduates. Here is yet another teacher struggling to communicate the poem to those who find no meaning or relevance in it: "Um, so what do we think Satan meant when he said, 'Better to reign in hell than serve in heaven?...Anything? Any ideas? Anybody?" The class remains as void of answers as Jennings's laconic group. Again following Sutherland's professor, a clearly frustrated Plecki tries to kindle interest by switching tack and trying to relate: "OK, alright. What, what if...you had a choice. What if...you could live in a mansion in Highland Park but you have to be the chauffeur. Or you can live in a shelter on lower Wacker Drive but you would be the king of that shelter, which would you choose?" One of the students asks for a qualification—"If I'm the chauffeur, what kind of car I drive?," before setting off a brief melee in the middle of class. After order is restored, the star pupil, Jolie Fitch (Jena Malone), finally offers a direct response: "Pride. That's what it's all about. Lucifer was too proud to play runner-up to someone he felt superior to, so he set up his own shop." When Plecki asks, in reply, "And what did Dante say was written on the gates of Lucifer's shop?," Fitch replies by quoting the famous inscription: "Abandon all hope, ye who enter here." To which another student quips, "That's what it should say on the door to this school." Fitch goes on to make a case for the Fall—that Adam and Eve just wanted knowledge, and that God was remiss in not telling them *why* they could not eat. "He was just, you know, 'I'm in charge here, do what I say.'"

And together, she and Plecki serve as the driving forces for the remainder of the film—they recruit the decathlon team and heavily influence their decision to cheat, with Fitch throughout playing Beelzebub to Plecki's Satan.

Indeed, the strongest Miltonic imprint on the film is the idea of Plecki as a romantic Satan, fighting against a corrupt system and convincing himself that his battle is a righteous one. During the opening classroom scene, one of the marked contrasts with the *Animal House* sequence is the writing on the chalkboard. Unlike Jennings with his dramatic and singular scrawl ("SATAN"), Plecki has filled the space with intriguing discussion questions—a teacher who has not only put some thought into his lesson plan, but also clearly disagrees with the central *Animal House* premise: that Milton is boring, unfunny, irrelevant. The questions themselves articulate Plecki's iconoclasm: "What is the primary source for *Paradise Lost*? Is everything in this poem the Gospel truth?" Should we take, in other words, authority at its word? The film is generally balanced in its treatment of the Plecki character and the system against which he is fighting, noting, for instance, the stultifying U.S. Academic Decathlon slogan, "Building skills that work in corporate America," while also problematizing Plecki's moral choices—he seems driven as much by personal demons (such as the unrewarded life of his immigrant father) as any revolutionary vision about the fairness of the public school system.

The film, in short, presents Plecki as potentially both a sympathetic and deplorable Satan. He is leader of the fallen (the student who finally blows the whistle on the cheating declares, "I now know what it's like to sell my soul to the devil") and a champion of the downtrodden. In one self-reflexive sequence, the whistle-blower is offered a movie deal in which he will be shown as the upright hero against the surrounding "disciples of darkness," while other media spin Plecki's defiance as bravery, a romantic spirit attacking all of life's inequalities. The characterization of Plecki as Satan continues to the end: one investigator, interrogating a Catholic student, demands of him, "remember what the Bible says: 'Repent so that your sins may be blotted out, lest Satan take advantage of us, for we are not ignorant of his devices.'" And after the combination of Acts and Corinthians convinces the student to confess, the investigator triumphantly declares to the press that Plecki was the "leader of this cult," brainwashing the kids into cheating, and that he "made sure they'd follow him to the gates of hell, and then break them down for him."

In the wake of this fall, and all the "lost innocence" projected onto his students, Plecki eventually looks to go underground, but not before one last surreptitious meeting with them. He tells them he is leaving and that he has come to understand their experience as "civil disobedience." The students, in turn, present him with "a little something": a copy of *Paradise Lost,* inscribed to "the best teacher we ever had." In this last gesture, the film makes a case for Milton's Satan as a prototype for defiant titanism, political agitation, and the triumph of will. The system has by this point stripped Steinmetz of its trophies and title, but the students' gift suggests that they have in actuality neither repented nor changed. Their minds are their own, and in the film's epilogue Fitch tells us that for her the fall was a fortunate one (she has since enrolled in college — "a good one" — and is considering becoming a teacher), and that she would succumb to the same temptation again in a heartbeat.

Beyond building an alliance with satanic subtexts, another of the prevailing reasons films turn to or invoke *Paradise Lost* is not for Milton's visualization of heaven or hell but for his depiction of the earthly paradise (a compulsion evident more superficially in the environmentalist appropriation of the phrase/title "paradise lost.") The overall approach to Milton's Eden is often oblique, as with *King Kong,* where the cinematography owes more to the illustrations of Doré than Milton's poetical descriptions.[9] I have not found, for instance, any film concerned with Genesis that makes use of Milton's striking Creation sequence, when "The grassy Clods now Calv'd" and a menagerie of animals erupt from the earth, as "the swift Stag from under ground / Bore up his branching head" (*PL* 7.463, 469–70). C. S. Lewis's *The Magician's Nephew* uses Milton's details in its Creation chapter, when the "grassy...humps moved and swelled till they burst," right down to the "stags" whose "antlers came up a long time before the rest of them." If the book is ever adapted, as was announced in 2011, perhaps Milton—at one step removed—will also come to light.[10]

However, two citations of Milton's Eden in Charles Dickens's *Great Expectations* (1861) have been transposed into film adaptations of the novel. When Pip is first headed to London at the end of the First Stage, his narration closely echoes the expulsion of Adam and Eve from the garden: "And the mists had all solemnly risen now, and the world lay spread before me."[11] (Milton writes, "The World was all before them, where to choose / Thir place of rest, and Providence thir guide: / They hand in hand with wand'ring steps and slow / Through *Eden* took thir solitary way" [*PL* 12.646–49].) At the end of the novel, the echoes return as Pip and Estella are rejoined: "I took her hand in mine, and we went out of the ruined place, and as the morning mists had risen long ago when I first left the forge, so, the evening mists were rising now, and in the broad expanse of tranquil light they showed me, I saw the shadow of no parting from her."[12] Dickens's allusion to the finale of *Paradise Lost* also extends to a slightly earlier passage describing the arrival of the angels:

> The Cherubim descended; on the ground
> Gliding meteorous, as Ev'ning Mist
> Ris'n from a River o'er the marish glides,
> And gathers fast at the Laborer's heel
> Homeward returning.[13]   (12.628–32)

The evening mists rising are meant to recall not only Pip's earlier passage but also Milton's entire simile: the mists advance upon the laborer who has finished his work, as Pip has seemingly come to the end of his arduous journey.

In the 1998 modernized *Great Expectations,* director Alfonso Cuarón makes the Milton citations explicit. The decayed mansion of Ms. Dinsmoor (Dickens's Miss Havisham) is called "Paradiso Perduto," and the film itself was released under this title in Italy. (In the novel, Havisham lives in "Satis House," a title explicated at some length by Estella as "mean[ing] more than it said," and sounding not a little like "Satan's House.")[14] Cuarón's final sequence condenses the close of the novel with the Miltonic subtext: Finn sits in the sprawling Florida estate of Paradise Lost, surrounded by Spanish moss and ladybugs and frogs but also cherubic statuary, the angelic guard come to guide him out. There is a shot of birds rising from the dilapidated ruins and soaring into the heavens, and in the final shot Finn takes Estella's hand as they gaze out over the sun-dappled Sarasota Gulf. The end of the David Lean adaptation (1946) makes the citation even more explicitly visual, as Pip and Estella run hand-in-hand from Satis House and, with one look back, pass through the iron gate and into the panoramic world beyond, eager to "start again, together." In both cases the final shots are romantic and sublime—Cuarón's might have been painted by Caspar David Friedrich—but build to this as Milton might by framing the pictorial energy of flowing, impenetrable mist against the earthy immediacy of a laborer's heel.

Traces of Milton's Eden appear elsewhere, albeit briefly. In *Mother Ghost* (dir. Rich Thorne, 2002), for example, a line from book 4 appears on a tombstone: "Flowers of all hue and without thorn the rose" (*PL* 4.256). A more interesting infiltration occurs in Michael Radford's adaptation of Shakespeare's *The Merchant of Venice* (2004). The film ends with a song not from the play but from *Paradise Lost:* "With Wand'ring Steps," taken from the epic's final lines and sung by German countertenor Andreas Scholl.[15] Similar interpolations with Shakespeare's texts had been done not long earlier in another film—the opening of Richard Loncraine's *Richard III* (1995) features a version of Marlowe's "Passionate Shepherd" (with Raleigh's response folded in for good measure). But how did Milton's Adam and Eve, even extradiegetically, get into *The Merchant of Venice?* While the song plays over final shots of Antonio and Shylock, both alone at the end, the very last sequence shows a troubled Jessica darting through the towering garden of Belmont, angelic statuary above her as if guarding the gate. A close-up follows, showing that she still wears the turquoise ring her father thought sold; the image seems to redeem her love for the abandoned Shylock. The lyrics "They hand in hand with wandering steps and slow" thus offer an interpretive model for this Shakespearean father/daughter, forging a spiritual link between their (ringed) hands, akin to Adam and Eve departing after the Fall. The supplementation from Milton further implies some inadequacy, or indeterminacy, in Shakespeare's own conclusion.

Another highly influential scene—the opening of hell's gates onto Chaos—has contributed to *Paradise Lost*'s attribution as a seminal work of science fiction, and science fiction films have been some of the most avid appropriators of Milton.[16] (It is one of those moments that distinguishes his cinematic sensibility from Shakespeare's—Puck may girdle the globe, but Shakespeare does not invite us to go along with him.) Thus, Satan's voyage becomes a space odyssey ("Satan is one of the first space-travelers," affirms one critic).[17] Subsequent moments in the poem celebrate and ponder other worlds—from the chorus of angels praising the Maker and imagining, at Creation, "every Starr perhaps a World / Of destin'd habitation" (*PL* 7.621–22) to Raphael's hypothesizing about life on the moon, a lunar landscape with its own fruits and rains, its own "Fields and Inhabitants" (8.145), and about whether this moon may be but one of many found with "other Suns" (8.148).[18]

In *Perestroika* (dir. Slava Tsukerman, 2009), a film preoccupied with ideas of revolution, the story picks up at an international conference on the "structure of the universe." The head of the conference, Professor Gross (F. Murray Abraham), kicks off with a poetic invocation: "I would like to read a brief passage from Milton's *Paradise Lost*. In this passage, the angel Raphael is speaking to Adam and Eve." The lines, significant for a gathering of astrophysicists, are from book 8, lines 66–80: "To ask or search I blame thee not, for Heav'n / Is as the Book of God before thee set, / Wherein to read his wond'rous Works, and learn / His Seasons, Hours, or Days, or Months, or Years." The professor continues, "the rest / From Man or Angel the great Architect / Did wisely to conceal / . . . to move / His laughter at thir quaint Opinions wide / Hereafter, when they come to model Heav'n / And calculate the stars." Gross then takes on the role of a subversive, technocratic Satan as he challenges whether the "Great Architect's" secrets will remain hidden much longer, and casts with defiance his final lines, "He who laughs last laughs longest."

Despite Raphael's interdiction not to pursue such fanciful theories—"Dream not of other worlds," he tells Adam, "what Creatures there" (*PL* 8.175)—Milton's poem has prompted numerous tropes for extraterrestrial adventures. The well-worn mission of the starship *Enterprise* in the original *Star Trek* series, "to explore strange new worlds, to seek out new life and new civilizations, to boldly go where no man has gone before," shares in the intrepid rhetoric of Satan's own expedition (if not Milton's invocation) its opening scene of drifting star fields matching his view onto the cosmos. In the first season, the episode "Space Seed" makes an explicit allusion to *Paradise Lost*. The villainous and superhuman Khan (Ricardo Montalbán), offered the option of exile to a "savage" and "inhospitable" planet over imprisonment in a Federation "reorientation center," asks Kirk, "Have you ever read Milton, Captain?" To this literary challenge Kirk responds, "Yes. I understand." The satanic Khan's choice to turn his exile into an empire may be clear to the literate captain, but he must explain the allusion to his officers. Scotty, standing in for the general audience, chimes in, "It's a shame for a good Scotsman to admit it, but I'm not up on Milton." And so Kirk paraphrases what he takes as the implicit reference, in a fairly broad gloss: "The statement Lucifer made when he fell into the pit: It is better to rule in hell than serve in heaven." That Kirk is up on Milton suggests a kind of intellectual affinity between himself and Khan, though the (mis)quote also underscores that the circulation of Milton in popular discourse is almost always distinct from the text itself. In the second *Star Trek* feature film, *The Wrath of Khan,* the story picks up 15 years after his banishment, and Khan has maintained his love of the classics: we see a partial library including not one but two copies of *Paradise Lost*, as well as *Paradise Regained,* the *Inferno, King Lear,* the Bible, and *Moby Dick*. Literary allusions figure prominently throughout the script, and the sacrificial act in *A Tale of Two Cities*—the book is exchanged as a gift between Spock and Kirk—eventually comes to supplant Khan's satanic reading of *Paradise Lost* as the film's dominant moral code.[19] The film has Khan successfully stealing away the "Genesis Device," technology that can remake entire planets into teeming gardens or vast wastelands, and *The Wrath of Khan* builds in a number of parallels suggestive of Satan's own comparable assault on Eden.[20]

A tendency toward ambivalence in the Miltonic film extends even to that most favored subject of earlier eras, Pandaemonium. Otto Preminger's *Carmen Jones* (1954), based on the 1943 Broadway opera with libretto by Oscar Hammerstein, makes one of the most interesting uses of Satan's capitol in the lyrics to "Whizzin' Away along de Track." In the ensemble piece, Carmen is being urged to take a train to Chicago with her friends when she suddenly reveals her love for Joe:

> Anudder night I might've come
> To raise some pandemonium
> But now de mockin' birds are hummin':
> "Carmen's in love,
> Carmen's in love!"[21]

The application of "pandemonium" here sounds at first like a euphemism along the lines of "raising hell" or "raising Cain," expressions meant to convey raucous and wild festivity. But Hammerstein's substitution of "pandemonium" conveys a much more specific and specifically literary (if not literal) act, identifying Carmen and her fellows with Satan and his fallen angels as well as with the majestic poetry of Milton himself. Jeff Smith observes that the film attempts a "cultural balancing act" between "primitivism and sophistication," "one intended to exploit the local 'color' and exoticism of rural African-American culture (voodoo, jazz, roadhouses, sexuality) while simultaneously preserving the aesthetic dominance of opera." The film "could revel in the entertainment values associated with black popular performers like Dandridge, Bailey, and Belafonte while enjoying the cultural pedigree offered both by Bizet and by classically trained opera singers."[22] The Milton allusion affirms this tension—a nod to white cultural normativity, subsumed in a single phrase and image that simultaneously undoes the structure of that hierarchy by releasing into it demonic energies, here coded as black. The dueling signification is preserved in Dandridge's delivery of the line, which she accentuates with sultry hip thrusts. She makes Milton sensuous and primal: the erecting of Satan's palace underwrites an erotic staging of repressed desire, while Carmen herself emerges as both playfully diabolical and complexly savvy, at once building and upending a tower of high culture by claiming ("anudder night I might've come") to want nothing to do with it.

BEYOND THE EPIC

Aside from *Paradise Lost,* other borrowings from Milton's poetry surface periodically in the cinema. In many of these instances, the adaptive moment is sudden and decontextualized. Even more than *Paradise Lost,* Milton's other works have themselves become detached from the kind of recognizability that would make the source contextually important to the average film viewer. The Alec Guinness comedy *The Horse's Mouth* (dir. Ronald Neame, 1958) ends with the destruction of a mural called "The Last Judgment" and a line from *Lycidas,* "To fresh woods, and pastures new." (Guinness's crotchety artist, Gulley Jimson, spends the first part of the film on a painting of Adam and Eve.) These lines return in the 1996 made-for-television drama *Sharpe's Siege* (dir. Tom Clegg), centering on a British soldier, Richard Sharpe (Sean Bean), during the Napoleonic Wars. After Sharpe admits in bed to his lover that he will be married to another in the morning, she replies, "To fresh woods and pastures new," prompting Sharpe to snuff out a candle and declare, "Bugger Milton."

The 1972 television movie *Look Homeward, Angel* (dir. Paul Bogart), based on the Thomas Wolfe novel of the same name, takes its title from *Lycidas,* though Wolfe by that point had arguably already displaced Milton as the recognized source for the line. Similarly, the five-episode BBC miniseries *Eyeless in Gaza* (dir. James Cellan Jones, 1971), adapted from the eponymous Aldous Huxley novel, draws its title from *Samson Agonistes.*[23] Marin Fulgosi's 1998 film *They Also Serve* alludes to Milton's Sonnet 19, "When I consider how my light is spent," and the famous end line, "They also serve who only stand and wait."[24] This line also appears in the space adventure *The Black Hole* (dir. Gary Nelson, 1979) and the World War II spy film *The Man Who Never Was* (dir. Ronald Neame, 1956). In the former instance, a U.S. spaceship searching for habitable worlds in deep space encounters a similar craft, the USS *Cygnus,* apparently adrift near the edge of a black hole. As the crew prepares to board, the captain orders a young and restive Lieutenant Pizer to stay behind and guard their ship. At the lieutenant's objection, the resident robot V.I.N.C.E.N.T. (voiced by

Roddy McDowall) quips, "Don't worry, Mr. Pizer, they also serve who only stand and wait." When Pizer cracks back, "Vincent, were you programmed to bug me?," the robot corrects him: "No, sir, to educate you." Even this short exchange makes a typically dual application of Milton, here as a source of wisdom—a corrective educationalist—and of bother, a fountainhead of truisms suited for programmatic, *artificial* intelligence but not for a real-life, red-blooded astronaut, for whom standing and waiting are as antithetical to heroism as a black hole itself. A further variation on Milton's famous line can be heard in Sam Peckinpah's classic thriller *Straw Dogs* (1971), "They also serve who sit at home and wait," while the screwball comedy *The Miracle of Morgan's Creek* (dir. Preston Sturges, 1943) puts an irreverent twist on it (playing up perhaps a certain obsolescence of Milton): "They also serve, you know, who only sit and...Well, whatever they do, I forget."

A few films borrow from Milton's *L'Allegro*, though as with Lonsdale's phantasmagoria, the poem's companion piece, *Il Penseroso*, has suffered in comparison. The best-known citation is likely *My Fair Lady* (dir. George Cukor, 1964), in which the line about Shakespeare "warbl[ing] his native woodnotes wild" serves as an intertextual marker for the interplay between natural and learned abilities. (The 1951 romantic comedy *Love Nest*, directed by Joseph M. Newman, puts the line to similar use.) *My Fair Lady* follows Shaw's play *Pygmalion* verbatim in its quotation of Milton, while elsewhere Henry Higgins claims English to be the tradition of "Shakespeare, Milton, and the Bible." Further, the song "I'm an Ordinary Man" posits a discussion of "Keats or Milton" as an exclusively male drive, in opposition to "talk of love." A lesser-known film, still in the bildungsroman tradition, called *The Corn Is Green* (dir. Irving Rapper, 1945), challenges this rigid gendering of an education in Milton. Bette Davis stars as Lilly Moffat, a teacher in a Welsh mining town who takes upon herself the instruction of the town's illiterate population (one old-timer believes "Shakespeare" is a place and not a person). She finds one diamond in the rough, a star pupil named Morgan Evans (John Dall), to whom she devotes special care in the hopes of securing him a competitive scholarship to Oxford. His curriculum ranges from translating Greek and Latin to reading Voltaire, Adam Smith, and Milton. After his successful trip to Oxford, Evans relates to Moffat a vision he had at the university: "I saw this room. You and me sitting here studying, and all those books. And everything I'd learned from those books, and from you, was lighted up like a magic lantern. Ancient Rome, Greece, Shakespeare, Carlyle, Milton, everything had a meaning because I was in a new world, my world, and so it came to me, why you'd work like a slave to make me ready for this scholarship." In addition to imagining Milton cinematically via the magic lantern, the film here frames Evans as the romantic sentimentalist, finally transcending the scholarship for a greater understanding of the world enabled by Moffat's motherly guidance. In the 1979 made-for-television remake with Katharine Hepburn in the lead role, coincidentally also directed by George Cukor, Evans's visionary line is largely delivered as in the Davis film. (One author is cut, but in a refreshing twist it is not Milton but Carlyle.)

Additional lines from Milton can be heard in the British pop group The Pet Shop Boys' surrealist musical, *It Couldn't Happen Here* (dir. Jack Bond, 1988), integrating Milton's poetry alongside various Edenic visual cues (e.g., a woman riding a train with a boa constrictor coiled about her neck). Near the end of the film, a limousine chauffeur dressed as a royal footman delivers three passages — *Paradise Lost* 1.44–49 ("Him the Almighty Power . . .") and 4.108–10 ("So farewell Hope . . ."), as well as *Lycidas* 123–27 ("Their lean and flashy songs . . .") — as a kind of running commentary while the car navigates a dark tunnel and exploding bombs, the latter seen "headlong flaming from th'Ethereal Sky." And in the adaptation of James Michener's *Hawaii* (dir. George Roy Hill, 1966), Max von Sydow (as the awkward missionary Abner Hale) takes stabs at appropriately romantic, vernal lines from both Virgil and Theocritus while wooing his bride-to-be, Julie Andrews's Jerusha Bromley. During an especially nervous tea, he is about to add citations from Milton to the classical poets — "One is also reminded of the divine Milton" — when he suddenly drops his teacup onto the floor before he can offer a single verse. It serves as yet another example of Milton interrupted.

Part of the opening speech from *A Mask Presented at Ludlow Castle* appears in *Indiana Jones and the Kingdom of the Crystal Skull* (dir. Steven Spielberg, 2008), where an impending interaction with seemingly immortal alien life forms inspires the cryptic clue, "Yet some there be that by due steps aspire; / To lay their just hands on that golden key; / That opes the palace of Eternity." Two film adaptations of *Sabrina* (Billy Wilder in 1954 and Sydney Pollack in 1995) also substantially frame their heroine as the eponymous water nymph of Milton's masque.[25] The story in each case involves two brothers, one mirthful and the other melancholic, vying for Sabrina's love. Both films incorporate numerous water tropes, and both also have a central gag involving broken champagne glasses, a device that mirrors the climactic moment in the masque when the brothers shatter the glass of Comus. Although the Wilder film is less explicit, Pollack's refers back openly to passages in *Comus*. When Linus Larabee (Harrison Ford), the elder of her suitors, asks Sabrina how she got her name, she replies, "My father's reading. It's in a poem." She then recites the song:

> Sabrina fair,
> Listen where thou art sitting
> Under the glassy, cool, translucent wave,
> In twisted braids of Lilies knitting
> The loose train of thy amber-dropping hair.   (*Comus*, 859–63)

Later, Linus returns to the subject, asking her what the "little poem" means. Sabrina glosses it (in a rather Sabrina-centric way) as "the story of a water sprite who saved a virgin from a fate worse than death." Linus responds, "And Sabrina's the virgin," and she corrects him: "Sabrina's the savior." In addition to straining the masque into a lyrical poem, the citation is also notable for a pattern evident in other films of excising mention of Milton by name.

Unquestionably among the most jangling appropriations of Milton's verse, including *Comus* and *L'Allegro*, is the soft-core Showtime production *Easy Six* (dir. Chris Iovenko, 2003, and for video marketing purposes later known as *Easy Sex*). This low-end production begins with an English professor, Packard Schmidt (Julian Sands), on his way to teach his last Milton seminar of the semester. The film opens with Professor Schmidt calling out to a student passing by on the quad, "Milton awaits!" And the film is unique in the range of citation and centrality of Milton, though it winds up in the same place as other post–*Animal House* films in mostly rejecting Milton as academic, old-fashioned, and anti-thetical to romance and rebellious, satanist values. The film is also unusual in that, while it is based on a literary novel (*Mustang Sally* by Edward Allen), the director suggests in the DVD commentary that he added all of the protagonist's Milton characterizations himself. The novel does, however, provide the informing note: there is another professor of Milton, of whom the narrator says quite ungenerously, "Like most Miltonists, he keeps his academic speciality scrupulously isolated from the other parts of his life."[26] The film typifies in this way its own Milton professor, who has not yet learned well enough how to compartmentalize. Milton becomes associated with Schmidt's other puritanical hang-ups, from which Schmidt must break free to live a life more hedonistic.

In the opening sequence, set on the mishmash fictional campus of "Princeton College in Salem, Florida," Schmidt is readying to attend an annual Milton conference in Las Vegas. Fallen on hard times, the Milton conference has tried to jazz up attendance by calling itself invitingly, if improbably, "Milton Mania." Schmidt packs a copy of *The Oxford Book of English Verse*, edited by Christopher Ricks, and underneath not a volume of Milton's poem but John Collier's *Paradise Lost: Screenplay for Cinema of the Mind*. (It is not clear whether this is intended to relate to the topic of Schmidt's paper, which seems to be on "Milton and Imagery," nor does the narrative ever acknowledge openly this embedded instance of Milton-on-film.) As Schmidt prepares his final Milton class, the camera follows him transcribing the concluding lines from *Comus* on the chalkboard: "Mortals that would follow me, / Love virtue, she alone is free, / She can teach ye how to climb / Higher than the Sphery chime" (108–21). To his dismay, only one student shows up for the class, and he concedes defeat, concluding the Attendant Spirit's speech with a simple recitation, "Or if Virtue feeble were, / Heav'n itself would stoop to her" (1022–23). Despite the lack of student interest, the film uses *Comus* as a framing text—clumsily, to be sure—as it develops themes of "virtue and freedom" (another of Schmidt's upcoming lecture topics). And Schmidt's own "feebleness" as an instructor and as a kind of fuddy-duddy stick-in-the-mud (he swears to his friend he will not be gambling or having sex in Vegas—"it's not a vacation, it's a conference," for Pete's sake) is translated into the tragic flaw from which he must be redeemed.

The *Comus* links continue in what becomes the film's main plot. Along with attending the conference, Schmidt has been asked by a colleague to track down his daughter, Sally. A former student of Schmidt's, Sally has run away from or otherwise purposefully lost touch with her father, later revealed to be mad and abusive, and Schmidt is given a scrap of a lead to follow. When he finally locates her, she is working at the Paradise Inn, a legal brothel on the outskirts of Vegas. Schmidt very quickly falls in love with the student turned heart-of-gold prostitute-heroine, the film's attempt to refigure the Lady of Milton's masque, and she instructs him in the film's conjoined romantic values of uninhibitedness and exhibitionism. A kind of spiritual chastity is ironically envisioned in the brothel's sign objecting to "kissing" ("Paradise Policy"), while Professor Schmidt seeks to rescue her from falling into complete perdition by bringing her home and restoring her to a morally responsible condition: he eventually marries her. The fact that he first succumbs to the gambling bug in order to save up enough money to pay for sex with her is, in the film's schematics, an incidental, if necessary, act to begin the redemption of both figures.

The Milton conference itself stands in for the kind of staid and fruitless academics from which the film wants its protagonist to detach. Transpiring in a dark and depressed recess ("the Dugout Room") of an otherwise glitzy casino, this conference, as the organizer acknowledges, will be "the last Milton conference." Even dubbing the conference "Milton Mania," as Schmidt observes, has not saved the event: "The new name didn't help, eh?" Nor apparently does his own presentation, a joint effort with the conference organizer (played by University of Southern California playwright Donald Freed), called "Erotic Images in Milton." The presentation is not scholarly, but features a slideshow of such images as Botticelli's Venus with accompanying, illuminating verse. Freed's character recites from *L'Allegro* during the Venus slide: "But come thou goddess fair and free / In heaven yclept Euphrosyne, / And to [*sic*] men, heart-easing Mirth, / Whom lovely Venus at a birth / So rosy, so pink [*sic*]." As one might expect, the recitation is imperfect at best, and by the end trails off into a strangely non-Miltonic hybridization or improvisation. That final substitution ("so rosy, so pink")—as if the speaker's own latent erotic longings overwhelm the actuality of the verse—fairly represents the use of Milton throughout. In *Easy Six,* the love of Milton serves primarily as a fixation for which there must always be a substitution: no students show up for Schmidt's seminar, but the loss is exchanged for the lusty return of Sally. The Milton conference is in its final throes, but Schmidt shows no interest in resuscitating it. Instead, at Sally's beckoning, he exits in the middle of the "Erotic Images" slideshow and walks off carelessly down the street, choosing the living Venus over its (Miltonic) facsimile. Thus, not even a last-ditch attempt to transform Milton into a voice-over for gratuitous nudity—one could say this is also the design of the film in its entirety—appears able to make Milton desirable.

A more elegant ambiguity about Milton's desirability occurs in the film adaptation of Virginia Woolf's *Mrs. Dalloway* (dir. Marleen Gorris, 1997). One of the guests at Clarissa Dalloway's crowning party is an expert on Milton—Professor Brierly (Edward Jewesbury). As Clarissa (Vanessa Redgrave) fears her party, still warming up, will be a failure, Brierly can be overheard holding court with a small group of listeners. Brierly begins drily, and so inauspiciously, "The essential condition for a study of Milton, an in-depth study of Milton...," when suddenly a breath of fresh air blows into the room and a curtain billows about him. "Oh!," he cries, with a frisson of pleasure, "A momentary sensation of an embrace!" And thus the unfinished pronouncement on the essential condition for a study of Milton is rescued from any number of distressingly sober endings by the playful and humanizing effect of gossamer. With that swerve, the party itself is rescued: Clarissa sees that the celebration will be fine, better than fine, and the ice is broken.

The move from serious, stuffy, and pontifical to breezy and unencumbered puts Milton in a compromising position. Must Milton be modified or discarded before the real party can start? Or does Milton fit naturally here—the essential condition for his study is an embrace of freedom, a poetics of spontaneity that functions without restraint and beyond social status quo? In brief, does Milton interfere with or inaugurate the celebration to come? Woolf characterizes the thorny Brierly only briefly in the novel: "prodigious learning and timidity," a "wintry charm without cordiality," an "innocence blent with snobbery." In contrast to the film's frisky reaction to the billowing curtain, in the novel the professor "quivered if made conscious by a lady's unkempt hair." (Depending on one's reading of "quivered," this might also presage the delight in disorder experienced by Brierly in the film.) In Woolf's description, Brierly's promotion of "some slight training in the classics in order to appreciate Milton" comes off as a prickly pomposity. Dalloway saves the moment only by interrupting and changing the subject to Bach.[27] Gorris's film seems to allow for the possibility, at least, that the subject of Milton need not be changed entirely. A momentary embrace of Milton can also be a reminder that his seriousness and seeming inaccessibility are merely the first, superficial encounters in a joyous study.

Milton's prose tracts make only scarce appearances on screen. In the coming-of-age tale *The Education of Charlie Banks* (dir. Fred Durst, 2007), Charlie (Jesse Eisenberg) strives to adapt his rough-around-the-edges upbringing to an elite liberal arts college, a process complicated by the prolonged stay on campus of a menacing bully from his youth. In the course of negotiating this tense arrangement, Charlie courts Mary (Eva Amurri), a well-heeled and literate love interest who prefers bad boys—in this case, Charlie's childhood nemesis (Mick). Her father, as it happens, admires Milton. In a change-up, the intertext here is not *Paradise Lost*—the father has not fostered a love of the Romantic Satan in his daughter—but a rare borrowing from Milton's *Of Education* (1644). As Mary explains to him during a visit to their friend's mansion retreat, "You made me think of my father's favorite quote: 'Inflamed with the study of learning and the admiration of virtue; stirred up with high hopes of living to be brave men, and worthy patriots, dear to God, and famous to all ages.'" Charlie does not recognize the quote (she identifies it for him—"Milton"), nor does its placement in the film seem transparently meaningful beyond the film's bildungsroman structure and the general subject of Milton's text. Mary's understanding of the quote is a further remove from this easy link: "My father always dredges it up when we fight about the kind of men that I date." It is a consoling moment: she has just spent a weekend choosing the satanic rebel over Charlie, the studious and virtuous alternative, but concedes Charlie the paternalistic overprotector role. The invocation of Milton consolidates their shared literary interests, a privileged moment that she cannot extend to Mick. But why is it a quote "dredged" up? A sunken and stagnant sort of exhumation, a quote plied over and over by her father, and one that—given Mary's contextualization—seems to stand primarily for the kind of man her father has idealized as her lover: not "childish" and "ill-taught," as Milton added, but manly and learned. The quote, at any rate, suddenly empowers Charlie, whose next line suggests Milton worked as a palliative, a sense of superiority: "sitting there on the lawn, watching Mick immerse himself in great literature, I realized I wasn't scared of him anymore." Charlie's brief identification with Milton's educated man—and with the kind of man for whom Milton's literariness means something—pulls him out of his doldrums, and Milton's vision of bravery inflamed by study becomes the film's heroic mode.

Several films in the silent era adapted Milton's biography (and with haphazard results), and other dramatized biopics have since been made: in 1972, for instance, BBC-TV produced *Paradise Restored,* a 90-minute telecast of Don Taylor's play about the miseries of Milton's domestic life, with John Neville as the intensely unhappy poet.[28] More often, aspects of Milton's personhood are appropriated only in brief. In the post–World War II drama *A Matter of Life and Death* (also known as *Stairway to Heaven,* dir. Michael Powell and Emeric Pressburger, 1946), there is a passing reference to Milton during the "trial in heaven" as part of the pantheon of great English writers, along with Shakespeare and a laundry list of other poets (Donne, Dryden, Pope, Wordsworth, Coleridge, Shelley, Keats, Tennyson, Bridges). A comparable sentiment is offered in *The Treatment* (dir. Chris Eigeman, 2006), in which Ian Holm plays a Venezuelan psychoanalyst, Ernesto Morales, who at various inopportune moments haunts his patient's subconscious. In the final scene, Morales pops out of a bedroom closet and proclaims himself "the last in a line" of "moral visionaries," "stretching from Moses to Aristotle, to Cicero, to Milton." The film *One True Thing* (dir. Carl Franklin, 1998), based on the Anna Quindlen novel about a Harvard-educated writer (Renée Zellweger) dealing with her mother's terminal illness, lavishes praise on the poet's untiring vocation. As the daughter looks over her father's unfinished novel, which he has been "working on for years" (her father, played by William Hurt, is a famous professor of American literature), she remarks hopefully, "Took Milton ten to finish my favorite poem."

Relatively frequent allusion is also made to Milton's blindness. In Fred Zinneman's film noir *Eyes in the Night* (1942), Edward Arnold plays a blind detective assisted by his guide dog, Friday. When a butler evinces surprise at a blind detective, he shoots back, "Many great men were blind. Milton, Homer, they were blind, weren't they?" The suspiciously educated butler counters by arguing that they all "complained" about it, and quotes (conflating the poet with his poem) lines 67–69 of Milton's *Samson:* "O loss of sight, of thee I most complain! / Blind among enemies, O worse than chains, / Dungeons [*sic*], or beggary, or decrepit age!" The detective laughs, "Milton, huh? Say, you're quite a butler. Tell Mrs. Lawry I'm here and don't stand around spouting poetry." In *The Miracle Woman* (dir. Frank Capra, 1931), a radio evangelist offers a tirade against despair, declaiming that Beethoven composed his greatest work while deaf, Oscar Wilde wrote his best poem while in jail, "And Milton, a blind man, gave us *Paradise Lost.*" Conversely, the absurdist comedy *Pure Luck* (dir. Nadia Tass, 1991) briefly makes light of Milton as a supposed exemplar (along with Delacroix) of misfortune. A quack psychologist, Doctor Monosoff (Harry Shearer), delivers an anecdote about the poet to showcase his theory about the accident prone: "What about Milton, the English poet? Just before he goes blind, his dog drags all of his manuscripts into a fire." What perhaps works here comically is that Milton is a weighty-enough name to register the seriousness of the doctor's claim while remaining obscure enough to allow the fiction of the dog and the papers to pass. (The humor further depends on a kind of gravitas in Milton to be so reduced by the burlesque of an untrained canine.)

Similarly, in the Vietnam era counterculture flick *Getting Straight* (dir. Richard Rush, 1970), Milton becomes implicated in the dangers of inherited wisdom. "Don't trust anyone over 300" might have been a suitable tagline, as the main protagonist, Harry Bailey (Elliott Gould, not channeling Chaucer's Host), breaks down during his master's oral exam in English literature. After attending serviceably to the political allegory of Spenser's *Faerie Queene,* Bailey falls apart as one demagogical professor demands he agree with his (condemningly) queer reading of *The Great Gatsby.* Bailey's breakdown plays out as a frantic leap onto the table and tossing of papers; he begins frantically spouting crude limerick upon limerick (insisting on the limerick as the essential English verse form). His profanation of Milton is a dirty limerick referencing his blindness, and the terrified, humorless pedants around him are not amused. One cries out "How dare you do that in here!" and the revolution is on. Seconds later the entire campus seems to echo Bailey, erupting in explosions of protest as the film reaches its climax.

GLORY OBSCURED: DEPOPULARIZING MILTON

As part of the touch-and-go alliance between Milton and the cinema, appropriations of Milton often suggest serious anxieties about the poet and the movies, particularly for mainstream, popular films aspiring to be seen as literary lions. Several recent films with literary pretensions evince just such a displacement of Milton even as they briefly bring him aboard. In *Sylvia* (dir. Christine Jeffs, 2003), the courtship of Sylvia Plath (Gwyneth Paltrow) and Ted Hughes (Daniel Craig) includes rapid-fire Shakespeare recitations, and a shared exchange from *Romeo and Juliet* proves a potent matchmaker. During a romantic punting on the river Cam, Hughes jokes that even the Cambridge bovines are poetry lovers, as the couple encounters along the riverbank some "very intelligent cows." When Plath asks, "What do you think they'd prefer? Milton or Chaucer?," Hughes responds without missing a beat, "Chaucer. Obviously." Plath then stands in the skiff and recites from *The Wife of Bath*. In a film that depends on poetry to mobilize all of its cinematic gravitas, and that elsewhere wants to claim that "poets are shamans" and poems "weapons," it is a compounding vote against Milton. The herd—even Cambridge cows, but especially mass culture—are not much for the grand style, but *Sylvia* adds an extra twist of the knife by rejecting Milton from its ultraliterate circle, as well.

Similarly, in the John Keats biopic *Bright Star* (dir. Jane Campion, 2009), where one might expect some substantial and perhaps even reverential citations of the "Old Scholar of the Spheres," and which again dramatizes a courtship through the sharing of verse, Milton is encountered through an act of non-reading. Fanny Brawne (Abbie Cornish) asks Keats (Ben Whishaw) to instruct her in poetry. When she arrives for her lesson, books stacked in hand, Charles Brown (Paul Schneider) interrogates her over her ambitious reading list. In the past week she claims to have read "All of [Chaucer]. Also, Mr. Spenser, Mr. Milton, and the *Odyssey*," as well as "all Mr. Keats has written." As proof, she is able to recite "The Eve of St. Agnes" verbatim. The skeptical Brown—"that's a lot to read in one week"—condescendingly tests her on the rest of the material, hoping to embarrass her and drive Keats from her side:

> BROWN: And what, Miss Brawne, did you make of *Paradise Lost*?
> BRAWNE: I . . . I liked it.
> BROWN: Did you? You didn't find Milton's rhymes a little pouncing?
> BRAWNE: No.
> BROWN: Did you not?
> BRAWNE: Not very.

Brown thereby traps her into later revealing that she has not read *Paradise Lost* at all, since there are no rhymes, pouncing or otherwise, and concludes that Brawne is not worth Keats's time: she "only knows how to flirt and sew." Keats is unaffected by Brown's cheap display, not least because Brawne has, understandably, preferred his poetry to that of Milton. But the excision of *Paradise Lost* once again suggests that it is a book everyone should read—it remains all well and good for tutorials on the importance or craft

or *seriousness* of poetry—but few are able to connect with it intimately. In melodramatic works, the epic is hardly ever preferred
over the lyric (even *Endymion* takes a few hits in *Bright Star*), and
whatever else *Paradise Lost* may signify, it has no popular application as an aphrodisiac. In the rules of attraction, the rejection of
Milton's poem has become as romantic a gesture as the spontane-
ous delivery of a sonnet.

An almost identical move happens in the second episode of the
2009 BBC adaptation of Jane Austen's *Emma* (dir. Jim O'Hanlon),
which opens with a slightly consternated Emma announcing, "I
have managed two pages of Mr. Milton." At which point she shuts
the book and earnestly quotes from the first 25 lines, "I may assert
the ways of God to man, and justify eternal providence." She then
tosses the book onto a shelf and declares spiritedly, "I think we
have done enough reading for today." It is a triple displacement
of Milton: Emma's quote is a pretty badly mangled misquote, and
her eager rejection of reading Milton at all consolidates her character as not only poor at memorization but feckless and irresolute,
far more interested in the romantic scrapbook she is filling than in
the poetic theology of *Paradise Lost*. But it is unmistakably also a
resounding haymaker thrown by one literary heavyweight against
another—the film does not develop Emma's tossing aside of
Milton as a critique of her seriousness but instead as an act of desire
for more entertaining fare, a welcome move from Milton's tedious
justifications and assertions to Austen's rippling matchmaking.
As Emma puts it, "such lofty thoughts require a moment's pause
to reflect on their value." And so this four-hour epic film pauses,
humorously, for less than a second to contemplate Milton before
rushing back into unmitigated Austen.

Insofar as Milton has been overdetermined as a signifier for
the tedious and effete in cinema's negotiations of both high and
low culture, there has been correspondingly a steady muting or
excision of Milton in popular films.[29] Most striking may be Chris
Weitz's adaptation of Philip Pullman's *The Golden Compass* (2007).
Pullman's novels have done immense work in drawing Milton into
the popular imagination, and the influence of *Paradise Lost* upon
Pullman's *His Dark Materials* series is well documented. Indeed,
the opening of the first novel begins with an epigraph from book 2

of *Paradise Lost*—Satan's view from the brink of hell into the "wild abyss" where the almighty's "dark materials" mass in confusion.[30] The use of the epigraph is not only an homage to Milton, but a signal that Pullman is taking up the charge of the Almighty himself, reworking and adapting the raw elements of *Paradise Lost* so as to "create more worlds," worlds founded on a strongly Romantic reading of their source.[31] Pullman's books are scaffolded with a number of paratextual markers, including numerous chapter epigraphs from Milton and Blake that strengthen the ties to this legacy. The epigraph also puts the reader squarely in the position of Satan, who stands in Milton's text poised to launch into the full depth of his narrative, even as readers of *The Golden Compass* prepare to engage Pullman's newly created worlds. This framing device is in keeping with Pullman's idea that he wanted to "tell the same story," even to tell (as he once conceived it) "*Paradise Lost* for teenagers in three volumes." His clear intent is to align the reader with Satan as a revolutionary, romantic spirit: "All of the imaginative sympathy of the poem is with Satan rather than with God."[32]

Weitz's film adaptation of *The Golden Compass* replaces the opening epigraph with an opening shot of cosmic soup: galaxies and nebulae passing by, while a voice-over by the Witch, Serafina Pekkala (Eva Green), announces that "there are many universes, and many earths."[33] In this particular universe, there is no Milton. By excising the epigraph, Weitz positions the film far more conservatively, rejecting from the start Pullman's idea of orienting his audience to sympathize with Satan, while also managing to eliminate completely the shadow of Milton (and any problematic intertextual parallels). That this does not signify an even more totalizing revolutionary impulse, but rather an attempt to unproblematize the narrative, can be gleaned from the consistently cautious decisions the film makes regarding the book's religious heterodoxies. In this case, if Pullman's Milton is of the devil's party (Pullman boasts that he himself is "of the devil's party and knows it"), the film wants no part of the union.[34]

A related treatment of Milton—as a sort of indeterminate figure, obscure and uncertain, easily unsettled and dispensed with as overly academic or arcane—appears in an earlier Chris Weitz film, *About a Boy* (2002, co-directed with Paul Weitz). The film begins with a kind of embedded epigraph, a television clip of a woman playing the UK game show "Who Wants to Be a Millionaire?" Her question is "Who wrote the phrase, 'No man is an island'? John Donne? John Milton? John F. Kennedy? Jon Bon Jovi?" The film's protagonist, Will Lightman (Hugh Grant), answers quickly, "Jon Bon Jovi. Too easy," while turning off the TV with his remote. Lightman proceeds to critique the island metaphor itself, which he finds "a complete load of bollocks," establishing his celebrated bachelordom and fashioning himself a rogue and a playboy but also a revolutionary—willing to upend Bon Jovi, at least—by imagining himself as a "little island paradise." ("I like to think I'm Ibiza," he concludes.)

But how does the film mean this instance of Milton? Perhaps most people would suspect that the author of the quote is not Jon Bon Jovi, and laugh along with or at the film's flip protagonist. But how many in a mass audience will choose correctly between the other Johns? Does the question, moreover, suggest that "John Milton" and "John Donne" are essentially interchangeable? Would Will have been so defiant about the metaphor if he had correctly identified the source as a revered literary figure? The matter is more interesting since the published shooting script sets up merely a generic game show announcer, asking the same question but with only three choices—Donne, Kennedy, and Bon Jovi.[35] The final cut of the film, using archive footage from "Millionaire," includes the fourth multiple-choice option. (There is no mention of Milton at all, and no comparable scene, in the original Nick Hornby novel. This is a reversal of most filmic instances of Milton in which a literary source generates the link prior to its somewhat begrudging inclusion in the cinematic adaptation.) Here, "John Milton" seems to function as a kind of empty signifier, one of a long and indeterminate list of famous "Johns" whose primary purpose is to authorize an endless parade of pithy sound bites and familiar clichés. Will's turning off of the TV further emphasizes that knowing the "right" answer to this question of authorship (the film audience never hears the correct response) is less important than resisting and destabilizing these old and tired saws — regardless of who came up with them.

The film returns to the question at the very end — once Will has come to understand the bonds of human relationships differently — and it is the boy, Marcus (Nicholas Hoult), who affirms finally, "It's like that thing he told me Jon Bon Jovi said: 'No man is an island.'" The continued Bon Jovi attribution is another, and decisive, change from the published shooting script, in which Marcus recalls "this thing we were reading at school. John Donne. Something about people being islands."[36] In this version, the unanswered question of the opening is finally (if circumspectly) brought to closure. The film, perpetuating the Bon Jovi gag, supports Will's initial impulse — that quotation, ripped from its authorial context, has a life of its own, and that it is the (literary) author who is not only dead but, more important, dull and beside the point. But beyond that, the film seems to make a case that John Milton, in particular, stands in perfectly for all those stuffy irrelevancies.

Woody Allen's *Deconstructing Harry* (1998) does not go so far as to cut Milton completely, but its appropriation of the author again unsettles the relationship between Milton and his cinematic audience. At one point, Allen's alter ego in the film, Harry Block, fantasizes a descent into the underworld (via elevator), where he is given a glimpse of his possible infernal afterlife. The setting begins with a Dantean superstructure — the elevator passes a series of levels where various sinners are grouped and punished (the sixth floor, for instance, is occupied by "right-wing extremists, serial killers, [and] lawyers who appear on television") — but ends in the ninth circle, where Harry encounters a vaguely Miltonic Satan, played by Billy Crystal. When Harry realizes that this level of hell seems more full of play than punishment (compare the war games and false harmonies of *Paradise Lost,* book 2), he remarks to Satan, "Better to rule down here than serve in heaven, right? That's Milton, I think." The scene is carefully explicated by Knoppers and Semenza, who argue that

> Harry's uncertainty about the source of his preference for reigning in hell / the world of the imagination — "That's Milton, I think" — is crucial because it suggests how little he knows about the

context from which the lines are taken. Specifically, the qualification reminds us that Harry is only *partly* correct in his attribution, for actually he is quoting Satan, not Milton himself. The appropriation works simultaneously, then, to sanction Harry's rebellious lifestyle by invoking the authority of Milton and to undermine it by suggesting that Harry is misquoting and potentially misreading Milton.[37]

As with the Milton of *About a Boy,* Harry's unsteady recollection of the lines from *Paradise Lost* also presents us with a devaluation of the author. Harry can deliver his point without knowing exactly where it came from, and without the anxiety that an audience *expects* him to know. *Is* it Milton? Or perhaps it was John Donne. What difference does it make? Harry's qualification suggests once more the unsteady appeal of Milton for a mass audience.

Likewise, in Dan Brown's novel *Angels and Demons* there is a central exegesis in which John Milton figures prominently—this time as a secret member of the Illuminati—that the film specifically rejects.[38] The symbologist-hero, Professor Robert Langdon, finds a poem signed "John Milton" scrawled in the margins of an original Galileo manuscript—presumably the product of one of the poet's *sub rosa* meetings in Italy: "From Santi's earthly tomb with demon's hole, / 'Cross Rome the mystic elements unfold. / The path of light is laid, the sacred test, / Let angels guide you on your lofty quest." Both the iambic pentameter verse and the fact that it is written in English—and so in a language alien to Vatican tongues ("a polluted, free-thinkers language for profane men like Chaucer and Shakespeare")—prompt Langdon to interpret the four lines as the essential clues to guide him through the Illuminati's puzzle: "*Milton was an Illuminatus. He composed the poem for Galileo to publish in Folio 5...far from the eyes of the Vatican.*"[39] Never mind that Brown/Langdon blunders the parsing (he repeatedly describes a single iambic foot as a "couplet") or that Milton sounds particularly bland here—the novel tries to register Milton as a kind of adventuring "savant," an exciting covert operative who wields his poetry for the forces of good. It encodes him in the broader discourse of the novel as a type for Langdon himself, an adroit semiotician endlessly caught up in the politics of faith. Langdon follows Milton's metrical footsteps not merely as a literary scavenger hunt but as an alternative to that "profane" language of Chaucer and Shakespeare—no one charts a sacred path in English like Milton—and the same movement can be seen in the couplets themselves, from the abysmal reaches of the "demon's hole" to the heavenly guidance of angels. Milton, in Brown's rendering, is not primarily of the devil's party, but rather one who can speak with balance to both spiritual extremes.

The film adaptation of *Angels and Demons* (dir. Ron Howard, 2009) cuts all ties with Milton, though the doggerel verse remains crucial. The script does not mention Milton at all, though it does carry over Shakespeare and Chaucer as exemplars of English, now "the language of radicals."[40] By reformulating the authorship question, the film implies that the lines were written by Galileo himself, in his best English (a take that perhaps makes better sense of the quality of the verse.) It thus rejects outright not only Milton but the *particular* Milton constructed in the original novel: a man of mystery and intrigue, the shadowy poet of angels and demons.[41] The implicit Milton lingering in the film's omission is the staid and doctrinaire patriarch familiar from *Animal House:* nonradical, canonical, the very Anglicization of the film's Vatican villains. His only shadowiness comes from his being obscured by those earthier, more "free-thinking" fellows Chaucer and Shakespeare, conveniently lumped together.

Finally, a lumbering but no less revealing instance of Miltonic appropriation combines many of the above issues—conjoined literary and popular aspirations, a conspicuous "book-dropping"—into a productive interpretive moment that depends at once on Milton's recognizability and his obscurity. The scene arrives early on in Roland Joffé's *The Scarlet Letter* (1995), when Demi Moore's Hester Prynne surprises the Reverend Dimmesdale (Gary Oldman) in the library:

> HESTER: What are you reading?
> DIMMESDALE: *Comus.* It's by John . . .
> HESTER [finishing the thought]: John Milton. Yes, I know. I've read it.
> DIMMESDALE: Have you?
> HESTER: Well I'm not all counterpanes and coverlets. Every spare moment, I am reading something.

At this point in the film, Hester and Dimmesdale have already shared several chance meetings, each more hot and bothered than the next, including one in the forest outside Salem, during which Dimmesdale rescues Hester from a horse-cart stuck in the mud. Dimmesdale, recognizing the dangerous feelings Hester has aroused, has rushed to the library intent on mortification. The selection of *Comus* here, then, signals a good Puritan reading, and is shelved alongside such tracts as *A Short Description of the Great and Last Judgement, Platform for Church Discipline,* and *The Goodwife's Manual for Animal Husbandry.* Dimmesdale's taste for a text that celebrates the virtues of chastity against the depredations of a monster in the woods further indicates that this reading choice is not arbitrary: he hopes to chasten himself of the lust he felt in the forest by reminding himself of Milton's arguments.

When Hester reveals that she not only has read the same text but also remembers its author, her response triggers at least three simultaneous shocks in Dimmesdale — that *she* has read this book, that she has *read* this book, and that she has read *this* book. That the woman about whom he has been fantasizing should not be the unlettered damsel in distress of the masque but an independent woman asserting her own interests seems the plainest sense of Dimmesdale's loaded remark. The film also wants desperately to authenticate Hester as progressive, to identify her as a literate and experienced intellectual, the reverend's equal, and one who can pleasure herself in whatever way she sees fit. Dimmesdale is thus supposed to be confounded that a woman, of all persons, should be engaged in such activity (and not as a dilettante but at "every spare moment.") Last, Dimmesdale projects his own inner demons here: if Hester too has read *Comus,* perhaps she has read it for the same reasons he has. She has had the same libidinous fantasies (in this notoriously prurient adaptation of Hawthorne, this is actually true) and has had to scourge them from her flesh. A corollary of the shock at the material is that Dimmesdale stands in for the mass of audience surprised that anyone, even Puritans, would be reading *Milton.* This is partly noted in the film's tripping over the name. Identifying the author of *Comus* at once underlines its obscurity and coaxes out of the encounter as much cultural capital as the scene can bear. In this mode, it is actually preferable if not everyone has read Milton, or even heard of him—the film's ambitions as high art (Joffé argued that his adaptation was "a dialogue with Hawthorne's book" and that he "wanted his title all over it") depend on such unfamiliarity.[42]

Milton's ambivalent cinematic presence, or absence, sorts with the varying opinions on the effectuality of Milton's visual imagination more generally. If Milton can be potent, rich, transporting, dynamic, energizing, he can also be flat, dull, overblown, ponderous. Films or genres that feed off the former—horror, fantasy, science fiction—find themselves far more at home with a sublime (or even quasi-gothic) Milton. Romantic or comic works naturally get more mileage out of rejecting Milton as boring than embracing him as radically hyperkinetic. And because the epic nature of *Paradise Lost,* like film itself, nimbly embodies so many generic modes, these dual discursive histories are often interwoven and sometimes confused.

The Greatest Motion Picture Never Made: John Collier's *Paradise Lost*

In 1967, the tercentennial of the first publication of *Paradise Lost,* John Collier began seriously pitching to Hollywood an idea he had been nurturing for some years: an epic film of Milton's poem that would become no less than "the most spectacular motion-picture ever made." A prolific writer of short stories, most tending toward the bizarre or fantastic, the London-born Collier had drifted to screenwriting after moving to Hollywood in the 1930s. His efforts included an early, never-used draft for *The African Queen* (dir. John Huston, 1951), a range of teleplays, including a number for *Alfred Hitchcock Presents,* and credits for such feature films as *I Am a Camera* (dir. Henry Cornelius, 1955) and the Charlton Heston vehicle *The War Lord* (dir. Franklin J. Schaffner, 1965). *Paradise Lost* was to be his crowning achievement, an irresistible admixture of space travel, horrific monsters, "exciting adventure," and "romantic love." Satan could be played by Paul Scofield or Richard Burton, and Fellini should direct. In fact, Collier promised that the film held "a compelling appeal to every band in the spectrum of the potential box-office," and that with its "thrilling and disturbing sound effects—violent, outrageous, sometimes enchantingly beautiful" and its visuals drawn from state-of-the-art technical innovations, the film would also stand as "an experience unique in the history of the cinema." The pitch was a triumph. Martin Poll, who at the time was producing Anthony Harvey's masterful *The Lion in Winter* (1968), quickly contracted Collier to draft a screenplay and wrote him a giddy letter enthusing over the possibilities of putting Milton on screen. Over the next several years, however, Collier and Poll increasingly battled with each other over the script until the project eventually collapsed. Determined to see his efforts come to light, and hoping to stir new interest in a film adaptation, Collier ended up publishing the final screenplay in 1973 as a mass-market trade book, *Paradise Lost: Screenplay for Cinema of the Mind*.[43] The book was, unfortunately, a resounding flop. However, the checkered history of Collier's adaptation illuminates a number of the issues that have plagued virtually every other attempt at mounting a feature film of *Paradise Lost*.[44]

In a letter dated July 24, 1967, and addressed to Collier's agent, Howard Hausman, Martin Poll first worked out the terms for Collier's work on the film. Gushing praise for the possibilities of the project, Poll says he is "enormously excited" about its "scope and potential" and "even more impressed" with Collier's own contributions. In a fantastic aside, he writes wistfully, "I wish I could be in a room with him, telling him all of the things that his presentation has depicted and visualized for me."[45] The producer highlights his interest in "making a film in a truly modern style that would have epic dimensions" and suggests that "the technical aspects and the boundaries of film techniques must be expanded." He even offers that Collier's should be the primary "point of view," not wanting a director to intervene at too early a stage and muddy the waters of the author's "clear vision." Poll names Freddie Young, who had shot both *Lawrence of Arabia* and *Doctor Zhivago*, as the ideal cinematographer, and his friend Robert Gottschalk, the founder and then president of Panavision, as a revolutionary who could "experiment and create new lenses and effects" needed for such a film. The late 1960s timing, moreover, was exactly right: "The film must be tomorrow in its style," Poll writes. "We would have an opportunity to achieve this as the world-wide audience in 1970 will be oriented and demand and accept visual and aural innovations....We can utilize the psychedelic and the impressions created must make everyone feel they are on a trip." Collier had also encouraged the trippiness when he proposed in his first treatment that Pandaemonium—which he described as "like the Pentagon, only larger, and gilded"—should look "as insubstantial—and also as vivid—as a dream, or as an L.S.D. trip."[46] He also sold Poll on the idea that the technical demands could be done on the relative cheap, since much of the film could be "a figment of [Satan's] paranoid imagination," and that "the blur and distortion accompanying such a change of focus can be used to disguise any point where our technological resources are not completely adequate."[47] For scripting this progressive and innovative odyssey, Collier was offered installments totaling $300,000 plus a 10 percent share of any profits, an arrangement he called "utterly fantastic."[48] Years later, he would bitterly recall this letter as being one "full of promises, some of which were kept."[49]

If Poll first played the Passionate Shepherd (his heart pouring out his fancies to Collier), his affections cooled as the screenplay advanced. Within a year, Collier was accusing him of ruining the spirit of the project (and the poem) and soon thereafter of numerous breaches of contract. The first cracks began to show in a letter dated September 11, 1968, in which Collier acknowledges Poll's "misgivings" about the script.[50] In Collier's account, these amount to objections over Adam and Eve's "prosaic gardening" and a perceived "fundamentalistic religious approach" to the Fall. Adam and Eve, Poll urged, needed to *do* more than just tend the roses. A few weeks later, after speaking again with Poll, Collier decided that "the one area that might possibly yield an extra dimension to the Adam and Eve story is a more protracted and complicated struggle against temptation."[51] In the same letter, he also announced that he had completed a final revision on the screenplay.

Meanwhile, Poll had been consulting with the artist Jan Stussy on Collier's earlier draft, possibly with the idea that Stussy would serve as artistic director for the film. (Stussy, moreover, was involved in a parallel Milton project at this time: his resume lists that in 1969 he was "commissioned by Hayworth Production Co. to write a space-science adaptation of Milton's 'Paradise Lost' as a screenplay called 'Again and Again.'")[52] In separate letters to Stussy and (more candidly) to Poll, Collier responded to Stussy's notes and his suggested visualizations with barely restrained contempt. To Stussy, he begins by asserting his authority over the original: "Naturally I am much closer to the poem than anyone else is likely to be, having spent a year going over it.... It is not our business to emulate Mulciber in his determination to create. The discipline in this particular operation is to keep as close to the text as possible, only introducing new elements when absolutely necessary. Otherwise, why make *Paradise Lost?*"[53] Collier was already moving rather far from Milton's original; the claim to an authentic text here seems mostly intended to fend off Stussy's analyses by invoking Milton's authority and implying its transfer onto Collier's attentive reproduction of the Miltonic text.

Most offensive to Collier's sensibilities were two changes promoted by Stussy: one, that heaven should be visually and dynamically rendered at the start of the film; two, that Satan and the other fallen angels should have horns. As to the first, Collier again brings in Mulciber, the architect of Pandaemonium, whom he characterizes as the frustrated "prototype of all artists": "This poor fellow... has thrown his lot in with Satan because in Heaven he is not allowed to create, to make something new. This is inevitable — a perfect place will be filled with perfect buildings, possibly varying in size and function, but artistically '*all exactly the same.*' ... Mulciber's motivation will become senseless if we have already seen a Heaven in which all the architecture is in different styles." (Collier does not seem aware of the irony in celebrating Mulciber's creative license a few lines after chastising Stussy for inadvertently following in his footsteps.) Collier also objected to any visualization of heaven (even a "single vague glimpse of the squareness") on the grounds that it would somehow risk losing the audience, who (Collier thought) had a strongly preconceived expectation of what should be in heaven: "palaces and temples in some vague mixture of the Acropolis and a Renaissance palace; one person's fancy differing from another's only in details, and these all tactfully dissolved in a Turneresque golden haze." He argues to Stussy (again critiquing his innovation), "It is very important, therefore, that what we show them is consistent with what they think they already know....If we present a different picture they won't believe in anything we show them." As to the horns, Collier rebuts Stussy by again citing Milton's authority:

> The devil with horns was the magician of the later Paleolithic caves, whose costume was worn by those peasants who celebrated the old rites as well as the new, official Christian religion in the dark and middle ages. The church uttered a specific warning against men "who go about in the mask of a stag or a bull, or put on the skins of herd animals or the heads of beasts, and turn themselves into devils." Milton describes the fallen angels very clearly. "His form had not yet lost all her original brightness, nor appeared less than archangel ruined, and the excess of glory obscured." This is how they were from the creation of the universe to the fall of man, some five billion earthly years later. Only then did they take on the forms that men were to create them in.[54]

Collier ends by suggesting that Stussy's greatest contribution to the film would be to create effects so realistic that his own "inventions" would become self-effacing, and the audience would feel as if they saw no special effects at all. Even here, Collier seems to want Stussy to disappear from the project.

To Poll, Collier responded with more heated derision. "A few days ago I read over the pages written by Jan Stussy," he remarks. "I must confess my hair stood on end."[55] He calls Stussy's visualization of the story a "catastrophe," accuses him of not "study[ing] the script," and declares that his interpretation will make "nonsense of the story and nobodies of the characters, and end up burying the real production under a heap of gimmicks." Poll, however, seemed to think Collier's script did not have enough gimmicks, and most certainly did not deliver on his *idée fixe* of a psychedelic trip for tomorrow's people. Hausman conveys that Poll and Russell Thacher, brought on as a potential co-producer, "are *not* content with the first draft screenplay. Their objections seem to go much deeper than merely to minor line or scene changes....Their central concern lies in the fact they feel the script has remained in a fairly literal, realistic pattern of presentation, also they feel there is insufficient conflict." Hausman finally advises Collier that Poll will not put up more money for revisions and that he should not consider further work on this assignment but to look for "other activities."

Collier reports back that he delivered a completed final script to Poll on September 29, 1968, with a revised final act, and that Poll seemed content at that point, telling Collier, "I expect to be sending you good news by the end of the month [i.e., October]." Collier has not heard from him since.[56] In addition to requesting that all accounts be settled, Collier supplies his agent with an exasperated point-by-point response to Poll's critique of the literalism and conflict, blaming Poll's apparent change of heart on two external consultants—Thacher and Malcolm Boyd, author of *Are You Running with Me, Jesus?*, whose criticisms Collier believed Poll to be channeling. On the question of "literalism," Collier writes,

> "Literal" can only mean following Milton to the letter. I had it in mind to give that impression to people who were unfamiliar with the poem, but actually to develop a much more modern view from certain dormant seeds which Milton unconsciously scattered through his pages. How anyone who has read both poem and script can think that I have followed Milton to the letter is something which utterly baffles me....I admit that the whole thing could be modernized in what is thought by the innocent to be a very up-to-date fashion, by making blacks and hippies of Satan and his followers, and squares and fuzz of the good angels. But this sort of modernism is at least forty years old, and if anyone wanted it they should have said so when the treatment was under discussion. But at that time the call was for character and story....I may add that when Marty and I went over the script together in August, his one and only criticism was that in this line or that I had been too contemporary. For example, I had a line for Adam—"I don't know what ails me"—which I should have thought was closer to 17th Century diction than to the modern. But Marty thought it too modern, so I changed it.

Collier's position is an intriguing one: not wanting to copy Milton, but to *imply* enough similarity to kick-start the project; conversely, he also does not want to stretch his adaptation so far that it transforms the "dormant seeds" of Milton's unconscious modernism into something self-consciously modern. Ironically, Collier was later lambasted for failing in just this way: John Updike thought *Screenplay for Cinema of the Mind* reached its nadir during the Fall: "Mr. Collier's Eve...is conceived unsteadily: eating the apple on her knees like a drugged porn queen, voting for life like some vociferous Shavian heroine, sniveling like a groupie when the angelic fuzz arrives, jerked through a series of attitudes by the dead strings of Genesis 3."[57]

Further defending to Hausman his treatment of Adam and Eve, Collier continues,

> From a line in a letter of his, I am inclined to think that Marty now considers Adam and Eve in particular as too realistic. He suggests they should be more like the good angels. It seems to me that since they are human, they should be depicted as such, in contrast to the monsters that represent the forces of Heaven and Hell. This was clearly stated in the first presentation, and in the "expanded presentation," and in various conversations and letters. They were written in this manner when I went to Paris in May, and both Glenville and Marty were well pleased when he read a further stretch in July, up to where Eve tells Adam of her dream Marty told me he was "so excited he was almost crying." And he was right. Whatever ineptitudes may have existed at that time in other areas, that particular scene is the best thing I've ever written in my life.

As to whether there is sufficient conflict, Collier details scene after scene in which he asserts its presence (particularly as inner conflict—he avoids any hint of battling angels, since "Who wants fisticuffs?"). He contends that the drama of Adam and Eve is less "Tarzan and Jane" and more "Torvald and Nora Helmer," referring to Ibsen's *A Doll's House* and what Collier calls "the most talked of play of its century despite the absence of Satan." When Adam and Eve "are approached by a forty foot archangel brandishing the sword of God, who drives them out of the Garden, and, more important, into the world," Collier wonders whether his producers "desired that Adam should pick up a sword and start fencing?" He concludes by announcing for the first time his intention of publishing the script, "partly because I want no confusion between what I have done and what may be added by anyone else."[58]

An offer from Doubleday to publish the script arrived in November 1968, though Collier was wary of the question of property rights. He hoped that Poll would release the script back to him, and expressed in a letter to his editor at Doubleday, Lee Barker, his pride in the work: "I don't know if the script is terrific or not. I do know that it's an immensely intricate machine, designed to evoke strong feelings in a very large audience, and some interesting thoughts in a rather narrower one. It's certainly the best thing I've ever done, in any medium. And, since I was standing on Milton's shoulders when I did it, perhaps I can allow myself to fancy that it's rather more like a work of art than the ordinary run of things produced either by me or by Hollywood."[59] In a subsequent letter to Hausman inquiring about the property rights, Collier also suggests his vision for the published book, which could include Stussy's artwork: "If Marty would let go of the property, I think I could publish a book embellished with some of Jan Stussy's wonderful designs and with an introduction by someone prominent in letters, or possibly in the film world, or even in the church. I feel that such a book might evoke a good deal of critical interest and this in turn could attract the attention of one or other of the makers and backers of real films."[60] He also admits a "paralyzing mixture of uncertainty and disgust which results from the *Paradise Lost* fiasco."

An article a few weeks later in the *Hollywood Reporter* illuminates some of Poll's objections and the relative "literalism" of Collier's artistic vision. According to the piece, which is based on exclusive interviews with Poll and Stussy, *Paradise Lost* was to incorporate "frame after frame of abstract art and photography. Much of the film will use manikins cut up and reassembled alongside live models, with images—stuffed animals, furniture, automobile parts, to name a few—projected on their bodies. As much as 85% of the film, according to production artist Jan Stussy, will be bathed in semi-surrealistic images, composed of superimpositions and multiple front projection."[61] The extreme abstraction of forms laid out by Stussy is also dependent entirely on his own technical innovations:

> His [Stussy's] approach to Milton's myth...is that "everything must be metamorphosed into a new gestalt." If you're going to film

"Paradise Lost," you can't shoot Hell on Pismo Beach. My multiple projection machinery will include from five to 15 projectors all running simultaneously. This movie is about the final vengeance of Satan in his battle with heaven and Adam and Eve. The Palace of Pandemonium will be a hypnotic manifestation. Legs will grow out of pillars and heads out of domes. A tiny bird will be flying around in the body container of a woman. But the multiple images will be carefully programmed. During production, some images will be thrown on the screen and some of the actors, simultaneously. The viewer's one to one relationship will be suspended so there will be no horizon lines, no measuring stick. A woman walking toward you may change into a field of butterflies. She may become the size of a mountain or a pebble.[62]

While the general treatment is not entirely beyond what Collier had presented in his script—particularly in the template of a surrealist Pandaemonium—the overwhelming insistence on "Stussy's personally developed front projection technique," which Poll underscores "will differ from the scotch light front projection used in '2001: A Space Odyssey,'" suggests that Stussy's artistic vision had by this point come to supplant Collier's own.

Indeed, Collier is given rather brief and subordinate coverage, the article implying his screenplay may even be derived from Stussy's imaginative exploits: "Novelist, short story writer John Collier, an Englishman who recently resided in Westwood and now lives in the south of France, has completed the screenplay of Milton's classic—and an unconventional screenplay it is. An old friend of Stussy's, Collier has suffused his script with just the amount of ambiguous suggestion that Stussy for years has exercised in his art. Some of the film will suggest Picasso, and all of the principals involved are concerned with erasing the old, realistic Biblical image from the film."[63] As one of the principals, Collier was certainly invested in this erasure, but as he points out in his letter to his agent, the erasure was less representational than ideological. Above all, Collier wanted to preserve something of Milton's own vision. The article also points out that, with production a year away, Poll had still not secured any financing or distribution.

Poll and Collier attempted to mend fences the following year. In January 1969, Poll offered to renegotiate a new contract based on the final script submitted by Collier in late September. Collier wanted to retain full rights to publish the screenplay in book form (again mentioning his hope to include plates by Stussy) and mentions Fellini as one of the "three or four great directors" who might take on the project.[64] By May, Collier and Poll had met up in Cannes for the premiere of Poll's film *The Appointment* (dir. Sidney Lumet), which they agreed had travestied the screenplay. This "had the effect of an epiphany" on Poll regarding Collier's work on *Paradise Lost;* accordingly, Poll now "appreciated the script, and would not have a word changed."[65] By this point Collier saw the need for additional touch-ups, which he suggested he would perform gratis, but after months of going back and forth on renegotiations he had also developed a skepticism about Poll's commitment. To Hausman, he confided, "If that contract ever stands, we shall end up with some equivalent of Omar Sharif playing Satan and with a Hell as tatty and untrue as Rome appeared in *The Appointment.*" Once again he also expressed the wish to publish the screenplay as a book, aiming to have it on bookshelves before Christmas.

For his part, Poll continued to shop the project around, albeit with sagging expectations. In April of the following year, Hausman informed Collier that Poll still intended to proceed but had not come close to financing the film.[66] Moreover, "He [Poll] is now contemplating a radically changed approach: the inclusion of an up-to-date modern story of Adam, Eve, and a tempter, perhaps with a New York City background. This would be framed by Milton's story of God and Satan, either based on [Collier's] script or a substantial abridgement or portions of it." Collier responded harshly that Poll had still not paid him for the screenplay, and that the producer "never had the faintest idea of what any part of the thing was about." Meanwhile, Poll had indeed been pushing for a modernized version of the story, this time under the direction of Stussy.[67] Collier wrote a brusque letter to Stussy in May, inquiring whether rumors were true: "I heard the extraordinary news that you are making a test piece of film for Marty Poll for a different version of *Paradise Lost.*"[68] He assured Stussy he had not abandoned his rights and, while not doubting the artist's scruples, reiterated that he did doubt Poll's. "The thought of *Poll Paradise Lost,*" he tells Stussy, "reminds me of *Fellini Satyricon*," in which "the whole essence of the book was ignored." The same day he wrote to Stussy, Collier also followed up with Hausman to see whether, indeed, Stussy was working up a new strip of "experimental foot-age," a modern story surrounded "with something from Milton," and also whether Poll was not renewing his option on Collier's screenplay.[69] Hausman replied that Poll would not go forward with Collier's version, but also would not give up his rights to the screenplay.[70] (He did, however, agree to relinquish rights to the publication of the book.) Hausman also informed Collier that the Stussy film would be "a completely modern story with the theme loosely based on Milton, but with none of the lines or scenes taken from Milton's poem, or from your material. His hope was that he could use some of Stussy's film effects in this story" and include "some nods toward the essential moral confrontations contained in Milton's poem."

After more back and forth over the book publication rights, in September Poll finally decided not to exercise the option on *Paradise Lost*, freeing it up entirely for Collier to do with as he pleased. Poll's last letter on the matter captures a compelling sense of both the ambition of the project and its recurring frustrations:

> The screenplay was submitted to many directors who were inter-ested in the subject, but were not interested in it after reading the screenplay despite my discussing it with them. They had negative comments that were so basic that it was impossible to discuss rewrit-ing or their meeting with you to explore the problems. Among them were: Federico Fellini, Ingmar Bergman, Mark Rydell, Sydney Pollack. When MGM dropped the option, I submitted your screen-play of "Paradise Lost" to all the other American motion picture companies, and they were not interested. Most agreed that your attempt and work as a writer is brilliant, but as a screenplay for a film, they found many unresolvable dramatic problems. Warmest regards to you and your family. I'm sorry that we are not going to be working together.[71]

This dismissal—and rejection by the entire American motion pic-ture industry—did not end Collier's own efforts to mount the film, nor the contentiousness with Poll. A few weeks after Poll ceded his rights, Hausman wrote an enticing note to Collier, suggesting that television producer Fielder Cook might be interested in purchasing an option, and reiterating his own faith in the project: "I continue to believe you have a truly great property, which will make a superb picture, and that we must and shall find a way to mount it."[72] Moreover, Hausman reports, "I saw Christopher Plummer two days ago and chatted with him briefly. When I mentioned this material he ignited. I think he is almost as 'satanic' as O'Toole, or as Burton might be, though perhaps not as easily financable [*sic*]." With such luminaries still in play, Collier was perhaps rightly suspicious when he heard that Poll was continuing on with a project called *Hell Breeds No Angels*. He suggested to Hausman that "it could be a step towards realizing Marty's notion of up-dating *Paradise Lost*," and told him (with more than a little artistic paranoia), "I need to be promptly informed of every move he makes in this direction, as I shall almost certainly be suing him on a number of counts if he embarks on such a production."[73] Collier also noted that a friend was passing along the script to director John Schlesinger, who had recently helmed both *Midnight Cowboy* (1969) and Thomas Hardy's *Far from the Madding Crowd* (1967) (and would later go on to appropriate Milton for the conclusion of *Sunday Bloody Sunday*). Joining Fellini, Bergman, Rydell, and Pollack before him, Schlesinger too would pass.[74]

Meanwhile, more snags in the contract Collier had signed with Poll emerged, endangering the publication of the screenplay as a book. In the fall of 1970, Collier arranged for the publication of the book with Doubleday, which would also publish in 1972 *The John Collier Reader,* edited by Anthony Burgess. In his letter to his agent, Collier argues that the publication of the book should proceed despite the problematic contract with Poll, since the contract "refers specifically to the disposal of the *screenplay*. What I hope to publish will not be the screenplay at all."[75] In his later preparation of the manuscript for publication, he again affirms that "it is the writer's intention to edit it in such a manner as to make it suitable for publication in book form, and not as a printed screenplay," and notes that he will thus remove "all technical cinematic terms, all discussion of the manner of cinematic presentation...and of certain clichés which have been included because they are current cinema parlance."[76] He further offers that the book might be published "in a format appropriate to the great prestige of the poem on which the present work is based. It is suggested that it might be paged on quarto, and possibly with one or more illustrations by a very modern painter acceptable to both publisher and author." It seems clear that Collier's alterations were not solely for aesthetics but for the sake of getting around the legalities and economics of the contract; in fact, the differences between the finished film script and *Cinema for the Mind* ended up being quite superficial. In the interim, he continued to search for high-profile names to back the film—"I think I can get Paul Scofield and Joe Losey to read it, and I'd like to get it to Zeffirelli, but I've no channel"—while completing his disenchantment with Poll by mocking him as the producer of such films as *The Lion in Brooklyn* and *The Disappointment.*[77]

Ultimately unable to secure any further backing for the film, Collier began to explore the theater as an alternative means of production. He writes to his literary agents, Harold Matson and Anthony Jones, that "the high spots" from his screen adaptation could make "a novel and sensational theatrical spectacular."[78] The pitch echoes much of the language of his film presentation: "the theme of *Paradise Lost* is singularly suited to attract the wide audience, and especially the young audience, of today. It is quasi-religious, quasi-scientific, and deeply humanistic, being the thrilling story, with which we can all identity, of how innocent, vegetarian Proconsul or Pithecanthropus was caught up in the guerilla war waged by Satan against the authoritarian dictatorship which orders the universe, and how he emerged as moral and immoral, curious, inspired, murderous and suffering Man." Allowing that "at first sight the project may seem to involve almost insuperable technical difficulties and a prohibitive cost," he calls these challenges that should invigorate the creative spirit. To save expense, there would be "no real rabbits on the lawn of Eden! No real fire in Milton's Hell!," but instead "a big, rough, ostensibly slap-dash production, dazzling with light effects, deafening with sound and sometimes enchanting with music, and above all bursting with energy so that it breaks out of the conventional frame of proscenium and foot-lights and often out of the frame of conventional dramatic form."

His plans, indeed, sound quite similar to such earlier stagings as Loutherbourg's Eidophusikon, though Collier does not indicate any knowledge of this or other dramatic precedents. He further contends that the problem of nudity in Eden—one that also concerned Collier in his film treatment—might be more easily solved on stage:

> The first point to be dealt with is their nudity. It would seem desirable to disarm curiosity by giving the audience the fullest and plainest view to begin with, so as to leave nothing to watch for, and thereafter to render it scarcely noticeable, and therefore soon accepted and forgotten. This will be the easier to accomplish in that both of them will be deeply sunburned, and Eve's skin is several shades darker than the average, and both are seen most of the time under the flickering shadow of light foliage, or under the vine-covered trellis of the bower where they sleep. Most of their scenes, also, are played at night, or in less than full day-light.

Such a theatrical spectacular, with its extravaganza of light and sound and energy, and its clearly contradictory submersion into the "flickering shadow of light foliage" in a somnolent, twilit Eden, also never materialized.

What did finally emerge from Collier's years of professional tribulation, *Screenplay for Cinema of the Mind,* is a most unusual adaptation of *Paradise Lost.* Perhaps the most interesting element of the book's production is the back cover blurb: a glowing assertion that "the audacity of John Collier's 'screenplay' of Milton's great epic poem is matched only by its success," and that "the master fantasist, Collier, uses the characteristic medium of our time to bring us closer to the greatest art of another epoch." Collier's anxiousness for the fulfillment of his script is evident in the protestations of success—though in the same breath the ironic setting off in quotes of "screenplay" begins to unravel exactly what Collier has here achieved and recalls his argument to Hausman that this publication "will not be the screenplay at all." It certainly does not seem to be "the characteristic medium of our time," unless the publishers are contending that failed movie scripts recycled as mass market paperbacks have become the new hallmark. Rather, the cover wants to confirm that Collier has succeeded in turning Milton's art into *film*. And this Collier has clearly not done. *Cinema of the Mind* is, however, ultimately difficult to categorize (one critic even refers to it as a "stand-alone poem").[79] At times an exuberant phantasmagoria and at others a melodramatic hallucination, it comes closest to establishing something of a modern closet drama, "a parade of scenes based on Milton's glorious and appalling images."[80] It maintains most of the narrative arc of Milton's original while also cutting some of the most recognizably Miltonic parts of the poem (for example, the war in heaven and Michael's prophetic visions of biblical history are omitted entirely). Notable, too, is the absence of the sinuous syntax and dense allusiveness of Milton's verse, though Collier also appropriates plenty of it. As a literary *rara avis, Screenplay for Cinema of the Mind* drew immediate attention, but Updike's excoriating review in the *New Yorker* was the final blow to Collier's dreams of a *Paradise Lost* spectacular.[81]

The final act for Collier may yet be staged, however. In 2009, four years after Vincent Newman announced his intention to produce *Paradise Lost*, Martin Poll reentered the picture. He claimed to have renewed the option on Collier's original script "over the years" and had plans to go forward, this time as an independent feature to counterpoint the Newman blockbuster. It promised a "multiethnic cast," with two unknowns (David Dunham and Patricia Li Bryan) to play Adam and Eve, and a budget of at least $30,000,000, backed by a Bollywood producer.[82] The film never entered the production stage, and Poll's real purpose in announcing the film may have been in the small print: he also claimed to have registered the title *Paradise Lost* and could have negotiated with bigger-budget films for its use. Poll passed away in April 2012, leaving the status of a Collier-scripted film adaptation in even greater limbo.[83] The project remains the strongest example in the twentieth century of Milton's simultaneous appeal and difficulty for the cinema.

Although *Paradise Lost* has yet to be adapted as a feature film, and while the presence of Milton on film has never fully released the primary tensions with which a popular Milton has always been freighted, two prominent filmic genres have grown substantially dependent on Milton as referent. An array of films in the late twentieth and early twenty-first centuries has been occupied with millennial or apocalyptic end-of-days scenarios, often packaged as a cosmic Armageddon. As if responding to Eisenstein's advice about Milton being exemplary for battle scenes, these films have turned to Milton as a source for ultimate war, especially drawing on his war in heaven as a quasi-historical or ultramythical template for *cinematic* combat. Even more immersed in Milton are horror films, which redefine (or re-redefine, returning to the English Romantics) Milton as primarily a poet not of the sublime and ineffable but of the grotesque, the hellish, the charmingly satanic. The following chapters discuss Milton's significant presence in both of these cinematic genres, angelic warfare and diabolical horror.

Winged Warriors and the War in Heaven

The war in heaven has been a favored subject of those adapting Milton since at least Niccolo Servandoni's lavish production in Paris of *The Fall of the Rebel Angels,* and it was a popular part of the medieval dramatic cycles long before. Luigi Maggi's *Satana* and D. W. Griffith's *Sorrows of Satan* were the earliest efforts at dramatizing these scenes and Sergei Eisenstein, of course, found the battle scenes intensely cinematic. John Milton was drawing on other epic traditions of celestial combat as well, notably the wars of the gods and titans in Greek mythology as written in Hesiod and Homer.[1] Moreover, as Henry More observed, there was no shortage of naturalized visions of such phenomena in Renaissance Europe, what he called "the Appearance of *armed men fighting* and encountring one another in the *Sky,*" many of which battles seeming to confirm, if not reenact, the kind of ethereal fighting described in 2 Maccabees and reiterated by Milton:

> There are so many examples of these Prodigies in *Historians,* that it were superfluous to instance in any. That before the great

slaughter of no less then fourscore thousand made by *Antiochus* in *Jerusalem*, recorded in the second of *Maccabees* chap. 5. is famous. The Historian there writes, "That through all the City for the space almost of fourty daies there were seen *Horsemen* running in the *Aire* in cloth of Gold, and arm'd with Lances, like a band of Souldiers, and *Troops* of Horsemen in array encountring and running one against another, with shaking of shields and multitudes of pikes, and drawing of swords, and casting of darts, and glittering of golden ornaments, and harness of all sorts."

...The like *Apparitions* were seen before the Civil wars of *Marius* and *Sylla*. And *Melanchthon* affirms that a world of such Prodigies were seen all over *Germany* from 1524 to 1548. *Snellius* amongst other places doth particularize in *Amortsfort*, where these sightings were seen not much higher then the house tops; as also in *Amsterdam*, where there was a *Sea-fight* appearing in the *Aire* for an hour or two together, many thousands of men looking on. And to say nothing of what hath been seen in *England* not long agoe.... And they being resolvable into no natural causes, it is evident that we must acknowledge supernatural ones, such as *Spirits, Intelligences* or *Angels,* term them what you please.[2]

The promulgation of such visions suggests a deep and long-standing psychological fascination with angelic combat—a fascination exploited in the conjurations of modern cinema, where even a sea fight over the rooftops of Amsterdam is easily manufactured. More's suggestion that these celestial visions were a part of life in Milton's England is further supported, if somewhat idiosyncratically, by a testament of the royalist supporter Walter Gostelo, who describes in 1658 a mystical vision above the streets of London involving an onslaught of flying demons: "I saw over the East part of this City London, in the Aire, many strange figures of furious Satyrs, as Executioners of Gods Wrath and vengeance; they had all shapes like Devils, not like men."[3] Milton refers in *Paradise Lost* to this tradition of spiritual forces battling in the skies when he has the fallen angels contend above the plains of hell,

> As when to warn proud Cities war appears
> Wag'd in the troubl'd Sky; and Armies rush
> To Battle in the Clouds, before each Van

> Prick forth the Aery Knights, and couch thir spears
> Till thickest Legions close.   (*PL* 2.533–37)

In addition to the reminder of millenarianism subsumed in Gostelo's description and so active in the period during which Milton was working on *Paradise Lost,* the kinds of unbelievable heavenly battles detailed poetically in 2 Maccabees and recast in Gostelo and Milton, all evince an anxiousness that the war in heaven will spill over onto earth.

Since the 1990s, an explosion of films capitalizing on the kinds of energies unleashed in the epic tradition and its visionary legacy—and driven no doubt by similar millennial forces as the twentieth century turned—has transformed Milton's "winged warrior[s]" (4.581) into earthbound action heroes: *The Prophecy* (also known as *God's Army,* 1995) and its sequels, *Spawn* (1997), *Dogma* (1999), *Constantine* (2005), *Gabriel* (2007), *Legion* (2009), and *I, Frankenstein* (2014) all take on the war in heaven as the central dramatic tension. Though Milton's warriors must be likewise extracted from the long history of angelic battles in art and literature (dominated by Michael and the serpent, but extending also to Jacob's angelic wrestler in Genesis and the apocalyptic combat of Revelation), there is sufficient difference in Milton's treatment to suggest clear examples of influence and inspiration. These angelic warrior films imply, if not favor outright, a Molochian drive toward "open War" (*PL* 2.51), often mitigated by the battle being a kind of proxy war fought by souls lost and found on behalf of the angelic hosts. Indeed, it is notable that most of the warrior angel films do not actually dramatize the war *in* heaven. Rather than taking on the endless scope of celestial realms, the implied grand design becomes transmuted into an earthly emulation. In this regard, the films follow Milton's own acts of accommodation, as when Raphael testifies that he will tell his story "By lik'ning spiritual to corporal forms, / As may express them best, though what if Earth / Be but the shadow of Heav'n, and things therein / Each to other like, more than on Earth is thought" (5.573–76).

The closest visual analogue to the aerial combat imagined in *Paradise Lost* may be the campy 1980 film *Flash Gordon* (dir. Mike Hodges, 1980), in which armies of Hawkmen wielding low-tech maces and spears, arrayed against a colorful, incandescent sky and looking much like the host of angels in Griffith's *Sorrows of Satan,* battle the satanic cannons of Ming the Merciless and his "war rocket Ajax." In addition to this invocation of the epic *Iliad,* Flash rides in on a flying machine in imitation of the Son on his chariot. Vincent Newman, producer of the most recent *Paradise Lost* film adaptation, describes his "fascination with the angelic warrior" as going back to the book of Daniel and the angelic visitant who makes mention of his battles with the prince of Persia. What amounts to a tantalizing aside in Daniel—the angel more or less announces, "I would have been here earlier if not for twenty-one days of epic combat"—led Newman to explore Milton's war in heaven as a more developed template for representing angelic combat on film.[4] Certainly the terrifying appearance of the angel in Daniel 10:5–7, with his "face as the appearance of lightning, and his eyes as lamps of fire," also figures as part of the mix in other filmic adaptations of the warrior angel. Should Newman's vision of a full-blown Miltonic war in heaven come to pass, all of these various traditions would be gathered under one banner—an adaptation of *Paradise Lost*'s celestial battles informed by apocalyptic literature and synthesizing the cinematic subgenre of the angelic war movie.

For all of their allure, the war books of *Paradise Lost* have also proven to be some of Milton's most controversial.[5] As Robert H. West notes, "Milton had three general problems with his angels: first, how to keep them largely suited to the staid Protestant interpretation of the Bible in spite of the fact that he needed more details than such interpretation provided; second, what 'authentic' speculation, his own or borrowed, beyond the strict warrant of the Bible he might make use to fill out his scheme of them; third—and this, of course, was the basic problem of literary manipulation and invention—how to treat graphically these essentially unpicturable beings without abandoning or discrediting either the doctrine or the speculation about them."[6] The problem of angelic representation in *Paradise Lost* is thus a long-standing one. In the nineteenth century, the Reverend Charles Leslie charged Milton with producing a "scene of licentious fancy" when he "dressed angels in armour, and put swords and guns into their hands, to form romantic battles in the plains of heaven."[7] Nor can Milton resist the kinds of poetic flourishes evident in Maccabees, with its horsemen in "cloth of gold," its "shaking shields" and multitudinous swords and darts and pole-arms, its "glittering of golden ornaments" and harnesses. So Milton's angels have "fiery foaming Steeds" (*PL* 6.391), "brazen Chariots" (6.211), and are adorned in "Golden Panoply" (6.527). They battle one another in imitation of classical Homeric warfare, with long parlays and Satan's host marching in "Legions" with "rigid Spears, and Helmets throng'd, and Shields / Various, with boastful Argument portray'd" (6.64, 83–84), recalling the ekphrastic display of the shield of Achilles. They attack under the "dismal hiss / Of fiery Darts in flaming volleys" (6.212–13), threaten to drag one another "bound" at their "Chariot wheels," and in the wake of battle leave behind "shiver'd armor" and overturn both "Chariot and Charioter" (6.389, 390). Finally, after Satan's invention of gunpowder and cannon momentarily sways the battle in his favor, the angels revert collectively to a primal cannonade, hurling the "seated Hills with all their load, / Rocks, Waters, Woods" (6.644–45), crushing and burying one another until "horrid confusion heapt / Upon confusion rose" (6.668–69).[8] It is what West calls a "purely literary debt," a paraphrase of Hesiod's depiction of "titanic conflict and disaster."[9] The heroic arrival of the Son in his "Chariot of Paternal Deity" (6.750) spares the heavens any greater wrack as he vanquishes the rebel armies with "ten thousand Thunders," "lightning," and "pernicious fire" (6.836, 849), and herds them "Into the wasteful Deep" (6.862). This climax is yet another borrowing from Hesiod, when Zeus lets fly his "full might," with "thunder and lightning, trailing supernatural flames" and drives the Titans into the abyss, where they fall for nine days until reaching Tartarus.[10] The war in heaven scenes are among the poem's most memorable sequences, though the mixture of classical typology and poetic fancy—putting "swords and guns" into the hands of angels—has proven both an inspiration and an offense.

Milton's many poetic licenses in the war were strenuously objected to by Johnson, who accused him of having "unhappily perplexed his poetry with his philosophy," foremost in a "confusion of spirit and matter, which pervades the whole narration of the war of heaven" and "fills it with incongruity."[11] He points out, for instance, that

> The vulgar inhabitants of Pandaemonium, being *incorporeal spirits,* are *at large, though without number,* in a limited space: yet in the battle, when they were overwhelmed by mountains, their armour hurt them, *crushed in upon their substance, now grown gross by sinning.* This likewise happened to the uncorrupted angels, who were overthrown the *sooner for their arms, for unarmed they might easily as spirits have evaded by contraction or remove.* Even as spirits they are hardly spiritual; for *contraction* and *remove* are images of matter; but if they could have escaped without their armour, they might have escaped from it, and left only the empty cover to be battered.[12]

Similar questions might be submitted against the crumpled chariots and, especially, the "fiery steeds." Are these spiritual horses also angelic? Or, as Bruce Boehrer wonders, are they even equine?[13] What advantage does an angel gain in riding one into battle? Are there other animals inhabiting heaven? Most of these complaints and questions could be dismissed for failing to register the degree to which Raphael, who tells the story of the war in heaven, must accommodate his narrative to human understanding. Raphael is openly concerned with this problem and wonders to Adam, "how shall I relate / To human sense th' invisible exploits / Of warring Spirits" (*PL* 5.564–66). He decides ultimately that he "shall delineate so, / By lik'ning spiritual to corporal forms, / As may express them best," though he also supposes that heaven and earth may after all be more alike "than on Earth is thought" (5.572–74, 576).[14] But neither of Raphael's gestures frees Milton from criticism entirely. Among other remaining incongruities is the question of how Raphael imagines he will make his story easier for Adam to comprehend by "likening spiritual to corporal forms" when Adam has never encountered such alien constructions as fashioned metal, swords and helmets and shields, chariots and spears, bits and harnesses.

But the central problem in adapting Milton's war is less the picturability of angels—cinematic representations tend to be broadly brushed anyway, with imbricated feathers for the good angels, coriaceous bat wings for the fallen, and an easy divide between the feathery and leathery—or the Johnsonian cavils about consistency than the fact that the angelic battles are essentially conflict without drama. Most significantly, despite all the hissing darts and slashing swords, there are no angelic deaths in heaven, as Milton declares after Satan is first wounded and then heals fully a mere ten lines later: "Spirits that live throughout / Vital in every part [. . . / Cannot but by annihilating die" (*PL* 6.344–47). West argues that while "a demonic death or two might have spiced the battle in heaven, still the fact that angel could slay angel would have meant that the blisses of heaven and pains of hell were terminable and so would have thrown out of gear Milton's whole purpose to tell of God's eternal grace and wrath."[15]

But if there is no immediate consequence to the havoc of war, what does it matter how fierce the fighting or how foaming the steeds? Most adaptations of the angelic warrior have concluded that these battles need spicing up with at least the threat of termination. What applies singly to the angels applies perforce to the hosts at large. In Milton's treatment the rebel angels can at least experience some duration of pain, and each side can be disrupted and dislodged, but ultimately each remains entirely the same day after day. Northrop Frye points out the implication of such an arrangement: "The remark the devils make about the war in heaven, that they have sustained the war for a day 'And, if one day, why not eternal days?' opens up a perverted vision of eternity as a Valhalla of endless strife."[16] But unlike Valhalla, in which the fighting (and the nightly rehashing of it in the mead hall) *is* the glorious end, even two days of bloodshed and regeneration in Milton's heaven are enough to provoke a kind of boredom. God proclaims that "War wearied hath perform'd what War can do," and rather than tolerate "perpetual fight" he sends his Son on the third day to resolve the conflict absolutely (*PL* 6.695, 693). This proper return to God's omnipotence is itself problematic in adapting the action to the dramatic. Even Milton saw the need to intensify the tension of the outcome, though it caused one of his most implausible lapses in representation. In book 5 he presents God as worried over the new "King in the North"; the Almighty stoops to urging the Son, "Let us advise, and to this hazard draw / With speed what force is left, and all imploy / In our defense, lest unawares we lose / This our high place, our Sanctuary, our Hill" (5.729–32), thus compromising his omnipotence, omniscience, and virtually every other divine attribute. Adaptive treatments of the angelic warrior thus have to come to terms with the paradox of angelic death, with some following Milton's premise of annihilation and others making special allowances for angelic deaths that occur on earth, as well as the overriding problem of an all-powerful opponent.

THE WINGED WARRIOR FILM

The cinematization of rebellious warrior angels conducting a war on earth against their creator in the style of *Paradise Lost,* particular in a semiapocalyptic or dystopian future, begins with Ridley Scott's futuristic film noir, *Blade Runner* (1982).[17] Miltonic subtexts were first proposed by David Desser in his 1985 essay "*Blade Runner:* Science Fiction and Transcendence." Desser describes the "heatless, soulless neon lights, the misting, acid rain and the teeming mass of humanity that populate this Los Angeles of the future" as the "very vision of hell as Milton saw it," and argues that Roy Batty (Rutger Hauer), the leader of a quartet of artificial humans or "replicants," built as surrogate soldiers, laborers, and "pleasure models," but now rebelling and creating havoc throughout the solar system, is "Satan, Adam, and Christ all rolled into one."[18] Elaborating further, Desser also sees Milton's Eve as a model for the film's femme fatale, Rachael (Sean Young), a replicant who becomes involved with the central protagonist, Rick Deckard (Harrison Ford), whom Desser regards as a new Adam.[19] It is Deckard's task as a blade runner to eliminate replicants who are on earth illegally. Rachael, Decker suggests, challenges *noir* conventions in the same way that Milton "attempted to redress the prevailing notion that Eve was simply the evil temptress."[20] Laura Lunger Knoppers and Gregory M. Colón Semenza pick up on these tropes as well, arguing that *Blade Runner* "extensively reworks Miltonic themes of alienation, fallen angels, humanity, and companionship in the hell-like atmosphere of a dark and crowded Los Angeles."[21]

The most significant articulation of these themes is actually delivered not via Milton directly but by a paraphrase of William

Blake's *America: A Prophecy,* which itself reworks and revises the fall of Satan and his "rolling in the fiery Gulf" (*PL* 1.52).[22] In tracking the head of the Tyrell Corporation that created him, Batty locates one of the subsidiary laboratories specializing in the manufacture of artificial eyes. Breaking in to the subzero workshop to interrogate the eye-maker, Chew, the replicant recites the lines, "Fiery the angels fell, deep thunder rolled around their shores, burning with the fires of Orc." The intertext is meant partly to affirm Chew's accusation that the replicants are illegal aliens, not meant to be on earth but exiled to off-world sites. It carries a thinly veiled threat—we are damned, but we are also experienced in great violence; we bring with us the fires of Orc. For Batty does not merely paraphrase but reverses Blake's original, in which "the Angels rose," and reverts to a Miltonic paradigm of warriors confounded but not conquered. The replicants are fallen from their designated place in the heavens, but they have also been freed from their servitude (both the literal slave labor they conduct and the programmatic determinism built into their construction). In seeking out their creator, they are not so much waging war against him as seeking freedom from a termination clause: this newest "Nexus 6" generation of replicants are so humanlike and emotional that, in order for humans to "control them better," they are given artificial memories and a four-year life span. Batty has been given "optimum self-sufficiency"—sufficient, that is, to have stood, though in a consequence seemingly unforeseen by his human creator, also free to fall. If Batty is Satan, Adam, and Christ in one, it is because he is channeled through the Romantic Satan, fallen but vital, a revolutionary freedom fighter against the tyranny of Tyrell.

The script makes explicit the hellish cityscape: in fact, the screenplay begins with a fade-in to "EXT. HADES—DUSK"; it is replete with "menacing shapes" and "stacks belching flames five hundred feet into the sky the color of cigar ash."[23] Amid this set, the pyramidal Tyrell Corporation looms like one of those "works of *Memphian* Kings" (*PL* 1.694), a Pandaemonium surrounded by the "combustible / And fuell'd entrails" of "thund'ring *Aetna*" (1.233–34, 233). And in addition to the satanic associations of the rebel angels turned earthly warriors, *Blade Runner* works other satanic devices into the narrative. One of the replicants, Zhora, a

trained killer described as "beauty and the beast," has been working incognito as an exotic dancer, performing as "Miss Salome and
the Snake." During the scene in which Deckard hunts her down,
an announcer encourages patrons to "watch her take the pleasures
from the serpent that once corrupted man." She is herself serpentine, dusted with scales and a cobra tattoo, entwining with her
artificial python, finally hissing and constricting Deckard's throat
with his tie. She is, in short, both the fallen Eve who has taken in
the snake and another embodiment of Satan, here both tempter
and destroyer, with echoes of Milton's Sin.

Finally, when Batty at last confronts his maker, Eldon Tyrell,
to ask for "more life," Tyrell responds that Death has become a
necessary adjunct to life: "You were made as well as we could make
you." He assures the replicant that his rapid fall into mortality is
because he has, like Lucifer, "burned so very, very brightly." In
this instance, the justification of God's ways rings so hollow that
the creature destroys the creator, as Batty gouges out Tyrell's eyes
and crushes his skull. Despite this brutal turn, Batty ends his life in
a powerfully sympathetic soliloquy, sparing the life of Deckard and
meditating on all that he has witnessed—including, most insistently, war in the heavens: "I've seen things you people wouldn't
believe. Attack ships on fire off the shoulder of Orion. I watched
C-beams glitter in the darkness at Tannhauser Gate. All those
moments will be lost in time like tears in rain. Time to die." It is
a eulogy not just for a romantic rebel but also for a warrior angel,
one who pines for battle with lyrical nostalgia even as he seeks
fruitlessly to overcome his own destructive desires.

While the threat of wide-scale war in *Blade Runner* can be felt
in Roy Batty's vivid elegy, the intergalactic conflicts are mostly
"off-world." Later films are more insistent on the collateral dam-
age of a heavenly war upon earth. Eventually growing into a five-
film franchise, *The Prophecy* (dir. Gregory Widen, 1995) was the
earliest of a string of films to depict the archangel Gabriel as a
divine soldier on earth, here played with a kind of crass aplomb
by Christopher Walken. Widen's production notes reveal that
the "story was inspired by 'Paradise Lost,'" and throughout the
film there are various debts to Milton, mostly oriented around his
presentation of angelic warriors.[24] In his negative review of the

film, the *New York Times* critic Stephen Holden opined that angels had "proliferated in popular culture in such profusion lately that maybe they needed a comeuppance," and that "a few more movies like 'The Prophecy' should stop the whole celestial bandwagon right in its tracks."[25] Holden's prognostication was fairly wide of the mark. For not only did the film eventually result in four sequels, but its central premise of the war in heaven transposed to earth, to be fought by angelic brigades, became the defining trope for a host of other films that followed.[26]

The arresting opening shot of *The Prophecy* pans down through a vaguely Martian landscape to the skeleton of an angel, implanted in red dust like a fossilized archaeopteryx. Standing next to the remains is the archangel Simon (Eric Stoltz), who offers an elegiac backstory drawn from Milton: "I remember the First War, the way the sky burned, the faces of angels destroyed. I saw a third of Heaven's legion banished and the creation of Hell. I stood with my brothers and watched Lucifer fall. But now my brothers are not brothers, and we have come here where we are mortal to steal the Dark Soul, not yet Lucifer's, to serve our cause. I have always obeyed, but I never thought the War would happen again." This second "war in heaven" has reached a stalemate, and Gabriel, the satanic antagonist in this work, jealous of man and eager to undo his creation, is plundering the earth in search of this Dark Soul—a human power that will lead the rebel angels to a decisive victory. Images and sounds of angelic battle strafe the ensuing scene, which cuts to a Catholic ordination ceremony. One of the novitiates, Thomas Daggett (Elias Koteas), is haunted by these gruesome visions: blood-spattered wings, dark and anguished astral forms, raptorlike screeches. Too agonized to complete the ceremony, he is dragged from the church. When the story picks up years later, Daggett (now a detective with a latent fascination for angels) relates how he lost his faith because "heaven show[ed] him too much." He also claims to be haunted by a passage from Paul, "perhaps the strangest passage in the bible" (and which is the film's invention) that informs the brutal theology of the entire *Prophecy* series: "Even now in heaven there were angels carrying savage weapons." Interestingly, almost all of the angelic combat in the film is hand-to-hand.

Immediately upon entering his apartment he is confronted by Simon, squatting like a gargoyle on the back of a chair. This is the standard pose for angels throughout the film, perched like birds of prey as they spy on humanity, a trope taken directly from Satan in *Paradise Lost,* who is not only discovered "Squat like a Toad" (*PL* 4.800) but who "sits in the shape of a Cormorant on the Tree of Life, as highest in the Garden to look about him" (book 4, "The Argument"). Simon reports to Daggett that he has a role to play in the cosmic battle, that he knows of his former visions, and that "heaven isn't heaven anymore." Daggett's seminary thesis "On Angels in Religious Scripture" is also introduced, a reminder of his deep knowledge and wavering faith. Simon, meanwhile, is tracked to his own apartment by Uziel (Jeff Cadiente, looking much like an Ozzy Osbourne impersonator), who sniffs him out like a bloodhound and then roosts like a raven, waiting outside his window. Simon detects his presence in the same way—by scent—just before Uziel leaps through a window to attack him. The angels throw each other about the room, crashing into furniture, digging and clawing into one another's flesh (these angels bleed—profusely—and feel pain), until Uziel is skewered on the broken shards of window glass. Simon finishes him off by removing Uziel's sunglasses to reveal dark, eyeless sockets, and then hurling him four stories down.

The materiality of the angels is lingered over during Uziel's autopsy. He has "No optical fibers," never had eyes, and bears the same chemical makeup as an "aborted fetus." His bones, "most of them sticking out of his chest anyway," have no growth rings. The angel, in other words, is "new born" and apparently created in totality, all at once. In keeping with Milton's design of angels who "can either sex assume, or both" (*PL* 1.424), Uziel is also a hermaphrodite: "he's got both male and female sex organs." Mirroring the film's earlier use of pseudobiblical writings, Uziel also carried an old, handwritten Bible bookmarked at the twenty-third chapter of Revelation. This chapter describes a basic apocryphal tradition drawn from the fourth century Life of Adam and Eve, in which Satan explains to Adam his motivation for his rebellion as a refusal to bend the knee to a human: "When God blew into thee the breath of life and thy face and likeness was made in the image of God, Michael also brought thee and made us worship thee in the sight of God.... And since Michael kept urging me to worship, I said to him, 'Why dost thou urge me? I will not worship an inferior and younger being (than I).' "[27] In *The Prophecy,* Daggett's reading from the extra chapter of Revelation paraphrases this as "there were angels who could not accept the lifting of man above them, and like Lucifer rebelled against the armies of the loyal archangel Michael. And there rose a second war in heaven."

The choice of Uziel is a further connection to *Paradise Lost.* In the poem, Uzziel is Gabriel's chief officer, "next in power" to him in the guardianship of Eden, and entrusted with half of the cherubim to search the southern perimeter (*PL* 4.782–84). So too in *The Prophecy,* Uziel is identified in a book on angelology (*Hebrew Cabalist Writings*) as a "lower soldier angel and [lieutenant] to the seraph or archangel Gabriel." (The accompanying woodcut is taken from Albrecht Dürer's engraving of the expulsion of Adam and Eve.) Consistent with his function in the poem, Uziel operates primarily as a scout in preparation for Gabriel's more developed representation. In the same cabbalistic text, Gabriel is glossed as "the angel of death, vengeance, revelation, annunciation," and shown with spear in hand conquering a satanic dragon. Gabriel is initially revealed to have superior senses—he can see, taste, and (especially) smell, and he employs all three in tracking the blood of Simon and Uziel. Eventually locating them in the desert of Arizona, Gabriel descends upon the town of Chimney Rock after catching a whiff of a graveyard as he is driving past; he then tracks down Simon by his angelic odor.

More than a little tongue-in-cheek, not least when it shows Gabriel teaching a young boy to blow his trumpet (which shatters a nearby window), the film's final visions are fairly dark. The plot hinges on a kind of metempsychosis, with angels sucking the soul from one body and breathing it into another. In a syncretic blend of quasi-Catholicism and Native American ritual, the film ends with an attempt to drive the Dark Soul from a young Navajo girl, Mary. Lucifer (Viggo Mortensen) appears during the ritual, announcing that he has come to earth to join the battle against

Gabriel (not wanting another fallen angel to inherit a rival hell). He explains that Gabriel plots to acquire the Dark Soul because humans "know more about war and treachery of the spirit than any angel," and thus Gabriel needs to have, ironically, a human lead his legions. Lucifer gives Daggett the film's gloss on hell, both Miltonic and anti-Miltonic/Dantean: "Do you know what hell really is? It's not lakes of burning oil or chains of ice. It's being removed from God's sight, having his Word taken from you." Thus, while it rejects Milton's lake of fire as an allegorical ploy, it also embraces Satan's view that "myself am Hell; / And in the lowest deep a lower deep / Still threat'ning to devour me opens wide" (*PL* 4.75–77). In this film, Lucifer arrives in the nick of time to prevent the destruction of Mary, tear out (and eat) Gabriel's heart, and bring him "home" to hell. Walken's Gabriel makes a game play at maintaining his characterization in Milton as an "Insulting Angel" (4.926), stabbing at Lucifer even as he is about to be dragged almost in chains to hell: "Lucifer, sitting in your basement, sulking over your break-up with the boss. You're nothing." But Lucifer prevails, with the assistance of Daggett, and the Dark Soul is removed from Mary in a belch of protoplasmic miasma, which in turn disintegrates when the sky opens and heavenly light beams down. "The enemy ghost is gone," intones one of the Navajo healers. But Gabriel will return: in at least two subsequent features, generally regarded as a stand-alone trilogy in the *Prophecy* series, he continues to wage his war.

An inferior direct-to-video production, *The Prophecy II* (dir. Greg Spence, 1998) starts with images from Gustave Doré's *Paradise Lost,* a leitmotif throughout the film. They are part of the collected papers of Thomas Daggett, who, since the events of the first film, has become a monk obsessed with the angelic prophecies. The sequel fairly quickly eliminates his character. Gabriel, reprised by Walken (the only principal actor to return for this film), has been released from hell by Lucifer, who claims that the place was not big enough for the two of them. Early on, he turns Daggett to ashes, the first of many such incinerations at his hands. (These are supplemented by more heart-ripping battle sequences, inflected now with wire-work martial arts, as when Gabriel destroys Rafayel [William Prael].) The film redirects the narrative away from the

Dark Soul warrior and toward the lusting angels of Genesis 6. Thus, the film includes an explicit sex scene between one good angel, Danyael (Russell Wong), and a woman, Valerie (Jennifer Beals), during which the angel assumes the role of benevolent incubus and impregnates her with a child whose birth forms part of the prophecy of the second war. The abbot of Daggett's monastery informs Valerie that Daggett's notes on the prophecy describe this birth as a second coming of the Nephilim—"a child born of an angel and a human." The child, as Danyael eventually discloses to Valerie, will unite the angelic host and bring an end to the war. The pregnancy is preternatural from the start, accelerated into days instead of months for the sake of dramatic unity. Valerie's investigation into Daggett's writings also prompt yet more images from Doré and a miscellany of Nephilim pornography, masculine angels in coitus with mortal women.[28]

The sequel resorts to some of the staler conventions of schlock horror: the relentless pursuer (Gabriel), the indomitable final girl (Valerie), and the gratuitous jump-scares punctuating their game of cat-and-mouse. It does nonetheless offer a few additional Miltonic nuances: angels are befuddled, for instance, by technology. Walken reacts with charming naïveté to computers, DOS, walkie-talkies, and, especially, guns; his barely concealed whimsy recalls Satan's own jocosity during the confrontation in book 6, when the angelic host is first assaulted by his cannons and mistakes them for hollowed tree trunks: "to our eyes discover'd new and strange" (*PL* 6.571). The first *Prophecy* alludes to this technological gap as well—Gabriel cannot drive cars and needs a human gopher for various errands—but there it is framed as a point of superiority, that angels ought to be chauffeured. The second film also introduces Eric Roberts as the archangel Michael and stages a rather bizarre climactic showdown in "Eden" (or "what man has made of it"), a superindustrialized concrete jungle where Michael and his warriors have continued to reside. Still a gated community (and with the tree of knowledge still bearing fruit), Gabriel has only moderately more difficulty than Milton's Satan in negotiating his way through. This time Eve conquers the serpent, as Valerie succeeds in ravishing Gabriel by telling him she can hear God's Word, and then leaping from a dangling platform with him clutched in her embrace. During the fall she reverses their position so that she ends up landing on top of him, and he ends up impaled. (Michael turns him into a human for good measure). It is a classic "final girl" move, the victim becoming the (masculinized) victor or, in this case, the submissive succubus turned conquering angelic incubus, a reversion to and revision of the earlier shots of Nephilim intercourse.

The third installment, *The Prophecy 3: The Ascent* (dir. Patrick Lussier, 2000), was billed as the "final, most thrilling chapter," and picks up 18 years after *The Prophecy 2*. It features another angel—Milton's Zophiel—as Zophael (Vincent Spano): "of Cherubim the swiftest wing" (*PL* 6.535). In the film, Zophael is glossed as the "Spy of God, bridge between rebel and loyal factions within heaven. His true allegiance is unclear from religious texts." Joseph (Steve Hytner), the beleaguered coroner in all three films, takes it upon himself to research the history of Zophael, the Nephilim, and the "second" war in heaven by plowing through a pile of angelology texts. The visuals in the montage sequence are a mixture of recycled imagery from the previous films with a much heavier dose of Doré's illustrations from *Paradise Lost* (as well as, rather incongruously in this case, the *Divine Comedy*, freely substituting for Milton as in the old magic lantern shows). In several shots Joseph can be seen actually consulting an illustrated edition of the poem as part of his investigation, presumably in the case of Zophael reaching beyond those "religious texts" that are "unclear" on the angel's disposition. Of course, Milton would have offered something of a counterexample to the film's Zophael, who is a replacement villain for the earlier films' Gabriel. (Walken appears as Gabriel here, too, now absurdly as a human who has "let himself go" and who sympathizes with the human "monkeys" he had been so eager to destroy.) As his name suggests, in *Paradise Lost* Zophiel is also something of a spy, or a scout at any rate, and returns posthaste from his patrol to report to the heavenly host on Satan's military movements: "Arm, Warriors, Arm for fight, the foe at hand, / Whom fled we thought, will save us long pursuit / This day, fear not his flight" (*PL* 6.537–39). In the film, Zophael at least is versed in his poetic ancestry, as he quotes from Satan's flight through the Paradise of Fools (*PL* 3.474) as a way of condemning humanity: "'Embryos, and Idiots.' I hate this place." In the last battle, Zophael's plans to unleash the "Angel of Genocide" are foiled by Danyael, the Nephilim boy produced by the union of angel and woman in the second film. At film's end, Gabriel, having seen the error of his ways, explodes into a flight of doves and is at last welcomed back into heaven.

Also occupied with an ongoing war that has swept earth along with it, *Spawn* (dir. Mark A. Z. Dippé, 1997) is based on the comic book series by Todd McFarlane. In the film's prologue, a dizzying montage of combustion and atomic devastation plays out while the character of Cogliostro (Nicol Williamson) provides a voice-over on the current state of affairs: "The battle between Heaven and Hell has waged eternal, their armies fueled by souls harvested on Earth. The devil, Malebolgia, has sent a lieutenant to Earth to recruit men who will turn the world into a place of death in exchange for wealth and power, a place that will provide enough souls to complete his army and allow Armageddon to begin. All the Dark Lord needs now is a great soldier, someone who can lead his hordes to the gates of Heaven and burn them down." This "great soldier" is Al Simmons (Michael Jai White), an elite covert ops agent who is double-crossed and burned to death by his superior, Jason Wynn (Martin Sheen) and sent to hell for all of his killing. The film favors a fiery wormhole as the implied conduit from earth to hell, and a vertiginous fall past flames and images of the damned is played as the opening title sequence. This recurs when Simmons actually makes the plummet, and the impact is sug-gestively Miltonic as he lands prone on the burning marl, him-self scorched and unrecognizable from his own burning above. Simmons must bargain with its presumed ruler, Malebolgia, the "Dark Lord" of the prologue with the satanic designs and Dantean name (an oddly underwhelming one, after the "evil ditches" of the *Inferno*'s eighth circle). If Simmons will lead the hellspawn armies, souls reaped from centuries of evil on earth, then he can return to the upperworld to avenge his death and, inverting the path of Orpheus, behold his beloved, Wanda, on earth once again. He readily agrees, and at this avowal an army of infernal spawn rises up from the reaches of hell, strongly echoing the first book of *Paradise Lost* when Satan views "his Legions, Angel Forms," and summons them to "rouse and bestir themselves," and they react from their positions "twixt upper, nether, and surrounding Fires" by appearing "on the firm brimstone" until they "fill all the Plain" (*PL* 1.301, 334, 346, 350).

After five years "secluded in darkness," Simmons slumps back to earth via a kind of holy halfway house, Rat City, a dank and moldy ruin, an architectural morass that is part sprawling cathedral, part urban squalor. There he meets both Cogliostro, once a knight and now a holy warrior in God's army, and Clown (John Leguizamo), a grotesquely evil entity who answers to Malebolgia. Together these two serve as the battling angel-on-the-shoulders of Spawn, with Cogliostro urging him to make his own choices and Clown manipulating him into fulfilling his promise to lead the legions of hell. When Clown leads Spawn to visit his own grave (to prove that Simmons is truly rebirthed from hell), they encounter a trio of would-be satanists performing a clumsy ritual; approaching Spawn, one of the cultists asks, "Did, like, Satan send you guys?" Spawn, just coming to grips with his reincarnation, drives off the worshippers, and Clown gleefully dubs him "General of Hell's Armies." (Later in the film, the same character remarks, "If we hadn't recruited him, the other side would have.") Among Spawn's new powers, he wears "necroplasmic" armor, an ultraflexible, symbiotic exodermis that divides and coalesces like angelic substance, Milton's "liquid texture" (*PL* 6.348). The armor is controlled by Spawn's will and is so ductile as to serve as both shield and weaponry, becoming whatever chains, hooks, or spikes he can imagine. It appears just the thing that will permit Spawn, as Clown puts it, to "lead us to the Holy Land, so we can burn it down." This line is, of course, pure Moloch, who urges the fallen "arm'd with Hell flames and fury all at once / O'er Heav'n's high Tow'rs to force resistless way," until even the throne of God is "mixt with *Tartarean* Sulphur, and strange fire" (2.61–62, 69). It is naturally in keeping with the majority of these warrior angel movies that the expeditious, crusading plans of Moloch are preferred over the more reserved devices of his infernal peers.

The necroplasmic armor suffices, at any rate, to enable Simmons to avenge his death, destroy Clown when he transforms into a giant insectoid demon, and save the world from the release of a biological toxin that would decimate the human race. Thus, in the film's somewhat distracted logic, the lost souls will complete the armies of hell—though presumably the ranks of the heavenly host will also swell with new recruits. In keeping with the Miltonic subtext on free will, Spawn also accepts the teachings of Cogliostro, who has been repeatedly urging him to make an active choice to refuse the orders of Malebolgia: "The War between heaven and hell depends on the choices we make. And those choices require sacrifice. That's the test." (Williamson reverts here to his turn as the paternalistic counselor Merlin in *Excalibur*.) In the end, Spawn foils Malebolgia's plan not only by choosing not to lead his army, apparently reneging on the earlier promise that got him out of hell in the first place, but by making one last trip to the fiery marl and blasting most of the hellspawn army with bolts of lightning that emanate from his symbiotic armor. That he also gives up his loved ones (Wanda has remarried—Simmons's best friend—and has a child that Spawn is also drawn to protect) seems a secondary sacrifice to the refusal of cosmic glory and dark-side evil that Spawn leaves behind when he takes control of his anger and sides with Cogliostro against the fallen. The extreme mayhem of *Spawn*, at its height in this final battle, which substitutes a war in hell for one in heaven, exploits some of the same fantasies expressed in the exceeding violence of *Paradise Lost*. The superhero's apotheosis turns him into a type for the Son, devastating foes with unlimited power, the triumphant crush anticipated in God's lines, "bring forth all my War, / My bow and Thunder, my Almightie Arms" (*PL* 6.712–13). It is a dramatic catharsis, a divine housecleaning, but one full of bewildering spectacle—the Son "grasping ten thousand Thunders" (6.836), crushing "helmed head" under his chariot wheels, while the eyes installed upon the chariot proper "glar'd lightning, and shot forth pernicious fire" (6.848–49). There is a pleasure in the effect, but an inescapable irony, too, as Johnson saw, that spirits should be mangled so terribly.

Kevin Smith's "comedic fantasy" *Dogma* (1999) plays off just this tension, as it uses the war in heaven as both a precipitating event and climactic parody. Smith thanks John Milton in the credits as one of his "disparate spiritual" influences and one of the "sundry storytellers and word-smiths" responsible for shaping the film.[29] The story follows Matt Damon and Ben Affleck as fallen angels Loki and Bartleby, cast out of heaven for a dereliction of duty (Loki had been the Angel of Death but had a crisis of conscience). Banished to Wisconsin, they discover that they can reenter heaven by "transubstantiating" into humans, passing through a blessed arch to receive a "plenary indulgence," and then dying as sinless mortals. The villain, the demon Azrael (Jason Lee), is trying to end all existence by manipulating Loki and Bartleby into undoing the universal laws with their "indulgence" loophole. Azrael recalls the war in roughly Miltonic terms, especially Raphael's line that "Angel should with Angel war" (*PL* 6.92): "Lucifer got restless and started his little war for the throne. Heaven became divided into two factions—the faithful and the renegades. The ethereal planes were chaotic with battle, angel against angel." Because Azrael would not choose a side, he too was sent to hell once the war had ended. At various times Loki and Bartleby are shown winged, with silvery armored breastplates, as they wreak divine justice upon any human beings with a trace of sin. They are in turn shot at, stabbed, and finally blown up. A sonic blast from God (Alanis Morissette) explodes Bartleby's head, a homage to the squashed heads of Milton's war in heaven done with ridiculous gratuity. The film revels in the crudeness of such violence and in the collision of high and low sensibilities—bloody angels, crimsoned wings—and like the food fight in *Animal House,* builds on Milton's war in heaven by calling upon its grossest absurdities.

One of the final comic lines of *Dogma*—"This is not a drill. This is the apocalypse"—could be the serious tagline for most of the angelic warrior films that followed it. By the time of *Constantine* in 2005 (dir. Francis Lawrence), the antihero embroiled in a cosmic war has morphed into Keanu Reeves as John Constantine, a chainsmoking, hardboiled "Hellblazer" based on the *Hellblazer* D. C. Comics series.[30] Constantine works prolifically as an exorcist/exterminator of the semi-angels and half-devils who reside on earth and who seek to possess the bodies of humans. These hybrid figures, visible as such only to Constantine and select other visionaries, are representatives on earth of a vast Manichean struggle between God and Satan. This is a dominant trope in other films in this genre.

For instance, the film version of Kevin Grevioux's graphic novel *I, Frankenstein* (dir. Stuart Beattie, 2014) similarly positions its hero, the Creature of Mary Shelley's original novel. Angelic combat is carried out by "the Gargoyle Order," first "commanded into being by the great archangel Michael." These winged figures "wage war against the demon horde, 666 legions of hellspawned creatures unleashed by Satan after his fall from heaven." The Creature becomes the central and determining agent in this "brutal unseen war." And as in Shelley's original, he takes on the name Adam, though there is no explicit mention in the film of the connection between this act and Milton's *Paradise Lost*. In *Constantine*, by universal agreement, fully fledged angels and fallen angels must keep to their own side of the earthly divide. As laid out in the film, "demons stay in hell, angels in heaven…the great détente of the original superpowers." Constantine calls this arrangement a "standing bet for the souls of all mankind" that will be determined at the end of time, a divine wager to see who ends up with more human poker chips. The angelic hybrids are sanctioned to intervene on behalf of the superpowers so long as they do not compromise any conditions of free will. This Miltonic staple is one of several borrowings from *Paradise Lost,* as the film imagines a secret pact, in defiance of the universal balance, between an angelic hybrid, Gabriel, and the demon Mammon, that will bring forth hell on earth.[31]

Driven about in an Angel City taxi, Constantine's first act is to drive out a "soldier demon" possessing a young woman. The presence of this warrior of the fallen immediately suggests to Constantine that the old laws have been changed. He consults first with Beeman, the film's version of James Bond's gadget maker Q, but with holy water ampules and dragon's breath instead of wristwatch lasers and submersible cars. Beeman assures him of the demonic code: "They can work us, but they can't come through onto our plane." Next he meets with Gabriel, played by Tilda Swinton as an androgynous figure whom Constantine first sees flashing momentarily a pair of dark, powerful wings—an image inspired by the dusky angels of Caravaggio.[32] Constantine is upset that despite all of his exorcisms he has received no credit toward salvation—credit he needs because he technically committed suicide as a teenager but was resuscitated and brought back from the dead. He complains to an unsympathetic Gabriel about all the "laws and regulations" before declaring, "You don't even understand us. You're the one who should go to hell, half-breed." This turns out to be foreshadowing, as Gabriel's covert pact with Mammon to end the world is revealed in the film's final act, and Gabriel falls from her heavenly state.

After being attacked in the open by a pure demon, Constantine visits with the former witch doctor Papa Midnite (Djimon Hounsou), once a soldier against the forces of hell but now retreated into neutrality and running a bar "for those who rise and fall." Constantine tells him, "This isn't the usual game, I can feel it. Something's coming." That "something" turns out to be Mammon, in this incarnation no less than the son of Satan. According to the final chapters of the film's invented version of Corinthians (from the "Bible of hell"), Mammon stands to fulfill a prophecy that the "sins of the father" will be "exceeded" by those of the son, and moreover that "Mammon has no patience for his father's rule and yearns to forge his own kingdom of fire and blood." This impatience is an almost perfect reversal of Mammon's plans of "endurance" in *Paradise Lost:* "dismissing quite / All thoughts of War" (*PL* 2.282–83) in order to remake hell in heaven's image, "to found this nether Empire, which might rise / By policy, and long process of time, / In emulation opposite to Heav'n" (2.296–98). But the plot is also an almost perfect transposition of Beelzebub's rebuttal of Mammon, when he urges the fallen to invade that "happy seat / Of…man," and "by sudden onset, either with Hell fire / To waste his whole Creation, or possess / All as our own" (2.347–48, 364–66). The Mammon of *Constantine* has taken Beelzebub's exhortations to heart.[33]

Because of a loophole in the cosmic cold war, Mammon can enter the earthly plane if he has assistance from the other side: "the help of God." This arrives through an ancient relic, the famed "Spear of Destiny," the blade that pierced Christ's side and that still bears spots of divine blood. The weapon alone, however, is not enough; Mammon must also have a human vessel potent enough to contain him, and Gabriel finds the perfect fit in Constantine's love interest, Angela Dodson (Rachel Weisz). In the climactic confrontation, Gabriel reveals her motivation in bringing Mammon to earth: jealous of the love God shows humans, she has been seeking to enact another fortunate fall by bringing about her own Armageddon: "I've been watching you for a long time. It's only in the face of horror that you truly find your nobler selves. And you can be so noble. So I'll bring you pain. I'll bring you horror. So that you may rise above it. So that those of you who survive this reign of hell on Earth will be worthy of God's love." It is a perversion of Michael's prophetic message in the last book of *Paradise Lost,* that a "new Earth" will be "raise[d] / From the conflagrant mass, purg'd and refin'd" (12.547–48) after the Second Coming, but it is also an attempt to imitate and honor God's divine plan in book 10. When the orders of angels view Sin and Death invading the world, he tells them, "See with what heat these Dogs of Hell advance / To waste and havoc yonder World" (*PL* 10.616– 17), though it is justified when by the Son "Heav'n and Earth renew'd shall be made pure / To sanctity that shall receive no stain" (10.638–39). The choice in Constantine to focus on the greedy Mammon aligns him with those Miltonic "Hell-hounds" and the "ravenous Jaws" they share with the very mouth of Hell (10.630, 637).

At the last possible moment, Lucifer intervenes. Drawn by another Constantine suicide attempt (he reportedly covets Constantine's soul so strongly that he makes the visit in person), he is informed of his son's plot and promptly turns into the angel of Abraham and Isaac, preventing the sacrifice of Angela and sending the wayward Mammon back to hell. As Lucifer explains to Gabriel, before blowing her almost to kingdom come: "This world is mine. In time. You best of all of us Gabriel should understand ambition." This exchange rather oddly implies that Gabriel here is actually meant to be seen not as the half-breed Constantine thinks her to be but as the true archangel—one who knows even the "old names" of Lucifer, and one with whom Lucifer himself has a backstory. In suggesting that Gabriel becomes the one who "best of all of us...should understand ambition," Lucifer merges his own misapplied ambitions with hers. But it also marks her as one of Milton's "grievous Wolves, / Who all the sacred mysteries of Heav'n / To thir own vile advantages shall turn / Of lucre and ambition" (*PL* 12.508–11), especially one who has attempted to "force the Spirit of Grace itself" (12.525). For these sins, when Gabriel attempts to strike at Lucifer she realizes God has forsaken her. Her piteous cry of "Father?" is answered by (apparently) Lucifer blasting her with fire and a torrent of water: her wings are incinerated and she ends virtually drowned. Not destroyed, she has, like other angels in these films, fallen into a completely human state. Her wings are cartilaginous stumps, her eyes no longer glow, and she can now experience the full range of the human condition, including the "pain" and "horror" she was herself promising to deliver. Lucifer, meanwhile, brings Constantine back from the brink of heavenly salvation so that he will have the chance once again to fall into damnation. Gabriel tries to accelerate this when she begs him to destroy her with a "holy shotgun": "Be the hand of God. It's your choice. It's always been your choice." Instead of succumbing to temptation and vengeance, he instead punches her hard in the mouth. "That's called pain," he says, "get used to it." It is a moment that recalls Michael's devastating strike through Satan's right side (when Satan "first knew pain" [*PL* 6.327]) even as it lifts Constantine from the world of the fallen.

Two years after *Constantine,* the impressively low-budget Australian film *Gabriel* (dir. Shane Abbess, 2007) resembles *The Prophecy* in pitting angel against angel, pushing the centrality of combat even further and adopting as its own antihero not an earthly intermediary like Deckard or Spawn or Constantine but the angel Gabriel (Andy Whitfield). The film begins with Gabriel traveling down a wormhole, "falling" through nebulae to reach Purgatory, where "even angels fear to tread," a realm situated between those of absolute light and dark. Purgatory is further contested by those powers—powers the film curiously chooses to keep nameless, so that God and Satan (and, for that matter, heaven and hell) are never mentioned. The accompanying voiceover recounts the other "Arc" [*sic*] Angels who have already made the journey to battle with the seven Fallen Angels who now have an unprecedented stranglehold on Purgatory. These other Arcs are Remiel, Uriel,

Amitiel (a female angel), Ithuriel, Raphael, and Michael; leading the fallen train is Sammael, an indubitably Miltonic Satan figure whose first word in the script and recurring motivation is "freedom," and his underlings are Asmodeus, Lilith, Ahriman, Balan, and Moloch. (The insubordinate Belial is slain by Sammael in one of the film's opening scenes.) The presence of Ithuriel here is an especially telling trace in regards to Milton's influence. As West points out, "Two of Milton's names, Ithuriel and Zophiel, do not appear in the Bible at all. Ithuriel scarcely appears, either, in the literature of angelology, unless we take some liberties in transliteration."[34] The names are clearly collected from a range of sources, from Zoroastrianism to the book of Enoch, but Abbess singles out Milton's epic in describing his preparation and influence: "We did...lots of research into angels and all the mythology behind them—read all the books, like *Paradise Lost*, and looked at all the best and most popular angels and took from them and made our own versions of them."[35] Ithuriel would surely be gratified to be included on this top 14 "most popular" list—according to IMDb this is the only use of that name in any film. Nonetheless, his appearance signals an open attachment to the Miltonic tradition, in particular to its role in shaping angelic warriors like Gabriel's spear bearer.

Gabriel, a young Mad Max clone with a fierce tattoo twining up his neck and impossibly blue colored contact lenses (a favored cosmetic device in the film's costuming), is the last of the Arcs—at least he receives a note from Michael telling him so, and alerting him that the others have failed. He then sets off into the woeful, dystopian Purgatory, a rainy, crepuscular urban space populated by hopeless "unclaimed souls," only to discover immediately that his mind gives off a kind of acoustic signal to his enemy angels, who promptly mobilize a preemptive assault. In keeping with his impatient characterization in *Paradise Lost,* the guttural, hairless Moloch—a dead ringer for F. W. Murnau's Nosferatu—is the first to attack Gabriel, and he does so in pell-mell fury. He rushes out from a blind corner and straight at the angel as Gabriel casually fires away at him with double-barreled semiautomatics. But Moloch is a cannier fighter than he first appears, vanishing and surprising Gabriel from behind; the two begin hand-to-hand combat, Moloch with blades and Gabriel at first with only his natural martial arts, stylized very much after the fight choreography in the *Matrix* films. In fact, one reviewer, while observing that *Paradise Lost* set the precedent for Gabriel as "tough guy," quipped that Abbess's film was still "more *Matrix* than Milton."[36] Gabriel finally secures one of Moloch's blades to use against him, plunging it into his flesh—all angels who make the journey to the "midworld" must become essentially human—before finishing him off in a hail of gunfire. And so the film establishes immediately its organizing principle: this is mortal combat (via *Mortal Kombat*), a video game–like series of angelic gladiatorial fights to the death.[37]

In between these set pieces, the film works a *Blues Brothers* angle: Gabriel is on a mission from God to put the band back together. He first finds Uriel, living in a state of paranoia in a fortified trailer, who has "turned his back on the order" and foresworn himself as a "servant of the light." Next is his former lover, Amitiel, who has been defeated by Sammael and forced not only to become fully human but also an addict and a prostitute. Ithuriel has retreated to the untroubled confines of a soup kitchen, while in the catacombs beneath the city Raphael lies dying in a barren cell. Michael has simply disappeared completely. One by one, Gabriel rescues them from their individual purgatories. And one after another, the angels are pitted against each other in epic permutations, a plot basically derived from the condensed action of *Paradise Lost* 6.354–72, when Gabriel "pierc'd the deep array / Of *Moloch* furious King," Uriel and Raphael "mangl'd with ghastly wounds" Adramalech and Asmadai (i.e., Asmodeus), and Abdiel "scorcht and blasted" the "Atheist crew" of Ariel, Arioch, and violent Ramiel. The film's fight card includes Balan versus Amitiel, Gabriel versus Balan, Gabriel versus Ahriman, Lilith versus Uriel, Sammael versus Raphael, and Gabriel versus Asmodeus (the latter an especially vicious bloodbath: Gabriel overcome with bloodlust, repeatedly smashing Asmodeus's skull with the butt of his rifle, until both fighters are splattered with gore). Seemingly conflicted by his own rampages and the deaths of the angels he has brought out of hiding (all perish but Amitiel), Gabriel nonetheless decides to finish off the border war (after finishing off Lilith by punching her full of fatal drugs) by challenging Sammael to single combat.

The film ends with a twist: Sammael, it turns out, actually *is* Michael, who after falling to Purgatory was so overcome by hate that he went to the dark side, overwhelming Sammael and replacing him as leader of the fallen. As part of their final confrontation, which ranges from ferocious to tender, Gabriel and Michael exchange dueling manifestos, with Michael's patterned very much after Milton's Satan: "We were born in a world controlled by fear and rules. We were slaves to a higher purpose. Tell me, what is the point of being created just so we could serve someone else's wishes? All I've done is set myself free. Now I beg you to do the same." The rough paraphrase of Satan's "Here at least we shall be free" speech (*PL* 1.258–70) also shows touches of Satan's speech at the start of the war in book 5, denouncing heaven's "Law and Edict" and urging his comrades to "cast off this Yoke" (5.798, 786). Michael, in short, hopes to convince Gabriel to join him in rebellion against their "master," and to rule alongside him in Purgatory until eventually becoming strong enough to assault even the heavenly realm of light: "In time we could grow powerful enough to crush it completely. These people are free, and now so are you." It is another Miltonic gloss, this time of Satan's plot to "possess / All as our own" and "Seduce" the "puny habitants" of earth "to our Party" (2.365–68), so that in time, "with neighboring Arms / And opportune excursion we may chance / Re-enter Heav'n" (2.395–97). When Gabriel refuses, Michael drives a pipe straight through him. Gabriel, however, can also quote Miltonic scripture for his purpose, and when Michael asks him, "Why, Gabriel? I give you everything and you still deny me?" (momentarily channeling Milton's God), Gabriel gasps, "Free will. It's not about control. It's about choice. We came here to guide these people. Nothing more." At that, Gabriel embraces Michael in a cosmic collision, driving the pipe through him as well, and they fall down to die together. Apparently struck by Gabriel's interpretation of free will, Michael uses his last scrap of power to heal his brother's fatal wound. Gabriel rises, but not before he too is moved from his orthodox position by Michael's words.

Railing at the heavens, Gabriel cries out over Michael's corpse and accuses God: "In time, you will form new works and all of this will be forgotten. I can't let that happen." Echoes of Roy Batty's poetical end in *Blade Runner* ripple here, especially in the lament for what will be forgotten. Gabriel's last protest, like Batty's, is not against the fallen but against his master: "You threw me far from grace, and now I fall unto it. I hope I see you again." Striking the inevitable cruciform pose, Gabriel throws himself from the roof. This fall will transform him from angel to man and allow him not only the experience of mortal love but to retain a memory of all that has happened. As he falls a voice-over says, "Falling is the last thing an angel feels. A distant voice still echoes inside my head. But for the first time, it is my own. Forgive me." The film is modeled very much after another Australian film, Alex Proyas's *Dark City* (1998), even ascribing to Gabriel the dual purpose of "destroy[ing] the Fallen and bring[ing] light back to this place." In its visual styling, it is also indebted to Proyas's *The Crow*, as well as *Blade Runner;* Wim Wenders's *Wings of Desire* (1987) is also never far away from films with angels falling to become human.[38] The messianic ending of *Gabriel*—clouds break, light returns to city—is not uncomplicated: Gabriel's self-sacrifice is also self-serving and invites a reading as a satanic fall ("the mind is its own place," the angel finally seems to say, when the voice in his head is finally "his own"). A postcredits coda in the theatrical release makes it clear that Gabriel has fallen to become fully human, just as Amitiel did (and whom he smilingly rejoins in the final shot), and to keep alive the memory of the tragic tale in which he had been compelled to participate.

Another film to set Gabriel against Michael, *Legion* (dir. Scott Charles Stewart, 2009) moves the war in heaven now fully to earth, with Michael (Paul Bettany) taking on the role of rebel angel.[39] In consequence of his refusal to take orders from God, his wings have been chopped, and he appears on earth on the verge of an apocalyptic end of days. God, it seems, has once more become "tired of all the bullshit," and the contractual limits of his previous covenants have apparently worn out. He is ready to exterminate the human race not with fire or flood but by sending his angels to possess human beings, beginning with the weak and working up. The film takes place almost entirely at a desolate diner called Paradise Falls and continues its Miltonic citations by repeatedly noting how the only people who show up at this truck stop in the "middle of nowhere" are those who are "lost." Paradise Falls has become the front line for salvation because a waitress there, Charlie (perhaps with reference to *Charlie's Angels*) is pregnant with a child who will once more redeem humankind. To drive the point home, the film is set at Christmas. Charlie (Adrianne Palicki) is a much-diluted version of Linda Hamilton's tough and gritty *Terminator* heroine, Sarah Connor. Meanwhile, an array of villains comes along to claim the unborn, including an elderly woman with a walker who has become the film's signature antagonist. She spews filth, eats raw meat, bites through a man's jugular, climbs walls, and generally savages the diner, all while wearing a housedress.

The film is really a zombie fusion, with the possessing angels standing in for the walking dead, along with rampant citations of the first *Terminator* movie (when the warring sides were humans and machines). In general, the film is heavily derivative—a possessed child, for instance, is modeled unmistakably after the "Chucky" doll villain—and its ambitions to become a cult film, doing for angels what George Romero's *Night of the Living Dead* did for zombies, are driven by set pieces from other works. Michael's appearance without wings is even linked early in the film to Clarence in *It's a Wonderful Life:* the holiday film plays in the background as Jimmy Stewart can be heard mumbling, "I don't know whether I like it very much being seen around with an angel without any wings." Michael's amputations are a bit more grisly than Clarence's, though perhaps not as bad as Bartleby's in *Dogma* or Gabriel's in *Constantine,* and he has to stitch the wounds together. The angel has also been stripped of his armor, and his new warrior panoply depends on an assortment of human weapons that he ransacks at the start of the film: a range of rifles, semiautomatics, submachine guns, and hunting knives. In a central scene, the story flashes back to a debate in heaven between Michael and Gabriel, his nemesis in the final battle. There both are garbed in the angelic gear of medieval frescoes—Roman legionnaire attire—underneath the canopy of their formidable wings. Michael suggests that he will not answer God's order to destroy humanity (apparently by targeting the unborn child directly) because he has *not* lost faith. In fact, he feels his own heart must be that of God's as well, and suggests that he gives God "what he needs," while Gabriel only bends to what he wants.

By rewriting Michael as satanic, as an angel who admires humanity's ability to hope against hope, to fight even when all is lost, the film conflates a number of uneasy alliances. Michael and Gabriel call each other "brother," and Michael is distinctly fashioned as the prodigal one—leaving home for earth, only to eventually return even more glorious for this seeming betrayal—a point Gabriel cannot understand. In one fight sequence, when Gabriel has Michael on the hip, he challenges him, "You wanted to live like one of them, now you will die like one of them." He invokes the narrative from Enoch of angels descending to participate in the variety of human experience, a point the film emphasizes with the tattoos on Michael's body, reportedly Enochian writings—the language of angels in the lexicon of John Dee. But it is not clear that Michael wants anything other than to fight. He arms himself and the rest of those in the diner, but he never stops to eat, drink, and certainly not to fall in love.

The climactic battle between Michael and Gabriel is confined to the dim diner. Gabriel attacks with a massive mace, one that he pumps up even more for his battle with Michael, and Michael fires back with a machine gun (fig. 5.1). Gabriel uses his wings as both shields (apparently bulletproof) and weapons—his favored attack is to pirouette with the wings slashing like scythes. In this treatment, angels can feel pain but also bruise, bleed, and die. So Michael is slain by Gabriel, which provokes a paradox—what happens to a dead angel? The answer arrives in the final scene, when Michael descends once more, now as the *deus ex machina* and with his fabled sword in hand, just in time to save the new Joseph and Mary from Gabriel, who seems utterly perplexed at how his dutifulness has come back to undo him. (Michael tells him it is because he showed no mercy.) Gabriel is likewise confused at this celebration of romantic satanism: he asks Jeep, the Joseph figure,

Fig. 5.1. Gabriel and war mace, from *Legion* (2009). *Courtesy of Sony Pictures.*

"Why do you continue to fight when you know all hope is lost?" The battle between Michael and Gabriel leans on some Miltonic devices—the technological innovations of Satan against the classical weaponry of the heavenly host, for instance (the screenplay trumpets, "it's mace versus machine gun")—and there is some garbled discussion of issues of free will.[40] Charlie wonders whether she ever had a choice to end her pregnancy; Gabriel argues that the "baby was never meant to be born." In the end, the new holy family moves forward into an "unwritten" future, blank as the Mojave desert into which they drive, still armed for war.[41]

Finally, Nora Ephron's romantic comedy *Michael* (1996) pushes at the borders of the warrior angel genre, while nonetheless boasting one of the most Miltonic (and certainly the most materialistic) angels of them all: John Travolta's swarthy, sweaty, and wise title character. An exceptionally hirsute and paunchy Travolta plays Michael as a kind of very cool man with enormous wings: he first appears unshaven, smoking a cigarette and scratching his crotch through his boxer shorts. And like Gabriel Garcia Marquez's fallen angel, whose "huge buzzard wings, dirty and half-plucked, were forever entangled in the mud," so that "nothing about him measured up to the proud dignity of angels," this Michael's wings are dirty and disordered, his feet bare, his long, dark locks a mare's nest of grooming.[42] As one of the journalists investigating his appearance puts it, the angel looks as if "some great big bird made love to that guy's mother." The passing joke—perhaps a Sesame Street reference—encodes more than it lets on. The image calls up the rape of Leda by Zeus and more obliquely the interspecies mating of angels and mortal women, and locates Michael squarely in the latter tradition. The link is not accidental: in the spirit of the supernatural Nephilim and the angels who produced them, Travolta's Michael has a series of casual sexual encounters with women throughout the film. The film implies, contra Milton, that "there's no sex in heaven," and so Michael reports he must get what he can on his earthly visits. At once a deflation of the "proud dignity" of the resplendent angels of *Paradise Lost* and an embrace of the material indulgences Milton allows them, the film is an extended burlesque on Raphael's line to Adam in book 5,

"Wonder not then, what God for you saw good / If I refuse not" (491–92).

Christopher Miller first noticed that Travolta's "bad-to-the-bone" seraph "pays homage" to Milton in presenting a figure less "kindly enabler" and "wistful lost soul" than bold cosmic swashbuckler. In Miller's view, Milton's larger-than-life angels are "six-winged shapeshifters who patrol the galaxy, leaving a vapor trail of heavenly fragrance in their wake. When the archangel Michael does battle with Satan, their shields are like 'two broad suns,' and their clash is like the collision of planets."[43] Miller does not mean that these grand galactic images ever show up in the film (which downplays special effects throughout) but that Ephron's Michael captures something of the robust energy and gargantuan power of Milton's angels, even if such powers are passed along through a Rabelaisian filter. This seems most evident in Michael's appetites: he consumes massive quantities of sugar, with "keen dispatch of real hunger," and has an equally insatiable libido. The angel also describes some of those titanic clashes recalled by Miller when he reports that he has fought "6,360 battles" with "no injuries," including the cataclysmic moment when he fought Satan in heaven. But perhaps the film's most telling carryover from Milton, and the one that led Miller to read Ephron's angel as a particular homage to Milton, is, in fact, the "vapor trail of heavenly fragrance." Milton imbues this quality especially in his sociable spirit, Raphael: "Like *Maia's* son he stood, / And shook his Plumes, that Heav'nly fragrance fill'd / The circuit wide" (*PL* 5.285–87). West, citing Joseph Addison, singles out this passage on "the perfume of Raphael's wings" as "Milton's invention."[44] And the film makes extensive use of this singularly Miltonic device, first by using the smell of the angel to herald his arrival, and then by developing that same redolence into a type of sex pheromone that effortlessly stirs desire in those (women) with whom it comes in contact.

The plot of the film is straightforward: a group of writers from a Chicago-based national tabloid are alerted to the angel by the landlady, Pansy Milbank (Jean Stapleton), who has been keeping him tenant for six months. Desperate for a story for the Christmas issue, the once legitimate journalist Frank Quinlan (William Hurt), his opportunistic partner Huey Driscoll (Robert Pastorelli), and the newly hired Dorothy Winters (Andie MacDowell), pretending to be an "angel expert," all travel to the rural Iowan town where Michael has taken up headquarters. The remainder of the film becomes one long picaresque road trip, with Michael eventually fulfilling his ultimate purpose in coming to earth for this, his twenty-sixth and last hurrah: to serve as matchmaker for Quinlan and Winters. Thus, Michael's loose behavior becomes justified as it relaxes as well the heartless Quinlan and thrice-divorced Winters, who by following his lead somehow translate the angel's smoking, drinking, line dancing, and interspecies canoodling into the standardized forms of romantic heteronormalcy.

Michael's initial presentation as an angel soaking up all the unsparing delights earth can offer him becomes a parody of the preparation of Raphael's food in *Paradise Lost*, with its emphasis on "bring[ing] forth and pour[ing] / Abundance" (5.314–15). He begins breakfast by pouring Frosted Flakes into a large bowl, dousing it in milk (he has been residing at the Milk Bottle Motel), and then gilding the lily with heaping spoonfuls of sugar. It is a simple exaggeration of Eve's preparations, who for Raphael's dinner "on the board / Heaps with unsparing hand" (5.343–44). It is less clear whether Michael's excess is meant to critique human inadequacy (in order to approximate the ambrosial flavors of heaven, even sugar has to be sugared) or celestial: as there is no sex in heaven, so too there is nothing that compares to the taste of earthly sweets, and Michael loads up at every opportunity.[45] In either case, it is a play on Milton's basic idea that the "the grosser feeds the purer" (5.416), and a travestying of his notion that angels "concoct, digest, assimilate, / And corporeal to incorporeal turn" (5.412–13). As Raphael's heavenly fragrance has been reduced to the warm aroma of chocolate chip cookies, and his "gorgeous wings" (5.250) to the filthy, molting things clumsily affixed to Travolta's back, so too the angel-at-my-table sequence has become trivialized as an act of gross overconsumption. The humor of the scene (and the film in general), beyond the broad physical comedy of Travolta stuffing and slurping cereal into his mouth and onto his lap, depends, of course, on the incongruity of an angel behaving like a barbarian.[46] What the film reminds us is that Milton, for some readers, had already done this. His gormandizing angel has been found objectionable since the earliest commentators, who found such "keen dispatch of hunger," in C. S. Lewis's words, "poetically grotesque."[47] When Winters opines, "I thought angels were cleaner," Michael replies, "I'm not that kind of angel." It is a joke easy to make at Milton's expense, a crude extrapolation of his materialist theology. If Raphael sat on the mossy ground not for an afternoon but for months, would his "feather'd mail / Sky-tinctur'd grain" (5.284–85) not get dirty, too? But it is also an aligning with, if not an outright celebration of, Milton's own heterodoxies.

As Pansy explains, Michael "battled Lucifer and threw him out of heaven" (for which she cites Revelation 12:7, conflating a primordial war in heaven, à la Milton, with the prophetic future visions of Saint John). Michael demurs—"that was a long time ago"—but confirms that he has been fighting more localized battles while on earth—including the smiting of a bank that had been squeezing Pansy on her motel mortgage. Later, Michael himself describes the battle in heaven in apocalyptic terms: "I spun around, and the next thing that happened was he came as a hundred mouths open and stinking with decay. And he tore at my flesh from every angle in heaven. So I grabbed Beelzebub's blue tongue in my fist..." (an "old geezer" listening to the tale interrupts to ask who Beelzebub is, and Michael clarifies, "Beelzebub is Satan"). The film makes other periodic nods to the tradition of Michael as a militant warrior, mostly through the same kind of inglorious deflations by which it parodies heavenly fragrance and angelic gustation. In another apparent Miltonic citation, Michael tells Quinlan, "I once saw the world's biggest cannonball," a memory prompted by his now wanting to see the World's Largest Ball of Twine. Milton's Michael, of course, witnessed the world's biggest, and first, cannonball, during the war in heaven. At one point, Michael spots a lone black bull off in a field, whose appearance (perhaps the horns) prompts him to utter several cries of "Battle!"; in imitation of the beast, the angel snorts and stamps his foot, then charges and rams headlong into the animal. He ends up concussed, momentarily suggesting Michael may be nothing more than a winged Quixote, tilting at windmills. And in a subsequent bar scene, Michael's penchant for battle becomes entwined with his magnetic attraction for women.

Travolta's expected dance number is set at a local tavern called Joe's. Every woman who passes his table is instantly affected by his pheromonal chemistry. After Michael moves off with a pair of women to the dance floor, Winters asks their waitress, "Have you ever, ever heard of an angel that was interested in sex? Of course not. Angels do not have sex." This is yet another premise the film is eager to undo. For all of Michael's dalliances, there is never a suggestion that he has fallen. Rather, the film again takes as its informing model Raphael's notion that what God saw good for man should not be shunned by angels, and that this maxim does not apply solely to food but other corporal pleasures. Thus, the film promotes the preposterous inverse of Raphael's idea that "men / With Angels may participate" (*PL* 5.493–94): angels too may participate with men and women in licensed carnal relations.[48] And when Michael's seductive aura becomes so great that it overwhelms the entire population of women at Joe's, the result, as in Enoch, is war. Or at least Ephron's best stab at it: a bar fight breaks out among the men jealous over all the attention being lavished on the angel. Michael assumes once more the port of Mars, the mantle of an indomitable warrior, using weapons from the armory at hand: a pool cue for a sword and a garbage can lid for a shield. During the fight the women, watching, debate the brand of Michael's aura: for some, "It's caramels, he smells like caramels"; another contends, "No, it's cotton candy"; Winters corrects them: "it's cookies . . . and the smell gets stronger when he's in heat." But what seems to drive Michael into heat is not so much the presence of the women as the battle lust he experiences with the men. Like *Dogma* before it, Ephron's warrior angel film plays off what might seem most comical about Milton's war, even as it perhaps unwittingly celebrates the same perplexing poetic impulses.

All of these warrior angel films have their romantic impulses: underdog heroes, an all-powerful but absent deity who has left the fight to others, moral codes that favor individual sacrifice, incessant drive, and unabated hope. In this, the films ally themselves with the Milton of the Romantics, and citations of *Paradise Lost* do the work of coding the films as continuing to fight the good fight—resist tyranny, seize independence. But most of the films are also enmeshed in the problems of the spectacular Milton—how to deliver rocking, celestial combat to the masses—and so also typically contain and celebrate the kind of battle glory that the poet ostensibly eschewed, as when in book 9 he claims to pursue the "better fortitude / Of Patience and Heroic Martyrdom" against the tales of "long and tedious havoc" of "fabl'd Knights / In Battles feign'd" (30–32); or when in book 11 Michael condemns the vainglory of "Battle" and "Man-slaughter" (691–93); or even in the war itself, when Raphael glosses over the "thousands" of heroic actions for which angels "Seek not the praise of men" (6.373, 376). The cartoonish violence of *The Prophecy* or *Gabriel* or *Spawn* or *Legion* not only takes on the bloody manners of Moloch but also shows how difficult Milton's poem can be to reconcile to itself. For Milton surely is better—and more luxurious—in his graphic battle scenes than he lets on in book 9, when he claims to be "Nor skill'd nor studious" (42) in such presentations. *Blade Runner,* though it is in some ways the least openly Miltonic of any in this genre, still captures best the complexity of Milton's angelic warriors, when the eye-gouging, finger-crushing freedom fighter dies not blasted, beheaded, or blown apart, but in a quiet wisp of poetry.

"All Hell Broke Loose":
The Horror Film

The long-established affiliation of Milton with horror and the macabre can be traced through the magic lantern shows and phantasmagorias that appropriated the dynamics of hell from *Paradise Lost*. Since those early entertainments, a steady line of horror films have perpetuated Blake's infamous conception of Milton as being "of the Devil's party," assuming in Milton a kind of Virgilian guide to all things infernal.[1] From such early horror films as Victor Fleming's *Dr. Jekyll and Mr. Hyde* (1941) and Roger Corman's *The Pit and the Pendulum* (1961) to more current works like Michael Winner's *The Sentinel* (1977), Jack Clayton's *Something Wicked This Way Comes* (1983), Neil Jordan's *Interview with the Vampire* (1994), David Fincher's *Seven* (1995), Taylor Hackford's *The Devil's Advocate* (1997), Wes Craven's *Scream 3* (2000), and Patrick Lussier's *Drive Angry* (2011), the horror genre has represented Milton as a signifier for the diabolical.[2]

Indeed, so at home with Milton are horror films that they exhibit little of the restlessness with Milton evident in most other genres, sometimes even expressing an exclusivity or possessiveness over him. In one instance, at the start of the pseudoslasher film *April Fool's Day* (dir. Fred Walton, 1986), a group of college students is ferrying over to an isolated island. One studious standout is seen reading *Paradise Lost,* for a "course on the English epic." She calls it (ominously) "a dying form"—Milton's writing a victim of generic indifference, but in this case the slasher film is the savior (even as one wonders what other English epics appear on the syllabus for such a course). As the young student points out to a baffled friend, "not too many people read it nowadays. Even in college." This is a direct shot at the ambivalence of the *Animal House* tradition, and a powerful act of reterritorializing seen in other films in the genre. For the one place that such pronouncements about nonreading can be thrown out, the one place college students can be expected to know *Paradise Lost* front to back, is in the horror film.

The association has become commonplace enough in popular culture that in the horror-noir video game *Max Payne* (dir. Navid Khonsari, 2001), Max storms the satanic nightclub Ragna Rock and finds a copy of *Paradise Lost* piled alongside the *Necronomicon, Malleus Maleficarum,* and other books, "all dealing with the occult and the infernal."[3] Further emphasizing the genealogy, these grimoires are piled beside "stacks of horror videos and a couple of Ouija boards."[4] Similarly, the fantasy game *Diablo II* (Blizzard Entertainment, 2000) features a plane of existence called Pandemonium and, within it, Pandemonium Fortress, a contested stronghold and base of operations in the game's storyline of the war between heaven and hell. The horror genre has thus more or less standardized Shelley's opinion that "the Devil owes everything to Milton" and has often followed the romantic poets in recognizing Satan as derived from *Paradise Lost:* "Dante and Tasso present us with a very gross idea of him. Milton divested him of a sting, hoof, and horns, and clothed him with the sublime grandeur of a graceful but tremendous spirit."[5]

Extending this influence, James B. Twitchell suggests in 1985's *Dreadful Pleasures: An Anatomy of Modern Horror* that "modern monsters have Milton's Satan as their great progenitor."[6] Certainly horror films have been drawn to the idea of a sympathetic Satan, unsettling the audience not only by displaying monstrous fangs and hoofs and horns—the gargantuan abominations of Satan in Dante's *Inferno*—but by manipulating the audience's identification with a rebellious antihero doubling as evil incarnate.[7] This is most clearly the approach in such films as *Interview with the Vampire* and *The Devil's Advocate,* which depend on ultracharismatic villainy, but recurs even in such absurdist treatments as the Adam Sandler comedy *Little Nicky* (dir. Steven Brill, 2000). And though many trickster figures of Hollywood cinema often typologically incorporate a kind of Faustian Mephistopheles—a trend that prompted one film critic to ask, "Is the Devil American?"—the Milton-influenced horror film more often turns for its deviltry to the technophilic Satan of *Paradise Lost.*[8] The same villain who could invent gunpowder and cannonballs to outpace and overwhelm the quaint arsenal of the heavenly host also serves as a prototype for such techie fiends as Rotwang in Fritz Lang's *Metropolis* and Evil in Terry Gilliam's *Time Bandits* (1981).[9]

Yet while the idea of a rebellious and progressive Satan has been adapted compellingly in horror films, such films have also frequently returned to Milton's greatest spectacularization of horror. Since at least the designs of Addison's friend who wished on the banks of the Thames for a device that would "employ all the tricks of Art to terrify and surprise the spectator," the palace of Pandaemonium appeared again and again in virtually every precinematic Milton entertainment. Continuing this pattern, horror films have appropriated Milton's figure of demonic space as a means to develop the menace of bureaucracy, industrialization, materialism, and homogeneity. Such films reinforce the horrors of "personal space" being invaded—the distillation of most works of horror, perhaps—and imagine the shapes of Pandaemonium projected onto diverse cinematic landscapes, from the hivelike urbanization of *Metropolis* to the disturbing carnival of *Something Wicked This Way Comes.*[10] In Twitchell's ascription of modern monsters as variations on Milton's Satan, he contends that such beings "have their own unique existences, their own solipsistic codes, not just a 'room of their own' but their own self-contained worlds."[11] What seems most important here is less the idea that modern monsters have transcended the grotesqueries of medieval representations than that Milton, in having Satan establish Pandaemonium, anticipated those modern horrors that respond to or depend on preeminently the conditions of their spatialization. Twitchell's "self-contained worlds" are not only the habitations of monsters but also constructions of the monstrous, presenting the self with at once the vastest and most intricate imagining of its own destruction, a sublimity of terror that threatens to engulf the spectator utterly.

The Horrors of Pandaemonium

William Blake can be credited with inaugurating and popularizing an association between the Industrial Revolution and those "dark Satanic Mills" he imagines in his preface to *Milton*. As David L. Pike details in *Metropolis on the Styx: The Underworlds of Modern Culture, 1800–2001*, the droning labor behind Pandaemonium came to stand for the mindless advance of industrialism and urbanization. "Satan and his minions in Pandaemonium are industrious and full of productive energy," Pike observes, "providing wonders and entertainment along with the requisite temptations."[12] Thus, "it was as a portrait of the modern city that Milton's Pandaemonium inspired so many later imaginations," with Satan routinely caricatured as an "infernal industrialist."[13] Unlike Dante's Dis — "a damned city without a head in which no sane person would possibly live" — Milton's Pandaemonium stood out as "an infernal place that nevertheless remains inhabitable."[14] In the new underworlds of brick and steam, Milton's vision captured something of the violations being perpetrated on the idylls of nature. The poem provides some blueprints for this association: when Mammon and his crew open "into the Hill a spacious wound / And digg'd out ribs of Gold," it presages the "ransack[ing]" of "mother Earth" by "impious hands," "Rifl[ing] the bowels... / For Treasures better hid" (*PL* 1.686–90). The very inhabitability of such spaces is problematized by many horror films, even as they transfer the vulnerability of the land to those dwelling within it.

The history of the word "pandemonium" is itself suggestive of this degeneration of Milton's capital into a hellish metropolis. Though the construction of Satan's palace can certainly be seen as a string of competing signifiers—grotesque splendor, dissonant organization, contentious solidarity, even self-parodying mockery (starting with its ironic inversion of the pantheon)—only one strain has remained in contemporary usage. "Pandemonium" has come colloquially to mean radical disorder, the hive become a swarm, all hell breaking loose.[15] Ironically, the latter phrase is itself a Miltonic coinage—appropriated in countless film taglines—and posed in *Paradise Lost* by Gabriel, when he first confronts and mocks Satan in Eden: "But wherefore thou alone? wherefore with thee / Came not all Hell broke loose?" (4.917–18). No film better exploits the "hell broke loose" trope than *Drive Angry* (2011), in which Nicolas Cage plays a man named John Milton who escapes hell to avenge the death of his daughter and save his grand-daughter from a satanic sacrifice. The movie poster reads simply, "*Drive Angry:* All Hell Breaks Loose"[16] (see fig. 6.1). The opening sequence shows Milton bursting out of hell in a stolen Charger and careening down the Highway to Hell, eventually reaching earth, where Milton's car promptly crushes a serpent crossing the road. But Milton's depiction of Pandaemonium is on the surface hardly consonant with the jailbreak confusion it has come to signify: the capital of hell is an organizing principle, a (mock) restoration of the hierarchies of heaven. The bastardization of the term "pandemonium" into its very opposite sense parallels its appropriation as a new *locus classicus* for the displacement of an English pastoral ideal by the horrors of industry, and in turn its promotion as a site for all the pandemic horrors of modernity. The stately palace has become a deteriorated cluster of disparate, disconnected motifs, the sacred become the scarred.

Danny Boyle's appropriation of Pandaemonium for the 2012 London Olympics opening ceremony pulls from this industrialization reading, as does the Julien Temple film *Pandaemonium* (2000), a literary period piece not about Milton but Coleridge, Wordsworth, and their circle. Coleridge's laudanum-induced delirium is a recurring visual effect, an aspect of the pandemonic derangement; but the film also repeatedly visualizes various eighteenth century technological achievements as prophetic of unstoppable evolutions. Thus, Coleridge takes a hot-air balloon ride that briefly and disturbingly turns into a vision of jet planes, and the

Fig. 6.1. Nicolas Cage as John Milton, breaking loose in *Drive Angry* (2011). *Promotional poster courtesy of Nu Image, Inc., and Summit Entertainment, LLC.*

Romantic poets' progressive, pantisocratic philosophy becomes both a counterresponse to this uncontrollable change and another iteration of it, an embrace of radical social revolution. The film, paralleling this ambivalence, dramatizes the relationship of the Romantic poets to Milton as full of veneration and challenge. An early scene offers a passing encomium, for instance, when Coleridge's friend Tom Poole predicts that "Sam will prove our finest poet since Milton." (Dorothy Wordsworth objects: "The new Milton should aspire to some more terrific theme, not domesticity. We need epic.") Later, there is a lighthearted scene of Wordsworth inhaling helium from a leather balloon. Bursting into a squeaky falsetto, he is urged by Coleridge to "Do some poetry! Some Milton! Do some Milton!" Wordsworth balks, wanting neither to embarrass himself nor, apparently, to diminish Milton's magniloquence. Coleridge takes the initiative—"then I will!"—and after filling himself with gas, recites a high-pitched, Mickey Mouse mockery of Satan's fall: "Nor did he scape / By all his engines, but was headlong sent / With his industrious crew to build in Hell. / ... At Pandaemonium, the high capital / Of Satan and his peers." A film invested both visually and narratively in madness and hallucination, this particular conflation of novelties—the captured helium, Satan's construction of hell—suggests the lure and mind-altering danger of the pandemonic.

Various buildings have been suggested as models for Milton's Pandaemonium, including St. Paul's and St. Peter's Cathedrals, though the poem itself holds up the two most significant analogues: "*Babel,* and the works of *Memphian* Kings" (*PL* 1.694).[17] The aspiring heights of mortal towers and pyramids are humbled by the sudden ascent of demonic sites, which accomplish in a single hour "What in an age they with incessant toil / And hands innumerable scarce perform" (1.698–99). It is partly the fury of this pace that makes the building of Pandaemonium such an uncanny structure. The supernatural speed of the fallen angels in *Paradise Lost* returns Milton to the folklore of fiends in *L'Allegro,* where the "drudging *Goblin*" threshes corn in one night "that ten day-labourers could not end" (105, 109). The folkloric link is sustained when the infernal spirits later diminish to the size of "smallest Dwarfs," or "Faery Elves" (*PL* 1.779, 781). This conceit captures a kind of horror also evident in the more famous epic simile comparing the palace to a beehive, in which the bees "among fresh dews and flowers / Fly to and fro" (1.771–72) in seeming pleasure, while the "swarming" crowd implies the dangers behind such mindless flitting—the loss of individual will and scope.[18] The woodland "faery elves," Milton writes, inspire fear in those rustics who hear their "midnight Revels, by a Forest side / Or Fountain" (1.781–83). The horror of this effect produces simultaneously "joy and fear" (1.788), forerunning that modern sense of horror's "dreadful pleasure"—the seduction of scaring ourselves. Milton's "belated Peasant sees, / Or dreams he sees" (1.783–84) these revels—the scene is a product not just of the moonlit landscape but also of his own desires. And that desire, as such tales of trespass into the fairy world tend to underscore, is for the "jocund Music" to play forever—to lose the self in an imagined eternity that is simultaneously carefree and rewarding and illusory play. It is thus a micro-scene of temptation and damnation that anticipates the loss of Eden. If Pandaemonium is literally a "place of all demons" (and an inversion of the classical "pan-theon," gathering place of "all gods"), the sylvan faeries suggest it is also the place of the panic-inducing satyr-god Pan: the pastoral fallen into the infernal, revels perverted into the orgiastic.

The capitol of hell is also "Built like a Temple." But it is a temple that flaunts its baroque trappings: "*Pilasters* round," "Doric pillars," "bossy Sculptures," and a roof of "fretted Gold" (*PL* 1.713–17). Anticipating the magical dining hall of Harry Potter's Hogwarts, the "arched roof" is further pixilated with "many a row / Of Starry Lamps and blazing Cressets" to give light "as from a sky" (1.726, 729–30). In effect, everything about the place strives toward the mimetic; its architect is Mulciber, who once "built in Heav'n high Tow'rs" (1.749) for the other deities. He now labors, in Mammon's words, to make heaven and hell sufficiently "resemble" one another: "As he our darkness, cannot we his Light / Imitate when we please?" (2.268, 269–70).[19] This repetition compulsion comprises a kind of poetics of Pandaemonium itself: the politics of Milton's use of blank verse and avoidance of royalist-favored rhyme in *Paradise Lost* resound in the demons who try to "rhyme" heaven, to duplicate its celestial bounty with ersatz imitations. The strained couplet they form in their echoing of heaven's grandeur is one of the foremost grotesqueries of the new underworld.[20] These repetitions also signal for what Paul Oppenheimer, in a study of modern horror films, calls the "redundancy" of demonic space: "one is borne round and round in never-ending circles of the same rooms, fields, offices, or whatever, among the same sorts of objects, whose meanings gather toward a new, frightening imperialism of greed."[21] The honeycombed hive of Pandaemonium confirms this image with its implied replication of cells; the demons throng around their capitol's "Gates / And Porches wide" (1.761–62) like bees "about the Hive / In clusters" (1.770–71). Pandaemonium becomes the graphic image of the fallen spirits' inability to escape the hell within them, one marked by the failures of reason and intellect, as when some of the host gather on a nearby hill to attempt to understand their situation, "and reason'd high / Of Providence, Foreknowledge, Will, and Fate, / Fixt Fate, Free Will, Foreknowledge absolute, / And found no end, in wand'ring mazes lost" (2.558–61).

One of the additional effects of a Pandaemonium pockmarked with porches and gates is to continue a pattern of wounding in the building sequence: Mammon and his crew "Opened into the hill a spacious wound / And digged out ribs of gold" (*PL* 1.689–90); the designer, Mulciber (i.e., Vulcan, Hephaestos), is infamously a crippled god; and the great hall in which the fallen angels gather is "like a covered field, where champions bold / ...Defied the best of paynim chivalry" (1.763–65).[22] The latter image summons up injury and bloodshed on a level with such gory romances as *The Song of Roland*. Pandaemonium is also partly an extension of Satan himself; Milton describes him earlier as standing "like a tower" (1.591). But it is also a continuance of his disfigured visage, which "Deep scars of thunder had intrenched" (1.601). These almost oxymoronic instances of "wounded pride" suggest major countercurrents: that bold ventures are often alloyed with the vulnerability of overextension, and likewise that positions of vulnerability often produce rash and reactive ventures. The great precedent for all of this, of course, as Milton points out, is the Tower of Babel and its typological twins.[23] As in Marlowe's *Doctor Faustus,* it is not just Helen's famous "face that launched a thousand ships" that discloses her demonism, but the insuperable "towers of Ilium" that are at once "topless" and "burnt," their limitlessness becoming perversely involuted, a sign of infinite collapse. It will be recalled that, in Genesis, Babel does not fall: rather, after the Lord confounds the language of its builders, it is left unfinished—in *Paradise Lost,* Milton notes simply, "thus was the building left / Ridiculous, and the work Confusion nam'd" (12.61–62). The confusion of the people becomes emblematized in the gaping wound of a structure that aims to go everywhere and ends nowhere.

Pandaemonium is unquestionably a massively invested symbol, suggesting at once a collective obliviousness that threatens the loss of the individual; almost carnivalesque inversions of high and low, heaven and hell; a derangement through repetition; a defiant vulnerability; and, finally, the paradoxical seductiveness of horror itself. It is never itself but ever a copy, keenly aware of and frustrated by its indebtedness. The convolutions of repetition can be seen in Pandaemonium's spatialization of narrativity, akin to Michel de Certeau's citified "walkers...whose bodies follow the thicks and thins of an urban 'text' they write without being able to read it"; the busy urban traceries of Pandaemonium are similarly built upon "networks of these moving, intersecting writings" that "compose a manifold story...shaped out of fragments of trajectories and alterations of spaces" that remain "daily and indefinitely other."[24] Satan's capitol has shape and form only relative to its physical and textual Others—Babylon or Cairo, Babel or Memphis—and its architecture is equally driven by texts always prior to itself: the Homeric fall of Mulciber, the medieval romances of violent "champions bold" and "paynim cavalry," oral tales of elves and fairies, and even the commands and summons of the fallen angels, still serving as evangelical messengers.[25] Its horrors are those of an uncanny space at once undergirded by and straining beyond its own circumscriptions. Horror films have at times drawn on all of these significations while maintaining a sense of Milton's original and spectacular design. But Milton has also become erased in the process as the idea of pandemonium has become increasingly detached from *Paradise Lost*, devolving into a horror so abject it has lost all form.[26]

THE BEGINNINGS: *METROPOLIS*

Fritz Lang's silent epic *Metropolis* (1927), often recognized as the first science fiction epic, also applies many of the conventions of classic, gothic horror: a withered cathedral and subterranean chapel, crypts and catacombs, a mad, Faust-like scientist, a tyrannical and domineering father, uncanny doppelgangers, demonic incarnations, and a tableau of Death and the Seven Deadly Sins. It also shares with Milton's Pandaemonium the epithet "Metropolis," a term Milton uses for the demonic palace in book 10, as the fallen angels are gathered to await the return of Satan from his exploits in Eden:

> So these the late
> Heav'n-banisht Host, left desert utmost Hell
> Many a dark League, reduc't in careful Watch
> Round thir Metropolis, and now expecting
> Each hour their great adventurer from the search
> Of Foreign Worlds.   (*PL* 10.436–41)

The Metropolis of Lang's film subsumes much of Milton's own. The labyrinthine structure of the city, both above and below ground, figures in almost all of this. Further, the idea of Metropolis as literally the "mother-city" associates it with the film's dominant maternal figure: Hel, the dead wife of Joh Fredersen (the "master of Metropolis") and one-time love of Rotwang, the inventor. Hel is monumentalized in the film in a number of ways: as a giant bust enclosed by curtains, in the likeness of the Maschinenmensch, or "Machine-man," the robotic gynoid that Rotwang has built in Hel's image, and in the city itself, built by Fredersen as his own compensation for his absent love. The city as a monumental maternal force, one necessarily wounded and expended, further recalls Pandaemonium, whose birth begins with demons behaving like workers "rifl[ing] the bowels of their Mother Earth" (*PL* 1.689).

Equally pandemonic is Lang's description of his inspiration of the film, "born from my first sight of the skyscrapers of New York in October 1924," and his sense of the skyscrapers as figuratively birthing his own imaginative city affirms the perversely maternal power of Metropolis.[27]

That the woman Hel is also a goddess of the underworld and a type for hell is manifest in Lang's recollection of New York's towering, infernal vacuity: "while visiting New York, I thought that it was the crossroads of multiple and confused human forces, blinded and knocking into one another, in an irresistible desire for exploitation, and living in perpetual anxiety. I spent an entire day walking streets. The buildings seemed to be a vertical sail, scintillating and very light, a luxurious backdrop, suspended in the dark sky to dazzle, distract and hypnotize. At night, the city did not simply give the impression of living: it lived as illusions live."[28] The primary denotations of pandemonium are all active in Lang's narrative: the multiplication of confusion, the continual reiterations and replications of blind alleys and hypnotic streets, an impression of imitation and illusion rather than authentic life. The buildings themselves seem "pendant by subtle Magic" that dazzles like Milton's "Starry Lamps and blazing Cressets" that "yielded light / As from a sky" (*PL* 1.727–30). Much of this vision is transferred to the film, whose futuristic cityscapes are sometimes suspended within the frame as if detached from their bases, while the entire urban sprawl looks alternately like a pulsating hive and the arterial circulations of the body (it is the "heart machine" that keeps the entire place running). The displacement of the human being by the materials of production forms one of the film's central tropes, just as the surreal glimpses of soaring buildings help to shape Metropolis's expressionistic aesthetic.[29]

In the particular instance of Pandaemonium as Metropolis in book 10 of *Paradise Lost,* the fallen angels have convinced themselves that they are awaiting the triumphant return of Satan as messiah, a false hope quickly exploded when the gathered spirits are metamorphosed into serpents. In Lang's *Metropolis,* the messiah of the fallen arrives in truth: Freder (Gustav Fröhlich), the son of Hel (who died giving birth) and Fredersen (Lang's God), and thus the mediator between hell and heaven, combine both Milton's Messiah and his Satan.[30] Metropolis's central edifice, called the "New Tower of Babel," also shares with Pandaemonium that model of hubris and confusion. It is positioned so as to survey the entirety of Metropolis, and Fredersen reigns from its pinnacle as a cold and impassive deity, an intellectual brainiac out of touch with the workers, the "hands," that serve him. The film begins with a view of this downtrodden laboring class heading into the bowels of the earth during a shift change. Hundreds of elevator cells permit access to a seemingly interminable underworld of factories and steam machines, all run by the exertion of the zombified workers who blend with the machines they are manipulating, raising the obvious question of who exactly is controlling whom. While the Worker's City is deep underground, the Club of the Sons is a vision of paradise, "as far above as the city beneath." The club serves the sons of the industrial tycoons in charge of Metropolis and has libraries, museums, and athletic competitions under the open sky. The film's rebellious messiah is Fredersen's son, Freder, a name that makes the son sound like the father. He wins a race and the privilege of then visiting the Eternal Gardens, a prelapsarian pleasure palace of nymphs and groves and fountains. When the film's heroine, Maria, the prophetess of the revolution who later becomes subsumed into the Machine-Man, takes a group of working-class children to this paradise, Freder begins to see the error of his and his father's ways. They have been oblivious to the grave disparities between those above and those below.

When Freder first visits the City of Workers, he witnesses the clockwork repetitions of the laborers who are clustered around and upon a colossal, whirling, belching "M-machine." An accident ensues in which one operator, unable to keep up with the fierce pace of work, fails to maintain the right levels of pressure, causing an explosion of scalding steam that injures countless men. In one of the film's many surreal sequences, Freder then perceives the machine as transformed into the Temple of Moloch; those burned by the steam are hauled up the temple steps and cast into the open furnace, while shifts of workers are set to follow them by walking heedlessly into Moloch's gaping maw of gears and pistons.

It is the most spectacular example of the film's easy exchange between the industrial and the infernal, and an explicit reference to the "grim Idol" of *Paradise Lost*. The Moloch sequence further elaborates Milton's depiction of hell as "one great Furnace flam'd" (*PL* 1.62), a place of pointless labor and excruciating repetition.[31]

After his infernal vision, Freder speeds to confront his father about the workers' conditions. "What if one day those in the depths rise up against you?" he asks his father, not yet aware that he will help to promote that revolt himself. Fredersen, meanwhile, has the ability to damn those who fail him: "to be dismissed by the father," as one subordinate puts it, means to "go below ... into the depths." At the heart of this antagonism is not the war in heaven but the legend of Babel, reconceived in the film as a fable of worker exploitation. It is a conflict rendered through architecture rather than militarism. Maria in her role as priestess recites the story, which becomes the template for the overarching narrative: the minds that conceived Babel could not build it; the hands knew nothing of the brain that conceived it, so the hands tear it down. The sentimental moral: one must have a heart to mediate between head and hand. When the film's climax arrives—a Luddite rebellion that promises "Death to the machines!"—every child in the underworld becomes endangered. The children, in fact, have been left behind while their parents unthinkingly destroy the very machines sustaining life in their city, and in the din of destruction the parents cannot be brought to remember them. It is a danger foreshadowed in the looming presence of Moloch, "besmear'd with blood / Of human sacrifice, and parents' tears / Though for the noise of Drums and Timbrels loud / Thir children's cries unheard" (*PL* 1.392–95). The children are rescued from a steady deluge by Freder and Maria, even as her double, a figure that combines Sin, the Whore of Babylon, and the threat of robotic human replacement, has almost achieved revolution at the cost of the entire superstructure. In the end, Freder reconciles God and the workers by embodying the "heart," suggesting that the city must depend not on equality but on a new republic of particularization. But as many critics have complained, the romantic attempt to redeem the dismembered horrors of the city does not fully account for all of the wounds the film has unveiled.[32]

The Pandemonic Film: From *The Pit and the Pendulum* to *The Devil's Advocate*

In Roger Corman's *The Pit and the Pendulum* (1961), the menacing Vincent Price character, Nicholas Medina, imprisons his brother-in-law in one of the inquisitional torture chambers beneath his castle and includes "pandemonium" in a gushing litany of hellish spaces: "You are about to enter hell, Bartolome. Hell! The netherworld, the infernal regions, the abode of the damned, the place of torment, Pandemonium, Abaddon, Tophet, Gehenna, Naraka, the pit!" It is a compelling example of Milton's literary construct having achieved the status of a mythological past, disarranging it from a recognizable present into an immeasurable, chthonic underworld that masquerades under endless aliases.

A similar act of mythologizing (or a kind of fetishizing of the Miltonic text) occurs in Michael Winner's *The Sentinel* (1977). Preoccupied throughout with liminality, with the borders between this world and another unseen, the title derives from a central, mythical figure who oversees unceasingly this borderland and who appears derived not from Scripture or apocrypha but from Milton. In this film, Christina Raines's Alison Parker, dissuaded by the high rents elsewhere (an unconscionable $600 for one apartment), takes up residence in an impossibly economic Brooklyn Heights complex, peopled she believes with eccentric tenants and one fifth-floor voyeur, the eponymous and Tiresian Sentinel, the blind Father Halliran. The motley residents, she later discovers, are all devils, the revenants of convicted murderers, with the building itself suspended at the gate of hell. She is destined to take the good priest's place as the next Sentinel and discovers this when scouring a shelf of books that are "all the same." The endless repetitions, moreover, are explicitly Miltonic: the books contain lines from *Paradise Lost*, "to thee thy course by Lot hath giv'n / Charge and strict watch that to this happie Place / No evil thing approach or enter in" (*PL* 4.561–63). The informing narrative of *The Sentinel* is thus Milton's depiction of Gabriel in book 4 as overseer of the gates of Eden. The New York apartments, in turn, serve as the borderland between hell and Eden—the latter a place, unlike in *The Devil's Advocate* to follow, seen as worth protecting. *The*

Sentinel is notable for its presiding Roman Catholicism — Milton's *Paradise Lost* has even been transformed into a Latin text that must be translated back into English — while the climax offers a famous pandemonic sequence when the complex comes alive with hell-spawn on the night of the Sentinel's changing-of-the-guard.

Pandaemonium surfaces again in Jack Clayton's *Something Wicked This Way Comes* (1983), particularly as a site of con-tested literary authority. An itinerant carnival, the Pandaemonium Shadow Show, is run by Mr. Dark, a villain who combines Milton's Satan with a strain of Mephistopheles. Dark draws victims to his Pandaemonium with assorted temptations that tend to become extreme makeovers gone wrong. Adapted for the screen by Ray Bradbury from his own novel, the film begins with a woodland scene, a quiet pond through candy-colored foliage — immediately evoking that classic underworld trope of lost souls falling as leaves upon a shore — what Milton calls the "Autumnal Leaves that strow the Brooks / In *Vallombrosa*" (*PL* 1.302–03). A skiff silently crosses the surface as a voice-over describes October in Greentown, Illinois, an ominously violent time of year when "10,000 pump-kins lie waiting to be cut." The story proper begins with the arrival into town of a "seller of lightning rods," just ahead of a "terri-ble storm." What terrors that storm might bring are presaged in a montage of the town's Deadly Sinners: avaricious Mr. Tetley, "obsessed with money"; lusty Mr. Crosetti, the barber, "always talking about far away ladies"; proud Ed the bartender, "yester-day's football hero" now a paraplegic; and vain Ms. Foley, the schoolmarm, "once…the most beautiful woman in town." Their "hidden desires" are made manifest in the arrival of the exotic car-nival, which fulfills them only to capture and undo them.

Two 12-year-old boys are the main protagonists — the nar-rator, Will Halloway (that is, "hallow" or "holy" way), and Jim Nightshade, his best friend and "shadow." They champion the equivalent of a heavenly troop along with Will's father, Charles Halloway (Jason Robards), who also serves as local librarian. It is alone, however, that the children first encounter the lightning-rod salesman, Tom Fury, preaching in the streets about the com-ing "hellfire storm." The lightning rods, he asserts, are for those

people who might need "special protection." The devices, however, only indirectly protect the person; as Fury remarks, "I can tell
which of your old homes is in danger." The immediate threat of
this storm is to domestic space, and to the perception that buildings can be sanctuaries against divine wrath—the kind of disillusionment Satan undergoes when he returns to Pandaemonium in
book 10, thinking he has reached a safe harbor only to be punished
utterly. Fury sells a lightning rod to the boys, "once the lightning rod on the pyramids of Egypt. Trained for three-thousand
years to pitch the lightning back to the high heavens." The war
in heaven is clearly sounded here, or its aftermath, with Satan's
troops "Hurling defiance toward the vault of Heaven" (*PL* 1.669),
but the metaphor is mixed. Fury has given Nightshade a piece of
Pandaemonium—a relic of "those Memphian kings" whose monuments, along with Babel, serve as model and successor for the
demonic edifice. But it is the demons of Pandaemonium who most
need protection, still reeling from, as Satan puts it, "Sulphurous
Hail / Shot after us in storm," as well as "the Thunder, / Wing'd
with red Lightning" (1.171–72, 174–75). The transference of
the lightning rod from infernal palace to domestic haven suggests
the film's trajectory: both a dismantling of demonic power and a
reformation of the boys who, though free to fall (as the pageant
of sinners around them and even Nightshade's dark and vaguely
venomous name might portend), are sufficient to stand, so long as
their *home* is impervious.

   After entering the library, the children encounter another version of spatial horror: deteriorative, entropic disarray, only ever
incompletely organized, here fluctuating between check-ins and
check-outs, losses and retrievals. The prodigious multiplication
of books on the library shelves, recalling the unending copies of
Paradise Lost in *The Sentinel,* further manifest Oppenheimer's
redundancy of space, hermeneutic circles of Dewey decimals and
other data, insistently "available" and yet, in their totality, bewil-
deringly unreadable. Such unreadable, labyrinthine libraries recur
as signs of fallenness in such works as Umberto Eco's *The Name
of the Rose,* including the 1986 film adaptation, directed by Jean-
Jacques Annaud, and Jorge Luis Borges's "The Library of Babel."

In *Something Wicked* the titles themselves suggest an extensive-ness both sublime and terrifying. Charles Halloway offers his son virtual adventures, travels to the North Pole and Zane Grey, and to Nightshade the "Arabian Nights—full of magicians and mon-sters." When the boy declines *The Arabian Nights,* Halloway offers instead *Drums of Doom: The Saga of the Thunder Lizards.* In the novel, this is preceded by an offer to examine Gustave Doré's illus-trations of Dante's *Inferno,* and the film maintains the hellish sub-text. Both the pagan tales of Araby and the doom of the dinosaurs construct a world of mortal anxieties: the drama behind the *Arabian Nights,* for instance, is the impending execution of Scheherazade; the discourse of dinosaurs is disturbed by their eventual extinction. The prehistoric beasts recall, too, the Tartarean punishments of Satan and his host transformed into ash-eating reptiles in book 10 of *Paradise Lost.* Ultimately, though, textuality itself appears dan-gerous here, with its intertextual disintegrations and bottomless referents. We are alerted by another voice-over that the death of Charles Halloway, the librarian, may also be imminent because of a heart "too old and too tired, too full of yearning and regrets." Too full, in other words, of desiring fictions and reimagined histories that overwhelm both his body and the story he's living—as father, certainly, and even especially as a gatekeeper for other people's narratives.[33] Into this world of texts made material and menac-ing enters the ekphrastic palace of *Paradise Lost,* incarnate as the Pandaemonium Shadow Show.

When the carnival train arrives, advance fliers have already adver-tised such attractions as the Magic Mirror Maze and St. Anthony's Temple of Temptation. Like Satan's palace, Dark's Pandaemonium Carnival is "suddenly built," rising "like an Exhalation" over the fairgrounds in mere seconds in the dead of night.[34] Jim and Will race through a graveyard to watch its arrival; the cemetery sculp-tures include various angelic figures penetrated by beams of red light when the train passes, another citation of the war in heaven and the fallen host "shot forth" with "pernicious fire" (*PL* 6.849). The boys are entranced, even entering one trailer inhabited by an oracle and temptress known as the Dust Witch (played by Pam Grier), who also happens to have an assortment of spiders. They flee after spotting one of her tarantulas, but return with vigor the next morning to see that the spooky midnight carnival is apparently just a "plain, ordinary carnival," with the standard Ferris wheel, fortune teller, and sideshow tents. Soon, however, we see it has the power to fulfill those "hidden desires" of the townsfolk: Ed the ex-football player is lured into the Maze of Mirrors after seeing his limbs restored in his reflection; Tetley wins $1,000; Crosetti the barber gets his seraglio of dancing women; and Ms. Foley, the teacher, after leaving the Maze, later regains her youth. But as the Maze of Mirrors implies, all these are merely the distorted and fatal fulfillments of illicit desire, and the reward of their sins is death (or in this Disneyfied case, disappearance). Ed never exits the fun-house mirrors, Tetley vanishes after riding the Ferris wheel, Crosetti is swallowed up by his harem, and Ms. Foley's youth brings with it a consequent blindness.[35]

Along with the byzantine mirrors reflecting and repeating, distorting, and disorienting, a central component of Pandaemonium here is the carousel. When the curious boys sneak under a tent flap for a peek and a ride, Jonathan Pryce's Mr. Dark appears, dragging them from their horses and "back to earth." The carousel can control time, either advancing it or turning it back depending on which direction it runs. At various points in the film it reduces Dark's minions into demonic ankle-biters, threatens to diminish Will into "a little baby," and offers Nightshade the chance to skip his adolescence. Dark, meanwhile, has some of the standard diabolical accoutrements—black suit and hat, hissing cobra cane—and others less orthodox, such as a mesmeric ability to make his own flesh crawl with designs. In the midst of the confrontation with Dark, Nightshade makes an interesting slip—the boy asks this devilish figure if he's the Dark of Dark's "Pandominium" Carnival, rhyming the word with "condominium," as if to blend modern conformity into Milton's coinage. Dark accepts the designation, and his lair fittingly contains the closest visual markers of Milton's Pandaemonium—arched backdrops and alcoves, embossed walls and sculptures, a thronelike electric chair for torturing that seller of lightning rods. Dark, it turns out, fears the very same "Thunder, / Wing'd with red Lightning" (*PL* 1.174–75) that frighted the rebel host. He tells Fury that "lightning reveals our dark corners" and thus threatens Pandaemonium itself. As with the earlier invocations of the war in heaven, divine wrath is here imagined as directed at the *place* of horror. And Dark has plenty to hide: around him are those same dark corners, in which the boys spot Tetley and the other fallen citizens, now mannequin-like beings fixed in space and time.

After the boys "see too much," Dark goes hunting for them. He gathers his demonic followers for a march down Main Street, the spectacle intended to draw out the two boys but also to display conspicuously the demons' costumed conquests: Tom Fury's throne converted to a sedan, the barber now dressed as a sultana, and so forth. When questioned by Dark about the boys' whereabouts, Charles Halloway tries to conceal their identity with various parcels of misinformation, including an alias for Jim Nightshade: "Milton Blumquist." The librarian's naming of Milton here serves as a strangely self-referential act, in which Halloway seems to recognize he is appearing in some version of *Paradise Lost*. The devil picks up on it, too, however, attempting to displace such literacy and especially its implications for his own designs: "The town's librarian....All that time spent living only through other men's lives, dreaming only other men's dreams. What a waste." Dark's description makes explicit one of the primary conditions of Pandaemonium—a facsimile of heaven, a wounded replica of other mighty fortresses. Indeed, it is the devil's plight in this film to be concerned only with other people's dreams. One condition of the Miltonic hell is to be consumed with what others are doing—Satan with Adam and Eve, Dark with the populace of every town on his rail-line.

The final scene at the carnival begins with the storm, bolts of lightning jolting the sky as reiterations of heavenly retribution. To save his son from Dark, Halloway must solve the Maze of Mirrors. Here Oppenheimer's repetitions of space reach their height: infinite, honeycombed cells, filled with an excrescent gray mist. The mirrors reveal to Halloway a further sin—his own regret and despair—that he must conquer, revisiting a moment where he failed to rescue his son from drowning because of his own paralytic fear. His son's words of love allow him to shatter the moment and the mirrors. The once imprisoned sinners are freed and flee the collapsing carnival; the lightning-rod seller escapes and skewers the Dust Witch. Dark attempts to transform his "son" Jim on the carousel, but Jim is saved when the Halloways "jump around" in joy. In the novel, this bursting dance is described as "pandemonium commotion," expressly co-opting and counterpointing the demonic energy of Dark's own Pandaemonium Shadow Show.[36] Trampled by a carousel of red-eyed horses, winged cherubim, and the trumpeting angels of Revelation, and finally electrified by lightning, Dark becomes a withered corpse, surreptitiously carried off by one of the carnival crew. After the whole carnival assembly hurtles into the heavens, it leaves behind Halloway and the boys and a last line: "A memory that would live as long as sons tell sons about fathers they love." The film reinstates the celestial God/Son bond of *Paradise Lost* as a means of redeeming a town of sinners, a gathering place of demons, but it does so through the remediation of its central horrifying concept—that the same story should be repeated over and over, *ad infinitum.*

In Taylor Hackford's *The Devil's Advocate,* Lang's city of Metropolis is renewed and updated as New York City, rendered as a twentieth century Pandaemonium. Keanu Reeves plays Kevin Lomax, a small-town Florida lawyer whose "unblemished record" as a trial attorney draws the attention of the Goliath Manhattan firm of Milton, Chadwick, Waters. Al Pacino impersonates John Milton impersonating a lawyer as the firm's diabolical head.[37] The opening credits appear against a virtual lake of fire, crackling at the bottom of the frame, while the image of a simple orb of light rises from it. The orb slowly recedes as it becomes the sun over waves of rolling clouds, the brimstone flames transformed into ashen brume. This establishes the basic conflict between heaven and hell and a visual alignment with *Paradise Lost* at the outset. The ensuing church scene, similarly, offers a hymn derived from Romans 16, "The God of Peace will soon crush Satan," which elaborates further the battle at hand. Like the Miltonic Pandaemonium films before it, *The Devil's Advocate* foregrounds the demonization of space as one of its particular horrors. Lomax also makes a Faustian bargain with the big-city firm, but even that is inflected by a prevailing Miltonic discourse on free will. For along with the film's self-conscious millenarianism—Pacino's John Milton calls it "Round 20" of his cosmic heavyweight bout—it also takes more seriously (some might say too seriously) its moral commentary on the twentieth century. Hackford repeatedly insists throughout his DVD commentary that this is a "moral tale"; this insistence culminates with his statement near the end, "we tried to make it about free will, not make it a special effects piece, a ghoul piece, a monster piece, but make it about something."

To some degree Hackford does succeed in repressing the monstrous: Pacino plays the sympathetic Satan, smooth and streetwise.[38] His diabolism becomes incorporated into the director's vision of a contemporary Pandaemonium (and one that recalls Lang's own New York City fantasia in the 1920s)—an urban cluster of skyscrapers, subways, and city streets that offer the temptation of infinite variety even as they comprise a labyrinth of dead ends.[39] Lomax's assimilation into the citified hive looms as the greatest threat to his soul, while his confrontations with the ghoulish and abominable are largely naturalized through his trial work. His zealously religious mother anticipates as much when she warns him of the move from Florida: "Let me tell you about New York. 'Fallen, fallen, is Babylon the Great. It has become a dwelling place of demons.'" Her allusion to Revelation 18 figures forth the apocalyptic end of Lomax's dream opportunity, which will be consumed in a conflagration by the finale, even as it succinctly defines New York City as Pandaemonium, "a dwelling place of demons."

Oppenheimer observes that the first representations of Babel in the Middle Ages seem "nothing so much as a tall, rectangular, and modern office building," a correlation that recalls Lang's design of Metropolis and is reproduced in the visuals of *The Devil's Advocate*.[40] Bruno Rubeo, the latter's production designer, further implies the demonism of the space: "This set was designed to be seductive, yet sexy and mysterious, so you can't really tell where it goes."[41] The same draw toward derangement is signified by *Paradise Lost*'s elvish midnight revels (charmingly threatening), by the fall of Babel into confusion, by the ultimate metamorphosis of

Satan and his followers into one universal hissing mass of serpents. The cinematography heightens this disorientation: time-lapse photography animates the cityscape in a flutter of light and motion, Hackford begins several shots with skyscrapers angled horizontally across the screen, and the interior of the law firm is covered in a repeating façade of uniform prefab concrete.

Moreover, there are two extended scenes—one upon the precipice of Milton's office building and another later on the girders of a construction site—intended to induce vertigo in the viewer. As part of this panoramic effect, such scenes, suggests Anna K. Nardo, "repeatedly invoke the pinnacle temptation of *Paradise Regained*."[42] There is a stress, too, on buildings in process, on remodeling and scaffolding, supporting one of Milton's extended rants in which he accuses humankind of seeking to "build egos the size of cathedrals," yet another Pandaemonium citation, allegorized as vaulting pride. A significant dimension of New York life for Hackford seems to be the paucity of available (and affordable) apartments, thus sharpening the value of and obsession with space itself. The apartment of Alex Cullen, a client accused of murdering his wife, is a notable example. Not only is Cullen a notorious real estate developer, but Hackford also proudly relates in his commentary that the apartment location—full of "glass, marble, brass, gold-leaf"—is, in fact, the real-life penthouse of Donald Trump, occupying the top four floors of Trump Tower. It is glaringly evocative of what William McClung, referring to the "roof" of Pandaemonium, calls the "gilded, paneled ceilings that are the staple of depraved interior decoration."[43] The ceiling also evokes the war in heaven with its collage of divine charioteers riding through clouds and blue sky.

The apartment complex, which houses most of the partners and Milton himself as majordomo is a "great building" that takes most workers in the firm years of waiting to get into. In the film's economy of space, Lomax and his wife, Mary Ann (Charlize Theron), are at first more than willing to trade up. As Mary Ann puts it, the dream apartment makes the "condo in Gainesville" and "weekend shack at Gulf Shores" seem positively philistine. But soon the panoptical effect of living in an apartment complex that erases boundaries between work and home, public and private, erodes first Mary Ann's enthusiasm and later her mental stability. As she begins to feel more and more out of place—a number of montages cross-cut her failed attempts at interior decorating with Lomax's meteoric rise at the firm—she confronts Lomax: "I don't like it here." He responds not by citing their wealth, prominence, or cultural opportunities; rather, he shoots back, "What about the apartment?" And despite his wife's retort, "This is not about the apartment! I hate this stupid place!" the domestic space becomes more menacing as the film unfolds, increasingly the cause of Mary Ann's derangement.[44] Even her eagerness to become pregnant early in the film is concretized by the apartment's prodigious bedrooms; with Lomax's absence from the household making sex scarce, she begins turning one of these potential nurseries into a law library. Finally, the permeability of the apartment undoes her utterly: raped by Milton, she reveals to Lomax that "he let himself in."

One of the awkward ironies of the film is that while Lomax can quote Scripture with the congregation, he seems oblivious to the literary significance of his mentor's name. (An uneducated foil for *Something Wicked*'s hyperliterate Halloway.) Nonetheless, it is Lomax who later offers the only direct quotation of *Paradise Lost* in the film: "Better to reign in Hell, then serve in Heav'n" (1.263), suggesting that he may have been deviously playing along with his "father" the whole time, and is intertextually savvy.[45] In the shooting script, the line is more sensibly delivered by Milton himself: "Work for someone else?—Hey, I couldn't hack it. 'Better to reign in Hell than serve in Heaven.'"[46] The film, in fact, is full of these dramatic ironies, all lost on Lomax: he and Milton are followed by a man carrying an enormous box labeled "Halo Lighting," the firm's headquarters is situated in Penta Plaza, as in "pentagram," and Lomax joins Milton for an enthusiastic scene in "the Garden": that is, Madison Square Garden, where they attend a boxing match.[47] There is even a Beelzebub figure: Eddie Barzoon, a name that hums with the buzz of Beelzebub's Hebrew epithet, "lord of the flies." As managing director of the firm, Barzoon has been Milton's second until the arrival of Lomax, and he governs especially the shredding, or "housekeeping," of the firm's paper trails.

In Andrew Neiderman's novel, Lomax's ignorance on the subject of *Paradise Lost* is clarified when a priest, Father Vincent, alludes to the poem as "a great literary work about good and evil…by the English poet John Milton." When the Lomax character (called Kevin *Taylor* in the novel) hears the name John Milton, he laughs: " 'It's his joke, his in joke, his own sick sense of humor. Father Vincent, John Milton is the name of the man I work for.' 'Really?' Father Vincent's eyes brightened. 'This is getting interesting. Obviously, you didn't recall the poetic narrative before this.' 'It must have been one of those things I fudged at college, bought those summarized versions to read instead of reading the work itself.' " The priest concludes, " 'It's not an easy thing to read.'"[48] By cutting this explanation of Lomax's curious (il)literacy, the film places him in the difficult position of protesting his innocence of any satanic affiliation while implicating himself in Satan's master narrative.

The most compellingly Miltonic scene in the film pits Lomax against Milton in a final confrontation. Satan wants Lomax to beget the Antichrist via his half-sister Christabella. The implied incestuous relationship between Milton and Christabella, to be reenacted with Lomax, recalls the intertwining of Satan, Sin, and Death in *Paradise Lost*. Meanwhile, the austere surroundings of Milton's abode have become inspirited. A dominant bas relief behind Milton's altar/desk is animated with the naked forms of men and women in sensual play. The sculpture owes something both to Rodin's *Gates of Hell* and Blake's languid illustrations of *Paradise Lost*, especially the depiction of the "Downfall of the Rebel Angels," where one demon with hands on head is an identical image.[49] And Hackford's imagining it to have "broke[n] off some temple someplace" takes us back directly to Pandaemonium, also "built like a temple."[50] God, says Pacino's Milton, is an "absentee landlord"; thus, he claims "the twentieth century is all mine." And given his metaphor, we must suppose he especially means the radical reconfiguration of space rather than the genocidal evils Hackford *claims* to have been invoked here: the world as urban condominium, the devil as squatter. The soundings of *Paradise Lost* are fast and loose here; when the devil proposes Lomax mate with Christabella, he declares, "This is revolution!" And in a sense, the offer does turn over the rest of the film; unable to procreate with his earthly wife, Lomax has the chance to join his own demi-devildom with another, to finally make manifest the Antichrist. The catch, Lomax deduces, is that he has to "volunteer." But as Lomax points out to Milton, "in the Bible, you lose, we're destined to lose"; Milton, for the first time now figured as an *author,* responds, "we're going to write our *own* book." Confronted with no other apparent options, Lomax finally kills himself, effectively canceling the collaboration. The devil is consumed in flames, Christabella withers into a mummy, the immured souls combust. In the last shot of the devil, he seems to take on his "true" shape — a kind of Keanu/Pacino hybrid with effulgent angel wings. The narrative returns meekly to its origins — the satanic angel thwarted — with, after all, no rewrite.

The film ends with a rather predictable return to the opening courtroom, as if Lomax has imagined or foreseen the narrative action almost instantaneously (a device used with much greater sophistication in *Jacob's Ladder* [dir. Adrian Lyne, 1990]). Pacino morphs back as well, ready to try again, playing on Lomax's new-found goodness but residual vanity. The credits roll over The Rolling Stones' "Paint It Black," which might seem an odd choice over the more obviously Miltonic Stones anthem, "Sympathy for the Devil." On the other hand, the song is perfectly consistent with the film's interior decorating montage. It is a song, after all, partly about making a hell of heaven, a heaven of hell, by redesign-ing the space: "I see a red door and I want it painted black." The song may also have been chosen to reinforce Hackford's vision of the film as a morality play — there is no sympathy for the devil intended, and in this way he is one of the few to purport an unro-mantic reading of Milton's intent: Satan is charming, seductive, and ultimately wrong.

The extraction of pandemonium exists outside the horror genre, as well, though even there the horror tropes lurk beneath the sur-face. The fraternity of misrule in *Animal House,* with John Belushi's Bluto recalling the underworld god Pluto, loosely paraphrases in its title the capitol of fallen spirits (*anima*), and the Delta Tau Chi brothers embody the subversive, *non serviam* energies of their rebel brethren while also playing off the general idea of pandemonium as chaos. Monty Python's Flying Circus further reconceives Milton's work as that of failed engineers. In a sketch titled "M1 Interchange Built by Characters from Milton's *Paradise Lost*," a news crew reports on "an impressive piece of motorway interchange building." There, "working on the site," armed with picks, shovels, and hoes, "are six angels, three devils, and Adam and Eve." Despite the "impressiveness" of the motorway, it is discovered that the crew has been at odds: according to the foreman, "no one really got on. Satan didn't get on with Eve...Archangel Gabriel didn't get on with Satan...nobody got on with the Serpent, so now they have to work on a rota: forces of good from ten till three, forces of evil three to six."[51] This reduction of Pandaemonium *ad absurdum* nonetheless contains markers of the horrifying: the assimilation of the individual parts into a faceless collective, a road that leads precisely nowhere. The parodic allusiveness of the sketch shares with Satan's construction a desire to mock its source while it inadvertently revels in its own weaknesses.

RECASTING THE SATANIC VILLAIN

In Victor Fleming's *Dr. Jekyll and Mr. Hyde* (1941), Hyde (Spencer Tracy) secures the girl of his id-driven dreams, Ivy (Ingrid Bergman), and for his pleasure keeps her cooped up in his home. When she meekly suggests that they go out for an evening, Hyde stamps out the idea and menaces her with some of his favored stay-at-home pastimes: "Now, let's see, what shall we do? We could play cards. But you're probably tired of cards, aren't you?" Tracy's Hyde is famously unmonstrous in appearance, little resembling the hirsute hominid in earlier adaptations, including the 1931 film (dir. Rouben Mamoulian) that Fleming essentially remakes. In keeping with this more urbane diabolicism, he then offers to Ivy, "You might read to me. Yes, yes. Milton's *Paradise Lost* would be nice. But we haven't the book, have we? And I don't suppose you know it from memory, do you?" The lines ooze subtext: Hyde's request to be read to implies both an animalistic illiteracy and an assertion of dominance. The absence of the book suggests, moreover, that this request is a trace of Dr. Jekyll's refined reading tastes—one that Hyde is desirous of co-opting or ironizing, reading the poem as a devil's manifesto, one that would terrify his captive in its implications. (Such absence maintains too Johnson's old notion that *Paradise Lost* is a book everyone should read and no one does.) Hyde's last salvo—that Ivy has not committed Milton to memory—is a final act of intellectual abuse.[52] Her failure to know *Paradise Lost* will prove a mortal failing, not only because she has not internalized its lessons (beware smooth-talking beasts) but also because, unlike Scheherazade with her 1,001 tales, Ivy has no repertoire of involuted narratives to keep Hyde's interest and herself alive. Her failure to know *Paradise Lost* is a failure to sustain the horror narrative itself.

Not all films with satanic antagonists, however, are so insistent in summoning Milton as a diabolical affiliate. In keeping with the tradition of excising Milton from adaptations of even highly literary works, the *Frankenstein* films, notably the 1931 James Whale classic and the 1994 Kenneth Branagh reboot, which advertised itself as *Mary Shelley's Frankenstein,* rarely make explicit use of the book's numerous allusions to *Paradise Lost*.[53] A recent exception is Danny Boyle's stage play *Frankenstein,* which was also released cinematically in 2012. With Benedict Cumberbatch and Jonny Lee Miller alternating roles as Victor and the Creature, the production quotes *Paradise Lost* frequently and openly invites parallels between the two narratives.

Another exception is a *Frankenstein* analogue, *R.O.T.O.R.* (dir. Cullen Blaine, 1988), a (very) poor-man's version of the megahit *RoboCop* (dir. Paul Verhoeven, 1987). In this low-budget production, a new cyborg coded Robotic Officer of the Tactical Operations Research Unit is being designed as the ultimate police officer against "society's scum." When R.O.T.O.R. is unleashed before full functionality, he turns on his creators and begins killing people for speeding violations. The scientist in charge, Captain Coldyron (who spends his off hours as a Texas rancher), likens himself to a "modern day Doctor Frankenstein" whose technologies have run amok. He summons up a passage from Milton, presumably via the title page of Shelley's *Frankenstein* (where it appears as the epigraph), as part of a rather highfalutin "I told you so": "Remember what I said at R.O.T.O.R.'s christening? First prototype of a future battalion, on the battlefield highways of the future. He'll be the judge, jury, and executioner. Now I've got to wonder: were we playing God, breathing life into our artificial Adam? Or have we lost sight of paradise? What was it Milton said? 'Did I request thee, maker, from my clay to mold me man? Did I solicit thee from darkness to promote me?' Is it his fault he is what he is? Or is it ours?" It is a short conscription of Milton, and one uttered with apparent uncertainty, perhaps because the allusive vector is not fully set (did Milton say this? Or was it Mary Shelley?). But even in this shorthand it is clear the prevailing intent of appropriating Milton's lines in this way is to make the monster more sympathetic.

A run of films in the 1990s further cemented Milton's place in the horror genre, especially in developing a sympathetic antihero. In *Interview with the Vampire* (1994), an adaptation of Anne Rice's first novel in her popular *Vampire Chronicles* series, director Neil Jordan draws on the idea of a sympathetic Satan in *Paradise Lost* to help shape the characterizations of his seductive vampires: "I always remember reading 'Paradise Lost' when I was a kid and being fascinated by the figure of Lucifer. His dilemmas were far more fascinating than the dilemmas of the good angels."[54] Consequently, he reads Rice's novel, which is told primarily in the first-person narration of the vampire Louis, as conveying the same virtues as Milton's poem, "the perspective of somebody who is evil and doesn't know why he's evil, somebody who no longer comprehends what it was to be good. This is one of the few stories I've come across that speaks from the point of view of the monster."[55] The film echoes *Paradise Lost* throughout, particularly in framing the vampires' various existential crises about their origins and their status among the living and the dead. Louis (Brad Pitt) refers to himself as "the devil," while the doll-like vampire child Claudia (Kirsten Dunst) calls him her "dark angel," and Louis's fall from troubled human to equally consternated vampire is meant to parallel Lucifer's fall from archangelic light to demonic darkness. The film's most sage vampire, Armand (Antonio Banderas), informs

Louis that his "fall from grace" has mirrored the fall of his age, "the fall of a century." Early in the film, Louis himself complains to Lestat (Tom Cruise), the endlessly needy vampire who first bites and transforms him, "You've condemned me to hell." Like Satan claiming to Beelzebub that "the mind is its own place," Lestat replies, "I don't know any hell."

The most transparent use of Milton is Louis's rejection of this hard sell by Lestat. Grieving over his lost humanity and his transformation into a murderous monster, Louis intones, "But there was a hell. And no matter where we moved to, I was in it." This paraphrases Satan's "Which way I fly is Hell; myself am Hell" (*PL* 4.75), when he is perhaps for the first time confronting openly and honestly his condition. By transferring one of Satan's most intimate pronouncements onto Louis, Jordan creates for him sympathy largely absent in Lestat's strident protests. Or, to put it another way, the film draws on competing senses of Milton's Satan and his "dilemmas"—Lestat emerges as the defiant titan of the opening books, Louis as the angst-ridden outcast trying to contemplate his way out of damnation.

Some of what Jordan reads as Miltonic in the novel can be traced to the genealogy of the vampire genre itself. Seeing the vampire in its Gothic origins as an extension of the Byronic hero, James B. Twitchell argues, "The male vampire certainly should have been a most attractive demon to the second generation of Romantics, for here was the personification of a most peculiar kind of exiled man, eternally outcast yet dependent on others, a lover yet incapable of loving, a superhuman yet a pathetic weakling, a Napoleon among men. Here was the gothic Don Juan, Milton's Satan reborn, the Romantic artist himself."[56] In the twenty-first century's neogothic vampire glut, this reading seems increasingly validated in such series as *Twilight* and *True Blood*.[57] Rice herself also builds into the novel a number of touches that seem conscious of Milton's Satan as backdrop.[58] Some of this is incidental—at one point, as the vampires begin to predate more heavily on their Louisiana plantation, Louis observes that "the plantation was in a state of pandemonium."[59] At other times the connections are part of a general cobweb of intertextual links: when Louis and Claudia remove to

Paris, they enter a "subterranean ballroom" featuring a mural of "The Fall of the Angels," "with the damned being driven from the celestial heights into a lurid chaos of feasting monsters."[60] (Rice kept this reference to Brueghel's work in the screenplay though it does not appear in the film.)[61]

Continuing the theme, Armand tells Louis they are not descended from Satan, or if they are, "Satan is simply God's child, and…we are God's children also."[62] Most significant may be the novel's attention to free will as part of the fall, a Miltonic move that the film, channeling Milton explicitly, makes even more emphatic. In the novel, the interviewer asks Louis if he "decided to become a vampire," to which Louis responds, "Decided. It doesn't seem the right word. Yet I cannot say it was inevitable."[63] In the film, Lestat makes quite clear that Louis must choose to accept the "dark gift": "I'm going to give you the choice I never had." Lestat brings this up several other times—that he had no "choice" in falling into vampirism—and the film's final lines are, in fact, Lestat attacking the interviewer (Christian Slater), hissing at him the exact same lines, "I'm going to give you the choice I never had." And so as to leave no doubt about the film's dispositions regarding its Miltonic vampires, the final shot then shows Lestat turning on a car radio, blasting The Rolling Stones' "Sympathy for the Devil" (covered here by Guns N' Roses), which plays over the closing credits.[64]

Alex Proyas's supervigilante film *The Crow* (1994) also makes use of Milton to express the diabolical. The film's dark superhero, Eric Draven (Brandon Lee), is resurrected to avenge his death and that of his fiancée, Shelly (Sofia Shinas), who are killed in their apartment on the eve of their Halloween wedding. In a particularly disturbed flashback of Shelly's murder and rape, one of the head villains, T-Bird (David Patrick Kelly), reads from a folio copy of the poem: "Abashed the Devil stood, / And felt how awful goodness is, and saw / Virtue in her shape how lovely" (*PL* 4.846–48). He then viciously critiques the lines, leering into the camera: "It's pornography. Virtue?" It is a difficult sequence to parse because of the rapid cuts and strobe lighting, but the narrative suggestion seems to be that the book has been found by T-Bird in the apartment, and that his mad interaction with the text ironizes the content.[65]

In the poem, the lines occur during Satan's discovery and inter-
rogation by Zephon and Ithuriel. Satan is nearly overawed by the
"grave rebuke" he receives from the cherubim, reminded of the
potency of goodness and its pleasures, all of which are evident
in the angels' "youthful beauty" and lovely shape; the encounter makes him briefly "pin[e] / His loss" (*PL* 4.845, 848–49).
T-Bird turns the rape into a response to Satan's humiliation—as a
devil himself, T-Bird is similarly energized by the goodness of the
angelic form he is threatening. According to his excited or spiteful
remarks, the moment in Milton is "pornographic," a staging of
barely suppressed homoerotic longing in which Satan is engrossed
and stimulated by the beauty of his captors. T-Bird rejects that
suppression as he rejects the sense that Satan could be awed by
goodness at all: he acts violently on his desire, and spits on the
supposed power of "virtue" to overcome evil. In a later flashback,
before he is killed, T-Bird can be seen again from the point of view
of Shelly, again reading from the book, and this time forcing it into
the camera: "Does it get you sweaty?"

The implication that the book had been in possession of Eric
or Shelly forces a strange and arbitrary bit of perusal onto T-Bird:
in the midst of this chaotic home invasion, he has taken the time
to pick out a copy of *Paradise Lost,* turn to an especially relevant
quotation, and deliver a brutally succinct commentary upon it. But
T-Bird's pointed encounter with *Paradise Lost* returns moments
before he is killed, when he cites the same lines. If T-Bird's initial
recitation from *Paradise Lost* is meant to affirm the horrific fall
of the film's first couple, the loss of their innocent lives and the
promise of connubial love, the recirculation of the text is part of
the recuperation of that loss. Draven has him bound and driven off
a pier inside a car full of explosives when T-Bird, clearly terrified,
repeats, "Abashed the Devil stood, and felt how awful goodness
is . . . and felt how awful goodness is." It is a decisive reversal of his
earlier reading, realizing that goodness (with "goodness" in the
moral code of the film the same as divine retribution) does have
potency—enough to raise the dead and bring forth a savior.

David Fincher's *Seven* (1995), while relying more on Dantean
contrapasso than Milton's theology for its treatment of sin, nonetheless maintains Milton as a guide to the infernal.[66] The first note

left by the serial killer, who is programmatically enacting one of the Seven Deadly Sins for each of his victims, is a couplet from *Paradise Lost* (where Milton is himself echoing Virgil's *Aeneid*): "Long is the way, and hard, that out of hell leads up to light."[67] The lines are spoken by Satan in book 2 as he prepares to accept the heroic mantle and risk the "unknown dangers" presumably facing any who attempt to escape the "prison strong" (*PL* 2.444, 434). Like most of Satan's rhetorical peaks, it is also a somewhat disingenuous moment—Satan is reasserting and consolidating his rulership in hell by building up a self-fulfilling prophecy of hardship and renewal. The more perilous the fallen host perceives the undertaking to be, the greater Satan's glory will be when he returns, and the scene is meticulously orchestrated by Satan throughout. In the film, the note maintains some of this equivocation, as the killer plays a game of literary cat-and-mouse with the two detectives, Mills and Somerset, who try to catch up on the killer's reading. They hope that tracking models for his killings in such works as Dante's *Purgatorio* and Chaucer's *The Parson's Tale* will help their understanding of his methods and principles.

The precipitating note is first discovered pinned on the wall behind the "Gluttony" victim's refrigerator. Somerset (Morgan Freeman) brings it to the precinct and identifies it for Mills (Brad Pitt): "It's from Milton. *Paradise Lost.*" He interprets it to mean that the "long way" is just beginning. Somerset then hits the public library, scanning the shelves for *The Canterbury Tales, The Divine Comedy* (in multiple translations), and the *Dictionary of Catholicism,* even photocopying diagrams of Dante's schemata. He leaves a note to Mills to check out the same texts, but Mills is unable to follow the poetry and orders the Cliff's Notes versions instead. Later, when the detectives are revisiting the implications of the note, Somerset implies that the lines have come to signify the killer's methodical patience. Mills deflates Somerset's characterization: having a "library card" does not make him "Yoda"—that is, reading Milton does not make one a genius. On the contrary, it does seem to indicate sociopathic tendencies. Spurred by the Milton quote, the detectives decide to run these reading habits through the FBI's digital records. As Somerset puts it: "If you want to know who's reading *Purgatory* and *Paradise Lost* and *Helter*

Skelter, the FBI's computers will tell us." To which Mills replies, "Could get us the name of some college kid writing a term paper on twentieth-century crime." The ensuing Boolean search ferrets out the killer's location and his collection of books—this most literate of cinematic horror villains has also been reading Aquinas, the Marquis de Sade, and Truman Capote. His making a mantra out of Milton thus serves as the film's most salient indicator (though not an exclusive one) of the ways in which literary occultism seeps into the popular imagination. With the poetry-hating Mills and bibliophilic Somerset as its mouthpieces, the film depicts *Paradise Lost* at once as an arcane, almost impenetrable text—a mark of one's erudition—and as a nearly unparalleled influence and resource (Dante still wins out) for plumbing the depths of human horror.[68] *Paradise Lost*, like *Helter Skelter*, will invariably flag its reader as a dangerous mind, an unsettled radical if not a satanic emulator.

Becoming satanic, possibly by reading *Paradise Lost*, is the primary threat in *The Haunting of Molly Hartley* (dir. Mickey Liddell, 2008). A *Rosemary's Baby* knock-off, the film opens with the title character (played by Haley Bennett) beginning at a new prep school. On her first day, an evidently spiritless English class is already well into *Paradise Lost*, with one student listlessly reciting lines from Satan's monologue at the start of book 4: "Nay curs'd be thou; since against his thy will / Chose freely what it now so justly rues" (4.71–72). This is *Animal House*, but with a twist. The lines are selected to resonate with the central, Faustian premise of the film: Satan has been making deals with parents, to their later regret, for the souls of their children when they turn 18. It will later be revealed, moreover, that this particular student (played by Chace Crawford) is *already* an agent of Satan. The teacher asks somewhat plaintively for him to read the lines again, "with some feeling." On the chalkboard behind him can be seen three lists—"Milton," "Satan," and "Definitions." Under "Satan," for instance, is "Army of Angels," while in the center of the frame is the list of "Definitions": "Fall from Grace," "Sympathetic Character," "Cosmic Battle," and then to hammer home the point of the scene—the tedium of *Paradise Lost:* "Dead Ideas" and "Bored to Death." It is not clear if the students have suggested these as their own feelings or those of Satan and the fallen, or if it is merely directorial winking. (It is also not apparent why "Dead Ideas" and "Bored to Death" would need to be defined.) The satanic student does not exactly rise to the emotive challenge—perhaps the idea is that he might, in fact, succeed in boring someone to death—before being interrupted by the arrival of Molly. She causes a bit of a disturbance as the shiny new girl, and then the verse continues: "Which way I fly is hell; myself am Hell." This, too, is meant to resonate: Molly has no choice but to submit, and wherever she runs she brings along the hell inside her.

Later, the scene shifts back to the classroom, where the teacher has just finished reading the students' papers on *Paradise Lost* ("over the weekend") and, disheartened at the results, decides to change up the lesson plan. He starts handing out Bibles, since the students "don't have the necessary reference points to fully appreciate these iconic texts of English literature." In a subsequent scene, the class is shown taking a multiple-choice exam on the poem. The one random student whose answers are visible gets her questions wrong: "Which of the following [forms does Satan take]?: A) Angel B) Toad C) Cormorant D) He takes all of these forms." The student circles "B," and then locates the Fall in book 7. All in all, it is one repeated fail after another in the classroom, affirming that the real value of *Paradise Lost* for horror is not as an "iconic text of English literature" but as a mouthpiece for Satan himself. The "normal" classmates have, then, the orthodox, extra-horror response to the text: they will get through it only kicking and screaming.

Like his namesake in *The Devil's Advocate*, the suspicious and prolific movie producer John Milton (Lance Henriksen) in the self-parodic slasher film *Scream 3* (dir. Wes Craven, 2000) is supposed to be conversant in all manner of horror. As the producer of the film-within-a-film (*Stab 3*, based on the murderous plots of the earlier *Scream* films), he has been intimately involved in promoting the entire *Stab* franchise. Within the film's broad self-referentiality—it plays as Craven's homage to Pirandello's *Six Characters in Search of an Author*—Milton the producer's shepherding of this franchise links Milton the poet to a similarly foundational role in shaping the horror genre. Described in the script as a "bigwig horror producer, a creepy fifty-something with penetrating eyes and a menacing demeanor," his first lines in the film are a defense of the horror genre against those condemning its desensitization of violence and encouragement of copycat killing: "I've been making horror movies for thirty years, never had a psycho problem." As Milton becomes increasingly implicated in the murders happening on his movie set, he also becomes increasingly conflated with the Satan of *Paradise Lost*.[69]

When a studio archivist (Carrie Fisher) reveals that Milton was credited with a few schlock horror pictures back in his "heyday" that link him to the present-day murders, the two characters investigating are shocked. The archivist interprets their response to mean they somehow have not heard of Milton at all: "John Milton? The horror producer?" Later, confronted in his office over his role in the killings, Milton admits to a sordid past, seducing starlets and prostituting them to other studio executives. His defense sounds like an updated testimonial from Satan after the fall of Eve: "It was in the seventies. Everything was different. I was well known for my parties. . . . It was for girls . . . to meet men. Men who could get them parts. If they made the right impression. Nothing happened to her that she didn't invite, in one way or another. No matter what she said afterwards." Pressed further about what went wrong, Milton paints Hollywood as another lost paradise: "I'm saying things got out of hand. Maybe they did take advantage of her. You know, maybe the sad truth is this is not the city for innocence." Milton remains a suspect for most of the film, though one character, claiming "Milton's the key to everything," is shot down by another: "He's a pervert, he's not a killer." The final sequence takes place at Milton's Old Hollywood mansion, which includes a number of standard Gothic devices—secret passageways triggered by the tug of a book in the library, creepy basements filled with gargoyles and guillotines (relics of Milton's horror film oeuvre), and romantic paintings in the manner of Friedrich. In the end, the real killer at last drags Milton gagged and bound from a closet, presenting him to Sidney Prescott (Neve Campbell), the *Scream* franchise's survivalist heroine, as "the man who gave away your mother's innocence." It is a charge that links this Milton with

Milton's Satan, even as it modulates some of the typical slasher conventions. Milton/Milton's Satan *is* the real villain, stripping the universal "Mother of Mankind" (*PL* 5.388) of her innocence, promoting the devil's parties, and providing the backing for the entire horror film genre.

Last, the Adam Sandler vehicle *Little Nicky,* a mock-horror flick, offers a series of *Paradise Lost* citations, especially in the opening act set in hell. Yet again the palace of Pandaemonium is front and center. Lucifer (Rodney Dangerfield) lays claim to the Black Palace: "You know, I was the one who created hell." In the script, he is insistent on the point: "You know what was in hell when I came down here...? Nothing. No mountains. No castles. Looked like a giant parking lot. It wasn't even called Hell." The palace that emerges, surrounded by winged demons and flying jelly-fishlike creatures, reimagines Pandaemonium as a subterranean, Brueghelian Babel. Lucifer's claim to have "created hell" paraphrases Milton's lines, "The Mind is its own place, and in itself / Can make a Heaven of Hell" (*PL* 1.254–55), while there is even more ambitious terraforming staked out: creating mountains out of molehills, castles from a featureless plain. The last matter—that Lucifer has not only created hell but, more importantly, *named* it—also nods to Milton's (or Satan's) coinage of Pandaemonium, with its popular metonymic sense as representing hell in its entirety. Indeed, Lucifer's naming of hell is also a claim to the popular in general; what he seems most proud of here is the defining of the underworld's most recognizable, circulated, even mundane feature: the name people are calling it.

Lucifer has abdicated his throne long ago, and his son (Harvey Keitel), referred to throughout as alternately "the Devil," "Satan," "the Prince of Darkness," and "Dad," has decided to announce his own successor, just as his father, Lucifer, once did. Satan's three sons, Adrian (Rhys Ifans), Cassius (Tommy Lister), and Nicky (Sandler), play Goneril, Regan, and Cordelia to Dad's Lear, waiting to see how the kingdom will be divided. Only Nicky reacts with relief to the surprise announcement: Satan's successor will be Satan. For "stability" and to "maintain the balance of good and evil," he explains. The elder sons Cassius (the strong one) and

Adrian (the smart one) rail against the decision, and Adrian invokes Milton directly in his resentful response: "Twenty-thousand years ago, Grandpa Lucifer said, 'It's better to rule in hell than it is to serve in heaven' [*sic*]. Well, I'm tired of serving in Hell. We need somewhere where we can rule." Like the preferment of the Son in *Paradise Lost*, the resentment over succession in *Little Nicky* prompts rebellion, and Adrian's pride, restlessness, and ingratitude are close parallels to Satan's intensifying "envy against the Son of God" (*PL* 5.662).

Without naming Milton explicitly, and in keeping with its mock-horror approach, the film moves the words of Milton some 20,000 years—this is a *really* dated bit of wisdom—and into the mouth of "Grandpa" Lucifer. Milton, even in Adrian's slightly colloquial paraphrase, sounds like the oldest fogey. This displacement is consonant with a later joke, when Dangerfield's Lucifer retorts to his son, "the last time you said [everything is fine] the Renaissance happened," as if for the Sandler audience, the worst possible thing to introduce is the pretentious art, literature, and other humanist mumbo-jumbo of 500 years ago. Milton is implicated in this staleness, though the tenor of the joke is somewhat cryptic. Coming from Lucifer, is this a backhanded compliment? So much *good* came from the Renaissance that it upset all of hell? Or is Lucifer supposed to mean that poets like Milton—the source of his own discursive identity—actually were stealing their words from him? It is, then, not the devil in actuality but the poets who have been mainstreaming hell, the Renaissance as direct antecedent of the heavy metal fetishizing and soft-core satanism the film elsewhere exploits, Milton once again the wellspring of horror.

The film, through the rebellion of Adrian, promises at any rate to overturn Milton's well-worn adage. But this is one of the plainest slippages of such intertextual references. Satan's line, "Better to reign in hell, than serve in heaven," excised from Milton's text and translocated into the mass discourse of the film, is stripped of its rhetorical force and relocated in a bland historicism. A romanticist Satan might well believe in the poem's line as a flat statement of ideological truth, independent of its dramatic context. But other Satans naturally emerge and multiply when the line is recontextualized: Satan is blustering and impassioned and reactionary, say, or

Satan is ranting for Beelzebub's sake, the start of a conventional rallying cry—"The grapes were sour anyway!" The early suggestion of reigning in hell is, at least, a project to which Milton's Satan never seriously commits himself after the opening book. The film, in trying to underscore how tiresome and clichéd the idea of Satan reinventing himself in hell has become, fails to register the dynamic play in the original. Satan, too, ultimately found the promise of "ruling in hell" inadequate. There is no irony, then, when Adrian and Cassius describe their plotting as a rehashing of Milton's council in hell. They, too, decide that the proper course is not to reign in hell nor assault heaven, but to take earth for themselves:

> ADRIAN
> What do you think about...Earth?
> We could create our own hell there.
>
> CASSIUS
> You saying we go up there and kill everyone?
>
> ADRIAN
> Eventually, Cassius. But first we have to corrupt as many souls as we can so that when we do destroy them . . .
>
> CASSIUS
> . . . their damned souls will be ours.

The exchange is an approximation of Satan's council, and a device familiar from the angelic warrior genre, when Beelzebub urges the taking of earth, "either with Hell fire / To waste his whole Creation, or possess / All as our own, and drive as we were driven, / The puny habitants, or if not drive, / Seduce them to our Party" (*PL* 2.364–68), and again when Satan advises Sin that he seeks "A race of upstart Creatures, to supply / Perhaps our vacant room" (2.834–35). Adrian and Cassius immediately rush toward hell's portal, an infernal "fall" of cascading fire, crash past the Gatekeeper, who claims that "The fire flows in, not out," and dive through the flames. Their rebellious act—both the inversion of the stable order sought by "Dad" and the analogous revolt against their creator, breaking out of his imprisonment—apparently freezes the gate shut. The frozen flames have sealed hell off completely—no souls can pass in or out—and alarms erupt across hell. For without new souls, Dad will decompose. Nicky must travel to earth, trap his brothers, and bring them back through the gateway to restart the flow of souls.

The Gatekeeper (Kevin Nealon) becomes a parody of Milton's Sin—his punishment for allowing the escape of Dad's sons is to have breasts emerge from his head. This emasculation becomes a crude running joke, as the Gatekeeper transforms gradually into a hypersexualized, feminine being who eventually takes up with a nameless, speechless Monster that stands in for Death as his/her consort. On earth, meanwhile, Nicky joins up with a miniature Cerberus bulldog named "Beefy" who leads him to his first meal, Popeye's fried chicken. Nicky has a Raphael moment as he tastes, chews, swallows, and excretes for the first time. And in another reiteration of the angelic tropes of desire, he also falls in love with a human, Valerie (Patricia Arquette), with whom he will eventually settle on earth after proving that his "inner good"—it turns out his mother is one of the heavenly host—outweighs his inner evil.

As part of its popularizing discourse, the film is rampantly and casually referential, quoting at various times *The Exorcist, Silence of the Lambs, The Untouchables, Scarface, Superman, The Blair Witch Project,* and *The Wizard of Oz.* Its central demonic trope, the helter-skelter possession of random humans (the kind of comic metempsychosis lampooned in the Renaissance) also places it in the tradition of demonic horror films like Gregory Hoblit's *Fallen* (1998). The villain in that work is Azazel, Satan's ensign in *Paradise Lost* and a player in other post-Enochian writings, including the comics of Neil Gaiman and the television show *Supernatural.* In *Fallen,* Azazel is a promiscuous possessor of human beings, and he can skip from one vessel to the next with a simple touch. While the film makes no overt mention of Milton (the closest it gets is fusing its hero's name, John Hobbes, from two seventeenth century philosophers, John Locke and Thomas Hobbes), Azazel's haphazard possessions resemble Satan's shape-shifting in *Paradise Lost.* There, the fallen angel becomes "now one / Now other" (*PL* 4.397–98) of "the sportful Herd" (4.396), "as thir shape serv'd best his end" (4.398). At the end of the film, Azazel makes a final spiritual leap from a dying man into a nearby cat.

In *Little Nicky,* the final resolution is Nicky's return to earth, and Satan/Dad confirms that he will establish rule there, taking the "middle part" while his mother watches from above and he from below. The final scene indicates that Nicky's earthly regime will be defined by alternating heavenly self-sacrifice and demonic prodigiousness. The film ends with Nicky's newborn breathing fire at an old woman ogling him in his stroller, and Beefy points out that his son is "only a quarter" angel. Is this the beginning of the end? The final titles suggest that Nicky and Valerie are also planting a new garden, and so its comic version of *Paradise Lost* ends with paradise regained, though the threat of backsliding into full-blown, fire-breathing horror is not abandoned completely.

That the horror genre has become so fluent in Milton as to permit or gain from his mocking is the surest signs in the cinematic landscape that Milton has reached the approval of mass horror-going audience. For parody to work there must be a low threshold of recognition—nothing drives the wholesale caricature of Shakespeare and, increasingly, Austen, so much as their excessive familiarity. Mainstream satires like Seth Grahame-Smith's *Pride and Prejudice and Zombies* (2009) and Jerusha Hess's *Austenland* (2013) depend far more than standard adaptations on Linda Hutcheon's combination of "the comfort of ritual and recognition with the delight of surprise and novelty." The devilish Milton, disturbing Pandaemonium, and sympathetic Satan have reached a similar generic, if not a cultural, saturation point. Thus a middling horror film like *Parasomnia* (dir. William Malone, 2008) has its mind-bending villain simply utter the words "Paradise Lost" as he brings forth one sleeping victim with the expectation that its target audience will immediately understand that this is shorthand for a satanic stand-in. (In this case, the female victim is also dressed in angel wings in a tortured tableau the villain terms "lost angel.") Similarly, the film *The Mortal Instruments: City of Bones* (dir. Harald Zwart, 2013), an adaptation of the first book in Cassandra Clare's popular series for young adults, features a New York club with the neon name "Pandemonium." There humans, half-angels, and demons mingle in a kind of *Twilight*-meets-*Harry Potter*-meets-*Paradise Lost* crossover. Like Pullman's *The Golden Compass* before it, Clare's book also begins with a Milton epigraph—"I sung of Chaos and eternal Night, / Taught by the heav'nly Muse to venture down / The dark descent, and up to reascend."[70] And like the film adaptation of Pullman's novel, *City of Bones* cuts that express link with Milton. But in this case, the single citation of Satan's literary capital seems to do the intertextual work that *The Golden Compass* rejects entirely.

Indeed, it seems hardly coincidental that the neo-gothic film revival of the past decade, driven by *Twilight* and its hosts of imitators, with all its vampires and werewolves and ghostly apparitions, comes along at the same time as renewed interest in a feature-length *Paradise Lost*. That film was pitched for its supreme warrior-angel sequences, but the director first given the helm—Scott Derrickson—was at that point primarily known for his horror films *Hellraiser: Inferno* (2000) and *The Exorcism of Emily Rose* (2005). Alex Proyas, who later took over for Derrickson, had a similar background with *Dark City* and especially, as discussed earlier, *The Crow*. The horror genre, then, can be seen finally as spearheading other, more ambitious projects that hope to capitalize upon Milton's potential for mass appeal. His horror cachet makes the prospect of converting such appeal into box-office success seem eminently realizable.

Conclusion:
Blockbuster *Paradise Lost*

In January 2012, principal shooting was set to begin in Sydney, Australia, on the Hollywood-backed production of *Paradise Lost*, first announced in 2005. With a cast that included *People* magazine's 2011 "Sexiest Man Alive," Bradley Cooper, as Satan, Benjamin Walker as Michael, Diego Boneta as Adam, and Camilla Belle as Eve, the film had a budget upwards of $120,000,000 and an exacting production schedule: 20 weeks of preproduction, 8 weeks of principal photography, and 72 weeks of postproduction to compose the unprecedented special effects.[1] Director Alex Proyas, whose other films include at least two with Miltonic ties—*Dark City* and *The Crow*—had arranged a major deal to develop a special effects studio in Sydney that would handle the extensive computer-generated imagery (CGI). He spoke glowingly about the "unparalleled exposure" this "unique film" would bring to Australia, and especially the "cutting edge technology that will be used in the making of *Paradise Lost*."[2] As Proyas and other members of the crew stressed in the years leading up to production, this film would be unlike anything seen in the history of motion pictures, borrowing from Milton's epic the vaulting pursuit of "things unattempted yet in Prose or Rhyme" (*PL* 1.16). Scott Derrickson, the first director attached to the project, remarked in a 2008 interview that "If we did it, we would be trying to do something that was new and that hadn't been done before, you know?...But you only want to do that if you can do it well. And if...technology isn't up to date enough to do it, then it shouldn't be done."[3] Derrickson's remark shows again the perception of a lag between technological limits and the everlasting avant-garde manner of *Paradise Lost*. The interviewer, sensing the danger of a Milton adaptation done with anything less than before-its-time visuals, cautioned that "the risk is that it turns into *Spawn*" and that "we've seen many versions of this kind of thing, from *Prophecy* to *Max Payne*." He concludes by admitting that when it comes to *Paradise Lost*, "I cannot imagine what it would look like." The realization of the film would overturn this recurring sense of the unfilmability of *Paradise Lost*, and in so doing redefine Milton's popular legacy. After centuries of frustrated attempts to turn *Paradise Lost* into a spectacular event, from John Dryden to John Collier and beyond, this latest film looked poised, finally, to grant a triumphant resolution to the question of the poem's adaptability.[4] As screenwriter Stuart Hazeldine contended just prior to production, "We finally feel like the filmmaking technology is there with performance capture and 3-D...to make *Paradise Lost* for the first time on a big epic canvas."[5] And then suddenly, two weeks before principal shooting was to commence, Legendary Pictures delayed production, reportedly due to budgetary concerns. On February 9, 2012, the company suspended the project indefinitely.

What had gone wrong? If the filmmakers' rhetoric did not differ markedly from earlier efforts to cinematize the poem (recalling Collier's pitch for "the most spectacular motion-picture ever made," and Martin Poll's proviso that "the boundaries of film techniques must be expanded"), this film had nonetheless gone the farthest yet in securing major studio backing and generating significant industry buzz, though not all of it positive. Mainstream magazines were debating what kind of dreamy Lucifer Bradley Cooper would make and salivating over the prospect of a hunky Adam preparing for "a lot of running around naked."[6] On IMDb message boards, comments on casting threads were eagerly envisioning God as Sean Connery or Donald Sutherland (a fair exchange for his turn in *Animal House*) and Michael the Archangel as Matthew McConaughey. Fans of films like *The Lord of the Rings, 300,* and *Avatar* were expecting the next epic special-effects showstopper. Proyas offered a tantalizing synopsis in an interview a few months before production was stopped:

> It's not just armies battling in an epic war.... This is an adventure about the origins of good and evil after Lucifer's rebellion gets him cast out of Heaven and leads to a struggle with his brother archangel over the soul of mankind, starting with Adam and Eve. That is the scope of the narrative here, and we've tried to stay as faithful as possible to Milton's text, particularly its focus on Lucifer's evolution and the birth of evil. It's a family saga, about a group of brothers, two in particular, who are on divergent paths, and Lucifer's feelings of betrayal by his father and family that forge his descent into evil.[7]

Sweeping, effects-driven 3-D films were already popping up frequently at the cinema, often with a bent toward gigantomachia: the gaudy remake of *Clash of the Titans* (dir. Louis Leterrier, 2010), its sequel, set partly in Tartarus, *Wrath of the Titans* (dir. Jonathan Liebesman, 2012), and the *Immortals* (dir. Tarsem Singh, 2011). Biblical epics were likewise gaining momentum: Steven Spielberg was announced to direct a Moses biopic, *Gods and Kings,* also scripted by *Paradise Lost* screenwriter Stuart Hazeldine, and enormous productions like the Russell Crowe vehicle *Noah* (dir. Darren Aronofsky, 2014), a return to those Miltonic Deluge entertainments, were also in full swing. This last trend also represented a return to films like *The Ten Commandments,* the trailer for which advertised the "greatest adventure story ever told," full of "love, drama, majesty."[8] And a film featuring 3-D angelic warfare would extend what Kristen Whissel calls cinema's "new verticality," an exploitation of the limitless upward and downward movement and soaring space made possible by the medium. Such an extension into the heavens would join *Paradise Lost* with other gravity-defying, disorienting digitized epics like *Avatar, The Matrix,* and *Crouching Tiger, Hidden Dragon.*[9] This despite the longstanding appeal of 3-D angels—John Demaray sees an early source for *Paradise Lost* in the spectacular scenes of Giovanni Coppola's *Le nozze degli dei favola* (Florence, 1637), in which "circles of heavenly figures whirled round in colored light; and giant clouds descended with choruses of singing musicians," while "various infernal creatures, including winged, flying devils, soared and cavorted before Pluto, enthroned in his evil chair of state at center stage" (see fig. 7.1).[10]

When the announcement about filming *Paradise Lost* was made, it was following hard on the heels of Mel Gibson's lucrative *The Passion of the Christ* (2004), a film to which Hazeldine drew an explicit link in a March 2007 *New York Times* interview: "I wanted to make sure that for the faith audience, I guess, that they will see it more as 'The Passion of the Christ' than 'The Last Temptation of Christ.'"[11] The producer Vincent Newman added that the film "could be like 'The Lord of the Rings,' or bigger," and the film's extensive combat sequences echoed Sergei Eisenstein's proclamation that "Milton is particularly fine in battle scenes."[12] While

SCENA QVINTA D' INFERNO.

Fig. 7.1. Flying devils in fifth intermezzo of act 4 of *Le nozze degli dei favola* (1637). *Courtesy of Houghton Library, Harvard University, call number Typ 625.37.298.*

Collier cut the war in heaven to promote the triangulated tale of Adam, Eve, and Satan, Newman saw the film as "a war movie at the end of the day," one that needed "less Adam and Eve and more about what's happening with the archangels." This was the tack that convinced Thomas Tull, CEO of Legendary Pictures (the production company behind the *Titans* films), to help bankroll the film. Tull recalls his initial response to the pitch as "Well, that's going to make a lot of older folks relive bad college experiences," continuing the theme first struck by Sutherland in *Animal House*. He came around after deciding, "if you get past the Milton of it all, and think about the greatest war that's ever been fought, the story itself is pretty compelling."[13] And there, in short, lies the rub: the need to "get past the Milton of it all." Where does that bring us? Back to Genesis, or Revelation, or to other narratives of cosmic combat? Moreover, what exactly has "the Milton of it all" become a placeholder for, if not narrative—Allusiveness? Syntax? Elegance of thought? The desire both to capitalize on and dispense with one's predecessors marks any number of, perhaps all, acts of adaptation—but this uneasy relationship is particularly fraught with Milton and his dual legacy of canonicity and "bad college experiences."

Like preceding adaptations of *Paradise Lost*, this film arose partly on the promise of unimaginable spectacle, the very stuff of Milton's sublimity. However, the gap between Milton's sublime vision and cinema's attempts to catch up technologically seems to be a constant, even as the forms of technology and contours of that gap have continually changed. As with Dryden's opera, the paradox of staying "as faithful as possible to Milton's text," trying to describe the indescribable, may stall a production: for better or for worse, only next-generation technical evolution on a limitless budget seems fit to match the epic poem. Yet even without this apparently ontological issue, the production since its inception had been regarded by some commentators as merely another Hollywood travestying of a classic, a critique of Milton on film that goes back as far as the silent era. That this was an inevitable failure because of the quixoticism of capturing Milton's imagination was suggested by at least one blogger, who wrote that "the filmmakers might as well be adapting *Leaves of Grass*" (an idea in fact parodied in the 1997 comedy *Love and Death on Long Island*, dir. Richard Kwietniowski) and that, "with plot and style in the unfilmable column, a celluloid *Paradise Lost* looks hollower than a chocolate Easter bunny."[14]

Other objections to the movie were grounded in what Jennifer M. Jeffers identifies as the "'Hollywoodization' of British literature," an institutionalized discursive practice in which American films "reterritorialize" what signifies as "British" for global audiences, a by-product of the totalizing effects of American cultural hegemony. "The future of British literature," she laments, "seems to be contained in iconic images of Britain produced and circulated primarily for our entertainment."[15] Without grieving the loss of British literary independence, some stateside critics nevertheless noted a loss of authenticity in what was for them an issue of Leitch's "exceptional fidelity." As one film reviewer reflected, "News that Hollywood is to make the first feature film of Milton's epic 'Paradise Lost' fills me with mixed feelings: eager anticipation and foreboding. If the last such blockbuster, 'Troy,' is anything to go by, then promises...that his version will be faithful to the original should be taken with a pillar of salt."[16] Assessing the project for the *Atlantic,* Alyssa Rosenberg writes, "as someone who has five copies of John Milton's epic in my apartment, I suppose I ought to be raging, wailing, and tearing my hair over this. But...I can only give an epic shrug and accept the inevitable butchery of a terrific work." Her love for *Paradise Lost* is not unmixed: she admonishes the producers, "First, most of the characters are boring. Adam and Eve are hopelessly naïve and lovey-dovey. God's a bit of an impenetrable jerk. And the Son just sort of sits around and glows obnoxiously. If it takes aerial warfare to spice things up, fine. But cast a seriously phenomenal actor as Satan, because you're going to need it. Second, don't skimp on special effects. This isn't some cheap-angels-attack-a-diner-Legion-style penny ante conflict. This is the big one." Rosenberg concludes that, while the epic action seems a "hot mess of an idea," it does reveal a niche for "an awesome Milton biopic."[17]

Less highbrow outlets piled on, as well: the *Paradise Lost* film was skewered by the satirical *Cracked* in a piece called "The Brainstorm

That Led to Hollywood's Most Unlikely Remake."[18] In the piece, ultra-exploitative producers swoon over a work that has "literary esteem, mainstream American appeal, tits, asses, epic battles and sequel potential," not to mention "kind of a sexy, complicated devil; probably be shirtless most of the runtime."[19] As with the Patrick Dennis burlesque on the life of faux-starlet Belle Poitrine, *Paradise Lost* becomes most absurd by virtue of its sublimity. Dennis's humor played off the abasement of Milton in the hands of Hollywood opportunists, while toying with how ridiculous the revisions—flashbacks to Eden and rhinestone fig leaves—would inevitably become. But Proyas, conscientious about audience reception and the nature of this adaptation, defended the production even on the count of fidelity, noting, "When you go into something as deep and as beloved as Milton's *Paradise Lost*, you try to be as respectful of the source material as possible."[20]

From 2010 to 2012, I worked for Legendary Pictures as a script consultant on the Vincent Newman film. The story, of course, departed freely from Milton, but there were no rhinestone fig leaves. Rather, I would describe the script as maintaining an alternately faithful and inventive relationship to the poetic narrative. The director at the time, Alex Proyas, pointed out, among other differences, that the film's primary conflict is between Satan and Michael (who assumes most of the Son's role in the poem). And in keeping with the promotion of angelic aerial combat, the story was structured around three major battles—two in heaven and one on earth.[21] The Fall, and the travails of Adam and Eve, became essential but secondary arcs, discreet against the panorama of Satan's rebellion and revenge against the Almighty. Unlike Collier's screenplay, which cut all but the barest vestiges of the godhead, the script retained the character of God even with the accompanying representational challenges. The functions of the Son were transferred onto other characters—Michael steps into the breach, and Satan rebels against the promotion of Adam. In its dialogue, the script oscillated between the compact delivery of contemporary action films and long sequences of adhering to Voltaire's adage: "If God, if the Angels, if Satan would speak, I believe they would speak as they do in Milton."[22] At the San Diego Comic-Con in

2011, preliminary concept art was revealed for heaven and hell, including the raising of Pandaemonium. In it can be seen traces of Gustave Doré and John Martin. One major character is added—the Angel of Death (Djimon Hounsou was at one point cast for the part)—while a few are transferred almost verbatim from Milton's poem. Sin, in particular, was so insistently Miltonic in her speech as to be dubbed "like Yoda times a thousand."

That none of this has come to theaters yet is a disappointment, and *Paradise Lost* may ultimately be a text always already ahead of itself. Or, to put it another way, *Paradise Lost* is so perfectly filmic that any film attempting to match that perfection will inevitably seem inadequate. As Deborah Cartmell and Imelda Whelehan report about the 2001 film adaptation of *Harry Potter and the Sorcerer's Stone* (dir. Chris Columbus), the adaptation "disappointed viewers" not because of its departures, but because "it was a copy of the original which, as a copy, could not live up to the experience of the book, a book which is, effectively, more cinematic than its filmic adaptation and more comfortable with its status as fantastic narrative."[23] *Paradise Lost* may well be more cinematic than any cinematic adaptation. Nonetheless, in 2014 the producer Vincent Newman continued to work on remounting the film, determined to finish it "sooner than later." In the history of *Paradise Lost* adaptation, there is plenty of evidence to indicate the challenges involved. There is also considerable evidence to suggest that Milton will not go away quietly.

In the 300 years since Joseph Addison fantasized about Pandaemonium on a summer riverbank, the poet has had an indelible effect on the development of spectacular entertainment, from the epic to the comic, the operatic to the pantomimic, the grand sermonic to the phantasmagoric, the sublime to the grotesque. If thus far that leaves a fragmented, "phraseological" sense of *Paradise Lost* on film—a hell sequence here, a heavenly combat there—Milton's particularly strong pull upon the cinematic imagination argues for *Paradise Lost* eventually becoming a whole greater than the sum of those parts. But even given the full complement of just those parts, and the range of time and genre they represent, Collier's starry-eyed assertion about the "compelling appeal" of

Paradise Lost for "every band in the spectrum of the potential box-office" rings true in the end. Technology may never catch up to the perpetual inaccessibility of the poem. But seeing *Paradise Lost* on screen may finally depend less on such a convergence than on building upon the ways in which Milton is already there.

Notes

Notes to Introduction

1. *The Guardian,* no. 103 (July 9, 1713), ed. Alexander Chalmers (London, 1822), 2 vols., 2:99–101. The show was held before the Palace of Whitehall on July 7, in celebration of the Peace of Utrecht. The British Museum holds a mezzotint capturing the performance: see *A representation of the Royal Fire-work perform'd by the directions of Coll. Hopkey and Coll. Borgard on the River of Thames,* Museum number 1854,0614.232; available at www.britishmuseum.org (accessed May 9, 2014).

2. Roland Mushat Frye, *Milton's Imagery and the Visual Arts: Iconographic Tradition in the Epic Poems* (Princeton, NJ: Princeton University Press, 1978), 3.

3. The subtext of Boyle's lead sequence was a movement from the rural greens of England's bucolic past to the dark reaches of the Industrial Revolution: "Pandemonium" was expressed as a series of smokestacks rising like "exhalations" from the floor of Olympic Stadium. In an interview with American television host Meredith Vieira, Boyle had to explain that Pandemonium "is the capital of hell in Milton's *Paradise Lost.*" To Vieira's quip, "That's a cheery opening," Boyle replied, "Well there you go, there's a contrary nature to it. But actually it is a massive celebration as well." What Boyle meant by "massive celebration" is intriguing: certainly it was a massive celebration for Satan and the fallen angels to discover they could build a palace in hell. But Boyle seems to be responding to the pure spectacle of Milton's creation, its imaginative exuberance, and, not least, its strikingly cinematic effect: setting in expressionistic motion the very fundaments of "revolution." See interview with Meredith Vieira on *Rock Center* (aired July 26, 2012); available at rockcenter.nbcnews.com/_news/2012/07/26/12953391-mastermind-danny-boyle-shares-details-for-london-2012-opening-ceremony (accessed Sept. 20, 2014).

4. Michel Foucault, *Discipline and Punish: The Birth of the Prison,* trans. Alan Sheridan (New York: Vintage, 1995), 227.

5. Robert Burford, *Description of an Attempt to Illustrate Milton's Pandemonium; now exhibiting in the Panorama, Leicester Square* (London, 1829), 3–4.

6. Interview with Robert E. Welsh, "David W. Griffith Speaks," *New York Dramatic Mirror* (Jan. 14, 1914): 49, 54.

7. On the pitfalls of perfect imitation, see Deborah Cartmell and Imelda Whelehan, *Screen Adaptation: Impure Cinema* (New York: Palgrave, 2010), who argue that "any film which prioritises transposition over interpretation" will "spectacularly fail by freezing all the action and events in an impossible simulacrum of the past made present" (83).

8. Edward Weitzel, review of *Conscience* (dir. Bertram Bracken, 1917), *Moving Picture World* 34, no. 2 (Oct. 13, 1917): 251.

9. Diane McColley, "O Eve, in evil hour…," comment on Milton-L listserv, Nov. 21, 2005, lists.richmond.edu/pipermail/milton-l/2005-November/002872.html (accessed May 9, 2014).

10. Semenza quoted in Michael Joseph Gross, "It's God vs. Satan. But What about the Nudity?," *New York Times*, March 4, 2007, A18.

11. See Laura Lunger Knoppers and Gregory M. Colón Semenza, *Milton in Popular Culture* (New York: Palgrave, 2006); Joseph Wittreich, *Why Milton Matters: A New Preface to His Writings* (New York: Palgrave, 2006); Nigel Smith, *Is Milton Better Than Shakespeare?* (Cambridge, MA: Harvard University Press, 2008).

12. In *Milton in Popular Culture*, Knoppers and Semenza argue persuasively that it is "important to introduce students to some of the films, books, music, and digital materials that adapt and appropriate Milton in our own time. Armed with the resources of popular culture, the classroom teacher of Milton can discuss *Paradise Lost* alongside Steven Brust's *To Reign in Hell* or a viewing of the film *Blade Runner*…and can show clips from Martin Scorsese's film, *The Last Temptation of Christ*, to compare and contrast with *Paradise Regained*" (15).

13. Thomas Leitch, *Film Adaptation and Its Discontents: From "Gone with the Wind" to "The Passion of the Christ"* (Baltimore: Johns Hopkins University Press, 2007), 127, 133.

14. Andrew Marvell, "On Paradise Lost," lines 18–22, 25–30, in *John Milton: Complete Poems and Major Prose*, ed. Merritt Y. Hughes (New York: Odyssey, 1957).

15. Krzysztof Penderecki's opera began in Chicago and played later in 1978 at both La Scala and the Vatican. A short-lived comedy, *Paradise Lost: The Musical* (dir. Michael Merriam), ran for several shows in the Forum Theater at the Festival of the Arts in Laguna Beach, California, in the fall of 2002. The *Los Angeles Times*, September 27, 2002, called it a "scattershot spoof." Eric Whitacre's show *Paradise Lost: Shadows and Wings* (premiered 2007), a postmodern fairy tale (young angels, opposed by forces of darkness, must find their wings), blends a number of musical and visual forms, including anime, with slight appropriations of Milton. An acclaimed adaptation called simply *Paradise Lost* was put on at the Bristol Old Vic in early 2004 by director David Farr—the *Bristol Evening Post*, January 22, 2004, crowed,

"*Paradise Lost* has everything—flying, passion, nudity, and some very expensive mud." For a review of other musical stagings and adaptations, see Martha Winburn England, "John Milton and the Performing Arts," *Bulletin of the New York Public Library* 80, no. 1 (1976): 19–70; Stella P. Revard, "From the State of Innocence to the Fall of Man: The Fortunes of *Paradise Lost* as Opera and Oratorio," in *Milton's Legacy in the Arts*, ed. Albert C. Labriola and Edward Sichi Jr., 93–134 (University Park: Pennsylvania State University Press, 1988); P. G. Stanwood, "*Paradise Lost:* Epic and Opera," *Early Modern Literary Studies* 15, no. 3 (2011): 5.

16. Knoppers and Semenza, introduction to *Milton in Popular Culture*, 5.

17. On this divide between Shakespeare and everyone else ("John Milton, Jane Austen, Maya Angelou"), see Douglas Lanier, *Shakespeare and Modern Popular Culture* (Oxford: Oxford University Press, 2002), 1–20.

18. Barbara Lewalski, *The Life of John Milton: A Critical Biography* (Oxford: Blackwell, 2000), 461.

19. Amilcare A. Iannucci, ed., *Dante, Cinema, and Television* (Toronto: University of Toronto Press, 2004).

20. See, for instance, the best-selling video game *Dante's Inferno* (Electronic Arts, 2010), in which a muscle-bound Dante Alighieri crusades against the entirety of hell.

21. E. V. Lucas, ed., *Letters of Charles Lamb*, vol. 3 (New Haven, CT: Yale University Press, 1935), 394.

22. Alvin Snider, *Year's Work in English Studies* 89, no. 1 (2010): 503. In *Is Milton Better Than Shakespeare?*, 185, Nigel Smith opines that "Miltonic themes" have had "a substantial impact on cinema," though he asserts this entirely on the evidence in Knoppers and Semenza's *Milton in Popular Culture*.

23. Stanley Fish, "Afterword," in Knoppers and Semenza, *Milton in Popular Culture*, 237.

24. Anthony Burgess, "On the Hopelessness of Turning Good Books into Films," *New York Times*, Apr. 20, 1975, 15.

25. Hiroko Sano, "Milton Studies in Japan Now," in *Milton, Rights, and Liberties*, ed. Christophe Tournu and Neil Forsyth (Bern: Peter Lang, 2007), 494.

26. Ibid., 496, 497. Sano's vision was partly realized at the 2012 International Milton Symposium in Tokyo when *Samson Agonistes* was in fact adapted as a Noh play by Mutsuo Takahashi.

27. Vachel Lindsay, *The Art of the Moving Picture* (New York: Macmillan, 1915), 41, quoting Shaw in *Metropolitan Magazine*.

28. Ibid., 41, 39.

29. Sergei Eisenstein, *The Film Sense*, trans. and ed. Jay Leyda (New York: Harcourt, Brace, 1942), 58.

30. For the counterclaim and a critique of Eisenstein's patchy reading of Milton in *The Film Sense*, see Eric C. Brown, "Revisiting *Paradise Lost* and

Eisenstein's *Alexander Nevsky*," *Literature/Film Quarterly* 40, no. 3 (July 2012): 165–79. A recent quotation of the *Nevsky* sequence can be seen in the middle of the crusader epic *Kingdom of Heaven* (dir. Ridley Scott, 2005), during the battle with the Saracens for Kerak Castle.

31. Raymond Dexter Havens, *The Influence of Milton on English Poetry* (Cambridge, MA: Harvard University Press, 1922), 69–70

32. See Marcia R. Pointon, *Milton and English Art* (Toronto: University of Toronto Press, 1970). On the full range of illustrations of Milton, see also Joseph Wittreich, "Illustrators," in *A Milton Encyclopedia*, vol. 4, ed. William B. Hunter et al. (Lewisburg, PA: Bucknell University Press, 1978), 55–78; and Wendy Furman-Adams, "Visual Arts," in *Milton in Context,* ed. Stephen B. Dobranski (Cambridge: Cambridge University Press, 2010), 180–209.

33. John Knowles, *The Life and Writings of Henri Fuseli, Esq.,* vol. 1 (London, 1831), 236. On the Milton Gallery and its influence on the development of Milton as spectacle, see Luisa Calè, *Fuseli's Milton Gallery: "Turning Readers into Spectators"* (Oxford: Oxford University Press, 2006).

34. Ronald Haver, *David O. Selznick's Hollywood* (New York: Bonanza, 1980), 84. Cf. Ray Harryhausen and Tony Dalton, *The Art of Ray Harryhausen* (New York: Billboard, 2006).

35. Haver, *Selznick's Hollywood,* 84. Discussing the making of *King Kong,* George E. Turner singles out a few specific evocations: "The First Approach of the Serpent" and, in the "wonderful scene in which Kong surveys his domain from the natural balcony of his mountaintop home," both "Satan Overlooking Paradise" and "The Hermit on the Mountain," the latter from Chateaubriand's *Atala.* See George E. Turner, Orville Goldner, and Michael H. Price, *Spawn of Skull Island: The Making of King Kong* (Baltimore: Luminary Press, 2002), 154.

36. Author interview with Vincent Newman, Oct. 29, 2010.

37. Richard Wilbur, "A Poet and the Movies," in *Man and the Movies,* ed. William R. Robinson (Baton Rouge: Louisiana State University Press, 1967), 224. Milton's anticipatory cinematics is also the interpretive model for Bill Readings's essay on *Paradise Lost* and postmodern temporality, "Milton at the Movies: An Afterword to *Paradise Lost,*" in *Postmodernism across the Ages: Essays for a Postmodernity That Wasn't Born Yesterday,* ed. Bill Readings and Bennet Schaber (Syracuse, NY: Syracuse University Press, 1993), which is occupied with both the "phenomenology of the temporality of cinema" and "the conditions of experience that cinema imposes." Calling Adam's vision of history in the final books of the poem a "filmic revelation," Readings argues that, "If film theory gives us an experience of viewing in which interpellation is animated by the desire to see, Milton's is explicitly a cinematics of blindness, for Adam 'now enforc'd to close his eyes'" (89).

38. *The Literary Essays of Thomas Merton,* ed. Patrick Hart (New York: New Directions, 1985), 252.

39. Christopher R. Miller, "Winging It," *New York Times Book Review,* May 24, 1998, 23.

40. James Hynes, "'The Tale of Paradise Lost': The Devil and the Details," *New York Times,* Nov. 14, 2004.

41. Edward M. Cifelli, *Paradise Lost and Other Poems,* ed. Edward Le Comte (London: Penguin, 2003), viii.

42. John Shawcross, "'Shedding sweet influence': The Legacy of John Milton's Works," in *A Concise Companion to Milton,* ed. Angelica Duran (Malden, MA: Blackwell, 2007), 25.

43. Brian McFarlane, "Reading Film and Literature," in *The Cambridge Companion to Literature on Screen,* ed. Deborah Cartmell and Imelda Whelehan (Cambridge: Cambridge University Press, 2007), 26.

44. Jonathan Rosen, "Return to Paradise: The Enduring Relevance of John Milton," *New Yorker,* June 2, 2008, 72.

45. Patrick Dennis, *Little Me* (1961; rpt., New York: Broadway, 2002), 144.

46. In 1963, for a poll called "Great Ideas That Never Got Filmed," *Show: The Magazine of the Arts* 3 (Aug. 1963), surveyed a number of prominent Hollywood screenwriters. Harry Brown, an Oscar winner for *A Place in the Sun* (dir. George Stevens, 1951), jokingly recommends the *Aeneid* or the *Dialogues of Plato.* He finds Milton equally risible: "So, indeed, what great ideas *are* left? Well, there's 'Paradise Lost.' The problem here is one of money, notably when it comes to special effects. Still, a great deal of expense can be avoided if the Yugoslav army is used for fallen angels and a Billy Graham scrub team for the, so to speak, Good Guys." Explaining the issue of unfilmability, he adds, "though we are surrounded by scientific marvels, not one of them is able to make visual a literary style" (62).

47. For an instructive reading of comparable "difficult" films, see Christine Geraghty, *Now a Major Motion Picture: Film Adaptations of Literature and Drama* (New York: Rowman and Littlefield, 2007), 47–72.

48. Discussion at www.imdb.com/title/tt0484138/board/nest/71790 400?d=100814330&p=4#100814330 (accessed Mar. 10, 2010; no longer archived).

49. Samuel Johnson, *Lives of the English Poets,* 2 vols. (London, 1820), 1: 146.

50. Joseph A. Wittreich, *Visionary Poetics: Milton's Tradition and His Legacy* (San Marino, CA: Huntington Library, 1979), 25. On Milton's preference for such transcendental forms, see also Angus Fletcher, *The Transcendental Masque: An Essay on Milton's Comus* (Ithaca, NY: Cornell University Press, 1972). Fletcher links explicitly the masque to film, noting that "the overall form of the masque is a transition...from an early state of strong visual fixation to a later state of harmonious musical motion. Or, using our conceptions from film-making, from a still show to slow motion,

through sequences run at regular speed" (103–04), and more pointedly that "every account of successful masques indicates that scene makers…sought to approach the technique of film montage." Milton's own efforts with the masque sought "the liberation of the genre from its visual materials," a transcendental effect achieved by "mix[ing] all the modes already brought together in disparate genres of tragicomedy, ballets de cour, opera, pageant, and masque itself, and in a thoroughly original way…forc[ing] imagery from all the available media of masque into the verbal confines of his text" (115).

51. Ambrosio press book for *Satana* (Turin, 1912). My thanks to Elizabeth Simon for this translation.

52. Mike Fleming Jr., "Alex Proyas Setting Benjamin Walker to Play Archangel Michael in 'Paradise Lost,'" *Deadline Hollywood*, Aug. 3, 2011, www.deadline.com/2011/08/alex-proyas-setting-benjamin-walker-to-play-archangel-michael-in-paradise-lost (accessed May 12, 2014).

53. Johnson, *Lives of the English Poets*, 1:152.

54. Harold Bloom, *How to Read and Why* (New York: Scribners, 2000), 117.

55. See esp. Robert Stam, "Beyond Fidelity: The Dialogics of Adaptation," in *Film Adaptation,* ed. James Naremore (New Brunswick, NJ: Rutgers University Press, 2000), 55.

56. See "Milton I" (1936), and "Milton II" (1947), in *Selected Prose of T. S. Eliot,* ed. Frank Kermode (New York: Harcourt, 1975), 258–64, 265–74.

57. Eliot, "Milton II," 270.

58. Ibid., 270.

59. Ibid., 269–70.

60. Christopher Ricks, *Milton's Grand Style* (Oxford: Oxford University Press, 1963), 22.

61. T. S. Eliot, *The Sacred Wood: Essays on Poetry and Criticism* (New York: Knopf, 1921), 142.

62. Cf. Wayne Barlowe, who did concept art for both *Avatar* and the Vincent Newman *Paradise Lost:* "And then I read Milton. There, before me, was the most visual and magnificent depiction of the underworld that I think anyone has ever created. Filled, as it is, with larger than life characters and settings it set my mind aflame. Here was a world conceived in a fullness that would shame and confound any Hollywood director." See Robert Thompson, "Interview with Wayne Barlowe," Nov. 9, 2007, fantasybookcritic.blogspot. com/2007/11/interview-with-wayne-barlowe.html (accessed May 12, 2014_). In *Sci-Fi Art: A Graphic History* (New York: Collins Design, 2009), 144, Steve Holland and Alex Summersby note that Barlowe also wrote a screenplay for Fox Animation structured around his paintings of the poem.

63. Noam Reisner, *Milton and the Ineffable* (Oxford: Oxford University Press, 2010), 202.

64. Marshall Grossman, "Milton's Dialectical Visions," *Modern Philology* 82, no. 1 (1984): 24.

65. Miklos Peti, "A Heap of Broken Images or, Why Milton Is an Iconoclast?," *Classical Receptions Journal* 6, no. 2 (2014): 275–76. Cf. Joanna Picciotto, *Labors of Innocence in Early Modern England* (Cambridge: Cambridge University Press, 2010), who writes of *Paradise Lost,* "we are forced to refocus our vision repeatedly, performing radical shifts in scale" (447).

66. Julia Staykova, "Structures of Perception in the Similes of *Paradise Lost,*" *SEL* 53, no. 1 (Winter 2013): 159.

67. Ibid., 159. On Milton's manipulation of the voyeuristic gaze as cinematic, see also Regina M. Schwartz, "Rethinking Voyeurism and Patriarchy: The Case of *Paradise Lost,*" *Representations* 34 (Spring 1991): 85–103.

68. Northrop Frye, *The Return of Eden* (Toronto: University of Toronto Press, 1965), 17–18.

69. Wittreich, *Visionary Poetics,* 24–25.

70. On this and other citations of Milton in the novella, see June Sturrock, "Angels, Insects, and Analogy in A. S. Byatt's *Morpho Eugenia,*" *Connotations* 12, no. 1 (2002/2003): 93–104; and Jane Campbell, *A. S. Byatt and the Heliotropic Imagination* (Waterloo, Ontario: Wilfrid Laurier University Press, 2004), 156.

71. Julie Sanders, *Adaptation and Appropriation* (New York: Routledge, 2006), 3, notes some 40 critical terms used to describe the relation between source and adaptive texts, from "borrowing" and "stealing" to "paratext, hypertext, palimpsest, graft." Similarly, Stam in "The Dialogics of Adaptation" offers "a whole constellation of tropes—translation, reading, dialogization, cannibalization, transmutation, transfiguration, and signifying," all preferable to "fidelity" (62).

72. Sanders, *Adaptation and Appropriation,* 4.

73. Knoppers and Semenza, *Milton in Popular Culture,* 10.

74. Lanier, *Shakespeare and Modern,* 17–18. See also Paul Coates, *Film at the Intersection of High and Mass Culture* (Cambridge: Cambridge University Press, 1994).

75. Linda Hutcheon, *A Theory of Adaptation* (New York: Routledge, 2006), 173.

76. Ibid., 12.

77. Sanders, *Adaptation and Appropriation,* 45.

78. See Gérard Genette, *Palimpsests: Literature in the Second Degree,* trans. Channa Newman and Claude Dobinsky (Lincoln: University of Nebraska Press, 1997), 5.

79. Hutcheon, *A Theory of Adaptation,* 21.

80. Charles Whitney, "Appropriate This," *Borrowers and Lenders: The Journal of Shakespeare and Appropriation* 3 (Spring/Summer 2008): 1–23, terms such acts of appropriation "dynamic transactions" and argues that Renaissance theater audiences were themselves "opportunistic agents" prepared to "adapt and apply specific dramatic material creatively, according to a range of interests and purposes" (3).

81. Hutcheon, *A Theory of Adaptation*, 7, 9.

82. Gregory Machacek, "Allusion," *PMLA* 122, no. 2 (Mar. 2007): 522–36, 525. Machacek traces some of his theory of allusion to Milton himself, speculating that the "allusive density of *Paradise Lost* is not merely an accident of his vast learning" but that "the allusions are designed to offer the reader the opportunity to exercise a mental faculty that Milton regarded as essential to moral decision making"—that is, to avoid falling by remembering (531).

83. Thomas Leitch, "Adaptation Studies at a Crossroads," *Adaptation* 1, no. 1 (2008): 66.

84. Hutcheon, *A Theory of Adaptation*, 204, quoting Mark Axelrod, "Once upon a Time in Hollywood; or, the Commodification of Form in the Adaptation of Fictional Texts to Hollywood Cinema," *Literature/Film Quarterly* 24, no. 2 (1996): 201–08.

85. John M. Desmond and Peter Hawkes, *Adaptation: Studying Film and Literature* (New York: McGraw-Hill, 2005), 128.

NOTES TO CHAPTER 1,
MILTON AND THE STAGING OF SPECTACLE

1. Angus Fletcher, *The Transcendental Masque: An Essay on Milton's "Comus"* (Ithaca, NY: Cornell University Press, 1972), similarly calls Milton a poet of extravagance, but extravagance as the "means of virtuosic intensity" (136).

2. T. S. Eliot, *The Sacred Wood: Essays on Poetry and Criticism* (New York: Knopf, 1921), 142; Harold Bloom, *How to Read and Why* (New York: Scribners, 2000), 117.

3. William Prynne, *Histrio-mastix: The Player's Scourge; or, Actor's Tragedy* (London, 1633), 970–71. On the relationship between word and image in seventeenth century reformation, though, see William Madsen, *From Shadowy Types to Truth: Studies in Milton's Symbolism* (New Haven, CT: Yale University Press, 1968), 166–80.

4. Joad Raymond, *Milton's Angels: The Early Modern Imagination* (Oxford: Oxford University Press, 2010), 164. On Milton's accommodation, see Laila Ghermani, " 'That I may see and tell / Of things invisible to mortal sight': Representing the Invisible in *Paradise Lost*," in *Milton, Rights, and Liberties,* ed. Christophe Tournu and Neil Forsyth (Bern: Peter Lang, 2007), 255–62.

5. Raymond, *Milton's Angels*, 184.

6. *Paradise Lost* 12.9–10, in *John Milton: Complete Poems and Major Prose,* ed. Merritt Y. Hughes (New York: Odyssey, 1957). Unless otherwise noted, all quotations from Milton's works refer to this edition.

7. Stanley Fish, for instance, writes that "Milton rejects spectacle for quiet inner resolution in his work"; see his "Afterword," in *Milton in Popular*

Culture, ed. Laura Lunger Knoppers and Gregory M. Colón Semenza (New York: Palgrave, 2006), 244.

8. Laura L. Knoppers, *Historicizing Milton: Spectacle, Power, and Poetry in Restoration England* (Athens: University of Georgia Press, 1994), 87.

9. Ibid., 79. Douglas Bush, *English Literature in the Earlier Seventeenth Century* (Oxford: Clarendon, 1945), describes this view of Milton's increasing apoliticism: "[Milton's] earlier pamphlets had been largely directed towards militant action; the decline and collapse of that external hope left him feeling the need of a closer walk with God. In his late poems, in place of the old ardent confidence in public reform we find an 'un-Miltonic' emphasis on private experience, on humility, obedience, faith, and divine grace" (402).

10. Knoppers, *Historicizing Milton,* 80. On Milton's hell, see Merritt Y. Hughes, "'Myself Am Hell,'" *Modern Philology* 54 (1956): 80–94; Ernest Schanzer, "Milton's Hell Revisited," *University of Toronto Quarterly* 24 (1955): 136–45; Robert Myers, "'God shall be all in all': The Erasure of Hell in *Paradise Lost*," *Seventeenth Century* 5 (1990): 43–53.

11. On this figure, see James Dougal Fleming, "Meanwhile, Medusa in *Paradise Lost*," *ELH* 69 (2002): 1009–28, who makes a number of helpful readings, though he also reads Medusa and the fallen angelic host as coeval.

12. Angus Fletcher, *Time, Space, and Motion in the Age of Shakespeare* (Cambridge, MA: Harvard University Press, 2007), 141, describes Satan's space flight as having "magnificent rolling rhythms—the same oceanic effect Stanley Kubrick achieved in *2001,* when he suddenly shifted his musical score into Strauss's *Blue Danube Waltz.*"

13. Barbara Lewalski, *The Life of John Milton: A Critical Biography* (Oxford: Blackwell, 2000), 465.

14. Gilles Deleuze, *Cinema 1,* trans. Hugh Tomlinson (New York: Continuum, 2005), 194–95. See also Elizabeth Ely Fuller, *Milton's Kinesthetic Vision in "Paradise Lost"* (Lewisburg, PA: Bucknell University Press, 1983), who argues for "repeated instances of aesthetic distancing" (21) throughout *Paradise Lost,* including modulations of object, character, and tone that have the effect of "jarring the perceptual faculties out of their sensuous sloth" (34).

15. The work was entered in the *Stationers' Register* on April 17, 1674, under the title *The Fall of Angells and Man in Innocence,* and most surviving manuscripts of the opera prior to 1677 bear this same title. That Dryden's opera has little to do with the fallen angels after the first act, and nothing with the war in heaven, may have motivated the change in emphasis onto events in Eden when the quarto was released. *The State of Innocence* was reprinted frequently in the ensuing years, at least nine times between 1678 and 1703.

16. The *Monitor,* vol. 1, no. 17 (1713), quoted in *The Early Lives of Milton,* ed. Helen Darbishire (London: Constable, 1932), 335. John Aubrey relates the encounter in similar language: "Jo: Dryden Esq. Poet Laureate, who very much admires him, & went to him to have leave to putt his Paradise-lost into a Drama in Rhyme: Mr. Milton received him civilly, & told him he would give him leave to tagge his Verses" (*Early Lives,* 7).

17. Lewalski, *Life of Milton*, 508.

18. On subsequent oratorios, esp. of *Comus*, see Dustin Griffin, *Regaining Paradise: Milton and the Eighteenth Century* (Cambridge: Cambridge University Press, 1986), 67–71.

19. John Dryden, *The Works of John Dryden: The Plays*, vol. 12, ed. Vinton A. Dearing (Berkeley and Los Angeles: University of California Press, 1994), 86.

20. Ibid., 12:5.

21. Ibid., 12:86.

22. The epigraph is drawn from *Ovid's Metamorphoses: The Arthur Golding Translation of 1567*, ed. John Nims (Philadelphia: Paul Dry, 2000), book 5, and Calliope's praise of Ceres that Dryden seems to be transferring to the duchess: "Utinam modo dicere possem / Carmina digna Dea: certe est Dea Carmine digna" (*Met.* 5.344–45; Golding's translation: "would God I could resound / Hir worthie laude: she doubtless is a Goddesse worthie praise"). But the epigraph is doing more work than extolling once again the worthiness of Mary. The Ovidian tale that this introduces, the rape of Proserpina, prefigures Dryden's (and Milton's) treatment of Eve and Satan, while the lines immediately following the encomium to Ceres describe the classical war against the gods: "the Giant Typhon gave presumptuously assayes / To conquer Heaven" (*Met.* 5.439–40).

23. Dearing, *Works of Dryden*, 12:86.

24. Harold Bloom, *The Anxiety of Influence*, 2nd ed. (Oxford: Oxford University Press, 1997), 32; Jonathan Richardson (father and son), *Explanatory Notes and Remarks on "Paradise Lost"* (London, 1734), cxix–cxx. Cf. Lara Dodds, "Poetic Authority in Manuscript and Print: The Case of Milton's *Paradise Lost* and Dryden's *The State of Innocence and Fall of Man*," in *A Manuscript Miscellany* (A Summer 2005 Institute Directed by Steven W. May), www.folger.edu/html/folger_institute/mm/EssayLD.html (accessed Sept. 29, 2014): "But if Dryden here acknowledged Milton's authorship, the remainder of the preface asserts independence by translating the meaning of heroism—a central concern of Milton's epic—into the specific idiom of Dryden's verse. Milton's authorship is finally transcended and exceeded by Dryden's own." A survey of Dryden's ambivalent relationship with Milton can be found in Dearing, *Works of Dryden*, 12:342–43.

25. Lewalski, *Life of Milton*, 508. See also William John Lawrence, "Dryden's Abortive Opera," *Times Literary Supplement*, Aug. 6, 1931, 606.

26. Raymond, *Milton's Angels*, 331.

27. James Anderson Winn, *John Dryden and His World* (New Haven, CT: Yale University Press, 1987), 264, 269. Winn adds that a cheaper production, the French Opera *Ariane*, which had already been performed at court, was played at Drury Lane on March 30 ("just four days after the opening of the new house"), and that the King's Company was able to save additional monies by recycling the set from the earlier staging (262).

28. Johnson, *Lives of the English Poets*, 1:295.

29. *The Works of John Dryden: Illustrated with Notes, Historical, Critical, and Explanatory, and a Life,* vol. 5, ed. Walter Scott and George Saintsbury (Edinburgh: Paterson, 1883), 95.

30. See, for instance, Montague Summers, "Dryden's Abortive Opera," *Times Literary Supplement,* Aug. 13, 1931, 621. On the history of such representation, see Clifford Davidson, "Nudity, the Body, and Early English Drama," *Journal of English and German Philology* 98, no. 4. (Oct. 1999): 499–522.

31. William Tydeman, *The Medieval European Stage, 500–1550* (Cambridge: Cambridge University Press, 2001), 171–72.

32. William Tydeman, *The Theatre in The Middle Ages: Western European Stage Conditions, c. 800–1576* (Cambridge: Cambridge University Press, 1979), 213.

33. Ibid., 213.

34. On connections between Milton's treatment of conjugal love and its presentation in the reformed mystery play, see Gordon Campbell and N. M. Davis, "*Paradise Lost* and the Norwich Grocers' Play," *Milton Quarterly* 14, no. 4 (Dec. 1980): 113–16. Tydeman, *Medieval European Stage,* 459, also describes an Italian festival of St. John the Baptist, Florence (1454), in which "they performed the battle of the angels when Lucifer was cast out of Heaven with his fallen angels."

35. The turn to the local habitations of Adam and Eve helps to explain further some of Dryden's other substitutions, such as using Asmoday, and his role in the book of Tobit as inimical to wedded love, in the place of Milton's second, Beelzebub, who has been demoted to a minor councilor. The focus on Adam and Eve, and Dryden's additional emphasis on Milton's idea of the fortunate fall, allowing for a happy ending, may also have been in the service of political aims: the marriage of James, Duke of York, and Mary of Modena seems to have been the occasion for Dryden's efforts. In his 1677 dedication to the duchess, Dryden makes the link more explicit and rather fulsomely praises her, "your Person is a Paradice, and your soul a Cherubin within to Guard it" (Dearing, *Works of Dryden,* 12:84).

36. In his *Discourse of Satire* (1693), Dryden elaborates on the problem of dramatic tension in the Christian epic, arguing that angelic conflict would form the most suitable subject matter, and thereby circumvent the lack of suspense in dramatizing God's omnipotence and omniscience: "The perusing of one chapter in the prophecy of Daniel, and accommodating what there they find with the principles of Platonic philosophy as it is now Christianised, would have made the ministry of angels as strong an engine for the working up of heroic poetry in our religion as that of the ancients has been to raise theirs by all the fables of their gods" (Scott and Saintsbury, *Works of Dryden,* 5:276).

37. John Dryden, *The State of Innocence, and Fall of Man,* in Dearing, *Works of Dryden,* 12:98. Marion H. Hamilton, "The Manuscripts of Dryden's *The State of Innocence* and the Relation of the Harvard MS to the First

Quarto," *Studies in Bibliography* 6 (1954): 237–46, points out that the 1677 edition omits two directions found in earlier manuscripts: "thunder is heard and flashes of lightning seen" and "A shower of fire rains over the stage." Since Dryden used this very device in his adaptation of *The Tempest,* he may have wanted to avoid duplication.

38. Scott and Saintsbury, *Works of Dryden,* 5:97.

39. Lawrence, "Dryden's Abortive Opera," 606.

40. Dearing, *Works of Dryden,* 12:324, 323. Bernard Harris, " 'That Soft Seducer': Dryden's *The State of Innocence and Fall of Man*," in *Approaches to "Paradise Lost,"* ed. C. A. Patrides (Toronto: University of Toronto Press, 1968), also contends that "the delight in the balancing feats made available by stage machinery is a proper exploitation of the literal possibilities of the action, and reveal the extent to which Dryden's dramatic intentions could happily co-operate with the illusionist world of lifts, traps and flying machines" (128).

41. Dearing, *Works of Dryden,* 12:324.

42. Lawrence, "Dryden's Abortive Opera," argues that because the opera was intended to be shown before a sophisticated international audience in celebration of James and Mary, accustomed to the splendor of Italian opera, Dryden needed to come up with a subject that would make the English look less "primitive." Like Dearing, he seeks out stage effects comparable to Dryden's but finds them in French and Italian opera houses. Still, his examples (e.g., Molière's *Psyché,* showing at the Palais Royal throughout the early 1670s) are not much more convincing of Dryden working within any established tradition: "Two Angels descend; they take the Woman each by the hand and fly up with her out of sight." While this clearly shows the same need for machinery, the representational terms are far less demanding. Montague Summers, *Dryden: The Dramatic Works,* 6 vols. (London: Nonesuch, 1932), 3:589–90, provides analogues for the representation of heaven and hell in Restoration playhouses. On the development of the English opera in general, see Judith Milhous, "The Multimedia Spectacular on the Restoration Stage," in *British Theatre and the Other Arts, 1660–1800,* ed. Shirley Strum Kenny (Washington, DC: Folger Shakespeare Library, 1984), 41–66.

43. Dearing, *Works of Dryden,* 12:94. On Dryden's reformulations of Milton, see also Marcie Frank, "Staging Criticism, Staging Milton: John Dryden's 'The State of Innocence,'" *Eighteenth Century* 34, no. 1 (Spring 1993): 45–64.

44. Nat Lee, "To Mr. Dryden, on His Poem of Paradice" (ll. 35–37), in Dearing, *Works of Dryden,* 12:538.

45. See Harris, " 'That Soft Seducer,' " 125.

46. Dearing, *Works of Dryden,* 12:95. On Dryden and the imagination, see also 12:334–40.

47. Ibid., 12:94–95.

48. Lee, "To Mr. Dryden," line 13, p. 537. For further discussion of Dryden's prosody, see Morris Freedman, "The 'Tagging' of *Paradise Lost:*

Rhyme in Dryden's *The State of Innocence*," *Milton Quarterly* 5 (1971): 18–22.

49. Andrew Marvell, "On Paradise Lost," lines 18–50, in *John Milton: Complete Poems and Major Prose,* ed. Merritt Y. Hughes (New York: Odyssey Press, 1957), 209.

50. Lewalski, *Life of Milton,* 510.

51. Dearing, *Works of Dryden,* 12:104. The raising of Pandaemonium in *Paradise Lost,* the favorite spectacle of most precinematic adaptations of Milton, likely has its roots in stagecraft. Milton's description closely echoes that of the raising of the Palace of Fame in William Davenant's masque *Britannia Triumphans* (1637). Hughes cites the effects of the machinery: " 'the earth open'd, and there rose up a richly-adorned palace, seeming all of goldsmith's work, with porticos vaulted, on pilasters of rich rustick work; their bases and capitels of gold. Above these ran an architrave freese, and coronis of the same—the freese enrich'd with jewels.' (Quoted by Todd from *The Stage Condemn'd,* 1698)" (Hughes, *Complete Poems and Major Prose,* 229n). John G. Demaray, *Milton's Theatrical Epic: The Invention and Design of "Paradise Lost"* (1980; repr., Cambridge, MA: Harvard University Press, 1999), also argues convincingly for a number of precedents in Italian theater (see esp. 26–27).

52. Dearing, *Works of Dryden,* 12:107–08.

53. Ibid., 12:116, 123. Cf. Dearing's purported analogue from *Mithridates,* "An Image of Victory descends with two Crowns in her hands; but on a sudden the Engines break, and cast the Image forward on the Stage with such violence that they dash in pieces," which actually has very little in common with the illusory effect called for in Dryden's direction other than exemplifying "machines that break" (12:324).

54. Ibid., 12:122.

55. Ibid., 12:118.

56. Ibid., 12:120.

57. Ibid., 12:143.

58. Harris, " 'That Soft Seducer,' " 130.

59. Winn, *Dryden and His World,* 268.

60. Milhous, "Multimedia Spectacular," 52.

61. *Spectator* 302 (Feb. 15, 1712). Summers, "Dryden's Abortive Opera," 621, takes Powell's play to be Dryden's opera revamped. See also Raymond D. Havens, "An Adaptation of One of Dryden's Plays," *Review of English Studies* 4, no. 13 (1928): 88. George Speaight, *The History of the English Puppet Theatre* (New York: John De Graff, 1955), 325, however, thinks this puppet play a revival of an older work, renamed after Dryden but otherwise merely the long-running "The Creation of the World." Subsequent advertisements suggest it may have been a mixture of conventional and political influences. The *Daily Courant* of March 31, 1712, adds to the opera "a new Piece of Machinery after the British Manner, contriv'd and just finish'd by

Powell, which Represents a Paradice wonderful surprising. At the breaking of the Clouds rises several Triumphal Arches, which forms several most agreeable Prospects; beautify'd by Her Most Serene Majesty of Great Britain in Her Royal Robes, attended by Her Peers and Officers of State: Under their feet are Represented the Trophies taken from the French and Bavarians by Her Majesty's Arms this War."

62. William Goodman, *The Social History of Great Britain during the Reigns of the Stuarts* (New York: William H. Colyer, 1843), 1:302. An earlier production of the opera featured Punchinello "encountering a Lyon in the Amphitheatre"; see the *Daily Courant,* Jan. 18, 1712.

63. Denis Diderot, *Salon de 1765,* in *Diderot: Oeuvres,* 5 vols., ed. Laurent Versini (Paris: Robert Laffont, 1996), 4:349.

64. Louise Pelletier, *Architecture in Words: Theatre, Language and the Sensuous Space of Architecture* (London: Routledge, 2006), 34–35.

65. See Simon Werrett, *Fireworks: Pyrotechnic Arts and Sciences in European History* (Chicago: University of Chicago Press, 2010), 137, who also notes that the fireworks included "fixed and turning suns, serpents, grenades, balloons, rockets, and *jets de feu,* which sent up great fountains of fire in imitation of *jets d'eau.*"

66. See Wendell Cole, "The Salle des Machines: Three Hundred Years Ago," *Educational Theatre Journal* 14, no. 3 (1962): 224–27.

67. Pelletier, *Architecture in Words,* 26. See also Marian Hobson, *The Object of Art: The Theory of Illusion in Eighteenth-Century France* (Cambridge: Cambridge University Press, 1982), 139–95.

68. Marc Olivier, "Jean-Nicolas Servandoni's Spectacles of Nature and Technology," *French Forum* 30, no. 2 (Spring 2005): 33.

69. Quoted in Pelletier, *Architecture in Words,* 28.

70. Ibid., 28.

71. Olivier, "Servandoni's Spectacles," 32. Servandoni quoted in Pelletier, *Architecture in Words,* 28.

72. "La musique de Geminiani est, selon lui, détestable; le jeu des mimes, d'une médiocrité honteuse. Le merveilleux est du domaine seul du poète épique; à vouloir réaliser ses fantasies on tombe dans la puérilité" (Jeanne Bouché, "Servandoni [1695–1766]," [Paris] *Gazette des Beaux-Arts* [Aug. 1910]: 139). Unless otherwise noted, translations are my own.

73. "Doit produire sur les esprits tout l'effet que l'on peut attendre d'un Spectacle muet" (Jean-Nicolas Servandoni, *Description du spectacle de la chute des anges rebelles: Sujet tiré du poëme du Paradis Perdu de Milton* [Paris, 1758]). For a general review of Servandoni's efforts, see Jérôme de la Gorce, "Une initiative originale d'un Italien au XVIII siècle: Les spectacles de Servandoni dans la salle des machines des Tuileries," in *Les artistes étrangers à Paris: de la fin du Moyen Âge aux années 1920,* ed. Marie-Claude Chaudonneret (New York: Peter Lang, 2007), 121–36.

74. "Donne des formes corporelles aux choses spirituelles, et présente sous des figures sensibles ce qui surpasseroit la portée de l'esprit humain" (Servandoni, *Description du spectacle*).

75. Quoted in Laurence Chatel de Brancion, *Carmontelle's Landscape Transparencies: Cinema of the Enlightenment* (Los Angeles: J. Paul Getty Museum, 2008), 13.

76. Bouché, "Servandoni," 121–46.

77. Ibid., 140.

78. See Elie Catherine Fréron, ed., *L'année littéraire; ou, Suite des lettres sur quelques écrits de ce temps,* vol. 2 (Paris, 1758), 145–54.

79. "Qu'il est tombé sans ressource dès la première représentation" (Denis Diderot, *Correspondance, littéraire, philosophique et critique par Grimm,* vol. 4, ed. Maurice Tourneux [Paris, 1877], 12).

80. "Les candélabres qui l'éclairent ont l'air d'une lanterne magique par la forme, et non par l'effet" (Fréron, *L'année littéraire,* 2:149).

81. See Voltaire's *Essay on Epic Poetry* (1727), in *The Complete Works of Voltaire,* vol. 3b, ed. David Williams (Oxford: Voltaire Foundation, 1996), 382.

82. "J'en suis d'autant plus fâché et surpris que j'aime véritablement ces sortes de spectacles, et que je me rappelle toujours d'avoir vû précédemment avec beaucoup de plaisir *La Descente d'Enée aux Enfers, la Forêt Enchantée,* et plusieurs autres sujets dignes de la grandeur du lieu où ils étoient réprésentés, et des connoisseurs qu'ils y attiroient" (Fréron, *L'année littéraire,* 2:153–54).

83. "Comme le Chevalier Servandoni s'efforce de concilier les idées de son Auteur, il espére qu'on ne le blâmera pas d'exposer sur la Scéne des choses, qui dans tout autre Spectacle paroîtroient hazardées, et même hors de place" (Servandoni, *Description du spectacle,* 4).

84. See Louis Josse, *L'origine du monde et la chute du premier home, pièce en cinq actes tirée du Paradis perdu de Milton, spectacle de peinture, méchanique et musique qui en expriment les différentes actions, . . . composé et executé par le Sieur Josse* (Paris: Claude Herissant, 1763).

85. Martin Meisel, *Realizations: Narrative, Pictorial, and Theatrical Arts in Nineteenth-Century England* (Princeton, NJ: Princeton University Press, 1983), 175n21. Meisel, noting the nineteenth century stage's "insistent attempt to translate the sublime into the spectacular," further observes the pervasion of the paradise narrative: "Paradise in the nineteenth-century theater . . . was to be found in pantomime, fairy-play, and extravaganza, that cluster of related forms. . . . A grim opening and a dark scene, and the garish malevolence of a horde of imps and demons, served to set off the paradisal character of what everyone knew was to come and had come to see, whose climactic visual achievement became the underlying rationale of the form" (167, 184). Milton's narrative structure naturally lent itself to such contrapuntal design. Another particularly Miltonic example, the opera *La tentation* premiered on July 18, 1832, in Paris and included both a spectacular heavenly

battle, which one London reviewer called "wonderful, almost Miltonian," and a demonic council, set within a volcano, that also seems adapted from Milton (perhaps via Mulciber): "On one side is a stupendous flight of steps, reaching to the utmost height of the stage, garnished with monsters of every possible description: the other displays a distant view of extensive lakes of fire and brimstone. An army of demons, with their band, artillery, and all the paraphernalia of infernal warfare, descend the gigantic staircase in immense force" (review in *Morning Chronicle*, July 20, 1832).

86. Adolphe Philippe D'Ennery and Ferdinand Dugué, *Le paradis perdu*, in *Le théatre contemporain illustré* (Paris, 1856), 2.

87. "Un vaste édifice tout rayonnant de magnificences bizarres; il est soutenu par des colonnes de métaux en fusion et se termine par un cirque immense; sous l'arc de la voûte, pendent de longues files de lampes étince-lantes. Au milieu du palais, un trône splendide" (D'Ennery and Dugué, *Le paradis perdu*, 3).

88. "A nous les créatures maudites, poursuivons-les!...saisissons-les!"; "L'homme a péché!...la terre est a nous!" (ibid.).

89. John Forster, *The Life of Charles Dickens, Volume 3: 1852–1870* (1874; repr., Cambridge: Cambridge University Press, 2011), 107.

90. Ibid., 107–08.

91. Barbara Barker, ed., introduction to *Bolossy Kiralfy, Creator of Great Musical Spectacles: An Autobiography* (Ann Arbor: University of Michigan Press, 1988), xix.

92. Ibid., xix–xxi.

93. See ibid. for a full account of the Kiralfys' stage spectacles.

94. "Amusements: The City Theatres," *New York Times*, Sept. 8, 1874, 5.

95. See Barker, *Bolossy Kiralfy*, 94.

96. See "Amusements: Niblo's Theater," *New York Herald*, Sept. 8, 1874, 7.

97. Barker, *Bolossy Kiralfy*, 94.

98. "Amusements: The City Theatres," 5.

99. Barker, *Bolossy Kiralfy*, 94.

100. Joseph Roach, *Cities of the Dead: Circum-Atlantic Performance* (New York: Columbia University Press, 1996), writes of Milton's influence on Mardi Gras parades, particularly the Krewe of Comus, and reports on a similar application using *Comus* earlier in the century: "The first procession and tableau ball of the Mistick Krewe of Comus in 1857 impersonated 'The Demon Actors in Milton's Paradise Lost.' The great Protestant epic provided ample opportunity for costume and characterization—damned characters from the realm of eternal death, of course, but still at heart English: a classical hell, Tartarus, with harpies, furies, and gorgons; the expulsion, with Satan, Beelzebub, and Moloch; the conference of Satan and Beelzebub, with a cho-rus of seven deadly sins" (258).

101. See Cecil Smith and Glenn Litton, *Musical Comedy in America* (1950; repr., New York: Routledge, 1991), 28–29, who note the influence of the cyclorama in the 1870s upon the Kiralfys' development of realistic spectacle.

102. From the [Wellington, New Zealand] *Evening Post,* July 26, 1878, 2.

103. Ibid., 2.

104. On Loutherbourg's work with and influence upon the theater, see Christopher Baugh, "Philippe de Loutherbourg: Technology-Driven Entertainment and Spectacle in the Late Eighteenth Century," *Huntington Library Quarterly* 70, no. 2 (June 2007): 251–68; Amy Sargeant, "From *The Wonders of Derbyshire* to Wookey Hole," *Early Popular Visual Culture* 4, no. 2 (July 2006): 103–11; and Ralph G. Allen, *The Stage Spectacles of Philip James de Loutherbourg* (Ph.D. diss., Yale University, 1960).

105. Stephen Herbert, ed., *A History of Pre-Cinema,* 3 vols. (New York: Routledge, 2000), 29. On these innovations, see also Christopher Baugh, *Garrick and Loutherbourg* (Cambridge: Chadwyk-Healy, 1990).

106. "Theatrical Intelligence," *Morning Chronicle,* Feb. 16, 1776, 3.

107. Meisel, *Realizations,* 170.

108. Iain McCalman, "The Virtual Infernal: Philippe de Loutherbourg, William Beckford and the Spectacle of the Sublime," *Romanticism on the Net* 46 (May 2007), www.erudit.org/revue/ron/2007/v/n46/016129ar.html, calls it one of the "forerunners of today's cinema and virtual reality technologies" (par. 3).

109. From advertisement in *Morning Herald,* Mar. 14, 1781, 1. Iain McCalman, "Magic, Spectacle, and the Art of de Loutherbourg's Eidophusikon," in *Sensation and Sensibility: Viewing Gainsborough's "Cottage Door,"* ed. Ann Bermingham (New Haven, CT: Yale University Press, 2005), points out that "much of the repertoire for the first program of the Eidophusikon had been borrowed and adapted from earlier scenographic work," though de Loutherbourg "took pains to distance the Eidophusikon from obvious associations with theatricality or popular entertainment" in order to preserve the prestige of his reputation as an "elite British artist" (190).

110. William Henry Pyne, *Wine and Walnuts,* 2 vols. (London, 1824), 1:296.

111. "A View of the Eidophusikon," *European Magazine* 1 (Mar. 1782): 182. Ann Bermingham, *Sensation and Sensibility* (New Haven, CT: Yale University Press, 2005), argues similarly that with the Eidophusikon, "landscape became a changing event rather than a static object" (22).

112. See James Chandler and Kevin Gilmartin, eds., *Romantic Metropolis: The Urban Scene of British Culture, 1780–1840* (Cambridge: Cambridge University Press, 2005), 10.

113. Loutherbourg expressed a similar theme in such paintings as *Travellers Attacked by Banditti* (1781), one of a series of works focused on outlaws preying on the innocent.

114. See Iain McCalman, *The Last Alchemist: Count Cagliostro, Master of Magic in the Age of Reason* (New York: Harper, 2003), 144 and throughout.

115. Qtd. in Richard Altick, *The Shows of London* (Cambridge, MA: Belknap, 1978), 121.

116. Qtd. in ibid., 121

117. Pyne, *Wine and Walnuts,* 1:284. Altick, *Shows of London,* 521n20, cautions however, that the accuracy of Pyne's reminiscence is thorny at best:

his claims, for instance, of various backstage passes seem suspect, and at any rate he "was writing at the remove of at least two decades."

118. Pyne, *Wine and Walnuts,* 1:285.

119. Herbert, *History of Pre-Cinema,* 3:29.

120. From the *Morning Herald,* Mar. 12, 1782, quoted in Kenneth Friedenreich, "Loutherbourg's Eidophusikon and Two Scenes from *Paradise Lost,*" *Bulletin of the New York Public Library* 80, no. 1 (1976): 72.

121. McCalman, "Virtual Infernal," abstract.

122. Austin Dobson, *At Prior Park* (New York: Stokes, 1912), contains a list of dates, performances, and changes in interscenes in his appendix B, 277–81.

123. *London Courant Westminster Chronicle and Daily Advertiser,* Feb. 6, 1782, 3.

124. See McCalman, "Magic, Spectacle," 192. Ernest W. Sullivan, "Illustration as Interpretation: *Paradise Lost* from 1688 to 1807," in *Milton's Legacy in the Arts,* ed. Albert C. Labriola and Edward Sichi Jr. (University Park: Pennsylvania State University Press, 1988), notes, moreover, that "during the seventeenth and eighteenth centuries, *Paradise Lost* was the literary subject most frequently illustrated in England (there were twelve different illustrated editions alone)" (59–92).

125. Pyne, *Wine and Walnuts,* 1:302–03.

126. "A View of the Eidophusikon," 180–81. This rendering appears to be press copy generated by Loutherbourg himself—it evolves with slight revisions in other newspaper accounts in the ensuing years (e.g., *York Chronicle,* May 25, 1787, of a previous performance at the Merchant Taylors' Hall, York, England). Contrast, however, the account in the *London Courant Westminster Chronicle and Daily Advertiser,* Feb. 6, 1782, which appears distinct, if equally congratulatory: "poetry and painting have combined to give the most magnificent entertainment the senses are capable of enjoying.... Satan appears in the gigantic figure Milton describes, calling up the spirits from the vasty deep—vivid lightnings flash around—the cavern groans—in short, there is no doing justice to the scene, it is full of all the terrific grandeur that constitutes the sublime."

127. David Morris, "Gothic Sublimity," *New Literary History* 16, no. 2 (Winter 1985): 306.

128. Friedenreich makes the case that if Loutherbourg wanted to incorporate Milton, the Pandaemonium scene also offered a steady representational balance: "the war in Heaven demanded too much action," while "the Eden scenes might not have demanded enough of the artist" ("Loutherbourg's Eidophusikon," 75). While there is something to this—the seething fallen angels are more potential than kinetic in their action (their perpetual plight, really)—it seems ultimately too arbitrary to satisfy the question of choice.

129. Diderot quoted in Dobson, *At Prior Park,* 99–100.

130. Peter Otto, *Multiplying Worlds: Romanticism, Modernity, and Virtual Reality* (Oxford: Oxford University Press), also observes that "Satan's creation of the vast interior space of Pandemonium, with its pendent lamps yielding light 'as if from a sky,' is implicitly drawn into relation with the virtual spaces conjured by Loutherbourg's Eidophusikon" (169).

131. J. A. Broadbent, *Some Graver Subject: An Essay on "Paradise Lost"* (London: Chatto and Windus, 1960), for instance, sees the whole thrust of Pandaemonium as antitechnological.

132. Marcia R. Pointon, *Milton and English Art* (University of Toronto Press, 1970), 105. Pointon relates the effects of Loutherbourg's Pandaemonium scene to a broader sweep of sublime theatricality: "It was the sort of terror created by Shakespeare in plays like *Macbeth* and *Julius Caesar,* the terror of the owl at midday, of earthquakes, lamenting in the air and 'strange screams of death,' a terror originating in human horror of the unnatural" (102).

133. Sybil Rosenfeld made one of the first and only close analyses of Burney's picture in "The Eidophusikon Illustrated," *Theatre Notebook* 18 (Winter 1963–64): 52–54. She also observes, "Burney's pale colourings show little of this splendor": the mountains "have rather pallid flames," the buildings "are not gold but stone-coloured," and Satan's tunic is yellow (53). She provides an intriguing point on the mechanization of Satan and his troops, noting that Loutherbourg had previously used "battalions, composed of small figures, [who] march out in excellent order, into the front of their lines" as a theatrical effect for the Coxheath scene in Richard Sherridan's popular 1778 musical *The Camp* (54).

134. Pyne, *Wine and Walnuts,* recalls how Sir Joshua Reynolds "recommended the ladies in his extensive circle to take their daughters, who cultivated drawing, as the best school to witness the powerful effects of nature" (1:281–82).

135. Herbert, *History of Pre-Cinema,* 3:30. Martha W. England, "John Milton and the Performing Arts," *Bulletin of the New York Public Library* 80, no. 1 (1976), wonders whether such darkened atmospheres might have contributed to (or been symptomatic of) a shift in Miltonic reception more broadly: "Do you think one can trace the diverting of interest from Adam and Eve to an interest in demonic energy straight to the door of the movie house?" (53).

136. Altick, *Shows of London,* 125.

137. See also, among others, *Morning Chronicle and London Advertiser,* Mar. 30, 1784, 1.

138. *Morning Herald and Daily Advertiser,* Dec. 24, 1784.

139. Qtd. in Dobson, *At Prior Park,* 280.

140. Advertisement in *Morning Herald,* May 5, 1786, 1.

141. Charles Coleman Sellers, *Charles Willson Peale* (New York: Scribner's, 1969), 205.

142. Ibid., 206, 207.

143. Qtd. in ibid., 207–08.

144. Qtd. in ibid., 207.

145. Kenneth Silverman, *Cultural History of the American Revolution* (New York: Crowell, 1976), 453–54.

146. Altick, *Shows of London*, 125.

147. *Oracle and Daily Advertiser*, May 23, 1799.

148. See the *Morning Post and Gazetteer*, Mar. 24, 1800. A display called "the remains of Loutherbourg's Eidophusikon" appeared in 1819 as an exhibition at Spring Gardens, and reportedly included the Storm at Sea, the Midnight Sun at the North Pole, and other scenic depictions. Edmund Kean witnessed the show and sought to replicate the design of the tempest for his *King Lear*. See Speaight, *History of English Puppet Theatre*, 129.

149. London *Times*, Mar. 6, 1800.

150. Qtd. in Friedenreich, "Loutherbourg's Eidophusikon," 75.

151. Altick, *Shows of London*, 123. See also Michael Kitson, "Loutherbourg at Kenwood," *Burlington Magazine* 115 (July 1973): 481–85. On the technical aspects, see also Ralph G. Allen, "The Eidophusikon," *Theatre Design and Technology* 7 (Dec. 1966): 12–16.

152. The production team credited Loutherbourg's original as "simultaneously a disaster movie, newsreel, multi-media experience and experiment in virtual reality" (see www.edmstudio.com/eidophusikon/index.html). An intriguing video of the Australian Eidophusikon in motion ("Eidophusikon Re-imagined") can be viewed at vimeo.com/32698316.

153. Dorfeuille kept a folio scrapbook, now housed by the Cincinnati Historical Society, that contained plentiful sketches of "radical human and animal deformity," an interest that M. H. Dunlop, "Curiosities Too Numerous to Mention: Early Regionalism and Cincinnati's Western Museum," *American Quarterly* 36 (Autumn 1984): 530, sees as informing the scope of the Infernal Regions exhibit. On the further reception of the show, see also David J. Voelker, "Cincinnati's Infernal Regions Exhibit and the Waning of Calvinist Authority," *American Nineteenth Century History* 9, no. 3 (2008): 219–39.

154. From contemporary broadside, courtesy Cincinnati Museum Center (as advertised in the Cincinnati *Advertiser*, Mar. 28, 1829).

155. Displays of this sort—equally sensational if slightly less impious—were popular in Milton's lifetime as well, and Milton himself writes in *Areopagitica* of "a mere artificial Adam, such an Adam as he is in the motions" (Hughes, *Complete Poems and Major Prose*, 733). Joseph E. Duncan, *Milton's Earthly Paradise* (Minneapolis: University of Minnesota Press, 1972), 215–16, draws attention to a waxwork exhibition of the terrestrial paradise shown in London in 1661: "*Paradise Transplanted and Restored, in a Most Artfull Land Lively Representation of the Severall Creatures, Plants, Flowers, and Other Vegetables, in Their Full Growth, Shape, and Colour.*" Duncan also recounts

the motion of the figures: "Adam appeared naming the animals, which ranged from the elephant to the mouse and from the crocodile to the glowworm, and Eve appeared, taking the apple from the serpent" (216). G. L. Apperson, "The Early History of the Panoramas," *Antiquary* 40 (Oct. 1904): 299–304, adds that visitors to the exhibition were first greeted by the gaze of a basilisk guarding the door and that the exhibition also incorporated a set of spectating wax figures—including "five beautifull Ladies"—whom visitors routinely mistook for living souls. A similar show was on display on September 23, 1673, attended by John Evelyn: "we went to see Paradise, a room in Hatton Garden furnished with the representations of all sorts of animals, handsomely painted on boards or cloth, & so cut out & made to stand & move, fly, crawl, roade & make their severall cries, as was not unpretty: though in it selfe a mere bauble, whilst the man who shew'd, made us Laugh heartily at his formal poetrie" (quoted in Apperson, "Early History," 300). Altick (*Shows of London*, 58) speculates that the "formal poetry" being laughed at might have been the recently published Milton epic.

156. Andrea Stulman Dennett, *Weird and Wonderful: The Dime Museum in America* (New York: New York University Press, 1997), 111.

157. *Cincinnati Daily Gazette*, Mar. 3, 1838.

158. T[homas] Adolphus Trollope, "Some Recollections of Hiram Powers," *Lippincott's Magazine of Popular Literature and Science* (Feb. 1875): 207–09.

159. Ibid., 207.

160. Frances M. Trollope, *Domestic Manners of the Americans* (New York: Dodd, 1901), 90. On the circumstances of her involvement, see J. Roger Newstedt, "Mrs. Frances Trollope in Cincinnati: The 'Infernal Regions' and the Bizarre Bazaar, 1828–1830," *Queen City Heritage* (Winter 1999): 37–45.

161. "A New Exhibition," [Baltimore] *Sun*, Sept. 29, 1837.

162. "Reveries and Reminiscences," orig. published in *Baltimore Athenaeum* (1836); repr. in the *Cincinnati Daily Gazette*, Feb. 14, 1838, 2.

163. *Cincinnati Daily Gazette*, Mar. 3, 1838, 3.

164. "Reveries and Reminiscences," 2.

165. "Western Artists: Hiram Powers," *Western Monthly Magazine, and Literary Journal* 3, no. 4 (Apr. 1835): 246.

166. Dennett, *Weird and Wonderful*, 111.

167. Linus S. Everett, "A New Hell," *Trumpet and Universalist Magazine* (Mar. 14, 1829): 148.

168. William Henry Venable, *Beginnings of Literary Culture in the Ohio Valley* (Cincinnati: Robert Clarke, 1891), 315.

169. See Dunlop, "Curiosities Too Numerous," 544–48. See also an ad in *Morning Courier and New York Enquirer*, May 29, 1839. Edward P. Hingston, *The Genial Showman* (1870; repr., Barre, MA: Imprint Society, 1971), 16–18, recounts the pathetic last days.

Notes to Chapter 2,
Pre-Cinematic Entertainment

1. "Specification of the Patent granted to Mr. Robert Barker, of the City of Edinburgh, Portrait-Painter; for his Invention of an entire new Contrivance or Apparatus, called by him 'La Nature à Coup d'Œil,'" in *The Repertory of Arts and Manufactures: Consisting of Original Communications, Specifications of Patent Inventions, and Selections of Useful Practical Papers from the Transactions of the Philosophical Societies of All Nations,* vol. 4 (London, 1776), 165–67.

2. Ibid, 165, 167.

3. For the Panorama and its beginnings, see Stephan Oettermann, *The Panorama: History of a Mass Medium,* trans. Deborah Lucas Schneider (New York: Zone Books, 1997), 5–47, and Ralph Hyde, *Panoramania! The Art and Entertainment of the "All-embracing" View* (London: Trefoil/Barbican Art Gallery, 1988), esp. 57–64. On the emerging idea of infinity and the arts during the seventeenth century, see Marjorie Hope Nicolson, *Mountain Gloom and Mountain Glory: The Development of the Aesthetics of the Infinite* (New York: Norton, 1963).

4. On Barker's early designs, see Denise Blake Oleksijczuk, *The First Panoramas: Visions of British Imperialism* (Minneapolis: University of Minnesota Press, 2011). On contemporary developments abroad, as well as the resurgence of panorama popularity in the late nineteenth century, see Vanessa R. Schwartz, *Spectacular Realities: Early Mass Culture in Fin-de-Siècle France* (Berkeley and Los Angeles: University of California Press, 1998).

5. Oettermann, *The Panorama,* 21–22.

6. It has been claimed that Bouton produced a diorama with scenes from *Paradise Lost;* however, this seems unfounded. Mikhail Yampolsky, "Transparency Painting: From Myth to Theater," in *Tekstura: Russian Essays on Visual Culture,* ed. Alla Efimova and Lev Manovich (Chicago: University of Chicago Press, 1993), writes that "G. de Nerval in his review of *The Flood* exhibited by Charles-Marie Bouton...perceptively traced such motifs of this diorama as the fantastic city with obelisks and pyramids as well as the rainbow to Milton's *Paradise Lost*" (144). The claim, repeated by Bernard Comment, *The Panorama,* trans. Anne-Marie Glasheen (London: Reaktion, 1999), 59, likely sprouts from a misreading of Gerard Nerval's review of the diorama "The Flood," in which he advises that artists wishing to convey the "history of the battle of the rebel spirits against the Almighty and his holy legions" *should* follow *Paradise Lost* (and even more the book of Enoch, which Nerval thinks was an influence upon Milton), though Bouton, lamentably, did not. See Nerval's *Selected Writings,* ed. Richard Sieburth (New York: Penguin, 1999), 188–89.

7. Anne Friedberg, *Window Shopping: Cinema and the Postmodern* (Berkeley and Los Angeles: University of California Press, 1994), 28.

8. Alison Griffiths, "Shivers Down Your Spine: Panoramas and the Origins of the Cinematic Reenactment," *Screen* 44, no. 1 (2003): 1–37, is one of a number of film historians who see the panorama as a forerunner of the modern cinema: "three factors make panoramas unique as precursors to film reenactments: first, the mode of spectatorship invited by their scale (unlike viewing easel paintings or photographs, spectators gazed at huge canvases that filled the space before their eyes); second, their status as technologies of virtual transport and invocation of presence as a constituent feature of the panoramic experience, and third, in the case of moving panoramas, their exhibition context—a fixed, as opposed to an ambulatory, mode of spectatorship, in which audiences sat in a darkened auditorium for the duration of a performance, complete with musical accompaniment and explanatory lecture" (3).

9. Richard Altick, *The Shows of London* (Cambridge, MA: Belknap, 1978), 180.

10. Qtd. in ibid., 181. For Walter Benjamin, *The Arcades Project,* trans. Rolf Tiedemann (Cambridge, MA: Harvard University Press, 1999), the panoramas were "dream houses of the collective," along with such nineteenth century mainstays as "arcades, winter gardens,...factories, wax museums, casinos, railroad stations" (405). In this respect, the panorama's promise of transport served also to mask a kind of insistent somnolence—the surreal transformation of history into the mythical typology of dreams.

11. Altick, *Shows of London,* 181. On similarities with American Romanticism, see Henry M. Sayre, "Surveying the Vast Profound: The Panoramic Landscape in American Consciousness," *Massachusetts Review* 24, no. 4 (1983): 723–42.

12. [London] *Times,* Apr. 1, 1789, 3. Cf. Peter Otto, "Between the Virtual and the Actual: Robert Barker's Panorama of London and the Multiplication of the Real in Late Eighteenth-Century London," *Romanticism on the Net* 46 (May 2007): 40, who writes that "The sublime is a defining feature of all panoramas"; and Comment, who argues that "Fear, darkness, immensity, infinity were, according to Burke, some of the attributes of the Sublime. In one form or another, the panorama was based on such attributes: fear, through the theme of war or through simulations that went so far as to make people dizzy or seasick; darkness, which Robert Barker made a prerequisite when entering the rotunda, reinforced by the contrast between the darkened platform and intense lighting that fell from a concealed source onto the canvas; immensity and infinity, at the very heart of the panoramic programme" (*The Panorama,* 80).

13. Joshua Reynolds, as recorded in *Chambers's Journal of Popular Literature,* Jan. 21, 1860, 33.

14. William Wordsworth, *The Prelude: A Parallel Text* (New York: Penguin, 1996), 7.259, 277–80; hereafter cited in the text. On Wordsworth's and other early receptions of the panorama, see Markman Ellis, "'Spectacles within doors': Panoramas of London in the 1790s," *Romanticism* 14, no. 2 (July 2008): 133–48.

15. Gillen D'Arcy Wood, *The Shock of the Real: Romanticism and Visual Culture, 1760–1860* (New York: Palgrave, 2001), 109.

16. *Paradise Regained* 4.40–42, in *John Milton: Complete Poems and Major Prose,* ed. Merritt Y. Hughes (New York: Odyssey, 1957). Unless otherwise noted, all quotations from Milton's works refer to this edition.

17. Ibid., 105–06. Wood reads Wordsworth's rhapsody on the panorama as ultimately critical of an unnatural, "anti-sublime" contrivance.

18. Anne-Julia Zwierlein, "Pandemonic Panoramas: Surveying Milton's 'Vain Empires' in the Long Eighteenth Century," in *Milton and the Terms of Liberty,* ed. Graham Perry and Joad Raymond (Cambridge: D. S. Brewer, 2002), 193. For a suggestion that Milton based these visions on the moving pictures in Dante's *Purgatorio,* cantos 10–17, see Richard DuRocher, "Dante, Milton, and the Art of Visual Speech," *Comparative Literature Studies* 27 (1990): 157–71.

19. John G. Demaray, *Milton's Theatrical Epic: The Invention and Design of "Paradise Lost"* (1980; repr., Cambridge, MA: Harvard University Press, 1999), 37.

20. John Wilson, "The Fall of Nineveh," *Blackwood's Edinburgh Magazine* 27 (Feb. 1830): 172. James G. Nelson, *The Sublime Puritan: Milton and the Victorians* (Westport, CT: Greenwood, 1962), also notes Milton's fit with the broader aesthetics of the early nineteenth century: "paintings, sermons, and poetry…freed their minds from restraint and lifted them to a state of emotional transcendence. As a result, canvases, books, and sermons were filled with direct appeals to the visual imagination designed to arouse sublime feelings.…artists and poets crammed their works with enormous objects and panoramas, limitless space, vast and irregular landscapes, titanic beings, and cataclysmic occurrences" (42). On the politics of Milton's sublimity at the end of the eighteenth century, see Joseph Crawford, *Raising Milton's Ghost: John Milton and the Sublime of Terror in the Early Romantic Period* (London: Bloomsbury Academic, 2011). For a general discussion of Milton's literary reception, see also Erik Irving Gray, *Milton and the Victorians* (Ithaca, NY: Cornell University Press, 2009).

21. Martin Meisel, *Realizations: Narrative, Pictorial, and Theatrical Arts in Nineteenth-Century England* (Princeton, NJ: Princeton University Press, 1983), 168. On Martin, the sublime, and the panorama, see also William Feaver, *The Art of John Martin* (Oxford: Clarendon Press, 1975), 67–70, who sees "Martin's epics, scene painting, panorama, diorama, and, eventually, comparable aspects of photography and the motion picture" as "interlinked, above all in their attempts to establish sublime documentary values in narrative entertainment" (69).

22. Oettermann, *The Panorama,* 113.

23. For Robert Burford, see *Description of an Attempt to Illustrate Milton's Pandemonium; now exhibiting in the Panorama, Leicester Square* (London, 1829), 5. On his "naturalization of hell," see Ralph O'Connor, *The*

Earth on Show: Fossils and the Poetics of Popular Science, 1802–1856 (Chicago: University of Chicago Press, 2008), 277–80. O'Connor also spots this naturalization as stemming directly from Loutherbourg's treatment of hell in his Eidophusikon.

24. Burford, *Description of an Attempt*, 3.

25. Ibid., 3–4.

26. Zwierlein, "Pandemonium Panoramas," 212.

27. C. H. Adams's long-running Lenten orrery show, an astronomy lecture accompanied by a moving exhibit of the solar system, included poetical excerpts from Milton. In this fusion of the scientific and literary, which in its scope bore much resemblance to the panorama, the conjunction with Milton seems to have elicited a more generally warm response. Adams's opening remarks on the shape of the earth, the effects of gravity, and the planet's "diurnal revolution" and "annual motion" led to a spectacular demonstration: "the Seasons illustrated in a novel manner by means of a SPLENDID TELLURIAN. Representing the Earth in the Four Quarters of its orbit, and moving at the same time round the Sun, shewing in the clearest manner the cause of the Seasons—the whole encircled by A ZODIAC Sixty Feet in Circumference"; quoted in Simon Henry Gage, *The Theatrical Observer and Daily Bills of the Play*, vol. 1 (London: C. Harris, 1835), 28. This part of the lecture culminated in a reading of "Milton's expressive language," which was, in one report, "delivered in a manner that drew forth reiterated applause"; see *London Literary Gazette*, Mar. 23, 1833, 184.

28. Burford, *Description of an Attempt*, 4.

29. Ibid., 4.

30. Ibid., 6.

31. "New Panorama," [London] *Times*, Apr. 25, 1829, 2; "Panorama of Pandemonium," [London] *Examiner*, Apr. 26, 1829, 261.

32. Burford, *Description of an Attempt*, 3–5

33. Ibid., 10.

34. Reviewed in *Athenaeum* 78 (Apr. 22, 1829), reprinted in *The Athenaeum and Literary Chronicle, Vol. 1, Issues 63–92* (London: F. C. Westley, 1829), 253. Subsequent citations to *Athenaeum* are from this volume.

35. O'Connor, *The Earth on Show*, 277, suggests that this coiled dragon is likely culled from John Martin's *Belshazzar's Feast* (1821), which, along with *The Fall of Nineveh* (1829), were among the non-*Paradise Lost* works influential on the panorama design. On the possible influence of the Pandaemonium panorama on Thomas Cole's fourth painting in his *The Course of Empire* series, *Destruction* (1836), see Wolfgang Born, *American Landscape Painting* (New Haven, CT: Yale University Press, 1942), 81

36. *The Real Devil's Walk. Not by Professor Porson. Designs by Robert Cruikshank. With Notes and Extracts from the Devil's Diary*, 2nd ed., with additions (London: William Kidd, 1831), stanza 25.

37. "Panorama of Pandemonium," 261.

38. Altick, *Shows of London,* 182.

39. "New Panorama," [London] *Times,* Apr. 25, 1829, 2.

40. Reviewed in *Athenaeum* 78 (Apr. 22, 1829): 253.

41. Ibid., 253.

42. Ibid., 253.

43. Ibid., 253.

44. Throughout the late 1850s and early 1860s, a James Batchelder (sometimes "Batchelor") achieved success in England with a moving panorama of Dr. David Livingstone's travels in Africa, which at some points displayed as well scenes of America based on *Uncle Tom's Cabin.* He died in Manchester on December 16, 1865.

45. After the assassination of Abraham Lincoln on April 15, 1865, an anecdote making the rounds in America went as follows (as picked up by the *Manchester Times,* Sept. 2, 1865): "A gentleman about whose Teutonic origin there could be but one opinion, was passing along the street a few days since, when he came to a halt before one of the huge posters announcing the coming of the Panorama of Paradise Lost. He read this line, 'A Rebellion in Heaven,' when he broke forth, as follows:—'A rebellion in heaven; mine Got! That lasts not long now—Onkel Abel ish tare.'"

46. Advertisement in the *Argus,* Mar. 1, 1867. I have been unable to locate any evidence of a single performance in England, let alone one for all of Buckingham palace. The Royal Archives maintain no record of Queen Victoria ever having attended such a performance; that the queen did not attend any places of public entertainment after the death of Prince Albert in 1861 makes Bachelder's boast almost surely fraudulent.

47. Mimi Colligan, *Canvas Documentaries: Panoramic Entertainments in Nineteenth-Century Australia and New Zealand* (Melbourne: Melbourne University Press, 2002), 71. Colligan mistakenly reports the earlier run of London shows as "1280," but even the lesser claim of 280 seems to be spurious.

48. Ibid., 72.

49. [New Zealand] *Herald,* Nov. 30, 1869.

50. *Daily Southern Cross,* Dec. 1, 1869.

51. Ibid., 1.

52. *Wellington Independent,* Mar. 24, 1870.

53. For a reading of the cartoon and other aspects of Bachelder's panorama, including its filmic "actualisation of realms beyond human experience" (33), see Brian Opie, "Poets in the News: John Milton and William Golder in Early Wellington," *Journal of New Zealand Literature* 31 (2013): 11–43.

54. *Brisbane Courier,* July 21, 1870.

55. *Auckland Star,* Dec. 31, 1878.

56. On the development of the early lantern, see Laurent Mannoni, *The Great Art of Light and Shadow: Archaeology of the Cinema,* trans. and ed. Richard Crangle (Exeter: University of Exeter Press, 2000), 34–45.

57. Mannoni, *The Great Art,* 59. A good overview of similar optical devices, including the magic lantern, panorama, and diorama, can be found in Barbara Stafford and Frances Terpak, *Devices of Wonder: From the World in a Box to Images on a Screen* (Los Angeles: Getty Research Institute, 2001).

58. Charles Patin, *Travels thro' Germany, Swisserland, Bohemia, Holland, and Other Parts of Europe,* 2 vols. (London: 1696), 1:234–35.

59. The thirteenth century text *De mirabili potestate artis et naturae,* attributed to Roger Bacon, offers a comparable effect, this time with mirrors: "One can cause great terror in an enemy town by making multitudes of stars or men appear above it, such that its inhabitants scatter in terror" (quoted in Mannoni, *The Great Art,* 18).

60. Quoted in S. I. Van Nooten, "Contributions of Dutchmen in the Beginnings of Film Technology," *Journal of the Society of Motion Picture and Television Engineers* 81, no. 2 (1972): 117.

61. Quoted in Mannoni, *The Great Art,* 10.

62. Quoted in ibid., 11.

63. Jean Leurechon, *Récréation Mathématique* (Pont-à-Mousson, 1621), 98–99, 103, quoted in Mannoni, *The Great Art,* 12.

64. Kircher's second edition of *Ars magna lucis et umbrae* appeared in 1671, this time with an illustration of a lantern in operation, projecting an image of a naked male figure half-consumed in flames, presumably a soul lost to perdition. The image has been criticized for major errors in its depiction, namely the placement of the slides outside the lens and the orientation of the projection, which should be the inverse of the orientation of the slide. The illustration offers a glimpse of other images that would have been projected, most either morbid, pious, or both: "a man holding a staff, a skeleton with a scythe and hourglass, Christ on the cross, a man kneeling in prayer" (Mannoni, *The Great Art,* 58).

65. Quoted in ibid., 40.

66. From *The Diary of Samuel Pepys,* ed. Robert Latham and William Matthews (Berkeley and Los Angeles: University of California Press, 2000), 7:198.

67. Quoted in Mannoni, *The Great Art,* 53.

68. Quoted in ibid., 67.

69. On Milton and the "new optics," see Karen L. Edwards, *Milton and the Natural World: Science and Poetry in "Paradise Lost"* (Cambridge: Cambridge University Press, 2005), and Angelica Duran, *The Age of Milton and the Scientific Revolution* (Pittsburgh: Duquesne University Press, 2006). On the imaginative effects stimulated by the telescope, and with some consideration of other devices, see Marjorie Nicolson, "Milton and the Telescope," *ELH* 2, no. 1 (Apr. 1935): 1–32; she calls *Paradise Lost* "the first modern cosmic poem, in which a drama is played out against a background of interstellar space" (3).

70. Johann Christoph Sturm, *Collegium experimentale sive curiosum* (1676), quoted in Mannoni, *The Great Art,* 61.

71. Quoted in Mannoni, *The Great Art,* 73.

72. Lorenzo J. Marcy, *The Sciopticon Manual: Explaining Lantern Projections in General* (Philadelphia: James A. Moore, 1877), 51, 52.

73. On the literary history of the phantasmagoria, see Terry Castle, "Phantasmagoria: Spectral Technology and the Metaphorics of Modern Reverie," *Critical Inquiry* 15, no. 1 (1988): 26–61. Castle links the phantasmagoria's "association with delirium, loss of control, [and] the terrifying yet sublime overthrow of ordinary experience" with the nineteenth century poetic imagination (48). See also David J. Jones, *Gothic Machine: Textualities, Pre-Cinematic Media and Film in Popular Visual Culture, 1670–1910* (Cardiff: University of Wales Press, 2011); Robert Miles, "Gothic Romance and Visual Technology," in *Gothic Technologies: Visuality in the Romantic Era,* ed. Robert Miles, *Romantic Circles,* Dec. 2005, www.rc.umd.edu/praxis/gothic/intro/miles.html (accessed May 28, 2014); and X. Theodore Barber, "Phantasmagorical Wonders: The Magic Lantern Ghost Show in Nineteenth-Century America," *Film History* 3, no. 2 (1989): 73–86.

74. See Mannoni, *The Great Art,* 150–51; quoting Chanoine Lecnau, *Histoire de Satan* (Paris, 1861), 438.

75. "Le diable refusant de me communiquer la science de faire des prodiges, je me mis à faire des diables, et ma baguette n'eut plus qu'à se mouvoir pour forcer tout le cortège infernal à voir la lumière. Mon habitation devint un vrai *Pandemonium*" (Étienne-Gaspard Robert [Robertson], *Mémoires récréatifs, scientifiques et anecdotiques d'un physicien-aéronaute* [Paris, 1833], 1:145).

76. Quoted in Mannoni, *The Great Art,* 159.

77. Sir David Brewster, *Letters on Natural Magic* (London: Chatto and Windus, 1883), 158.

78. Henry Lemoine, "The Phantasmagoria," *Gentleman's Magazine* 72 (Jan.–June 1802), n.p. The poem itself is dated June 30, 1801.

79. Mark Pattison, *Milton* (New York: Harper and Brothers, 1880), reappropriated this fantasy of Milton in the phantasmagoria, arguing that "It was not in Milton's nature to be a showman, parading before an audience a phantasmagoria of spirits, which he himself knew to be puppets tricked up for the entertainment of an idle hour" (182), though even in Pattison's denial of Milton's phantasmagoric qualities he has reimagined the poet as a knowing attendee, as if it were impossible that Milton could *not* have been invested in phantasmagorias, if only to reject them.

80. *The Autobiography of John Britton,* 2 vols. (London, 1850), 1:101n.

81. Marina Warner, *Phantasmagoria: Spirit Visions, Metaphors, and Media into the Twenty-First Century* (Oxford: Oxford University Press, 2006), 148.

82. *Morning Chronicle,* Dec. 18, 1801.

83. *Morning Chronicle,* Jan. 1, 1802. For "The Hare and Many Friends," see *The Fables of John Gay* (London: George Routledge, 1854), 165–67.

84. Quoted in Altick, *Shows of London,* 199.

85. Edward Ziter, *The Orient on the Victorian Stage* (Cambridge: Cambridge University Press, 2003), 33.

86. *Autobiography of John Britton,* 1:101n.

87. Warner, *Phantasmagoria,* 147–48, sees the panoramas and dioramas as "forerunners of the wide-screen epic film," whereas the phantasmagoria anticipates the "great silent movies like F. W. Murnau's vampire movie *Nosferatu* (1917) and Robert Wiene's *The Cabinet of Dr. Caligari* (1919)."

88. See review in *London und Paris* (Weimar), 9, no. 1 (1802): 3–10. The reviewer, while at times swept away by the skill of the artists, finally concluded that the show was too disjointed and depended too heavily on lecture rather than spectacle.

89. Only a little more than a decade earlier, Milton's own grave had been ghoulishly robbed. See, for example, Carol Barton, "'Ill Fare the Hands That Heaved the Stones': John Milton, a Preliminary Thanatography," in *Milton Studies,* vol. 43, ed. Albert C. Labriola, 198–260 (Pittsburgh: University of Pittsburgh Press, 2004).

90. From the British Library Folder, *A Collection of cuttings from newspapers, play-bills, letters and other manuscripts, etc. relating to the Lyceum Theatre from 1781 to 1840,* clipping from Feb. 12, 1802.

91. Ibid., Mar. 16, 1802.

92. Quoted in Mervyn Heard, *Phantasmagoria: The Secret Life of the Magic Lantern* (Hastings: The Projection Box, 2006), 155.

93. Quoted in ibid., 156.

94. A generally favorable review in the *Monthly Mirror* 13 (June 1802), notes mostly the "risible" phantasmagoric elements. Lonsdale seemed ultimately unable to sustain the tension between them and his instructional lectures on the Egyptian scenery: "One cannot wonder that this divertisement became such a favourite lounge for the fashionables of the metropolis. . . . The action of the ghosts was animated and pleasing, and the corresponding transitions on the canvas highly curious. The terrors of a dreary heath formed a grand and magnificent scene, and little *Will o' Wisp* caused a considerable exertion of the risible faculties" (424).

95. *Autobiography of John Britton,* 1:101n. Cf. William Ayrton, "The English Opera House," *Harmonicon* 8 (1830): 129, who argues that Lonsdale's failure was finally one of popular appeal: "unequivocally praised by the well-informed as a most refined and classical evening's amusement, it was, to use the words of *Hamlet,* 'caviare to the multitude.' Like his predecessors, after having nearly ruined himself by his alternating and refitting of the theatre, he was obliged to vacate it at the end of the season."

96. Charles Musser, *Before the Nickelodeon: Edwin S. Porter and the Edison Manufacturing Company* (Berkeley and Los Angeles: University of California Press, 1991), 23.

97. *Frank Leslie's Illustrated Newspaper,* Mar. 8, 1879, 5, 7.

98. Judith Buchanan, *Shakespeare on Silent Film: An Excellent Dumb Discourse* (Cambridge: Cambridge University Press, 2009), 28.

99. *The Magic Lantern: How to Buy and How to Use It* (London: Houlston and Wright, 1866), written by "A Mere Phantom." This manual also quotes

Brewster's earlier description of phantasmagorias as reproducing Milton's "darkness visible" (19).

100. Marcy, *Sciopticon Manual*, v, xxiv.

101. *Dallas Morning News*, Oct. 14, 1885.

102. *Keystone Courier*, Mar. 27, 1885.

103. See Terry and Deborah Borton, *Before the Movies: American Magic-Lantern Entertainment and the Nation's First Great Screen Artist, Joseph Boggs Beale*, (London: John Libbey Publishing, 2014), citing T. H. McAllister, *Catalogue of Stereopticons, Dissolving View Apparatus and Magic Lanterns, with Extensive Lists of Views for the Illustration of All Subjects of Popular Interest* (New York, 1893). A 1907 McAllister catalogue also offers an image of Milton as one of its numerous "statuary" slides.

104. *Milton's Paradise Lost, Abridged for an Evening's Reading, To suit the illustrations by Gustave Doré and John Martin*, from a compilation of miscellaneous lantern readings entitled *Scott's Notes by the Way* (Kingston-upon-Hull: James and R. Scott, n.d. [1875–79?]), 98. Courtesy Richard Crangle, Magic Lantern Society Slide Readings Library.

105. A complete set of the 12 overpaintings of *Paradise Lost* are in the archives of the George Eastman House International Museum of Photography and Film in Rochester, New York.

106. The "Life of Milton" set, which came in both painted and plain versions, included such images as the "Medallion Portrait of John Milton," "Milton in His Study" (John Faed), "Milton and His Daughters" (Dekenser), and "Milton's Mulberry Tree; Christ's College, Cambridge." Another lantern set, produced by J. H. Steward (London) in the 1890s, for "lime light and electric light lanterns," offered as a set "An Hour with Some Popular Poets," and included Milton's "The Expulsion from Paradise." On a secondary Miltonic text and its place in the magic lantern tradition, see Deirdre Loughridge, "Haydn's Creation as an Optical Entertainment," *Journal of Musicology* 27, no. 1 (Winter 2010): 9–54.

107. Milton shows also had to compete with such popular sequences as those for T. S. Arthur's temperance novel, *Ten Nights in a Bar Room* (1854); one set contained an "effect" slide of heaven, along with a lavish illustration, that brought vibrant motion to the more staid Doré imagery.

108. Buchanan, *Shakespeare on Silent Film*, 39, argues that the sequencing of slides also naturally created new narratives in ways quite different from viewing any single picture independently, "re-injecting into a painterly moment" an "evolving dramatic force."

109. Olive Cook, *Movement in Two Dimensions* (London: Hutchinson, 1963), points out the publication of several instruction manuals available for hand-coloring glass plates at home, and a limited range of transparent pigments available (93–94). See also Edward Groom, *The Art of Transparent Painting on Glass* (London: Winsor and Newton, 1855).

110. *Fulton Times*, Feb. 14, 1906.

111. Ibid.
112. *Dobbs Ferry Register,* July 13, 1906, 4.

NOTES TO CHAPTER 3,
EARLY CINEMA AND THE CINEMATIC SUBLIME

1. Quoted in Charles Musser, *The Emergence of Cinema: The American Screen to 1907* (Berkeley and Los Angeles: University of California Press, 1994), 15. Compare C. W. Ceram, *Archaeology of the Cinema,* trans. Richard Winston (London: Thames and Hudson, 1965).

2. Raymond Lister, *British Romantic Art* (London: G. Bell and Sons, 1973), 143; Oliver Grau, *Virtual Art: From Illusion to Immersion,* trans. Gloria Custance (Cambridge, MA: MIT Press, 2003), 5. See also Ben Brewster and Lea Jacobs, *Theatre to Cinema* (Oxford: Oxford University Press, 1997); Stephen Herbert, ed., *A History of Early Film,* 3 vols. (New York: Routledge, 2000).

3. Musser, *Emergence of Cinema,* 15.

4. See Katherine Singer Kovacs, "Georges Méliès and the *Féerie,*" in *Film before Griffith,* ed. John L. Fell (Berkeley and Los Angeles: University of California Press, 1983), 244–57.

5. John Hagan, "Cinema and the Romantic Tradition," in Fell, *Film before Griffith,* 229–36, finds this to be a period of "heightened visual consciousness," evident in the works of Poe, Baudelaire, and other Romantic and Symbolist writers.

6. David E. Nye, *American Technological Sublime* (Cambridge, MA: MIT Press, 1996), 246, ironically argues that film and, especially, television representations of both technological and natural marvels remain inadequate to the sublimities of their subject. Early filmmakers displaced this very insufficiency onto prior art forms, appropriating instead the language of (scientific) advance and innovation to establish the singularity of the cinema as sublime.

7. Quoted in Leo Marx, *The Machine in the Garden: Technology and the Pastoral Ideal in America* (Oxford: Oxford University Press, 1964), 203.

8. Walter Benjamin, "The Work of Art in the Age of Mechanical Reproduction," in *Film Theory and Criticism,* ed. Leo Braudy and Marshall Cohen (New York: Oxford University Press, 2009), 673.

9. D. W. Griffith, "The Motion Picture and the Witch Burners" (1915), repr. in *Focus on "The Birth of a Nation,"* ed. Fred Silva (Englewood Cliffs, NJ: Prentice-Hall, 1971), 97.

10. Benjamin, "Work of Art," 680.

11. Luke White and Claire Pajaczkowska, eds., introduction to *The Sublime Now* (Newcastle upon Tyne: Cambridge Scholars, 2009), 239.

12. Griffith, "Motion Picture and Witch Burners," 97.

13. See also Vivian Sobchack, "Embodying Transcendence: On the Literal, the Material, and the Cinematic Sublime," *Material Religion* 4, no. 2

(July 2008): 194–203, who notes that "our sense of bodily transcendence and the sensuality of our bodily existence are often *amplified* at the movies—rather than *reduced* by the cinema's supposed lack of a full sensorium" (198).

14. F. T. Prince, "Milton and the Theatrical Sublime," in *Approaches to "Paradise Lost,"* ed. C. A. Patrides (Toronto: University of Toronto Press, 1968), 56.

15. Joseph A. Wittreich, *Visionary Poetics: Milton's Tradition and His Legacy* (San Marino, CA: Huntington Library, 1979), 24–25. Compare the aestheticizing of poetic language at the turn of the century in Carsten Strathausen, *The Look of Things: Poetry and Vision around 1900* (Chapel Hill: University of North Carolina Press, 2003); and Pasi Väliaho, *Mapping the Moving Image: Gesture, Thought and Cinema Circa 1900* (Amsterdam: Amsterdam University Press, 2010).

16. On Adam's transition, see also Barbara Lewalski, "Structure and the Symbolism of Vision in Michael's Prophecy, *Paradise Lost,* Books XI–XII," *Philological Quarterly* 42 (1963): 27–28.

17. Anthony Slide, *The Big V: A History of the Vitagraph Company* (Metuchen, NJ: Scarecrow Press, 1976), 18. See also William Uricchio and Roberta Pearson, *Reframing Culture: The Case of the Vitagraph Quality Films* (Princeton, NJ: Princeton University Press, 1993). On the breadth of early efforts at epic filmmaking, see Sheldon Hall and Stephen Neale, *Epics, Spectacles, and Blockbusters: A Hollywood History* (Detroit: Wayne State University Press, 2010).

18. From *The Vitagraph Bulletin,* March 15 (1910), qtd. in Slide, *The Big V,* 59.

19. *Moving Picture World* 10, no. 1 (Oct. 7 1911): 47.

20. *Moving Picture World* 10, no. 2 (Oct. 14 1911): 132.

21. As late as the *Film Year Book 1922–23,* ed. Joseph Dannenberg (New York: Wid's Films and Film Folks, 1923), 102, Mullin (by that time editor at Goldwyn Pictures) is credited as having been, in 1911, the "First scenario writer to adapt such recognized classics as 'Vanity Fair,' 'Lady of the Lake,' 'Pickwick Papers,' 'Ivanhoe,' 'Paradise Lost,' 'David Copperfield'— filmed by Vitagraph." That last clause—"filmed by Vitagraph"—is tantalizing, grouping as it does *Paradise Lost* with those other works for which production records exist. But no mention is made of *Paradise Lost* in any of Vitagraph's surviving publications, including their *Vitagraph Life Portrayals* series.

22. See *Wid's Daily,* June 16, 1921, and *Film Daily,* Aug. 11, 1927.

23. *Moving Picture World* 8, no. 8 (Feb. 25, 1911): 432.

24. *Moving Picture World* 12, no. 3 (Apr. 20, 1912): 256.

25. *Moving Picture World* 12, no. 6 (May 11, 1912): 527.

26. *Moving Picture World* 12, no. 11 (June 15, 1912): 1004–05.

27. Pathé Freres later produced a condensed, nine-episode version of the series, and surviving footage used in a dozen or so of the original episodes still exists in this re-edited release.

28. A full summary can be found in *Moving Picture World* 21, no. 3 (July 18, 1914): 488.

29. Two stills are reproduced in an advertisement in *Moving Picture World* 21, no. 2 (July 11, 1914): 320.

30. Jon Solomon, *The Ancient World in the Cinema* (New Haven, CT: Yale University Press, 2001), 4. See also Claudia Gianetto and Giorgio Bertellini, "The Giant Ambrosio, or Italy's Most Prolific Silent Film Company," *Film History* 12, no. 3 (2000): 240–49.

31. Take, for example, this account in *Moving Picture World* 15, no. 6 (Feb. 8, 1913): "Mr. Fred Martin, the manager of the Monopol Film Company, is well known to America and after his handling of the first 5,000-footer, 'The Mysteries of Paris,' needs no introduction to showmen here. His newest feature is 'Satan,' and in describing this in an interview in a daily newspaper he asserts that the day of the short film is doomed. Many managers not only here, but across the pond, will, I think, concur that Mr. Martin is jumping too much to conclusions. There are several shows in London alone where a film over 1,500 feet is never screened" (584).

32. Richard Abel charts some of the film's success over the first half of 1913 in *Americanizing the Movies and "Movie-Mad" Audiences, 1910–1914* (Berkeley and Los Angeles: University of California Press, 2006), 34–35.

33. From a two-page color spread in *Moving Picture World* 15, no. 1 (Jan. 4, 1913). The film was distributed in the United States by Ambrosio American Company, 15 East 26th Street, New York, NY. A musical score is suggested by the aptly named Clarence E. Sinn in *Moving Picture World* (Mar. 8, 1913): 985, who recommends commencing with either *The Damnation of Faust* or "The Storm" from *William Tell* until the title card "The First Sin."

34. *Moving Picture World* 15, no. 3 (Jan. 18, 1913): 243–44. Such acclaim was widespread: the *Daily Oklahoman,* Apr. 15, 1913, reports that "'Satan' Film Is Real Thriller," and "The scenes and effects produced in the picture are said to even surpass in every particular those of 'Dante's Inferno' which is supposed to be one of the greatest moving pictures of that character ever produced." Similarly, the *New York Dramatic Mirror,* Jan. 8, 1913, 31, describes the film as "notably ambitious and impressive," with "superbly artistic force and beauty," and concludes that it is "an achievement of which any company might well be proud. Such films are mighty forward steps in the world of photoplay. " The New York *Morning Telegraph,* Feb. 2, 1913, in a piece titled "Satan Brings Change of Heart to Former 'Knocker," opines that "ten years ago" such a film "would have been denounced as sacrilegious," but now it is "witnessed with great and solemn interest." It adds, "Other motion pictures more ingenious and elaborate have been seen in New York, but there have been none more artistic and effective."

35. My thanks to Elizabeth Simon for this translation. For a complete summary, see the press booklet for *Satana,* reprinted in Aldo Bernadini and Vittorio Martinelli, *Il cinema muto Italiano,* 1912 (Rome: Bianco e Nero/ centro Sperimentale di Cinematografia, 1995), 2:192–99.

36. *Lexington Herald,* Mar. 30, 1913.

37. Press booklet for *Satana.*

38. *Bioscope* 18 (London, Jan. 16, 1913).

39. W. Stephen Bush, review of *Satana, Moving Picture World* 15, no. 3 (Jan. 18, 1913): 243. The *New York Dramatic Mirror,* Jan. 8, 1913, 31, glosses this sequence as "Satan repelled by the angels from heaven."

40. Press booklet for *Satana.*

41. Most reviews of the film cite the Milton adaptation, with some more generous than others. *Bioscope* 18 (London, Jan. 16, 1913) reports that "it would be difficult to conceive any greater subject than the story of Satan" and that "the influence of Milton and Goethe are strongly in evidence through-out, and the adaptor has striven with great success to convey something of the great lessons which may be gathered from the study of these masters." *Moving Picture World* 16, no. 1 (5 Apr. 1913) reports that " 'Satan,' showing the birth of evil as told in Milton's 'Paradise Lost,' was exhibited at the Palace Theater, Boston, last week." Cf. Il Rondone, "La Vita Cinematografica," *Torino,* no. 24 (Dec. 25, 1912): "La riduzione cinematografica del poema di Mylton [*sic*] presentava indubbiamente non poche difficoltà.... Pochissimi sono I personaggi che possono formare soggetto a quadric speciali, atti per la grandiosità ad una rappresentazione cinematografica" ("The film adaptation of Milton's poem undoubtedly presented not a few difficulties.... There are very few characters that are suitable subjects for the unique pictures appropri-ate for the grandiosity of cinematic representation").

42. Press booklet for *Satana.*

43. Ibid.

44. Quotations are from the continuity script of *Conscience: A Photoplay in Five Reels,* written by J. Searle Dawley and E. Lloyd Sheldon, from a sce-nario by Adrian Johnson, Fox Film Corporation. All prints of the film itself have apparently been lost.

45. *Motography* 18, no. 16 (Oct. 20, 1917): 834.

46. Brockwell was billed as "The Woman of a Thousand Faces" or "a Thousand Expressions" in contemporary advertisements; in the court scenes she even played the judge; see *Moving Picture World* (Oct. 13, 1917): 164. The parts played by Brockwell were originally to have gone to Theda Bara (she is inked into the part in the continuity script), and the character seems devised with the famed actress's previous vamp roles in mind.

47. On Milton's development of the conscience trope, see Anthony Low, " 'Umpire Conscience': Freedom, Obedience, and the Cartesian Flight from Calvin in *Paradise Lost,*" *Studies in Philology* 96, no. 3 (1999): 348–65.

48. Charlie Chaplin's *The Kid* (1921) also features a war in heaven dream sequence that Gerald Mast, *The Comic Mind: Comedy and the Movies* (Chicago: University of Chicago Press, 1979), calls a "comic pantomime-ballet version of *Paradise Lost*" (94). The sequence transforms the Bowery into a mock heaven of frolicking cherubs with trumpets and harps, and even

a flying dog-angel. The Little Tramp and the Kid (Jackie Coogan) are flown about on wires, as well. Then "Sin creeps in," and the heavenly space is invaded by horned devils with pitchforks. They instigate a kind of civil war, urging on a love-triangle among the Tramp, a seductive female angel, and an antagonizing heavy from earlier in the film. Feathers fly like confetti in the ensuing melee. The Tramp tries to escape by soaring out of reach of an angelic policeman, who finally shoots him down with his pistol. The film arranges Chaplin as a type for a sympathetic Satan, his rebellion sown upon his tryst with the seductive angel, a type for Sin, and his expulsion conveyed through the peacekeeping officer, Michael with a firearm. It transforms Satan's fall into a tale of comic redemption, however, when the Tramp is awakened from his dream to be reunited with the Kid he thought had been lost.

49. R. W. Johnson, review of *Conscience, Motion Picture News* 16, no. 15 (1917): 2584.

50. Edward Weitzel, review of *Conscience, Moving Picture World* (Oct. 13, 1917): 251. Weitzel had been more generous with another film earlier the same year, Edward Warren's *The Warfare of the Flesh*, which he noticed "embraces suggestions from the Bible, Bunyan, Milton" and which "opens with Satan's fall into hell" (*Moving Picture World* [May 5, 1917]: 811). Warren's five-reel film, at times advertised as "based on Milton's *Paradise Lost*" (*Variety*, Apr. 18, 1919, 48) contained a number of Milton-inspired scenes, including an opening seven-minute sequence set in hell dramatizing Satan's fall that featured Satan and Sin overlooking their new home, with 500 extras as the fallen host. See Jenny Henderson, *The North Carolina Filmography* (Jefferson, NC: McFarland, 2002), 179. Satan and Sin then proceed together to Eden, where they combine to seduce Adam and Eve in the garden of Eden. In a significant departure, it is Sin who tempts Eve, transforming like Milton's serpentine model into the coiled serpent. Unfortunately, the hell sequence, which *Variety* praised as "exquisitely beautiful" (contra the rest of the film, a modern and melodramatic tale of temptation—see *Variety*, Apr. 27, 1917, 127), has been lost. However, some of the Eden sequence, including Sin's transformation, can be seen as the final five minutes of Dutch director Peter Delpeut's compilation *Lyrical Nitrate* (1991). The remainder of *The Warfare of the Flesh* also survives, archived in Amsterdam at EYE, the film museum.

51. *Motography*, 18, no. 16 (Oct. 20, 1917): 834.

52. Robert M. Henderson, *D. W. Griffith: The Years at Biograph* (New York: Farrar, Straus, and Giroux, 1970), 3.

53. See Russell Merritt, "Rescued from the Nest: D. W. Griffith's Escape from Theatre into Film," *Cinema Journal* 21, no. 1 (Autumn 1981): 29n9.

54. Mikhail Iampolski, "Intertextuality and the Evolution of Cinematic Language: Griffith and the Poetic Tradition," in *The Memory of Tiresias: Intertextuality and Film*, trans. Harsha Ram (Berkeley and Los Angeles: University of California Press, 1998), 93.

55. *The Man Who Invented Hollywood: The Autobiography of D. W. Griffith* (Louisville, KY: Touchstone, 1972), 88. Griffith was, of course, not the only filmmaker adapting poems: a sampling from Fox Film Corporation includes *A Fool There Was* (dir. Frank Powell, 1915), based on Rudyard Kipling; *Evangeline* (dir. Raoul Walsh, 1919), based on William Henry Longfellow; *The Ancient Mariner* (dir. Chester Barnett and Henry Otto, 1925), based on Samuel Taylor Coleridge; *Over the Hill to the Poorhouse* (dir. Harry Millarde, 1921), based on Will Carleton.

56. See Richard Schickel, *D. W. Griffith: An American Life* (New York: Simon and Schuster, 1984), 82–84. The poem appeared in *Leslie's Weekly* (Jan. 10, 1907); Schickel reprints it in its entirety along with Griffith's giddy account of seeing it in print for the first time.

57. Lary May, "Apocalyptic Cinema: D. W. Griffith and the Aesthetics of Reform," in *Movies and Mass Culture,* ed. John Belton (New Brunswick, NJ: Rutgers University Press, 1996), 26.

58. Ibid., 26.

59. Ibid., 31.

60. Ibid., 5.

61. Iampolski, "Intertextuality," 86.

62. Griffith, "What I Demand of Movie Stars" (1917), reprinted in *Focus on D. W. Griffith,* ed. Harry M. Geduld (Englewood Cliffs, NJ: Prentice-Hall, 1971), 53. The record of his commentary on the stage, however, reveals at times an underlying ambivalence. After controversy over racism in *The Birth of a Nation* and mixed critical support for *Intolerance,* Griffith intimated, perhaps petulantly, that he might abandon film altogether: "Of necessity, the stage must tell the truth more freely than any other method of expression. It is the only means existing today of even attempting to portray the truth. . . . I now contemplate turning to the stage in making an attempt to find freedom of expression" (Henry Stephen Gordon, "The Real Story of *Intolerance,*" *Photoplay Magazine* [July–Nov. 1916]: 40). On Griffith's complex relationship to the theater, see David Mayer, *Stagestruck Filmmaker: D. W. Griffith and the American Theatre* (University of Iowa Press, 2009).

63. Merritt, "Rescued from the Nest," 4.

64. Griffith, "What I Demand," 53.

65. While Griffith was intent on the singular poetics of film, the silent cinema did maintain the paradoxical application of written intertitles. Judith Buchanan, *Shakespeare on Silent Film: An Excellent Dumb Discourse* (Cambridge: Cambridge University Press, 2009), describes this as an outgrowth of prior wordless stage productions—pantomimes and spectacle shows—and observes that "when the new medium of cinema necessarily excised spoken language completely from its Shakespearean productions, it not only tapped into a non-verbal Shakespearean performance tradition in the pantomimic conventions of the minor theatres (and of nineteenth-century ballet): it also traded upon and extended the legitimate stage's tendency to erode the significance of language in preference to other forms of scenic

display" (49). That films were simultaneously envisioned and read suggests that this erosion was not entirely destructive of earlier language acts, but rather that, in Griffith's terms, the cinema had effectively appropriated and subordinated other art forms. The interstitial display of written texts was a conspicuous display of cinema's power to contain and convert the potency of poetic discourse.

66. Interview with Robert E. Welsh, "David W. Griffith Speaks," *New York Dramatic Mirror* (Jan. 14, 1914): 49.

67. Ibid., 49.

68. Ibid., 49.

69. Griffith, "Motion Picture and Witch Burners," 96–98.

70. D. W. Griffith, "Cinema: Miracle of Modern Photography," *Mentor* 9, no. 6 (July 1, 1921): 3.

71. Walter Lionel George, *A London Mosaic* (New York: Stokes, 1921), 30–31.

72. D. W. Griffith, "The Motion Picture To-day and To-morrow," *Theatre Magazine* 45–46 (Oct. 1927): 21, 58.

73. See esp. Tom Gunning, *D. W. Griffith and the Origins of American Narrative Film: The Early Years at Biograph* (Urbana: University of Illinois Press, 1991).

74. *Letters of Vachel Lindsay,* ed. Marc Chénetier (New York: Burt Franklin, 1979), 137.

75. Eileen Bowser, ed., *Biograph Bulletins, 1908–1912* (New York: Octagon Books, 1973), 290.

76. Scott Simmon, *The Films of D. W. Griffith* (Cambridge: Cambridge University Press, 1993), 152.

77. Karl Brown, *Adventures with D. W. Griffith* (New York: Farrar, Straus and Giroux, 1973), 46.

78. Ibid., 46–47.

79. Ibid., 48.

80. Marie Corelli, *The Sorrows of Satan* (London: Lippincott, 1895), 375.

81. May, "Apocalyptic Cinema," 40.

82. Ibid., 40. See D. W. Griffith, "Pace in the Movies," *Liberty* (Nov. 13, 1926): 19–23.

83. Schickel, *D. W. Griffith,* 518–19.

84. Ibid., 519.

85. Ibid., 519–20.

86. Press sheet, 14, from Margaret Herrick Library, Beverly Hills, CA, Academy of Motion Picture Arts and Sciences special collections, Paramount Pictures press sheets.

87. Schickel, *D. W. Griffith,* 521.

88. Paramount press sheet, 14.

89. Robert M. Henderson, *D. W. Griffith: His Life and Work* (New York: Oxford University Press, 1972), 263. For a detailed account of the production conflicts, see Schickel, *D. W. Griffith,* 517–24.

90. Doré's work is listed among the "mass of data and paintings" collected by the studio to guide the film's art direction (see Paramount press sheet, 5.) Another of Milton's illustrators, John Martin, had influenced with his *Belshazzar's Feast* (1821) the design of the Babylonian scenes in Griffith's *Intolerance*. See Schickel, *D. W. Griffith*, 313, 331.

91. Halsey's untitled treatment, 1, in the Norman Bel Geddes Theater and Industrial Design Papers, Harry Ransom Center, University of Texas at Austin.

92. Ibid., 1.

93. Forrest Halsey, *The Sorrows of Satan* continuity script, in the Norman Bel Geddes Theater and Industrial Design Papers, Harry Ransom Center, University of Texas at Austin, n.d., 5.

94. Ibid., 5, 6, 7.

95. Norman Bel Geddes, *Miracle in the Evening* (New York: Doubleday, 1960), 319.

96. Ibid., 320.

97. Ibid., 321.

98. Norman Bel Geddes, "Rough Draft for Allegorical Sequence," 3, in the Norman Bel Geddes Theater and Industrial Design Papers, Harry Ransom Center, University of Texas at Austin.

99. Ibid., 4.

100. The English rock group Bauhaus used the image as cover art for what has become a goth anthem, "Bela Lugosi's Dead." Jennifer Park, *Gothic: Dark Glamour* (New Haven, CT: Yale University Press, 2008), 117, points out that the back cover was taken from *The Cabinet of Dr. Caligari*, which has sometimes confused attribution of the Griffith image.

NOTES TO CHAPTER 4,
THE AMBIVALENCE OF THE MILTONIC FILM

1. Douglas L. Howard, "*National Lampoon's Animal House* and the Fraternity of Milton," in *Milton in Popular Culture*, ed. Laura Lunger Knoppers and Gregory M. Colón Semenza (New York: Palgrave, 2006), offers that "the film recalls some of the less inspired lectures that took place [at Dartmouth in the 1960s], as frustrated faculty were often forced to teach *Paradise Lost* to disinterested fraternity members as part of the English curriculum" (164).

2. Ibid., 166–67, 166.

3. The scene is echoed, for instance, in *The Skulls II* (dir. Joe Chappelle, 2002), when a professor comparing Milton to Dante cites the lines, "Long is the way, and hard, that out of hell leads up to light" as a mantra for surviving "the hell of staying awake through a particularly boring lecture," a lecture such as the one he appears to be giving.

4. Directed by George Gordon et al., *Paradise Smurfed* first aired on October 17, 1981, as part of season 1, episode 12.

5. Jack London, *The Sea-Wolf* (New York: Macmillan, 1904), 47.

6. Ibid., 249.

7. Of the numerous film adaptations of this novel, from the silent era onward, Curtiz makes the most out of London's use of Milton. In *The Legend of Sea Wolf* (dir. Giuseppe Verde, 1975), Milton is cut from the book sequence entirely. The 1993 television adaptation *The Sea Wolf* (dir. Michael Anderson, with Charles Bronson as Wolf) retains Larsen speaking the line, "Better to reign in Hell than serve in Heaven." In the television miniseries, *Sea Wolf* (dir. Mike Barker, 2009), Van Weyden finds a book open, but there is no identification of Milton; later he wonders of Larsen, "You can read Kipling, Milton, Browning, Plato…Shakespeare." See also Tony Williams, "Hollywood and *The Sea-Wolf*," in *Nineteenth-Century American Fiction on Screen,* ed. R. Barton Palmer (Cambridge: Cambridge University Press, 2007), 206–18.

8. *Thirteen Conversations about One Thing* (dir. Jill Sprecher, 2001) also borrows these lines ("the mind is its own place and in itself can make a Heaven of Hell, a hell of Heaven"). A literature professor (Barbara Sukowa) expels them between drags on a cigarette while dissertating with her lover, a physics professor (John Turturro), on the benefits of her husband's self-delusion.

9. A good example of the indirectness regarding Milton's Eden is *Pleasantville* (dir. Gary Ross, 1998), which Knoppers and Semenza see as "extensively but implicitly adapt[ing] Miltonic motifs" (*Milton in Popular Culture,* 10). The film is concerned with a literary Eden, situating its tensions over freedom and conformity in 1950s America, and it maintains a generally Miltonic influence in its critique of unreasoned authority and sterilizing social pressures. The film never mentions *Paradise Lost,* developing instead similar ideas through *Huckleberry Finn.*

10. See C. S. Lewis, *The Magician's Nephew* (New York: HarperCollins, 2002), 133–34.

11. Charles Dickens, *Great Expectations,* ed. Charlotte Mitchell (London: Penguin, 2003), 160. On parallels between *Paradise Lost* and Dickens's novel, see Jerome Meckier, *Dickens's Great Expectations: Misnar's Pavilion versus Cinderella* (Lexington: University of Kentucky Press, 2002), 173–79. Meckier points out that Pip's paraphrase of the final lines of *Paradise Lost* is even closer to Milton in Dickens's manuscript: "And the mists had all solemnly risen now, and the world was before me."

12. Ibid., 484.

13. See ibid., 507.

14. Ibid., 56. Michael K. Johnson, "'Not Telling the Story the Way It Happened: Alfonso Cuarón's *Great Expectations,*" *Literature/Film Quarterly* 33 (2005): 62–78, glosses the film's Edenic motif: "Finn…is an American Adam whose innocence is shattered…by his first meeting with Estella in the seemingly Edenic overgrown gardens surrounding Dinsmoor's house.

Although lush, fertile, and wild, these grounds are a paradise lost—Paradiso Perduto as the name over the gate proclaims—rather than an Eden, a fallen world where Finn will lose his innocence to a tempting Eve" (67). See also Brian McFarlane, *Charles Dickens' "Great Expectations": A Close Study of the Relationship between Text and Film* (London: Methuen, 2008), 111–26.

15. Julie Sanders, *Shakespeare and Music: Afterlives and Borrowings* (Cambridge: Polity, 2007), 56n, incorrectly identifies the lyrics as being from *Comus* and suggests that the song is meant to emphasize "the connections between seventeenth-century masque and musical adaptations of Shakespeare."

16. Harriett Hawkins, "Paradigms Lost: Chaos, Milton and *Jurassic Park*," *Textual Practice* 8, no. 2 (1994): 40–49, discusses *Jurassic Park* as "cognate to *Paradise Lost*" (45), particularly in the way they each "refer us directly to the uncontrollable world outside their texts where chaos operates not just in theory but in practice, and where the mundane and trivial, as well as the fearsome and destructive forces we cannot control (for which Milton's Satan and Crichton's velociraptors are appropriately mean and magnificent metaphors) are real" (47).

17. Colin Manlove, *Christian Fantasy from 1200 to the Present* (Notre Dame, IN: University of Notre Dame Press, 1992). Compare Marjorie Hope Nicolson, "The Discovery of Space," in *Medieval and Renaissance Studies: Proceedings of the Southeastern Institute of Medieval and Renaissance Studies, Summer, 1966,* ed. O. B. Hardison Jr. (Chapel Hill, NC: University of North Carolina Press, 1966), who observes, "Nowhere in poetry do we find more majestic conceptions of the vastness of space" (57). Such views are tempered by those who regard the interplanetary realms of Dante, Ludovico Ariosto, Thomas More, or Milton as largely uninterested in the kinds of inquiries that hallmark modern science fiction. Robert Scholes and Eric S. Rabkin, *Science Fiction: History, Science, Vision* (New York: Oxford University Press, 1977), write that these works "remain separate from science fiction because they are constructed on a plan derived from religious tradition rather than scientific speculation or imagination based, however loosely, on science" (43).

18. On Milton and space, see Maura Brady, "Space and the Persistence of Place in *Paradise Lost*," *Milton Quarterly* 41 (2007): 167–82; Lara Dodds, "Milton's Other Worlds," in *Uncircumscribed Mind: Reading Milton Deeply,* ed. Charles W. Durham and Kristin A. Pruitt (Selinsgrove, PA: Susquehanna University Press, 2008), 164–82; and Grant McColley, "The Astronomy of *Paradise Lost*," *Studies in Philology* 34 (1937): 209–47.

19. See Shari Hodges, "A Pedagogically Useful Comparison of *Star Trek II* and *Paradise Lost*," *CEA Forum* 24, no. 2 (1994): 4–7. Roger B. Rollin, "Beowulf to Batman: The Epic Hero and Pop Culture," *College English* 31, no. 5 (1970): 431–49, offers a series of analogues between the *Star Trek* television series and *Paradise Lost*.

20. This is a topos revisited in other *Star Trek* narratives: the episode "The Apple" (1967) features beings whose procreative urges are curbed by

a draconian overseer, and whom the crew must rescue from their ignorance; in the fifth film, *The Final Frontier* (dir. William Shatner, 1989), another type for Eden, "Sha Ka Ree," sits at the center of the galaxy and is occupied by a being that first resembles the deity but quickly devolves into something satanic. The film also includes a dystopian settlement called "Paradise City"— the "Paradise" inscription over the city gate has been graffitied into "Paradise Lost." Later series continue the theme: *Deep Space Nine*, for instance, has an episode called "Paradise Lost" (1996) in which the ideals of the Federation are seen to be imploding. As one critic puts it, the show "rewrites the earlier *Star Trek* mythos in order that a perfect society should give way to a morally and politically uncertain world." See Peter Linford, "Deeds of Power: Respect for Religion in *Star Trek: Deep Space Nine*," in *Star Trek and Sacred Ground*, ed. Jennifer E. Porter and Darcee L. McLaren (Albany: State University of New York Press, 1999), 86.

21. *Carmen Jones*, lyrics and book by Oscar Hammerstein II (New York: Knopf, 1945), 60. The pandemonium lyric is cut from "Whizzin' Away" in the original Broadway cast recording (1943, remastered Decca U.S., 2003).

22. Jeff Smith, "Black Faces, White Voices: The Politics of Dubbing in *Carmen Jones*," *Velvet Light Trap* 51, no. 1 (Spring 2003): 37, 38.

23. Carol Fry and Christopher Kemp, "Rambo Agonistes," *Literature Film Quarterly* 24, no. 4 (1996): 367–76, train their sights on this drama as a parallel to what they describe as the "patriotic adventure film" (368), specifically as embodied in the Sylvester Stallone *Rambo* franchise, despite their disclaimer that "it would be absurd to cite 'Samson Agonistes' as an analogue for the Rambo films" (367). See also the nuclear terrorism film *Seven Days to Noon* (dir. John and Ray Boulting, 1950), which incorporates the quotation "Dark, dark, dark, amid the blaze of noon." See too Gregory M. Colón Semenza, "The Ethics of Appropriation: *Samson Agonistes, Inglorious Basterds,* and the Biblical Samson Tale," *Adaptation* 7, no. 1 (2014): 62–81.

24. Fulgosi's film is an adaptation of the Mervyn Wall short story "They Also Serve...," first published in *Harper's Magazine* 181 (1940): 125–29, which his biographer calls a "charming satire of Civil Service bureaucracy." See Robert Goode Hogan, *Mervyn Wall* (Lewisburg, PA: Bucknell University Press, 1972), 22. The film follows Wall's comic treatment of an out-of-work Dubliner who, because of a clerical error, begins receiving monthly checks for doing nothing but waiting around in an unassigned government office.

25. On the *Sabrina* films, see Catherine Gimelli Martin, "*Sabrina Fair* Goes to the Movies: Milton, Myth, and Romance," and Julie H. Kim, "Sabrina...Or, the Lady?: Gender, Class, and the Specter of Milton in *Sabrina* (1995)," both in Knoppers and Semenza, *Milton in Popular Culture*, 139–50 and 151–62, respectively.

26. Edward Allen, *Mustang Sally* (New York: Norton, 1994), 143.

27. Virginia Woolf, *Mrs. Dalloway*, ed. David Bradshaw (1925; repr., New York: Oxford University Press, 2000), 149–50.

28. Reviewed in "Don Taylor's Play, *Paradise Restored*," *Milton Quarterly* 9, no. 4 (1975): 116–17.

29. There is sometimes a violent reaction to even the mention of Milton, especially if done with the slightest hint of condescension, as in the case of two films that received the Academy Award for Best Picture. In dialogue drawn directly from Henry Fielding's 1749 novel, *Tom Jones* (dir. Tony Richardson, 1963) offers this exchange between Squire Western and his sister: "Your ignorance, Brother, as the great Milton says, almost subdues my patience." To which the offended Squire retorts, "Damn Milton! If he had the impudence to be here and say it to my face, I'd lend him a flick." (This is a snarled reference, since Mrs. Western invokes an apparently apocryphal passage, so she is quoting "Milton" only for Milton's sake.) In the westward expansion epic *Cimarron* (dir. Wesley Ruggles, 1931), restless pioneer Yancey Cravat (newspaper editor, lawyer, sharpshooter, played by Richard Dix) compliments his wife Sabra's dress: "Why, Milton would have no words for such beauty." Later, in a different mood, Sabra (Irene Dunne) throws it back at him, ironically after hearing him quote Homer: "You and your miserable Milton."

30. Philip Pullman, *The Golden Compass* (New York: Ballantine, 1995).

31. On this influence in the books, see Stephen Burt, "Fighting Since Time Began: Milton and Satan in Philip Pullman's *His Dark Materials*," and Lauren Shohet, "*His Dark Materials, Paradise Lost*, and the Common Reader," both in Knoppers and Semenza, *Milton in Popular Culture*, 47–58 and 59–70, respectively; and Burton Hatlen, "*His Dark Materials*, a Challenge to Tolkien and Lewis," and Carole Scott, "Pullman's Enigmatic Ontology: Revamping Old Traditions in *His Dark Materials*," both in *His Dark Materials Illuminated*, ed. Millicent Lenz with Carole Scott (Detroit: Wayne State University Press, 2005), 75–94 and 95–105, respectively.

32. Philip Pullman, introduction to *Paradise Lost*, ed. Stephen Orgel and Jonathan Goldberg (Oxford: Oxford University Press, 2005), 9; Wendy Parsons and Catriona Nicholson, "Talking to Philip Pullman: An Interview," *The Lion and the Unicorn* 23 (1999): 126; Laura Miller, "Far from Narnia," *New Yorker*, Dec. 26, 2005, 58.

33. Only a handful of films borrow from Milton for their title—and *The Golden Compass* is not, technically, one of them. Pullman recalls that the series was originally titled

> *The Golden Compasses*, which is another line from *Paradise Lost*: "He took the golden Compasses, prepared / In God's eternal store, to circumscribe / This Universe, and all created things" (Book 7, ll. 225–27). It was referring to the idea of Creation and that Blake engraving of a figure leaning down and measuring. So before I formally called the first volume *Northern Lights*, I called it *Book One: The Golden Compasses*. Before I knew it, the book was published in America as *The Golden Compass*, referring to the *alethiometer* Lyra has been trusted with. Before I knew it, ten thousand copies had been printed with that title

and the compass on the cover. It was reprinted on the front cover of the Spring issue of *Publishers Weekly*. Enormous publicity! So I was stuck with it.

See Parsons and Nicholson, "Talking to Philip Pullman," 126–27. The title *The Golden Compass*, then, not only signals an erroneous conflation between Lyra's chronometer and the golden drafting compasses the Son employs in creating and circumscribing the universe, but alters Milton's phrasing to make the misreading fit.

34. On Weitz's remodeling of religion in the adaptation, see, among others, Sam Coates, "God Is Cut from Film of Dark Materials," *Times* (London), Dec. 8, 2004, Home News section, 3; and Hanna Rosin, "How Hollywood Saved God," *Atlantic*, Dec. 2007, 68–79.

35. See Peter Hedges, Chris Weitz, and Paul Weitz, *About a Boy: The Shooting Script* (New York: Newmarket, 2002), 1.

36. Ibid., 130.

37. Knoppers and Semenza, *Milton in Popular Culture*, 4. The line is quoted with greater accuracy in *Animal Factory* (dir. Steve Buscemi, 2000), a prison film set in San Quentin. The central character, Earl Copen (Willem Dafoe), who negotiates expertly the difficulties of the penitentiary, fails in an attempt at the end of the film to escape in a garbage truck. He utters with a mix of resignation and relief, "Better to reign in hell than serve in heaven, right?" His friend Vito (Danny Trejo), as if affirming the accuracy of the quote along with the sentiment, tells him, "You got that right." Contrastingly, Edward Bunker's novel upon which the film is based is less sure about the verse: contemplating the pros and cons of incarceration, and deciding to make "Everything in the prison world" his own, Copen tries to recall the literary precedent: "And what had Milton's Satan said when God hurled him from heaven to the abyss? Something about it being better to reign in the pit than serve in heaven." See Edward Bunker, *Animal Factory* (New York: Minotaur Books, 2000), 191.

38. A similar excision occurs in another thriller, Roman Polanski's *The Ninth Gate* (1999), an adaptation of Arturo Pérez-Revert's 1993 novel, *The Club Dumas*. In the book, the main character says he prefers to think of the devil as "Milton's fallen angel" and even gestures at popularizing him ("Anyone can read Milton. Even me"). See *The Club Dumas*, trans. Sonia Soto (Boston: Mariner, 2006), 215. Nothing in the film, though it is swept along by a strong current of bibliophilia, carries over any of the Miltonic references.

39. Dan Brown, *Angels and Demons* (New York: Simon and Schuster, 2000), 167, 169.

40. *Angels and Demons*, screenplay by Akiva Goldsman ("Draft White," Apr. 2008), 34, www.imsdb.com/Movie Scripts/Angels & Demons Script. html (accessed Oct. 5, 2014).

41. *Paradise Lost* does crop up as a kind of *Da Vinci Code* in an episode of the television series *The Unit*, created by David Mamet. In the finale of season 2

(broadcast May 8, 2007), the covert military group at the show's center is about to be shut down. When one member goes missing (Jonas Blane, played by Dennis Haysbert), he leaves behind a cryptic note for his wife. She deciphers the numbers to mean the location of pages, passages, and word orders in *Paradise Lost*. The ensuing season begins with two episodes titled "Pandemonium" and makes several other allusions to Milton. My thanks to Brittany Sharpe for pointing me to this reference.

42. See Chuck Crisafulli, "'Scarlet Letter' Director Defends License to Change," *Los Angeles Times*, Oct. 16, 1995, 1.

43. John Collier, *Milton's "Paradise Lost": Screenplay for Cinema of the Mind* (New York: Knopf, 1973). The screenplay exists in a number of drafts and outlines, held in the John Collier Papers at the Harry Ransom Center in Austin, Texas, which also houses Collier's fervent correspondence with Hollywood producer Martin Poll. Efforts to make the film lasted from early 1967 to November 1970, when Poll declined to renew the option on Collier's script, at which point Collier turned in earnest to the publication of the screenplay in book form with Knopf. Above quotations are from his manuscript "Notes on Certain Aspects of the Production" (n.d.).

44. On Collier's book, see Eric C. Brown, "How Fallen and How Changed: John Collier's *Paradise Lost: Screenplay for Cinema of the Mind*," in *Milton Studies*, vol. 51, ed. Laura L. Knoppers, 205–48 (Pittsburgh: Duquesne University Press, 2010).

45. Letter from Martin Poll to Howard Hausman, July 24, 1967, John Collier Papers, Harry Ransom Center, Austin, TX. Unless otherwise noted, all correspondence is from this source.

46. John Collier, "Preface and Outline of Major Scenes," Jan. 18, 1967, 6.

47. Collier, "Notes on Certain Aspects," 4. This was a point Collier consistently promoted: that *Paradise Lost* could be a relatively inexpensive film. He contended that "the advance of electronics in the last very few years, and the perfection of certain devices in other fields, has been such that technicians are unanimous in declaring that the most crowded and colossal scenes in Hell or in space will actually be cheaper to bring to the screen than some of the more limited and naturalistic settings in the Garden of Eden," and that "the Spectacle of a hundred million angels falling through space or writhing in a limitless sea of fire can be achieved by a comparatively simple multiplication of images" ("Notes on Certain Aspects," 2–3). Again, in an interview with *Time* magazine, Collier adds, "I've got pictures of Arizona. One could make hell out of almost any corner of the Grand Canyon with a little mist or smoke." See Timothy Foote, "All About Eve," *Time*, June 25, 1973, 93. As late as 1976, he held onto the story: "laboratory technicians assure me that electronic advances mean that there is no real need for such a vast budget." See Tom Milne, "The Elusive John Collier," *Sight and Sound* 45, no. 2 (Spring 1976): 108.

48. Letter from Collier to literary agent Harold Matson, July 1967.

49. Milne, "The Elusive John Collier," 108.

50. Letter from Collier to Hausman, Sept. 11, 1968.

51. Letter from Collier to Hausman, Sept. 28, 1968.

52. *The Jan Stussy Papers, 1950–1985,* Smithsonian Archives of American Art, Microfilm Reel 2200, "Biographical Information."

53. Letter from Collier to Stussy, Oct. 14, 1968.

54. All quotations in this paragraph are to ibid.

55. Letter from Collier to Poll, Oct. 17, 1968.

56. Letter from Collier to Hausman, Oct. 25, 1968.

57. John Updike, "Milton Adapts Genesis; Collier Adapts Milton," *New Yorker,* Aug. 20, 1973, 89. Contra Updike, Timothy Foote's review in *Time* magazine ("All About Eve," 92), urges that Collier's "film script, published in book form, is a symbiotic work of literary art, fast-paced, clever, well crafted, full of knowledge and delight. Everybody should read it, preferably with Milton as a trot." Foote is happy to see "on the cutting-room floor" a great deal of "highly expendable Milton," especially the "lofty jawboning sessions with angels who tend to sound like an unfortunate blend of Dean Rusk and Charlton Heston," and contends that in "describing the action for future cameramen, Collier creates prose that often matches and sometimes surpasses even Milton's great-ranging visual imagination." He offers, "One can indeed imagine Collier's *Paradise Lost* as a superflick, called *All About Eve II,* or *4560 B.C.,* done in the style of Stanley Kubrick" (93). In a short review, Joseph Anthony Wittreich Jr., "Beyond New Criticism: Literary History, Literary Criticism, and Milton Studies, 1973," *Milton Quarterly* 8, no. 1 (1974): 15–21, also praises Collier's publication, observing that "Collier's 'Cinema of the Mind' reminds us that Milton . . . is still very much alive in today's popular culture, which is capable, even in its 'foreign' media, of contributing significantly to our understanding of Milton" (19).

58. All quotations in this paragraph are from a letter from Collier to Hausman, Oct. 15, 1968.

59. Letter from Collier to Barker, Nov. 14, 1968.

60. Letter from Collier to Hausman, Nov. 15, 1968.

61. Ray Loynd, "Marty Poll Plans Pic Version of Milton's Epic, 'Paradise Lost,'" *Hollywood Reporter,* Dec. 23, 1968, 6.

62. Ibid., 6.

63. Ibid., 6.

64. Letter from Collier to Hausman, Jan. 23, 1969.

65. Letter from Collier to Hausman, May 26, 1969.

66. Letter from Hausman to Collier, Apr. 13, 1970.

67. Albert Boine, *The Odyssey of Jan Stussy in Black and White* (Los Angeles: The Jan Stussy Foundation, 1995), 162, asserts that in 1969 Stussy wrote "a screen adaptation of *Paradise Lost* in collaboration with Alex Haley and Quincy Jones," likely the sci-fi adaptation *Again and Again* Stussy later included on his professional resume.

68. Letter from Collier to Stussy, May 15, 1970.

69. Letter from Collier to Hausman, May 15, 1970.
70. Letter from Hausman to Collier, May 20, 1970.
71. Letter from Poll to Collier, Sept. 9, 1970.
72. Letter from Hausman to Collier, Sept. 28, 1970.
73. Letter from Collier to Hausman, Oct. 3, 1970.
74. On Fellini, Collier believed that at one point he "had agreed to do it" and claimed that "United Artists were willing to make the picture if he would do it." See Milne, "The Elusive John Collier," 108. Derek Jarman was also reportedly "engaged in discussions about a possible film version of Milton's epic poem"; see Rowland Wymer, *Derek Jarman* (Manchester: University of Manchester Press, 2005), 133. This was a remounting of the Collier script, begun in the late 1980s, and was to be produced by James MacKay and Sony Pictures, Japan. Tony Peake, *Derek Jarman* (London: Little, Brown, 1999), recounts how

> in Tokyo, Jarman and Mackay talked to Sony, then looking for suitable material to pioneer their new high-definition video system. Sony had bought *The Last of England* for release as a laser disc and seemed keen to explore how, using their new system, Jarman's brand of non-narrative, image-based film-making might be taken into the mainstream. There was the carrot of a great deal of money should the right project be found. Jarman wondered whether *Paradise Lost* might fit the bill. This adaptation of Milton's epic poem for the screen by the writer John Collier had been suggested to Jarman as a potential project by Nicholas Ward-Jackson. But Collier's script was too lavish for what Sony had in mind. Undeterred, Jarman and Mackay later began talking about altering it to suit Sony's needs, or, failing that, taking it elsewhere. (559n40)

75. Letter from Collier to Hausman, Nov. 22, 1970.
76. John Collier, "Screenplay Prepared for Publication as Book or Film, 'Uncut Version,'" John Collier Papers, Harry Ransom Center, Austin, TX.
77. Letter from Collier to Hausman, Nov. 22, 1970.
78. Letter from Collier to Matson and Jones, n.d.
79. James D. Bloom, *Hollywood Intellect* (Lanham, MD: Lexington Books, 2009), 141.
80. Collier, *Cinema of the Mind*, vii.
81. See also Jay Martin, "Praise for the Blighted and Blasted," review in *New Republic* 168, no. 25 (June 23, 1973): 28–29. Martin, seeing the book as a modern romance in the tradition of "Chrétien de Troyes or Marie de France," argues that "Collier's audience is likely to find his romantic conclusion to Satan's Complaint quite predictable and only mildly amusing" (29).
82. Gregg Kilday, "Classic Satan Tale Hot Again," *Hollywood Reporter*, Apr. 30, 2009, 4.
83. In 2012, Damian Collier, a producer on the 2005 *War of The Worlds* (dir. Steven Spielberg), and apparently no relation to John, began development on yet another *Paradise Lost* film, with the tagline, "The Untold Story of the Greatest Story Ever Told." As of 2014 this project showed no signs of entering production.

NOTES TO CHAPTER 5,
WINGED WARRIORS AND THE WAR IN HEAVEN

1. On Milton's sources for the war, see Stella P. Revard, *The War in Heaven: "Paradise Lost" and the Tradition of Satan's Rebellion* (Ithaca, NY: Cornell University Press, 1980); Neil Forsyth, *The Old Enemy: Satan and the Combat Myth* (Princeton: Princeton University Press, 1989); and George F. Butler, "Giants and Fallen Angels in Dante and Milton: *The Commedia* and the Gigantomachy in *Paradise Lost*," *Modern Philology* 95, no. 3 (1998): 352–64.

2. Henry More, *An Antidote against Atheism*, 3 vols. (London, 1653), 3:126.

3. Walter Gostelo, *The Coming of God in Mercy, in Vengeance; Beginning with fire, to Convert, or Consume, at this so sinful City London* (London, 1658).

4. Interview with Vincent Newman, Oct. 29, 2010. On the book of Daniel and Milton's account of the war, see esp. Feisal G. Mohamed, *In the Anteroom of Divinity: The Reformation of the Angels from Colet to Milton* (Toronto: University of Toronto Press, 2008), 141–64. See also Revard, *The War in Heaven*.

5. For a brief history, see Edward Le Comte, "Dubious Battle: Saving the Appearances," in *Milton Re-Viewed: Ten Essays* (New York: Routledge, 1991), 3–24.

6. Robert H. West, *Milton and the Angels* (Athens: University of Georgia Press, 1955), 106.

7. Charles Leslie, "The History of Sin and Heresy," in *The Theological Works of the Rev. Charles Leslie* (Oxford: Oxford University Press, 1832), 7: 439.

8. George Bernard Shaw's *Man and Superman* (1903; repr., New York: Penguin, 2000), critiques *Paradise Lost* via the gunpowder sequence, as the devil claims (erroneously, as it happens) that Milton "described me as being expelled from Heaven by cannons and gunpowder; and to this day every Briton believes that the whole of his silly story is in the Bible. What else he says I do not know; for it is all in a long poem which neither I nor anyone else ever succeeded in wading through" (143).

9. West, *Milton and the Angels*, 105.

10. Hesiod, *Theogony* and *Work and Days*, trans. M. L. West (Oxford: Oxford University Press, 1988), 23–24. On the imagery of the war in heaven, see Michael Lieb, " 'The Chariot of Paternal Deitie': Some Visual Renderings," in *Milton's Legacy in the Arts*, ed. Albert C. Labriola and Edward Sichi Jr. (University Park, PA: Pennsylvania State University Press, 1988), 21–58.

11. Samuel Johnson, *Lives of the English Poets*, 2 vols. (London, 1820), 1:152, 153.

12. Ibid., 1:152–53.

13. Bruce Boehrer, "The Horseless Epic," *Milton Quarterly* 43, no. 1 (2009): 1–16.

14. On resemblances between the celestial and earthly paradises, see John R. Knott Jr., "Milton's Heaven," *PMLA* 85, no. 3 (1970): 487–95.

15. West, *Milton and the Angels,* 107.

16. Northrop Frye, *The Return of Eden* (Toronto: University of Toronto Press, 1965), 23.

17. In a recent interview, Ridley Scott makes an explicit connection between Milton and his 2012 film *Prometheus:* "if you look at the Engineers, they're tall and elegant. They are dark angels. If you look at 'Paradise Lost,' the guys who have the best time in the story are the dark angels, not God. He goes to all the best nightclubs, he's better looking, and he gets all of the birds [Laughs]." This is a fairly strong misreading of the poem, at least after book 2, but Scott's comment actually captures very well the popular account of Satan as not only more interesting than Milton's God but as an Enochian, Azazel figure and progenitor of the human race. When asked directly whether Milton was then an influence on the film, Scott hedges a bit: "That sounds incredibly pretentiously intellectual. But in a funny sort of way, yes. I started off with a title called *Paradise.* Either rightly or wrongly, we thought that was telling the audience too much. But then with *Prometheus*—which I thought was bloody well intellectual—that wasn't my idea. It was Fox's notion, it came from Tom Rothman, who's a smart fellow. The more I thought about it, the more I thought it was a good idea. This is about someone who dares and is horribly punished. And besides, do you know something? A little bit of an education at the cinema isn't such a bad thing." See Sean O'Connell, "Dialogue: Sir Ridley Scott Explains 'Prometheus,' Our Past, and Teases Future 'Alien' Stories," June 5, 2012, www.movies.com/movie-news/ridley-scott-prometheus-interview/8232 (accessed Oct. 8, 2014).

18. David Desser, "*Blade Runner:* Science Fiction and Transcendence," *Literature/Film Quarterly* 13, no. 3 (1985): 173, 178.

19. David Desser, "The New Eve: The Influence of *Paradise Lost* and *Frankenstein* on *Blade Runner,*" in *Retrofitting Blade Runner,* ed. Judith B. Kerman (Bowling Green, OH: Bowling Green State University Press, 1991), 53–65. See also Sharon Gravett, "The Sacred and the Profane: Examining the Religious Subtext of Ridley Scott's 'Blade Runner,'" *Literature/Film Quarterly* 26 (Jan. 1998): 38–43.

20. Desser, "The New Eve," 60, is following here Diane K. McColley's interpretation in *Milton's Eve* (Urbana: University of Illinois Press, 1983). For a reconsideration of this typology, see also Karen L. Edwards, "The Mother of All Femmes Fatales: Eve as Temptress in Genesis 3," in *The Femme Fatale: Images, Histories, Contexts,* ed. Helen Hanson and Catherine O'Rawe, 35–45 (New York: Palgrave Macmillan, 2010).

21. Laura Lunger Knoppers and Gregory M. Colón Semenza, eds., *Milton in Popular Culture* (New York: Palgrave, 2006), 9.

22. See Alexis Harley, "*America, a Prophecy:* When Blake Meets *Blade Runner,*" *Sydney Studies in English* 31 (2005): 61–75. Harley points out that "Cinematic adaptations of Shelley's *Frankenstein*...have so popularised versions of Shelley's novella that it has become the primary intermediary between

Paradise Lost's fundamental mythic narrative—creature confronting creator—and an audience generally more literate in film than in Milton" (62). On the influence of Blake, see also Christiane Gerblinger, "'Fiery the Angels Fell': America, Regeneration, and Ridley Scott's *Blade Runner*," *Australasian Journal of American Studies* 21 (July 2002): 19–30.

23. *Blade Runner*, screenplay by Hampton Fancher and David Peoples (Feb. 23, 1981), 1.

24. Stephen Holden, "The Devil and God at War over Souls," *New York Times*, Sept. 2, 1995, A15. The Z-horror film *Fear No Evil* (dir. Frank LaLoggia, 1981) also features an earthly battle between Lucifer and the archangels Gabriel and Michael. In this case, Satan (a senior in high school) raises an army of zombies to hasten the coming of the Antichrist. He is opposed by Gabrielle and Mikhail— female incarnations of the celestial defenders (one his high school classmate, the other his elderly neighbor). In a low-tech finale they defeat him with a special cross that appears to fire holy laser beams.

25. Holden, "The Devil and God," A15.

26. Douglas E. Cowan, "Religion and Cinema Horror," in *Understanding Religion and Popular Culture*, ed. Terry Ray Clark and Dan W. Clanton Jr. (New York: Routledge, 2012), sees the film as part of what he calls a "metataxis of terror," an expression of "our fear that . . . the sacred order could be turned upside down in a matter of moments" (63). Carl Royer and B. Lee Cooper, *The Spectacle of Isolation in Horror Films* (New York: Routledge, 2005), commend *The Prophecy* series for "restoring a more traditional depiction of angels as the harbingers of justice, even as great pain and slaughter are strewn in their wake" (96).

27. Quoted in Joad Raymond, *Milton's Angels: The Early Modern Imagination* (Oxford: Oxford University Press, 2010), 75.

28. On the sensual impulses of Milton's angels, see Karma deGruy, "Desiring Angels: The Angelic Body in *Paradise Lost*," *Criticism* 54, no. 1 (Winter 2012): 117–49.

29. Milton also shows up in the script for Kevin Smith's epic of disenfranchisement *Clerks* (1994). The central character Dante is supposed to be highly literate: the opening scene shows off his collection of books—the *Inferno, Beyond Good and Evil, The Catcher in the Rye*—and later he "studies a copy of *Paradise Lost*" while working the store counter. In the filmed version of that scene, Milton has been dropped and Dante is reading a generic magazine. See Kevin Smith, *Clerks and Chasing Amy: Two Screenplays* (New York: Miramax, 1997), 33.

30. Alan Moore's series is often self-consciously Miltonic, as in two standalone graphic novels called *All His Engines* (2005), a reference to the fall of Mulciber in book 1 of *Paradise Lost*, and *Hellblazer: Pandemonium* (2010).

31. Among the critics to note the Miltonic traces, Scott Renshaw, "Stranger than Paradise," *Salt Lake City Weekly* (Feb. 17, 2005), is the bluntest: "*Constantine* acts less like a typical comic book adaptation than

it does an attempt to turn *Paradise Lost* into a blockbuster action movie" (45). Renshaw also claims that the film "delivers the most entertaining divine warfare this side of paradise" (45), though there are in fact very few dramatizations of divine combat. John P. McCarthy, "Paradise Misplaced," *Reel Talk Movie Reviews,* www.reeltalkreviews.com/browse/viewitem .asp?type=review&id=1180 (accessed Aug. 25, 2014), saw the film similarly as "Milton's 'Paradise Lost' as a slick video game."

32. Francis Lawrence, dir., DVD commentary to *Constantine* (2005). The androgynous representation also somewhat resembles Rosalinda Celentano's portrayal of Satan in Mel Gibson's *The Passion of the Christ* (2004). In *The Gospel according to Hollywood* (Louisville, KY: Westminster John Knox Press, 2007), Greg Garrett supposes that Gabriel's tour of duty in *Constantine* will be familiar to readers of Milton: "S/he has long served as an intermediary for God on the front lines of a cosmic battle involving angels and devils that many of us remember (we think) from John Milton's *Paradise Lost*" (6).

33. In an early draft of the screenplay, Mammon resembles Milton's Death in having been "conceived before his father's fall from grace but…born after." (Kevin Brodbin et al., *Constantine* [Nov. 14, 2002] 72). There is never any mention of a mother. See www.imsdb.com/Movie Scripts/Constantine Script.html (accessed Oct. 8, 2014).

34. West, *Milton and the Angels,* 155. On the general influence of Milton's angel names, see also John Shawcross, " 'Shedding sweet influence': The Legacy of John Milton's Works," in *A Concise Companion to Milton,* ed. Angelica Duran (Oxford: Blackwell, 2007), 27–28. An essential update on West's compendium is Raymond's excellent *Milton's Angels,* cited above.

35. See Clint Morris, "Interview: Shane Abbess and Andy Whitfield" (Nov. 14, 2007), *Moviehole.net,* moviehole.net/200712228interview-shane-abbess-andy-whitfield (accessed Aug. 25, 2014).

36. Richard Jinman, "Heavy Hand Keeps Action Hero Angels Grounded," *Sydney Morning Herald,* Nov. 15, 2007, 17.

37. Both the director and production designer, Victor Lam, confirm these video game analogies. Lam notes a "videogame influence" in the level of gore, while Abbess admits, "As for videogames, I'm sort of quite fanatical about it. When we wrote Gabriel, the first few drafts were through *Halo 2,* and…I also find that by playing games, I get into that 'new world.' " See separate interviews by Patrick Kolan, Oct. 16, 2007, and Oct. 3, 2007 (Abbess), both with IGN [Imagine Games Network] Australia, a web-based review site for video games, www.ign.com/articles/2007/10/16/exclusive-gabriel-concept-art-and-au-interview and www.ign.com/articles/2007/10/04/gabriel-au-inter-view-with-shane-abbess (accessed Oct. 8, 2014).

38. *Wings of Desire* offers plenty of glimpses of its own war in heaven: the Great War's bombardment of Berlin, elaborated in montages that intercut the beating of angelic wings with bombs igniting and the sky filling with fumes and warplanes. That the angels are also implicated in this war in heaven

is later implied when the one relic they are allowed to take to earth after becoming human is their suit of armor. Wenders's film also parallels its fallen angels with Milton's—in the scene of the angel Damiel's awakening, the graffiti "SATAN" can be seen clearly framed in the background, on a building behind a group of children who are spying on the fallen angel. As Damiel lies on the ground, an object suddenly crashes onto his head, bloodying him: his angelic armor. The pain from the armor, and the blood oozing from the wound, are his first sensory experiences (and perhaps there is a Johnsonian jab at Milton with the angel being crushed by the weight of his own armor). The entire sequence has been highly influential on later angelic films: for instance, Damiel pauses to lick the blood from his fingers and remarks, "it has a taste"; the angel Bartleby performs the very same act upon becoming human at the end of *Dogma*.

39. In the sentimental Western *Heaven Only Knows* (dir. Albert S. Rogell, 1947), the archangel Michael (Robert Cummings) comes to earth as a gun-toting cowboy in order to save a lost soul. The film features the Pair-o-Dice saloon and Michael punching his way out of trouble: "Never mistake kindness for weakness."

40. Peter Schink and Scott Stewart, *Legion* screenplay, final draft (Oct. 31, 2007), 90.

41. With similar apocalyptic leanings, *X-Men: The Last Stand* (dir. Brett Ratner, 2006) also features the angelic comic book superhero Archangel (Ben Foster), whose mutant powers include not only flight but also increased strength and speed. The film does not focus extensively on his character, though in popular culture he may be the best-known angelic warrior of them all.

42. Gabriel Garcia Márquez, "A Very Old Man with Enormous Wings" (1955), in *Collected Stories* (New York: Harper Perennial, 1999), 218, 219.

43. Christopher R. Miller, "Winging It," *New York Times Book Review*, May 24, 1998, 23.

44. West, *Milton and the Angels*, 104.

45. Compare the life-after-death comedy *Defending Your Life* (dir. Albert Brooks, 1991), in which celestial cuisine "is not only the best food you'll ever have but you can eat all you want." Such is the promise of Milton's heaven, where angels eat and drink "and in communion sweet / Quaff immortality and joy, secure / Of surfeit, where full measure only bounds / Excess, before th' all bounteous King" (*PL* 5.637–40).

46. Harold Bloom, *Fallen Angels* (New Haven, CT: Yale University Press, 2007), reports, "every angel is terrifying, wrote the poet Rilke, who had not confronted a screen upon which John Travolta cavorted as an angel" (24).

47. C. S. Lewis, *A Preface to "Paradise Lost"* (London: Oxford University Press, 1942), 106. For the broader resonance of this scene, see also Denise Gigante, *Taste: A Literary History* (New Haven, CT: Yale University Press, 2005), 22–46; and on Milton's purposeful, rather than ludicrous, presentation, compare Anthony Low, "Angels and Food in *Paradise Lost*," in *Milton*

Studies, vol. 1, ed. James D. Simmonds, 135–45 (Pittsburgh: University of Pittsburgh Press, 1969); John E. Parish, "Milton and the Well-Fed Angel," *English Miscellany* 18 (1967): 87–109; Jack Goldman, "Perspectives of Raphael's Meal in *Paradise Lost,* Book V," 11, no. 2 (1977): 31–37. On the (im)materiality of angelic consumption, as well as questions of their substantiality in general (often contra Raymond), see also Noel Sugimura, *"Matter of Glorious Trial": Spiritual and Material Substance in "Paradise Lost"* (New Haven, CT: Yale University Press, 2009), 179–86.

48. John Martin Evans, *"Paradise Lost" and the Genesis Tradition* (Oxford: Oxford University Press, 1968), reminds us that, "according to the maximal Fathers, it may be recalled, Man was created the equal of the angels. Besides being immortal and passionless, he fed with the archangels and was designed to procreate in some non-carnal angelic way" (245).

Notes to Chapter 6, "All Hell Broke Loose": The Horror Film

1. Even ultralow budget productions have adopted this position. See, for instance, *In medias res* (dir. Joe Perry, 2011), with God debating Satan on a beach, and the amateur short *Apostasy* (dir. Andrew Bellware, 1998). In a September 2011 interview with Mike Haberfelner, Bellware reflects ambivalently on his use of Milton: "Yes, it was based on *Paradise Lost.* In fact, it has sizable chunks of *Paradise Lost* in it. Why would anyone do such a thing?" See "An Interview with Andrew Bellware, Science Fiction Director, Head of *Pandora Machine,*" Sept. 2011, www.searchmytrash.com/cgi-bin/article creditsb.pl?andrewbellware%289-11%29 (accessed Aug. 26, 2014).

2. Steven Dillon, *Derek Jarman and Lyric Film: The Mirror and the Sea* (Austin: University of Texas Press, 2004), calls Derek Jarman's underworld visions in *The Angelic Conversation* (1985), a film accompanied by readings from Shakespeare's sonnets, "a Miltonic 'darkness visible'…construed through the outlines of flames and the suggestions of walls" (105). Several aborted attempts at bringing Milton to the screen also focused on his visions of the infernal. Saul Bass had plans for an "impressionistic series of images" as an epilogue to his cult apocalyptic film *Phase IV* (1974), reportedly inspired by Milton. The montage would have provided "a hallucinatory tour-de-force" under the titles *Paradise Lost* and *Paradise Regained;* see Jennifer Bass and Pat Kirkham, *Saul Bass: A Life in Film and Design* (London: Laurence King, 2011), 260–61, which also reprints sketches for the unfilmed sequences. The initial series of images, titled "Man Controlled," is that of "giant monoliths and tiny human figures who fall through space, lose their features and finally catch fire" (261). Andrew Pyper's *The Demonologist* (New York: Simon and Schuster, 2013), in the pipeline as a feature film, also centers on a Milton expert simultaneously caught up with supernatural horrors.

3. In another popular postapocalyptic video game, *Fallout 3* (Bethesda Game Studios, 2008), *Paradise Lost* also makes an appearance as an archaic tome that can augment a player's "Speech" skill. The book is proffered by a ghoulish merchant named Tulip, and her computer provides the player some longish excerpts from the poem (books 1, 4, and 8). However, the game is another instance of the popular miscibility of Milton with Dante's *Inferno*, as Tulip claims that the game's "Underworld" milieu is based upon "this old book called 'Paradise Lost.' It's about a guy who goes to Hell. Pretty interesting stuff." Moreover, the game underscores that the tale is not *that* interesting: Tulip gives copies away because "nobody around here wants 'em." My thanks to Andre Madore for this reference.

4. The 2008 cinematic adaption *Max Payne*, directed by John Moore, never articulates such an explicit connection with Milton. However, in its development of warring angels appearing on earth as part of an end-of-days conflict, the film shares some basic tropes with Miltonic warrior angel films like *The Prophecy, Constantine,* and *Spawn.* The film makes a mash-up of Norse and Christian mythology—using black winged, demonic "valkyries" as stand-ins for infernal dark angels—and as is typical of this apocalyptic genre, the hero discovers that "the devil is building his army," an army he must combat with an arsenal of advanced earthly weaponry.

5. Percy Bysshe Shelley, "On the Devil, and Devils," in *The Works of Percy Bysshe Shelley in Verse and Prose,* 8 vols., ed. Harry Buxton Forman (London, 1880) 6:390.

6. James B. Twitchell, *Dreadful Pleasures* (Oxford: Oxford University Press, 1985), 304n3.

7. That the sympathetic Satan (or unsympathetic God) also regularly appears in heavy metal and other rock-derived music (spawned first by the Rolling Stones' anthem "Sympathy for the Devil") has also made for numerous crossovers in horror soundtracks. Nick Cave's song "Red Right Hand," for instance, which quotes Belial's colorful warning in book 2 of future divine wrath ("or from above / Should intermitted vengeance arm again / His red right hand to plague us?" [*PL* 2.172–74]), is featured in the first three *Scream* films (1996–2000), the comic book adaptation *Hellboy* (dir. Guillermo del Toro, 2004), and *Cirque du Freak: The Vampire's Assistant* (dir. Paul Weitz, 2009). Cave released "Red Right Hand" on his 1994 album *Let Love In.* Another Nick Cave song, "Song of Joy," from *Murder Ballads* (1996), returns to this phrase and others from *Paradise Lost* ("Farewell happy fields / Where joy forever dwells, / Hail horrors hail") and refers to Milton directly:

> They never caught the man
> He's still on the loose.
> It seems he has done many, many more,
> Quotes John Milton on the walls in the victim's blood.
> The police are investigating at tremendous cost.
> In my house he wrote "his red right hand."
> That, I'm told, is from *Paradise Lost.*

These lyrics actually recall the plot of an episode in the television series *Man against Crime* (1949–54) called "Paradise Lost." In season 4, episode 6 (Nov. 1952), "Griffith Jackson, a private detective friend of Mike Barnett's, is stabbed to death by someone he knows very well. A copy of Milton's 'Paradise Lost' is found near his body. It's up to Mike to find the killer." See *IMDb*, "Paradise Lost, Plot Summary," www.imdb.com/title/tt0932004/plotsummary (accessed Aug. 26, 2014).

8. See Tony Williams, "Is the Devil American?: William Dieterle's *The Devil and Daniel Webster*," in *Horror Film Reader*, ed. Alain Silver and James Ursini (New York: Limelight, 2001). John T. Soister, *Up from the Vaults: Rare Thrillers of the 1920s and 1930s* (Jefferson, NC: McFarland, 2004), contrasting the pervasiveness of the Faust legend, says *Paradise Lost* "seems forever to be relegated to required reading lists for grad school survey courses, rather than to the proscenium arch or beaded screen" (40).

9. In the schlock horror anthology *Night Train to Terror* (dir. John Carr et al., 1985), God and Satan debate free will and the plight of souls while riding a train named Satan's Cannonball, a possible reference to Satan's fusillade of "Iron Globes" in book 6 of *Paradise Lost*. Satan's fondness for technology was also noted in a Reuters news item dated February 11, 2004, "Sicilian Town Battles 'Demonic' Mystery Blazes," in which "A Sicilian town is struggling to work out why dozens of household items from fridge-freezers to furniture keep mysteriously bursting into flame, terrifying locals and sparking theories of demonic intervention." A Catholic exorcist, Gabriele Amorth, relayed to the Italian press, "I've seen things like this before. Demons occupy a house and appear in electrical goods.... Let's not forget that Satan and his followers have immense powers"; see www.telegraph.co.uk/news/world-news/1567428/Aliens-caused-Sicily-fires-say-officials.html (accessed Oct. 8, 2014).

10. On horror as "boundary violation," see esp. Stephen Prince, "Dread, Taboo, and *The Thing*: Toward a Social Theory of the Horror Film," *Wide Angle* 10, no. 3 (1988): 19–29; Noël Carroll, *The Philosophy of Horror, or Paradoxes of the Heart* (New York: Routledge, 1990); and Isabel Cristina Pinedo, "Postmodern Elements of the Contemporary Horror Film," in *The Horror Film*, ed. Stephen Prince, 85–117 (New Brunswick, NJ: Rutgers University Press, 2004). Steven Jay Schneider, "Towards an Aesthetics of Cinematic Horror," also in Prince, *The Horror Film*, 131–49, observes that "a horrifying object or event may indeed be threatening, but what makes it a source of horror as opposed to fear (or even terror) is one's contemplation of, even fixation on, its violative status" (140).

11. Twitchell, *Dreadful Pleasures*, 1304.

12. David L. Pike, *Metropolis on the Styx: The Underworlds of Modern Culture, 1800–2001* (Ithaca, NY: Cornell University Press, 2007), 86. See also Humphrey Jennings, *Pandaemonium, 1660–1886: The Coming of the Machine as Seen by Contemporary Observers*, ed. Mary-Lou Jennings and Charles Madge (London: Picador, 1987).

13. Pike, *Metropolis on the Styx*, 86, 74. Drawing on Benson Bobrick's *Labyrinth of Iron: Subways in history, Myth, Art, Technology, and War* (New York: Henry Holt, 1986), Pike also observes that Milton indirectly came to be shaped by the process of urbanization: John Martin's influential rendering of the poem in his mezzotint "Bridge over Chaos" "incorporated an image of the Thames Tunnel into its conception" (75).

14. Pike, *Metropolis on the Styx*, 79.

15. The *OED* shows this sense of "utter confusion, uproar; wild and noisy disorder; a tumult; chaos" emerging in the mid- to late-nineteenth century, citing among examples Mark Twain's *Roughing It* (1872): "Natives from the several islands...had made the place a pandemonium every night with their howlings and wailings, beating of tom-toms and dancing"; and Thomas Hardy's *Tess of the d'Urbervilles* (1891): "Amid the...confusion as of Pandemonium, Tess untied her last sheaf." Contrastingly in Mary Shelley's *Frankenstein* (1818) it is still being invoked, without irony, as an "exquisite and divine...retreat." On film, the prize for most ironic citation goes to the period piece boxing drama, *Cinderella Man* (dir. Ron Howard, 2006), when the ringside announcers declare, "It's pandemonium here in the Garden!"

16. Patrick Lussier was editor on *Scream 3*, which also uses John Milton as a villain. Among countless other examples of hell breaking loose, see *Supernova* (dir. Walter Hill, 2000): "All hell is about to break loose"; *Underworld* (dir. Len Wiseman, 2003): "On September nineteenth, all Hell breaks loose"; *Season of the Witch* (another Cage flick, dir. Dominic Sena, 2011): "All hell will break loose"; and *Mansion of Blood* (dir. Mike Donahue, 2012): "All Hell Breaks Loose."

17. Romish allusions begin with Rebecca King, "The Source of Milton's Pandaemonium," *Modern Philology* 29, no. 2 (1931): 187–98; more recently, see Joseph Lyle, "Architecture and Idolatry in *Paradise Lost*," *SEL* 40, no. 1 (Winter 2000): 139–55.

18. For an extended interpretation of Milton's bee simile, see Cristopher Hollingsworth, *Poetics of the Hive: The Insect Metaphor in Literature* (Iowa City: University of Iowa Press, 2001), 85–99.

19. Steven Blakemore, "Pandemonium and Babel: Architectural Hierarchy in *Paradise Lost*," *Milton Quarterly* 20, no. 4 (Dec. 1986): 142–45, argues that "Milton's point is that evil can only imitate and parody goodness. Pandemonium itself is a perverse parody of heaven," as with its high golden roof recalling the low-cast pavements of heaven. For the literary history of the former image, see James A. Freeman, "'The Roof Was Fretted Gold,'" *Comparative Literature* 27, no. 3 (Summer 1975): 254–66. Roger Martin offers an imperialist interpretation of the architecture in "The Colonization of Paradise: Milton's Pandemonium and Montezuma's Tenochtitlan," *Comparative Literature Studies* 35 (1998): 321–55.

20. A similar additive garishness is evident in Milton's supposed response to Dryden's *State of Innocence:* "it seems you have a mind to *Tagg* my points," after the "foppish fad of wearing ribbons 'tagged' with bits of metal at the

end." See Barbara Lewalski, *The Life of John Milton: A Critical Biography* (Oxford: Blackwell, 2000), 508.

21. Paul Oppenheimer, *Evil and the Demonic: A New Theory of Monstrous Behavior* (New York: New York University Press, 1996), 7. Roger B. Salomon, *Mazes of the Serpent: An Anatomy of Horror Narrative* (Ithaca, NY: Cornell University Press, 2002), notes the persistence of this trope "of endless and reiterative nightmare" in such works as Arthur Machen's *The House of Souls* (London: Grant Richards, 1923), where it unfolds as "the repeated eruptions in nature of the terrible force he calls Pan, a force of decreation, withering, meltdown, and death" (Salomon, 98). See, too, Victor Sage's extension of this pattern to "narrative redundancy" in *Horror Fiction in the Protestant Tradition* (New York: St. Martin's Press, 1988), 127.

22. Mythological tradition also makes Vulcan suitable: he is the craftsman who forms Pandora out of clay, adorns her in deceptively beautiful trappings (including, in Hesiod's *Theogony*, a wondrous crown of gold), and thereby indirectly releases upon humanity all the "evil spirits" contained in Pandora's box. Thus, Pandaemonium becomes yet another inversion of divine precedence; the "gifts" implied (and already ironic) in Pan-dora's name here become demonized in totality.

23. Though Satan's "suddenly built" palace surpasses Nimrod's Babel, its design represents it. Compare Brueghel's painting *The Tower of Babel*, ca. 1563–64, and Maerten van Valckenborch's *Building the Tower of Babel*, 1595. For Oppenheimer, though "the Babel story, and its insight into empirical evil, have exerted a direct and an oblique but identifiable influence," his concern is primarily with the disintegration of language into a helpless silence, finding representative examples in works as diverse as Hitchcock's *Psycho*, with its "virtual disappearance of speech," and the Kafka-inspired Terry Gilliam's *Brazil*, "in which a gigantic tower-like building, a Ministry of Information, stoops with gloomy importance over a high-tech metropolis" (*Evil and the Demonic*, 153, 165, 166).

24. Michel de Certeau, *The Practice of Everyday Life*, trans. Steven Rendall (Berkeley and Los Angeles: University of California Press, 2002), 93.

25. The obverse of this fallen literariness can be glimpsed in *Wings of Desire* and its remake, *City of Angels* (dir. Brad Silberling, 1998)—the latter's title a reverse of Satan's City of Demons—where the angelic host loiters in libraries, one of the few earthly repositories where their infinite intellect can be stimulated.

26. This effect may account for such far-flung treatments as Alfred Sole's *Pandemonium* (1982), a slasher spoof starring Tom Smothers as a Canadian Mountie on the trail of a killer at a camp for cheerleaders.

27. Gretchen Berg, "The Viennese Night: A Fritz Lang Confession, Parts One and Two" (1965–66), repr. in *Fritz Lang: Interviews*, ed. Barry Keith Grant (Jackson: University Press of Mississippi, 2003), 68.

28. Ibid., 68–69.

29. A hard-boiled noir variation on *Metropolis*, Alex Proyas's film *Dark City* (1998) also evokes Milton's Pandaemonium in its labyrinthine cityscape, newly created every 24 hours as a scientific experiment in which human beings are the rats in an extraterrestrial maze. In its conflation of labs and labyrinths, this spiraling, artificial city, as one of its alien constructors describes it, is "fashioned...on stolen memories. Different eras, different pasts, all rolled into one." Milton develops a similar labyrinth motif in *Paradise Lost*, where the coiled and involuted machinations of Satan are the confusion of the human condition (as when Satan seeks the snake "in whose mazy folds / To hide me and the dark intent I bring [9.161–62], and locates him "in Labyrinth of many a round self-roll'd, / His head the midst, well stor'd with subtle wiles" [9.183–84].)

30. On the film's eschatology, see Åke Bergyvall, "Apocalyptic Imagery in Fritz Lang's Metropolis," *Literature Film Quarterly* 40, no. 4 (2012): 246–57. Bergyvall also argues for Edmund Spenser's *The Faerie Queene* as an "uncanny" analogue for the film.

31. Tom Gunning, *The Films of Fritz Lang: Modernity, Crime, and Desire* (London: BFI, 2000), 63, observes here "the demonic power of the city, embodied in the Moloch machine screaming to be fed."

32. H. G. Wells, reviewing the film in the *New York Times* (Apr. 17, 1927), may have been the first to respond harshly to the film's insufficiencies: "It gives in one eddying concentration almost every possible foolishness, cliché, platitude, and muddlement about mechanical progress and progress in general served up with a sauce of sentimentality that is all its own" (5M4, 22).

33. In one later dream sequence, the boys' bedrooms are invaded by spiders: there is a glimpse of one of their bedtime books as one tarantula ambulates over the cover: Percy Marks's 1924 novel *The Plastic Age*. A somewhat titillating coming-of-age tale, once banned, it is a very curious choice for a 12 year old. It opens with the founding of a fictional college by a hellfire Puritan who urges his students in twice daily sermons to battle with Satan, and later he offers one modern student's choice literary opinion: "Lord Almighty, how I hate Milton! What th' hell do they have to give us that tripe for?" (Percy Marks, *The Plastic Age* [New York: Grosset and Dunlap, 1924], 102).

34. Ray Bradbury's novel makes the parallels more explicit, as when "The great tents filled like bellows. They softly issued forth exhalations of air that smelled like ancient yellow beasts" (*Something Wicked This Way Comes* [1962; repr., New York: Avon, 1998], 54).

35. The film shares the idea of a sinful carnival with the 1935 film *Dante's Inferno* (dir. Harry Lachman), in which a sideshow features a lurid rendering of Dante's *contrapasso* punishments.

36. Bradbury, *Something Wicked*, 286.

37. In one of the more extraordinary adaptations of Milton, and a clear analogue for *The Devil's Advocate*, Fred Astaire's weekly television series *Alcoa Premiere* presented an episode (Nov. 1, 1962) in which Astaire played

Mr. Lucifer in a drama set in contemporary New York City: "According to poet John Milton, Lucifer's 'city and proud seat' is called Pandemonium, but these days, even the Devil needs an office on, or under, Madison Avenue, and Mr. Lucifer has one: his secretary is a retired moon goddess and his vice-presidents are all infamous fiends. The staff is having no trouble meeting its quota of souls, but the Boss can't rest easy in his Room at the Bottom; a certain young man is setting too good an example on behalf of the Competition, and Satan is out to get him" (from *TV Guide*, Nov. 1, 1962). The episode was directed by Alan Crosland Jr. and included such notable credits as Elizabeth Montgomery (Iris Hecate), George Petrie (Beelzebub), Milton Frome (Mammon), Hal Smith (Belial), and Gaylord Cavallaro (Moloch).

38. In a *Newsweek* interview Pacino conducted for his role as Roy Cohn in the Mike Nichols HBO adaptation of Tony Kushner's *Angels in America* (2003), he comments briefly on his familiarity with Milton and on his sympathetic portrayal of Satan (a link to Roy Cohn suggested in the interview by his co-star Emma Thompson):

> *Newsweek:* Al, do you think you made Roy sympathetic?
> *Pacino:* I don't think you set out to do that. I think it's innate in the characterization that Tony has made. It's impossible to do that character without getting to the humanity of it. He's already done that work, and so it's up to you to sort of find it in yourself and follow his lead.
> *Thompson:* You know, what he made me think of when I first read the play was Satan in Milton's "Paradise Lost." That's who he is. And you're so fascinated by Satan, he's the best character.
> *Pacino:* I played him once [in *The Devil's Advocate*].
> *Nichols:* I thought it worked. I quite liked it.
> *Pacino:* As a matter of fact, I did read Milton when I was playing that part. It was very helpful.
> *Thompson:* It's amazing, isn't it? I haven't read it for a long, long time, but my God, that's sort of who he is.
> *Kushner:* But the great trap is that when you fall in love with the Devil you're recapitulating the fall of the human race. That's why we fall.
> *Thompson:* And that's the point. It's so fascinating. You desperately want to be with him.
> *Nichols:* There is something to be said for the idea that one of the actor's main jobs is to make the best possible case for the character. Al does that playing a villainous person.

See David Ansen and Marc Peyser, "City of Angels," *Newsweek* 142, no. 23 (Dec. 8, 2003): 50.

39. Compare Paul Oppenheimer's sketch in *Evil and the Demonic: A New Theory of Monstrous Behavior* (New York: New York University Press, 1996), of demonic space as "a personified, stiff atmosphere and geography... Gothic and eerie with passion-endowed crags, grottoes, isolated farm houses, or for

that matter with busy avenues, factories, skyscrapers, and department stores suddenly looming with a terrible mischief" (6). Oppenheimer also describes the importance of the "haunted houses of diabolical films," buildings that "gush with doomed shouts, groans, hisses, and most often with no recognizable speech at all," a horror film sub-genre with Pandaemonium (or Babel) as precursor (6).

40. Ibid., 153.

41. "Devil's Advocate, VIII. Production," https://web.archive.org/web/20020106181528/http://movies.warnerbros.com/devils/cmp/production2-c.html (accessed Oct. 8, 2014). Also available on Special Features, "On Location," *Devil's Advocate*, DVD.

42. Anna K. Nardo, review of *Milton in Popular Culture*, in *Milton Quarterly* 41, no. 3 (Oct. 2007): 207

43. William McClung, "The Architecture of Pandaemonium," *Milton Quarterly* 15, no. 4 (1981): 109–12.

44. On the "Apartment as a Cell of Horror," one that permits filmmakers to explore "voyeurism, paranoia, and alienation," see Carl Royer and Diana Royer, *The Spectacle of Isolation in Horror Films* (New York: Routledge, 2005), 77–94.

45. On this line, and Pacino's/Milton's ambiguous response, see also Ryan Netzley, "'Better to Reign in Hell than Serve in Heaven,' Is That It?': Ethics, Apocalypticism, and Allusion in *The Devil's Advocate*," in *Milton in Popular Culture*, ed. Laura Lunger Knoppers and Gregory M. Colón Semenza, 113–24 (New York: Palgrave, 2006).

46. See Jonathan Lemkin and Tony Gilroy, *The Devil's Advocate: Revised Shooting Script* (Jan. 18, 1997), 135.

47. The film does not use the word "pandemonium," though it does appear in the source novel. There it appears only in its conventional sense of utter confusion, perhaps further ironized: after some inflammatory testimony in one of Lomax's cases, "pandemonium broke out in the courtroom." See Andrew Neiderman, *The Devil's Advocate* (New York: Pocket Books, 1990), 223.

48. Ibid., 278–79.

49. Warner Brothers encountered legal problems when it was accused of duplicating Frederick Hart's sculpture *Ex Nihilo*, which appears on the façade of the Washington National Cathedral in Washington, DC. The final settlement included the alteration of several early scenes involving the backdrop, though the filmmakers also ultimately denied any reference to Hart's work.

50. McClung observes that both Roland Mushat Frye, *Milton's Imagery and the Visual Arts: Iconographic Tradition in the Epic Poems* (Princeton, NJ: Princeton University Press, 1978), 134–35, and Amy Lee Turner, "Milton and the Arts of Design," in *A Milton Encyclopedia*, 9 vols., ed. William B. Hunter et al. (Lewisburg, PA: Bucknell University Press, 1978), 1:90–102, argue for Pandaemonium as "a mélange of varying styles and as an assemblage of discordant architectural elements, that is, as a monster" ("Architecture," 109); comparable grotesqueries emerge in Hackford's "ultra-modern" set

design—hybridized by "both an "Italian architect and a Japanese architect"—in a return to the fabric of Pandaemonium's disorder (Taylor Hackford, DVD commentary to *Devil's Advocate*).

51. *Monty Python's Flying Circus,* episode 35 (first aired Dec. 14, 1972). Quoted in *The Complete Monty Python's Flying Circus: All the Words,* 2 vols., ed. Roger Wilmut(New York: Pantheon, 1989), 2:167.

52. Abigail Burnham Bloom, *The Literary Monster on Film: Five Nineteenth-Century British Novels and Their Cinematic Adaptations* (Jefferson, NC: McFarland, 2010), regards Hyde here as "pointing out her limitations as a companion," an Adamic rejection of Eve, asking her to read "something that would be beyond Ivy's comprehension" (79).

53. See, however, Laura Lunger Knoppers, "Miltonic Loneliness and Monstrous Desire from *Paradise Lost* to *Bride of Frankenstein*," in Knoppers and Semenza, *Milton in Popular Culture,* 99–112. Knoppers makes a compelling argument that "a distinctive Miltonic loneliness continues to mark pop cultural representations of Frankenstein's Creature, and indeed that this pathos and sympathy distinguish the Creature from other long-standing fellow monsters such as Dracula, Wolfman, the Mummy, or Jekyll and Hyde" (108).

54. Janet Maslin, "'Paradise Lost' Inspires Meditation on Vampires," *New York Times,* Oct. 28, 1993, C15.

55. Ibid., C15. Two recent television series have made similar claims regarding *Paradise Lost: Supernatural* (2005–present on the CW) and *Carnivale* (HBO, 2003–05). The creator of *Supernatural,* Eric Kripke, remarked in a 2009 interview with the *CW Source* that the show's fifth season would feature a Miltonic Lucifer, one "that hasn't really been seen that often in movies and TV, which is sort of a gentle, almost sympathetic depiction. We're cribbing a lot—it's either an homage or we're stealing, depending on your point of view, from *Paradise Lost.*" The series has, at various times, featured such angels as Gabriel, Raphael, Uriel, and Azazel, and one named Anna Milton. Charlie McCollum described *Carnivale* in a review, "Carny Series Evokes Another Era, Dimension," *San Jose Mercury News,* Sept. 14, 2003, as "working from a template loosely based on John Milton's *Paradise Lost*" and presenting "a surreal tapestry of magic and spirituality, of temptation and redemption" (3E). Creator Daniel Knauf confirms, "What I drew on was all literary. I think of it as taking 'Paradise Lost' and using it as a template and layering it onto the Depression. And if you're going to steal, you might as well steal from the best" (3E).

56. James B. Twitchell, *The Living Dead: A Study of the Vampire in Romantic Literature* (Durham, NC: Duke University Press, 1981), 75. Alain Silver and James Ursini, *The Vampire Film: From Nosferatu to Interview with the Vampire,* rev. ed. (New York: Limelight, 2004), 55, also see analogies with Milton: vampires possess "revulsive appetites" and are "endowed with an epic quality like that of Milton's striding, primordial Death," who "with eternal famine pine[s]." They add that "the vampire is, like Satan, a ruthless stalker of men, attaining the life-blood of the body through the soul" (55).

57. With less emphasis on the vampiric, see Lisa Lampert-Weissig, "A Latter Day Eve: Reading *Twilight* through *Paradise Lost*," *Journal of Religion and Popular Culture* 23, no. 3 (2011): 330–41.

58. In a 2001 posting to her website, www.annerice.com/faq2001.htm, Anne Rice remarks, "I've never really read *Paradise Lost....* I began to read it while I was writing *Memnoch* [published in 1995] and I was absolutely overwhelmed by the beauty of Milton's language, and I want to read more of *Paradise Lost*." My thanks to Amanda DeGrace for this reference.

59. Anne Rice, *Interview with the Vampire* (New York: Ballantine, 1976), 26.

60. Ibid., 229.

61. Rice, screenplay for *Interview with the Vampire*, 2nd draft (Apr. 1992), 138, www.dailyscript.com/scripts/Interview_Vampire.pdf (accessed Aug. 28, 2014).

62. Rice, *Interview with the Vampire*, 236.

63. Ibid., 13.

64. A vampire film released two years after *Interview with the Vampire*, Robert Rodriguez's *From Dusk till Dawn* (1996) also references *Paradise Lost*, though somewhat circuitously. In the Quentin Tarantino-scripted film, two bank robbers flee to Mexico, where they stumble upon an out-of-the-way brothel. The establishment turns out to be a nest of vampires, including the star attraction, a dancer named Santanico Pandemonium (Salma Hayek), who performs a sensuous snake-dance on a stage meant to resemble an Aztec temple. Her name is based on a low-budget Mexican "nunsploitation" flick called *Satánico Pandemonium* (dir. Gilberto Martinez Solares, 1975), also known as *The Sexorcist*. In the latter film, Satan first tries to seduce the nun with an apple before succeeding in awakening her repressed fantasies of sex and violence.

65. The book was reportedly purchased by Kelly for the scene and came in as the second most expensive prop on the set. Kelly elaborates on the influence of the text: "The things that inspired me to create T-Bird were based in the 'Revolt of Angels' in John Milton's *Paradise Lost*. The concepts of light and dark, and why evil comes in, and the powers of ambition and greed, and the seven deadly sins; these evil things are completely dwarfed by the goodness that avenges them" (www.thecrow.info/castcrew.htm [accessed Aug. 28, 2014]).

66. The official website for *The Devil's Advocate*, https://web.archive.org/web/20011217082129/http://movies.warnerbros.com/devils, also adopted Dante rather than Milton as its spokesperson, a reversal of the film's centralizing and another instance of the favoring of Dante in most popular media.

67. See Andrew Kevin Walker, *Se7en (1995): Shooting Script*, electronic edition (Alexandria, VA: Alexander Street Press, 2003), 70–71; available through American Film Scripts.

68. Reviewing Fincher's body of work, David Denby, "Influencing People: David Fincher and 'The Social Network,'" *New Yorker*, Oct. 4, 2010,

observes, "Sympathy for the devil has always been a productive mood for an artist, and particularly for Fincher; he could probably make a thrilling version of Milton's 'Paradise Lost,' with Satan reigning heroically in Hell" (101).

69. On the conventions of the slasher film, see esp. Carol J. Clover, *Men, Women, and Chainsaws: Gender in the Modern Horror Film* (Princeton, NJ: Princeton University Press, 1992). The creepy Satan of book 4, who spies on the innocent lovers, follows them surreptitiously, and ends up attempting a spiritual rape in the guise of a toad, has much in common with the demonized killers of the slasher genre.

70. Cassandra Clare, *City of Bones (The Mortal Instruments, Book 1)* (New York: Margaret K. McElderry Books, 2008). The novels contain several references to Milton and *Paradise Lost,* including a Satan clone named Valentine Morgenstern (i.e., "Morningstar").

Notes to Conclusion

1. Bradley Cooper was interviewed about the project on *Charlie Rose* (May 25, 2011, www.charlierose.com/watch/50152088 [accessed Nov. 3, 2014]), and he credited Milton scholar Jason Rosenblatt with fostering his love for the poem as an undergraduate at Georgetown. He described an impromptu audition: recording himself as Satan in his kitchen, perched on a stool, and reading from the screenplay (which he called "almost in verse") in "a sort of mid-Atlantic accent." In a single take, he became hooked on the power of the lines and e-mailed the video to Proyas, who then replied approvingly, "Satan lives!"

2. Pip Bulbeck, "Sydney Secures Alex Proyas' 'Paradise Lost' Shoot," *Hollywood Reporter,* July 20, 2011, www.hollywoodreporter.com/news/sydney-secures-alex-proyas-paradise-213157 (accessed Sept. 2, 2014).

3. Patrick Lee, "Del Toro, Rourke, and *Paradise Lost,*" *SciFi Wire,* Dec. 8, 2008, https://web.archive.org/web/20081216011231/http://www.scifi.com/scifiwire/index.php?id=62650 (accessed Oct. 13, 2014).

4. In the early 2000s, a London-based production company called Wanton Muse also had designs on a feature-film version of *Paradise Lost,* though it aimed to update it and adapt it into science-fiction noir. The company, now dissolved, was headed by Pikka Brassey, Moira Campbell, and Philippa Goslett, who went on to script the Salvador Dali biopic *Little Ashes* (dir. Paul Morrison, 2008). The *Paradise Lost* project never materialized. In a 2001 interview, Goslett describes the transformation into an "almost sci-fi fantasy world," and one "without the pressured religious elements," as necessary to combat the poem being inherently "a bit long winded." See Tom Fogg, "Interview with Wanton Muse," Netribution Film Network, 2001, www.netribution.co.uk/features/interviews/2001/wanton_muse/1.html (accessed Sept. 2, 2014).

5. Claire Bueno, interview with Stuart Hazeldine, "The Craft of Screenwriting—Paradise Lost—Part III," Jan. 25, 2012, *Premiere Scene,* www.youtube.com/watch?v=vfYEZwtGoMU (accessed Sept. 2, 2014). The script was originally written by Byron Willinger and Philip de Blasi; Hazeldine worked from this script in making a major rewrite. As the script evolved, Lawrence Kasdan was also brought in for a polish, and Ryan Condal continued revisions until Legendary halted the project.

6. Diego Boneta, on being cast as Adam, acknowledged weeks of intensive training for such exposure: "I have to be ripped." See Marc Malkin, "Paradise Lost: 'A Lot of Running Around Naked,' Says Young Star," *E! Online,* Dec. 21, 2011, www.eonline.com/news/282350/paradise-lost-a-lot-of-running-around-naked-says-young-star (accessed Sept. 2, 2014).

7. Mike Fleming Jr., "Alex Proyas Setting Benjamin Walker to Play Archangel Michael in 'Paradise Lost,'" *Deadline,* Aug. 3, 2011, www.deadline.com/2011/08/alex-proyas-setting-benjamin-walker-to-play-archangel-michael-in-paradise-lost (accessed Sept. 2, 2014).

8. On the history of the epic, especially the trend toward "digital epic," see Constantine Santas, *The Epic in Film: From Myth to Blockbuster* (Lanham, MD: Rowman and Littlefield, 2008). J. Hillis Miller, *Theory Now and Then* (Durham, NC: Duke University Press, 1991), answering Cleanth Brooks's assertion that the grandeur of Milton's poem overwhelms its theological or moral conditions, defends the poem by placing it against the epic film tradition: "If *Paradise Lost* is no more than a 'wonderful story' and grand painted scenes, could not its function in the classroom be fulfilled just as well, perhaps better, by the screening of a Cecil B. DeMille spectacular, with a cast of thousands?" (333).

9. Kristen Whissel, "Tales of Upward Mobility: The New Verticality and Digital Special Effects," *Film Quarterly* 59, no. 4 (Summer 2006): 23–34.

10. John G. Demaray, *Milton's Theatrical Epic: The Invention and Design of "Paradise Lost"* (1980; repr., Cambridge, MA: Harvard University Press, 1999), 26–27.

11. Michael Joseph Gross, "It's God vs. Satan. But What about the Nudity?," *New York Times,* Mar. 4, 2007, A18.

12. Sergei Eisenstein, *The Film Sense,* trans. and ed. Jay Leyda (New York: Harcourt, Brace, 1942), 58.

13. Compare Marina Warner, *Phantasmagoria: Spirit Visions, Metaphors, and Media into the Twenty-First Century* (Oxford: Oxford University Press, 2006): "Movies, above all, have found in the Book of Revelation a quasi-organic iconology for its own kind of storytelling, not in content only, but in the very nature of Apocalypse's cast of characters: monsters and war, angels and engines, populate any number of visions of the end of days, and on the whole, the theme has become the staple of the most popular spectaculars" (342).

14. John Ott, "A Paradise Lost Movie? Really?," *Making the Movie,* Apr. 24, 2006, www.makingthemovie.info/2006/04/paradise-lost-movie-really.html (accessed Sept. 8, 2014).

15. Jennifer M. Jeffers, *Britain Colonized: Hollywood's Appropriation of British Literature* (New York: Palgrave, 2006), 38, 233.

16. Daniel Johnson, "Mixed Feelings over 'Paradise Lost' Film," *New York Sun*, Oct. 13, 2005, 5.

17. Alyssa Rosenberg, "'Paradise Lost': The 3-D Movie Adaptation," *Atlantic*,Sept.22,2010,www.theatlantic.com/entertainment/archive/2010/09/paradise-lost-the-3-d-movie-adaptation/63203 (accessed Oct. 13, 2014). There is an interesting lack of recognizability when it comes to Milton the man. Shakespeare's images—however problematically true to life—have been commodified and reproduced ad absurdum, while Milton's likeness has borne no such cultural circulation. Stanley Fish also argues in his afterword to *Milton in Popular Culture*, ed. Laura Lunger Knoppers and Gregory M. Colón Semenza (New York: Palgrave, 2006), that "it's time for a movie titled 'Milton in Love'" (237). Although the Milton biopic may not have much other momentum, early drafts of the Proyas adaptation of *Paradise Lost* did imagine Milton as narrator, a visualization that might at least have inched him closer to the iconicity of the Bard.

18. As Lauren Shohet reminds us in "*His Dark Materials, Paradise Lost*, and the Common Reader," in *Milton in Popular Culture*, ed. Laura Lunger Knoppers and Gregory M. Colón Semenza (New York: Palgrave, 2006), Milton's crisscrossing of high and low is part of a broader cultural permeability: "the audiences for 'elite' and 'popular' texts overlap. Although certain strands of conservative cultural critique (from seventeenth-century anti-aesthetic polemic to the culture wars of 1980s America) insist upon the separation of elite art and popular entertainment, we all are members of multiple interpretive communities" (59).

19. Robert Brockway, "The Brainstorm that Led to Hollywood's Most Unlikely Remake," *Cracked*, May 4, 2011, www.cracked.com/blog/the-brainstorm-that-led-to-hollywoods-most-unlikely-remake (accessed Sept. 9, 2014). Other satires on the film include Peter Bradshaw's poetic installment in the *Guardian*, released around the time of the first announcement in 2005, in which he imitates Milton's God: "Who've you got for SATAN? Robin Williams? / Or Johnny Depp? Mayhap some smarmy Brit? / And who'll be playing Me? That James Earl Jones?" See Bradshaw, "Milton Goes to Hollywood," *Guardian*, Oct. 12, 2005, www.guardian.co.uk/film/2005/oct/13/classics (accessed Sept. 10, 2014).

20. Carla Hay, "Bradley Cooper Gives a Sneak Peek of His Version of Lucifer in 'Paradise Lost,'" *Examiner*, July 24, 2011, www.examiner.com/celebrity-q-a-in-national/bradley-cooper-gives-a-sneak-peek-of-his-version-of-lucifer-paradise-lost (accessed Oct. 13, 2014).

21. See Fleming, "Alex Proyas Setting Benjamin Walker."

22. Voltaire, *Essay on Epic Poetry* (1727), in *The Complete Works of Voltaire*, vol. 3b, ed. David Williams (Oxford: Voltaire Foundation, 1996).

23. Deborah Cartmell and Imelda Whelehan, *Screen Adaptation: Impure Cinema* (New York: Palgrave, 2010), 83.

Filmography

The following films are discussed or cited in this book.

About a Boy (dir. Chris and Paul Weitz, 2002)
The African Queen (dir. John Huston, 1951)
Alexander Nevsky (dir. Sergei Eisenstein, 1938)
The Ancient Mariner (dir. Chester Barnett and Henry Otto, 1925)
The Angelic Conversation (dir. Derek Jarman, 1985)
Angels and Demons (dir. Ron Howard, 2009)
Angels and Insects (dir. Philip Haas, 1995)
Angels in America (dir. Mike Nichols, 2003)
Animal Factory (dir. Steve Buscemi, 2000)
Animal House (dir. John Landis, 1978)
Apostasy (dir. Andrew Bellware, 1998)
The Appointment (dir. Sidney Lumet, 1969)
April Fool's Day (dir. Fred Walton, 1986)
Arrival of a Train at a Station (Lumière, 1895)
Austenland (dir. Jerusha Hess, 2013)
Avatar (dir. James Cameron, 2009)
The Avenging Conscience (dir. D. W. Griffith, 1914)
The Birth of a Nation (dir. D. W. Griffith, 1916)
The Black Hole (dir. Gary Nelson, 1979)
Blade Runner (dir. Ridley Scott, 1982)
Bright Star (dir. Jane Campion, 2009)
Broken Blossoms (dir. D. W. Griffith, 1919)
The Cabinet of Dr. Caligari (dir. Robert Wiene, 1919)
Carmen Jones (dir. Otto Preminger, 1954)
Carnivale (TV show, 2003–05)

Cheaters (dir. John Stockwell, 2000)

Cimarron (dir. Wesley Ruggles, 1931)

Cinderella Man (dir. Ron Howard, 2006)

Cirque du Freak: The Vampire's Assistant (dir. Paul Weitz, 2009)

City of Angels (dir. Brad Silberling, 1998)

Clash of the Titans (dir. Louis Leterrier, 2010)

Clerks (dir. Kevin Smith, 1994)

Conscience (dir. Bertram Bracken, 1917)

Constantine (dir. Francis Lawrence, 2005)

Cordeliers Square in Lyon (dir. Louis Lumière, 1895)

The Corn Is Green (dir. Irving Rapper, 1945)

Crouching Tiger, Hidden Dragon (dir. Ang Lee, 2000)

The Crow (dir. Alex Proyas, 1994)

Dante's Inferno (dir. Harry Lachman, 1935)

Dante's Inferno (video game, Electronic Arts, 2010)

Dark City (dir. Alex Proyas, 1998)

Deconstructing Harry (dir. Woody Allen, 1998)

Defending Your Life (dir. Albert Brooks, 1991)

Demolition of a Wall (dir. Lumière, 1895)

The Devil's Advocate (dir. Taylor Hackford, 1997)

Diablo II (video game, Blizzard Entertainment, 2000)

Dogma (dir. Kevin Smith, 1999)

Dr. Jekyll and Mr. Hyde (dir. Victor Fleming, 1941)

Dr. Jekyll and Mr. Hyde (dir. Rouben Mamoulian, 1931)

Drawing Out the Coke (Lumière, 1896)

Drive Angry (dir. Patrick Lussier, 2011)

A Drunkard's Reformation (dir. D. W. Griffith, 1909)

Easy Six (aka *Easy Sex*, dir. Chris Iovenko, 2003)

The Education of Charlie Banks (dir. Fred Durst, 2007)

Emma (dir. Jim O'Hanlon, 2009)

Evangeline (dir. Raoul Walsh, 1919)

The Exorcism of Emily Rose (dir. Scott Derrickson, 2005)

Eyeless in Gaza (dir. James Cellan Jones, 1971)

Eyes in the Night (dir. Fred Zinneman, 1942)

Fallen (dir. Gregory Hoblit, 1998)

Fallout 3 (video game, Bethesda Game Studios, 2008)

Far from the Madding Crowd (dir. John Schlesinger, 1967)

Fast and Loose (dir. Edwin L. Marin, 1939)

Faust (dir. F. W. Murnau, 1926)

Fear No Evil (dir. Frank LaLoggia, 1981)

Flash Gordon (dir. Mike Hodges, 1980)

A Fool There Was (dir. Frank Powell, 1915)

Frankenstein (dir. Danny Boyle, 2012)

Frankenstein (dir. James Whale, 1931)

From Dusk till Dawn (dir. Robert Rodriguez, 1996)

Gabriel (dir. Shane Abbess, 2007)

Getting Straight (dir. Richard Rush, 1970)

Giovanni Milton (Itala Film, 1911)

The Golden Compass (dir. Chris Weitz, 2007)

Great Expectations (dir. Alfonso Cuarón, 1998)

Great Expectations (dir. David Lean, 1946)

Harry Potter and the Sorcerer's Stone (dir. Chris Columbus, 2001)

The Haunted Castle (dir. Georges Méliès 1896)

The Haunting of Molly Hartley (dir. Mickey Liddell, 2008)

Hawaii (dir. George Roy Hill, 1966)

Heaven Only Knows (dir. Albert S. Rogell, 1947)

Hellboy (dir. Guillermo del Toro, 2004)

Hellraiser: Inferno (dir. Scott Derrickson, 2000)

Henry Fool (dir. Hal Hartley, 1998)

The Horse's Mouth (dir. Ronald Neame, 1958)

The House of the Devil (dir. Georges Méliès, 1896)

I, Frankenstein (dir. Stuart Beattie, 2014)

I Am a Camera (dir. Henry Cornelius, 1955)

Il paradiso perduto (dir. Luciano Emmer and Enrico Grass, 1948)

Immortals (dir. Tarsem Singh, 2011)

Indiana Jones and the Kingdom of the Crystal Skull (dir. Steven Spielberg, 2008)

In medias res (dir. Joe Perry, 2011)

Interview with the Vampire (dir. Neil Jordan, 1994)

Intolerance (dir. D. W. Griffith, 1916)

It Couldn't Happen Here (dir. Jack Bond, 1988)

Jacob's Ladder (dir. Adrian Lyne, 1990)

John Milton: The Blind Poet (dir. George Kleine, 1912)

Judith of Bethulia (dir. D. W. Griffith, 1914)

Jurassic Park (dir. Steven Spielberg, 1993)

The Kid (dir. Charlie Chaplin, 1921)

Kingdom of Heaven (dir. Ridley Scott, 2005)

King Kong (dir. Merian C. Cooper, 1933)

La lanterne magique (dir. Georges Méliès, 1903)

The Last Days of Pompeii (dir. Luigi Maggi, 1908)

The Legend of Sea Wolf (dir. Giuseppe Verde, 1975)

Legion (dir. Scott Charles Stewart, 2009)

The Lesson (dir. D. W. Griffith, 1910)

The Lion in Winter (dir. Anthony Harvey, 1968)

Little Ashes (dir. Paul Morrison, 2008)

Little Nicky (dir. Steven Brill, 2000)

Loading a Boiler (dir. Lumière, 1896)

Look Homeward, Angel (dir. Paul Bogart, 1972)

Love and Death on Long Island (dir. Richard Kwietniowski, 1997)

Love Nest (dir. Joseph M. Newman, 1951)

Lyrical Nitrate (dir. Peter Delpeut, 1991)

Mansion of Blood (dir. Mike Donahue, 2012)

The Man Who Never Was (dir. Ronald Neame, 1956)

Mary Shelley's Frankenstein (dir. Kenneth Branagh, 1994)

The Matrix (dir. Andy and Lana Wachowski, 1999)

A Matter of Life and Death (aka *Stairway to Heaven,* dir. Michael Powell and Emeric Pressburger, 1946)

Max Payne (video game, dir. Navid Khonsari, 2001)

Max Payne (dir. John Moore, 2008)

The Merchant of Venice (dir. Michael Radford, 2004)

Metropolis (dir. Fritz Lang, 1927)

Michael (dir. Nora Ephron, 1996)

Midnight Cowboy (dir. John Schlesinger, 1969)

The Miracle of Morgan's Creek (dir. Preston Sturges, 1943)

The Miracle Woman (dir. Frank Capra, 1931)

The Mortal Instruments: City of Bones (dir. Harald Zwart, 2013)

Mrs. Dalloway (dir. Marleen Gorris, 1997)

My Fair Lady (dir. George Cukor, 1964)

The Name of the Rose (dir. Jean-Jacques Annaud, 1986)

Nero, or The Burning of Rome (dir. Luigi Maggi, 1909)

Night Train to Terror (dir. John Carr et al., 1985)

The Ninth Gate (dir. Roman Polanski, 1999)

Noah (dir. Darren Aronofsky, 2014)

Nosferatu (dir. F. W. Murnau, 1917)

One True Thing (dir. Carl Franklin, 1998)

Orphans of the Storm (dir. D. W. Griffith, 1921)

Over the Hill to the Poorhouse (dir. Harry Millarde, 1921)

Pandaemonium (dir. Julien Temple, 2000)

Pandemonium (dir. Alfred Sole, 1982)

Paradise Lost (dir. Andrea Di Stefano, 2014)

Paradise Lost (dir. Herb Freed, 1999)

Paradise Lost (dir. D. W. Griffith, 1911)

Paradise Lost (dir. Evelyn Lambart, 1970)

Paradise Lost (aka *Turistas*, dir. John Stockwell, 2006)

Paradise Lost: The Child Murders at Robin Hood Hills (dir. Joe Berlinger and Bruce Sinofsky, 1996)

Paradise Restored (BBC TV, 1972)

Paradise Smurfed (dir. George Gordon et al., 1981)

Parasomnia (dir. William Malone, 2008)

The Passion of the Christ (dir. Mel Gibson, 2004)

Perestroika (dir. Slava Tsukerman, 2009)

The Perils of Pauline (dir. Louis J. Gasnier and Donald MacKenzie, 1914)

Phase IV (dir. Saul Bass, 1974)

The Pit and the Pendulum (dir. Roger Corman, 1961)

A Place in the Sun (dir. George Stevens, 1951)

Pleasantville (dir. Gary Ross, 1998)

The Princess Bride (dir. Rob Reiner, 1987)

Prometheus (dir. Ridley Scott, 2012)

The Prophecy (dir. Gregory Widen, 1995)

The Prophecy II (dir. Greg Spence, 1998)

The Prophecy 3: The Ascent (dir. Patrick Lussier, 2000)

Pure Luck (dir. Nadia Tass, 1991)

R.O.T.O.R. (dir. Cullen Blaine, 1988)

Rambo (dir. Ted Kotcheff, 1982)

Richard III (dir. Richard Loncraine, 1995)

RoboCop (dir. Paul Verhoeven, 1987)

Sabrina (dir. Sydney Pollack, 1995)

Sabrina (dir. Billy Wilder, 1954)

Sally of the Sawdust (dir. D. W. Griffith, 1925)

Satana, or the Drama of Humanity (dir. Luigi Maggi, 1911)

Satánico Pandemonium (dir. Gilberto Martinez Solares, 1975)

The Scarlet Letter (dir. Roland Joffé, 1995)

Scream 3 (dir. Wes Craven, 2000)

Season of the Witch (dir. Dominic Sena, 2011)

The Sea Wolf (dir. Michael Anderson, 1993)

Sea Wolf (dir. Mike Barker, 2009)

The Sea-Wolf (dir. Michael Curtiz, 1941)

The Sentinel (dir. Michael Winner, 1977)

Seven (dir. David Fincher, 1995)

Seven Days to Noon (dir. John and Ray Boulting, 1950)

Sharpe's Siege (dir. Tom Clegg, 1996)

Shitsurakuen (*Paradise Lost,* dir. Yoshimitsu Morina, 1997)

The Skulls II (dir. Joe Chappelle, 2002)

Something Wicked This Way Comes (dir. Jack Clayton, 1983)

The Sorrows of Satan (dir. D. W. Griffith, 1926)

Spawn (dir. Mark A. Z. Dippé, 1997)

Star Trek II: The Wrath of Khan (dir. Nicholas Meyer, 1982)

Star Trek V: The Final Frontier (dir. William Shatner, 1989)

Straw Dogs (dir. Sam Peckinpah, 1971)

Sunday Bloody Sunday (dir. John Schlesinger, 1971)

Supernatural (TV show, 2005–present)

Supernova (dir. Walter Hill, 2000)

Sylvia (dir. Christine Jeffs, 2003)

Tabu (dir. F. W. Murnau, 1931)

That Royle Girl (dir. D. W. Griffith, 1925)

They Also Serve (dir. Marin Fulgosi, 1998)

Thirteen Conversations about One Thing (dir. Jill Sprecher, 2001)

Time Bandits (dir. Terry Gilliam, 1981)

Tom Jones (dir. Tony Richardson, 1963)

The Treatment (dir. Chris Eigeman, 2006)

Troy (dir. Wolfgang Petersen, 2004)

2001: A Space Odyssey (dir. Stanley Kubrick, 1968)

Underworld (dir. Len Wiseman, 2003)

The Warfare of the Flesh (dir. Edward Warren, 1917)

The War Lord (dir. Franklin J. Schaffner, 1965)

Waterworld (dir. Kevin Reynolds, 1995)

Way Down East (dir. D. W. Griffith, 1920)

What Drink Did (dir. D. W. Griffith, 1909)

Where Are My Children? (dir. Lois Weber, 1916)

Wings of Desire (dir. Wim Wenders, 1987)

Workers Leaving the Lumière Factory (dir. Lumière, 1895)

Wrath of the Titans (dir. Jonathan Liebesman, 2012)

X-Men: The Last Stand (dir. Brett Ratner, 2006)

Index